OXFORD HISTORICAL MONOGRAPHS

EDITORS

J. H. ELLIOTT M. H. KEEN
P. LANGFORD H. C. G. MATTHEW
H. M. MAYR-HARTING A. J. NICHOLLS
SIR KEITH THOMAS

Youth and the Welfare State in Weimar Germany

ELIZABETH HARVEY

CLARENDON PRESS · OXFORD
1993

Oxford University Press, Walton Street, Oxford OX2 6DP
Oxford New York Toronto
Delhi Bombay Calcutta Madras Karachi
Kuala Lumpur Singapore Hong Kong Tokyo
Nairobi Dar es Salaam Cape Town
Melbourne Auckland Madrid
and associated companies in
Berlin Ibadan

Oxford is a trade mark of Oxford University Press

Published in the United States
by Oxford University Press Inc., New York

© Elizabeth Harvey 1993

All rights reserved. No part of this publication may be reproduced,
stored in a retrieval system, or transmitted, in any form or by any means,
without the prior permission in writing of Oxford University Press.
Within the UK, exceptions are allowed in respect of any fair dealing for the
purpose of research or private study, or criticism or review, as permitted
under the Copyright, Designs and Patents Act, 1988, or in the case of
reprographic reproduction in accordance with the terms of the licences
issued by the Copyright Licensing Agency. Enquiries concerning
reproduction outside these terms and in other countries should be
sent to the Rights Department, Oxford University Press,
at the address above.

British Library Cataloguing in Publication Data
Data available

Library of Congress Cataloging in Publication Data
Harvey, Elizabeth.
Youth and the welfare state in Weimar Germany/Elizabeth
Harvey.
p.   cm.—(Oxford historical monographs)
Includes bibliographical references and index.
1. Youth—Services for—Germany.   2. Youth--Government policy—
Germany.   3. Germany—social policy—History—20th century.
4. Welfare state.   I. Title.   II. Series.
HV1441.G3H37   1993   93–18199
362.7'1'094309042—dc20
ISBN 0–19–820414–0

1 3 5 7 9 10 8 6 4 2

Typeset by Cambrian Typesetters
Frimley, Surrey
Printed in Great Britain by
Bookcraft (Bath) Ltd, Midsomer Norton, Avon

For my mother, and in memory of my father

ACKNOWLEDGEMENTS

Many colleagues and friends, both in England and in Germany, have helped me to prepare this book. I would above all like to thank Anthony Nicholls for his constructive criticism, moral support, and remarkable patience. Volker Berghahn, Jürgen Brühns, Richard Evans, Dick Geary, and Hartmut Pogge von Strandmann provided valuable comments on earlier versions and parts of the text. I also benefited greatly from conversations with Stephan Leibfried, Christoph Sachße, Florian Tennstedt, Christa Hasenclever, Rüdeger Baron, Walter Thorun, and Paul Weindling, and from the material which they made available to me. My conversations and correspondence with Jeanne Bauer, Alice Borchert, Gustav Buchhierl, Hanna Eisfelder-Grunwald, Henry Jacoby, Ella Kay, Hilde Köster-Richter, Lotte Lemke, and Anneliese Ubenauf gave me insights into youth welfare work in Weimar Germany which archives did not provide. I would also like to record my debt to two people whom I can no longer thank in person: Detlev Peukert, whose advice, knowledge, and enthusiasm helped me greatly, and Tim Mason, who supervised my work in its initial stages and whose encouragement was crucial.

The staff of the following archives and institutions gave me invaluable assistance: the Hamburg Staatsarchiv, Kirchenarchiv, Handelskammer, and Landgericht; the Zentrales Staatsarchiv in Potsdam and Merseburg; and the Bundesarchiv in Koblenz. My research in these archives was generously financed by the British Academy, the FVS Stiftung Hamburg, the British Council, and the German Historical Institute. Salford University's Research Committee provided assistance for further travel and research. Colleagues in Dundee, Salford, and Liverpool gave me practical help at various stages in preparing earlier versions and the final manuscript. Finally, I would like to thank Tony and Willi McElligott, Helga Stachow, Christa Hempel-Küter, Christian Führer, Alan Kramer, and Eva Bollbach, who provided help with this book and a lot more besides.

E. H.

Liverpool, 1992

CONTENTS

List of Tables	viii
Abbreviations	ix
1. Introduction	1
2. Public Policies and the Young Worker in Imperial Germany	28
3. Public Policies towards Apprentices and Young Workers, 1918–1933	62
4. Youth Unemployment and Policies towards Unemployed Youth, 1918–1933	103
5. New Approaches to the Problem Adolescent? The Reform of Youth Welfare and Juvenile Justice in the Post-War Period	152
6. Juvenile Crime and the Practice of Juvenile Justice	186
7. Reforming the Delinquent? Probation and Correctional Education	226
8. From Republic to Third Reich	264
Tables	299
Bibliography	317
Index	343

LIST OF TABLES

1. Occupational structure of the youthful labour force compared to the total workforce in the Reich, 1925 and 1933
2. Occupational structure of the youthful labour force compared to the total workforce in the City of Hamburg, 1933
3. Economic participation rates of the youthful population in the Reich, 1925 and 1933
4. Apprentices and unskilled young workers in Hamburg: survey of vocational school pupils, Dec. 1926
5. The unemployed as a proportion of the economically active population in different age-groups in the City of Hamburg and in the Reich in June 1933
6. Youth unemployment compared to total unemployment in Hamburg and in the Reich in July 1932
7. Youth unemployment rates in different sectors of the economy compared with total unemployment in the Reich, 16 June 1933
8. Education and punishment in the practice of the juvenile courts in the Reich and in Hamburg, 1924–1933
9. Educational measures ordered by the Hamburg juvenile courts, 1924–1933
10. Correctional education in Hamburg, 1919–1934

ABBREVIATIONS

AA	Arbeitsamt
AB	Arbeitsbehörde
ADGB	Allgemeiner Deutscher Gewerkschaftsbund
AfA-Bund	Allgemeiner freier Angestelltenbund
AFET	Allgemeiner Fürsorgeerziehungstag
AfS	*Archiv für Sozialgeschichte*
AVAVG	Gesetz über Arbeitsvermittlung und Arbeitslosenversicherung
AW	Arbeiterwohlfahrt
BA	Bundesarchiv
BAG	Berufsausbildungsgesetz
BDF	Bund Deutscher Frauenvereine
BDM	Bund Deutscher Mädel
BGB	Bürgerliches Gesetzbuch
Bl. DRK	*Blätter des Deutschen Roten Kreuzes*
BSB	Berufsschulbehörde
BWW	*Blätter der Zentralleitung für die Wohltätigkeit in Württemberg*
CB	*Correspondenzblatt der Generalkommission der Gewerkschaften Deutschlands*
DAF	Deutsche Arbeitsfront
DATSCH	Deutscher Ausschuß für technisches Schulwesen
DDP	Deutsche Demokratische Partei
DINTA	Deutsches Institut für technische Arbeitsschulung
DNVP	Deutschnationale Volkspartei
DVP	Deutsche Volkspartei
FAD	Freiwilliger Arbeitsdienst
FE	Fürsorgeerziehung
GG	Geschichte und Gesellschaft
HJ	Hitler-Jugend
HZ	*Historische Zeitschrift*
JB	Jugendbehörde
JGG	Jugendgerichtsgesetz
JGH	Jugendgerichtshilfe
JEH	*Journal of Economic History*

Abbreviations

JV	Jugend- und Volkswohl
KAH	Kirchenarchiv Hamburg
KJA	Kirchliches Jugendamt
KJVD	Kommunistischer Jugendverband Deutschlands
KPD	Kommunistische Partei Deutschlands
LAA	Landesarbeitsamt
LGH	Landgericht Hamburg
MM	*Militärgeschichtliche Mitteilungen*
NSDAP	Nationalsozialistische Deutsche Arbeiterpartei
NSV	Nationalsozialistische Volkswohlfahrt
RABl	*Reichsarbeitsblatt*
RAM	Reichsarbeitsministerium
RAVAV	Reichsanstalt für Arbeitsvermittlung und Arbeitslosenversicherung
RddJ	Reichsausschuß der deutschen Jugendverbände
RFM	Reichsfinanzministerium
RGBl	*Reichsgesetzblatt*
RJWG	Reichsjugendwohlfahrtsgesetz
RMdI	Reichsministerium des Innern
RStGB	Reichsstrafgesetzbuch
SA	Sturmabteilung
SAJ	Sozialistische Arbeiterjugend
SB	Sozialbehörde
SOWI	*Sozialwissenschaftliche Informationen*
SP	*Soziale Praxis*
SPD	Sozialdemokratische Partei Deutschlands
StAH	Staatsarchiv Hamburg
StJB	*Statistisches Jahrbuch*
StJB Hamburg	*Statistisches Jahrbuch für die freie und Hansestadt Hamburg*
USPD	Unabhängige Sozialdemokratische Partei Deutschlands
VjZG	*Vierteljahreshefte für Zeitgeschichte*
VO	Verordnung
VSWG	*Vierteljahresschrift für Sozial- und Wirtschaftsgeschichte*
WRP	Wohlfahrtspflege in der Rheinprovinz
ZBl	Zentralblatt für Jugendrecht und Jugendwohlfahrt
ZGS	Zeitschrift für die gesamte Strafrechtswissenschaft
ZStA	Zentrales Staatsarchiv

1

Introduction

The welfare state was a crucial issue in Weimar politics from the founding of the Republic to its collapse.¹ Social and welfare policies were central to the political compromise which the Republic's founders sought to establish as the basis for Germany's new parliamentary democracy after the revolution of 1918.² Little more than a decade later, the decline and demise of Weimar democracy were inextricably linked to the crisis of its welfare state.³ While the political significance of welfare issues for the development of the Weimar Republic has for some time been recognized, it is only recently that historians have begun to explore the complex and contradictory nature of the Republic's social welfare institutions, and their impact on the relationship between state and society in Weimar Germany. This book seeks to shed light on these issues by examining a cross-section of Weimar social and welfare policies targeted at a particular social group: young workers, that is, the

---

[1] The term 'welfare state' may seem an anachronism, given its specific associations with the post-1945 development of the welfare state in Britain; however, it is the English equivalent of the term *Wohlfahrtsstaat*, which, despite its pejorative connotations during the Weimar period, has been used in a neutral sense by recent historians of Weimar welfare and social policy; and it is also the nearest English translation of *Sozialstaat*, which other historians prefer to use when referring to Weimar. For a discussion of the terms *Wohlfahrtsstaat* and *Sozialstaat*, see Werner Abelshauser, 'Die Weimarer Republik—ein Wohlfahrtsstaat?', in id. (ed.), *Die Weimarer Republik als Wohlfahrtsstaat* (Stuttgart, 1987), 10–11; Gerhard A. Ritter, *Der Sozialstaat: Entstehung und Entwicklung im internationalen Vergleich* (Munich, 1989), 10–28.

[2] Heinrich A. Winkler, *Von der Revolution zur Stabilisierung: Arbeiter und Arbeiterbewegung in der Weimarer Republik 1918–1924* (Berlin and Bonn, 1984), 68–96; Detlev J. K. Peukert, *Die Weimarer Republik 1918–1933: Krisenjahre der klassischen Moderne* (Frankfurt am Main, 1987), 46–52.

[3] Heinrich A. Winkler, *Der Weg in die Katastrophe: Arbeiter und Arbeiterbewegung in der Weimarer Republik 1930–1933* (Berlin and Bonn, 1987), 313–20, 338–42, 379–80, 415; Peukert, *Weimarer Republik*, 247–63; Gotthard Jasper, *Die gescheiterte Zähmung: Wege zur Machtergreifung Hitlers 1930–1934* (Frankfurt am Main, 1985), 55–63; David Abraham, *The Collapse of the Weimar Republic: Political Economy and Crisis*, 2nd edn. (New York, 1986), 220–70.

mass of young people who were out of full-time education and on the labour market from the age of about 14. The measures which were adopted by central and local governments and which are analysed in this study range from vocational training and labour market policies aimed at the mass of young workers, to welfare and educational policies targeted at 'problem' adolescents—juvenile offenders and young people regarded as 'at risk' or delinquent. The common thread linking these disparate areas of policy was the conviction on the part of the state authorities that the transition from school to work marked the beginning of a phase of life where distinct forms of pedagogically conceived public intervention were called for: the state was to supplement, reinforce, or provide an alternative to the socialization of working-class youngsters through the family and the workplace.

Policies towards young workers formed an integral part of the strategy of Weimar governments to use social welfare to underpin the legitimacy of the Republic and to ensure the reproduction of a stable, disciplined workforce. At the same time, the drive to find ways of integrating young workers into the Republic's social and political order was given particular impetus by the prominence of youth issues in Weimar Germany. At one level, perceptions of the 'youth problem' were shaped by more general fears on the part of the German bourgeoisie connected with Germany's rapid industrialization and urbanization and the threat of the industrial working class, which found symbolic expression in images of the rebellious and deviant proletarian urban youngster. Young workers, seen as vulnerable but also volatile, became objects of fascination and fear, constructs on which to hang the fears of the respectable middle classes. But the high profile of youth issues in the Weimar period also had to do with the role of generational tensions in structuring social and political conflicts in the Republic.[4] The extreme rapidity of political change after the First World War and

---

[4] Hans Mommsen, 'Generationskonflikt und Jugendrevolte in der Weimarer Republik', in Thomas Koebner, Rolf-Peter Janz, and Frank Trommler (eds.), *'Mit uns zieht die neue Zeit': Der Mythos Jugend* (Frankfurt am Main, 1985); Elisabeth Domansky, 'Politische Dimensionen von Jugendprotest und Generationenkonflikt in der Zwischenkriegszeit in Deutschland', in Dieter Dowe (ed.), *Jugendprotest und Generationenkonflikt in Europa im 20. Jahrhundert: Deutschland, England, Frankreich und Italien im Vergleich* (Bonn, 1986); Elisabeth Domansky and Ulrich Heinemann, 'Jugend als Generationserfahrung. Das Beispiel der Weimarer Republik', *SOWI* 13/1 (1984), 14–21.

the crises and discontinuities in Weimar's development underlined the gaps between successive generations and fuelled inter-generational tensions. Such experiences sustained the idea of generational mobilization based on a myth of youth as a force for social and political renewal, a concept cultivated by the bourgeois youth movement in Wilhelmine Germany and taken up in the Weimar period as a rallying-cry against the Republic by youthful rebels across the political spectrum.[5]

Conflicting perspectives have been brought to bear on the history of the Weimar welfare state. One version places Weimar social and welfare policies in the context of the evolution in modern industrial societies of systems of social security and welfare, which provided increasing levels of protection for the working class against risks of poverty, sickness and old age. Industrial development and urbanization in the nineteenth century created new types of social need; traditions of state interventionism and 'reform from above' encouraged the state authorities to adopt policies to improve the condition of the working class, not least as a strategy to take the wind out of the sails of the labour movement, while bourgeois social reformers and organized labour pressed their own agendas for social policy.[6] Histories of social and welfare policies in Imperial Germany traditionally focused on central government and its role in pioneering social insurance; recent research has also highlighted the role of municipalities in developing modern systems of poor relief and local health and welfare services.[7] The First World War has been seen as a catalyst in the history of the German welfare state, breaking down obstacles to the expansion of public welfare and bringing organized labour into collaboration with the state authorities.[8]

[5] Frank Trommler, 'Mission ohne Ziel: Über den Kult der Jugend im modernen Deutschland', in Koebner et al. (eds.), Mythos Jugend.
[6] On the history of the welfare state in Germany, see Ritter, Sozialstaat; Florian Tennstedt, Sozialgeschichte der Sozialpolitik in Deutschland vom 18. Jahrhundert bis zum Ersten Weltkrieg (Göttingen, 1981); Volker Hentschel, Geschichte der deutschen Sozialpolitik 1880–1980: Soziale Sicherung und kollektives Arbeitsrecht (Frankfurt am Main, 1983); Rüdiger vom Bruch (ed.), Weder Kommunismus noch Kapitalismus: Bürgerliche Sozialreform in Deutschland vom Vormärz bis zur Ära Adenauer (Munich, 1985).
[7] Christoph Sachße and Florian Tennstedt, Geschichte der Armenfürsorge in Deutschland, i. Vom Spätmittelalter bis zum Ersten Weltkrieg (Stuttgart, 1980); ii. Fürsorge und Wohlfahrtspflege 1871–1929 (Stuttgart, 1988).
[8] Ludwig Preller, Sozialpolitik in der Weimarer Republik (Düsseldorf, 1978), 34–85.

The revolution of 1918 and the installation of parliamentary democracy have been identified as a further, decisive turning-point in the history of German social policy. The development of the welfare state during the Weimar Republic was to be driven by Social Democrats in alliance with the Catholic Centre party and the left-liberal DDP. Taking advantage of the temporary ascendancy of organized labour over the employers, the first governments of the Republic pushed through reforms in the sphere of labour legislation and social policy which were intended to consolidate working-class support for the moderate, reformist socialism of the SPD and free trade union leaders, and to dampen the movement for revolutionary economic change. Reforms such as the 8-hour day, the introduction of unemployment benefit and the legal recognition of collective agreements were introduced in the wake of the November revolution.[9] The National Assembly at Weimar included in the Republic's constitution pledges to uphold social rights and promote public welfare: the constitution proclaimed the right to work or maintenance and the right to organize in trade unions, and declared the state's commitment to housing reform and to health and welfare policies to protect motherhood and the family, children, and youth.[10]

Essential to the construction of the new democratic welfare state were public health and welfare services at local level: in the early Weimar Republic, newly-democratized local governments re-organized and expanded their welfare services and appointed a growing establishment of social workers and other professional experts. Local governments were directly confronted by the social dislocation, poverty, and ill-health resulting from the war and from the post-war inflation, and they played an important role in supporting the unemployed in the demobilization period, in developing services to assist disabled veterans, war widows, and orphans, and in providing for those impoverished by the hyper-inflation.[11] While central government guidelines aimed to ensure a basic nationwide provision of welfare at local level, the form and extent of local authority welfare services varied considerably according to the local political context; this has been highlighted by

[9] Ludwig Preller, *Sozialpolitik in der Weimarer Republik*, 226–38.
[10] Gerhard A. Ritter, 'Entstehung und Entwicklung des Sozialstaats in vergleichender Perspektive', *HZ* 243 (1986), 1–90, 61–4; Preller, *Sozialpolitik*, 242.
[11] Sachße and Tennstedt, *Geschichte der Armenfürsorge*, ii. 89–97.

recent research on innovatory health and welfare initiatives pioneered by reformers employed by Social Democratic local authorities.[12]

Some historians of Weimar Germany have stressed the degree of welfare state expansion and the burden it placed on the economy. While recognizing the political pressure to maintain the welfare state as a cornerstone of Weimar democracy, they criticize the Reich Labour Ministry (headed between 1920 and 1928 by the Centre Party politician Heinrich Brauns) for helping to bring about, through the mechanism of state arbitration in the second half of the 1920s, an unsustainably high level of wages. According to this view, local authorities also bore a share of blame for overloading public budgets and contributing to a crisis of public finance, spending beyond their means on a variety of ambitious projects—including welfare and public housing.[13] Other accounts, however, have stressed the limits to the expansion of public welfare in Weimar Germany and have pointed out that many expectations raised by the pledges in the constitution were not fulfilled. Excluded from power at national level for most of the 1920s, the SPD's influence on Reich legislation was limited. Particularly after the stabilization of the mark in 1923/4, while the fragile compromise in favour of social policy held sufficiently for the long-awaited legislation on unemployment insurance to be carried through in 1927, the rights of organized labour were coming under pressure from the organized employers and the political Right.[14] In the Depression, conflicts over social policy erupted into open battle as class conflict intensified. Those economic historians who see the pre-Depression economy as burdened by high wage costs and welfare expenditure view Brüning's forced deflation policy and his dismantling of the Weimar welfare state as the only option. Others see the economic

[12] For examples of such initiatives in the field of health care, see Eckhard Hansen, Michael Heisig, Stephan Leibfried and Florian Tennstedt, *Seit über einem Jahrhundert . . .: Verschüttete Alternativen in der Sozialpolitik* (Cologne, 1981).

[13] Knut Borchardt, 'Economic Causes of the Collapse of the Weimar Republic', in id., *Perspectives on Modern German Economic History and Policy* (Cambridge, 1991); Harold James, *The German Slump: Politics and Economics 1924–1936* (Oxford, 1986), 85–109; 209–213; id., 'Economic Reasons for the Collapse of the Weimar Republic', in Ian Kershaw (ed.), *Weimar: Why Did German Democracy Fail?* (London, 1990), 38–9; Heinrich A. Winkler, *Der Schein der Normalität: Arbeiter und Arbeiterbewegung in der Weimarer Republik 1924–1930* (Berlin and Bonn, 1985), 728. On the Borchardt debate generally, see Jürgen von Kruedener (ed.), *Economic Crisis and Political Collapse: The Weimar Republic 1924–1933* (New York, Oxford, and Hamburg, 1990).

[14] Winkler, *Schein der Normalität*, 484, 510, 517.

crisis as having been used by right-wing politicians and sections of industry to undermine union rights and to reduce wage costs in a politically-motivated offensive which drove large sections of the working class into a stance of hostility towards the Republic.[15] However, the ruling élites realized that a full dismantling of social policy gains would only be possible if the Republican order itself were demolished.[16] In their search for a new political and social order which would replace the Weimar Republic and which would eliminate the power of organized labour, the ruling élites turned to National Socialism: not, for the most part, as their first preference, but as a last resort.[17]

The history of the Weimar welfare state can therefore be analysed in terms of material gains made by the working class in the aftermath of revolution, subsequently defended by the reformist Left but increasingly eroded due to employer opposition and the financial constraints imposed on governments by the condition of the Weimar economy. However, recent research has increasingly brought to bear on Weimar welfare a perspective on the history of the welfare state which sees it as a motor of social change bringing not only greater material security for the working class but also more ambivalent or even negative consequences. It is argued, for instance, that in Germany the development of social insurance had the effect of differentiating and thus fragmenting the working class, creating a split between a core of regular (usually adult male) workers enjoying privileged protection and security through insurance, and a periphery including the non-working population and those workers, often young and/or female, who were employed casually or part-time on low wages. Those in the latter category were less likely to achieve the security of insured benefits and were in case of need more frequently forced to rely on the means-tested support provided through poor relief or more modern forms of

---

[15] Peter-Christian Witt, 'Finanzpolitik als Verfassungs- und Gesellschaftspolitik', *GG* 8 (1982), 386–414; Bernd Weisbrod, 'Die Befreiung von den "Tariffesseln": Deflationspolitik als Krisenstrategie der Unternehmer in der Ära Brüning', *GG* 11 (1985), 295–325; Dick Geary, 'The Industrial Élite and the Nazis', in Peter D. Stachura (ed.), *The Nazi Machtergreifung* (London, 1983), 95–8.
[16] Ritter, 'Sozialstaat', 66–7.
[17] Michael Geyer, 'The State in National Socialist Germany', in Charles Bright and Susan Harding (eds.), *Statemaking and Social Movements. Essays in History and Theory* (Ann Arbor, Mich., 1984), 199–203; Ian Kershaw, *The Nazi Dictatorship: Problems and Perspectives of Interpretation* (London, 1985), 42–3.

public assistance.¹⁸ This differentiation had, among other things, the effect of prescribing regular full-time work as the norm and discriminating against casual employment. In stressing the function of welfare as a mechanism for reinforcing behavioural norms, this interpretation of social insurance shares the perspective of research on the history of social and welfare policies which, influenced by the work of Gerhard Oestreich, Foucault, and others, has emphasized their 'social disciplining' functions.¹⁹ In the early modern period, the administration of public welfare already had the goal of inculcating virtuous and thrifty behaviour into paupers; since industrialization, state social and welfare policies have been a vehicle for efforts to instil into the industrial working class regular work habits, a consciousness of health and hygiene, and a willingness to organize daily life on 'rational' lines. In Imperial Germany, as already mentioned, it has been argued that social insurance regulations helped to enforce the norm of the adult male breadwinner with a stable working routine. Local poor-relief authorities sought, through the institution of means testing and home visiting, to impose sanctions against the feckless and disorderly poor,²⁰ while health care institutions set out to educate working-class women in the principles of rational housekeeping, hygiene, and child care.²¹ At the same time, as more punitive forms of policing the lower orders declined, welfare acquired new disciplining functions: education and welfare came to be seen as more effective and more humane methods of dealing with criminals, prostitutes, and vagrants than simple punitive treatment.

These approaches have also been applied to the history of the Weimar welfare state. Historians of German health policies have stressed how eugenic thinking and fears of biological degeneration underlay the development in the Weimar Republic of a technocratic

---

[18] Susanne Rouette, 'Zur Geschichte von Sozialpolitik und Sozialstaat in Deutschland: Einige neuere Veröffentlichungen', *SOWI* 18/1 (1989), 3–11, 6–8; Stephan Leibfried and Florian Tennstedt (eds.), *Politik der Armut und die Spaltung des Sozialstaats* (Frankfurt am Main, 1985), 13–32.

[19] For examples of this approach, see the contributions to Christoph Sachße and Florian Tennstedt (eds.), *Soziale Sicherheit und soziale Disziplinierung: Beiträge zu einer historischen Theorie der Sozialpolitik* (Frankfurt am Main, 1986).

[20] Sachße and Tennstedt, *Geschichte der Armenfürsorge* i. 214–22.

[21] Ute Frevert, 'The Civilizing Tendency of Hygiene: Working-Class Women under Medical Control in Imperial Germany', in John C. Fout (ed.), *German Women in the Nineteenth Century: A Social History* (New York and London, 1984).

strategy, backed by politicians and reformers across the political spectrum, which extended the influence of the state over the population. From the point of view of the professional health experts, reconstructing the *Volkskörper* after the devastation of the First World War necessitated imposing, through surveillance and coercion where necessary, healthy and orderly norms of behaviour on the working classes.[22] In their negative perceptions of the 'rough' working class, Social Democrats found much common ground with their bourgeois allies. This was nothing new: the Social Democratic movement had long cultivated values such as discipline, industriousness, and temperance, and its leaders and members had sought to distance themselves from what they saw as the undisciplined ranks of the *Lumpenproletariat*.[23] After 1918, Social Democrats together with politicians from the bourgeois parties accordingly built into the new Republic's social and welfare policies measures to discipline that section of the working class which was seen as embodying a threat to political and social stability. While on the one hand the state authorities were concerned to organize and secure the material existence and living standards of the 'orderly' worker, Weimar social and welfare policies—for instance those relating to unemployment benefit—also contained sanctions against those who failed to conform.[24]

This approach enables further light to be shed on the impact of the world economic crisis on the Weimar welfare state. Reductions in public spending did not only mean cuts in material benefits and social provision; the economic crisis also brought a qualitative change in the overall emphasis of social, welfare, and educational policies. Mass unemployment and poverty intensified the fear of the 'asocial' among ruling élites, and led to new ways of using the welfare state to police the poor.[25] This trend was given further

---

[22] Paul Weindling, *Health, Race and German Politics between National Unification and Nazism 1870–1945* (Cambridge, 1989), 305–57.
[23] Brigitte Emig, *Die Veredelung des Arbeiters: Sozialdemokratie als Kulturbewegung* (Frankfurt am Main and New York, 1980), 229–39.
[24] Karl Christian Führer, *Arbeitslosigkeit und die Entstehung der Arbeitslosenversicherung in Deutschland 1902–1927* (Berlin, 1990), 418–23.
[25] Rudolf Vierhaus, 'Auswirkungen der Krise um 1930 in Deutschland. Beiträge zu einer historisch-psychologischen Analyse', in Werner Conze and Hans Raupach (eds.), *Die Staats- und Wirtschaftskrise des Deutschen Reichs 1929–1933* (Stuttgart, 1967); Karl Heinz Roth, 'Ein Mustergau gegen die Armen, Leistungsschwachen und "Gemeinschaftsunfähigen" ', in Angelika Ebbinghaus, Heidrun Kaupen-Haas, and

impetus by the increasing influence in welfare circles of 'negative eugenics', which stressed not so much the need to improve the condition of the general population through expanding welfare measures as the necessity of cutting resources allegedly wasted on the unfit.[26]

The focus of this book is policy development; however, in attempting to provide a social history of social policy, it does address a number of questions raised by works on the social history of youth in Weimar Germany. The interest in youth as the object of historical study has been growing in recent years: a variety of concepts and methods from the social sciences have been employed to investigate such phenomena as the 'discovery of adolescence', generational conflict, youthful protest movements and youth subcultures in history.[27] Much of the work on youth in Weimar Germany has focused on the bourgeois youth movement, which originated in the pre-war *Wandervogel* and evolved after the First World War into the diverse, more tightly-structured organizations of the *bündische Jugend*.[28] While the memberships of the élitist *Bünde* were typically middle-class and educated, the bourgeois youth movement is nevertheless of relevance to this study, both indirectly, in so far as its proclamation of youth's mission of social renewal raised the profile of youth issues generally in the Weimar period, and more directly, in that activists from the youth movement became involved in lobbying on social policy issues concerning youth and in educational work directed at young workers. Meanwhile, the body of work specifically on young workers has been growing. Some of this has covered the history of

Karl Heinz Roth (eds.), *Heilen und Vernichten im Mustergau Hamburg: Bevölkerungs- und Gesundheitspolitik im Dritten Reich* (Hamburg, 1984), 8–10.

[26] Weindling, *Health, Race and German Politics*, 442–6.

[27] John Gillis, *Youth and History: Tradition and Change in European Age Relations, 1770–Present*, 2nd edn. (London, 1981); Stanley Cohen, *Folk Devils and Moral Panics: The Creation of the Mods and Rockers*, 2nd edn. (Oxford, 1980); Stephen Humphries, *Hooligans or Rebels? An Oral History of Working-Class Childhood and Youth 1889–1939* (Oxford, 1981); Dowe (ed.), *Jugendprotest*; Koebner et al. (eds.), *Mythos Jugend*; Deutscher Werkbund e.V. and Württembergischer Kunstverein Stuttgart (eds.), *Schock und Schöpfung: Jugendästhetik im 20. Jahrhundert* (Darmstadt and Neuwied, 1986).

[28] The best overall survey of the history of the bourgeois youth movement remains Walter Laqueur, *Young Germany: A History of the German Youth Movement* (London, 1962). On women in the youth movement, see Marion E. P. de Ras, *Körper, Eros und weibliche Kultur: Mädchen im Wandervogel und in der bündischen Jugend 1900–1933* (Pfaffenweiler, 1988).

the youth organizations of the labour movement;[29] other recent work has gone beyond organizational history in order to construct a social history of working-class youth 'from below'. The work of Eve Rosenhaft on working-class youth gangs in Berlin in the late Weimar period, and above all the study by Detlev Peukert of unskilled male working-class adolescents from the First World War to the Depression, have broken new ground in uncovering the distinctive subculture and lifestyle of proletarian youth in Weimar Germany and in analysing the impact of the Depression and mass unemployment on the socialization of young workers.[30] Research on young workers in Weimar Germany has tended hitherto to focus on young men; relatively little has been done on young women workers.[31] This is surprising, not least in view of the changes affecting the lives of young working women in this era of the 'New Woman': the acquisition of the vote, the expansion of white-collar

[29] Karl-Heinz Jahnke et al., *Geschichte der Arbeiterjugendbewegung 1904–1945* (Berlin, 1973); Erich Eberts, *Arbeiterjugend 1904–1945: Sozialistische Erziehungsgemeinschaft—politische Organisation* (Frankfurt am Main, 1979); Heinrich Eppe, *Selbsthilfe und Interessenvertretung: Die sozial- und jugendpolitischen Bestrebungen der sozialdemokratischen Arbeiterjugendorganisation 1904–1933* (Bonn, 1983); Martina Naujoks, *Mädchen in der Arbeiterjugendbewegung in der Weimarer Republik* (Hamburg, 1984).

[30] Eve Rosenhaft, 'Organising the "Lumpenproletariat": Cliques and Communists in Berlin during the Weimar Republic', in Richard J. Evans (ed.), *The German Working Class 1888–1933: The Politics of Everyday Life* (London, 1982); id., 'Die wilden Cliquen', in Deutscher Werkbund (ed.), *Schock und Schöpfung*; Detlev J. K. Peukert, *Jugend zwischen Krieg und Krise: Lebenswelten von Arbeiterjungen in der Weimarer Republik* (Cologne, 1987); id., 'The Lost Generation: Youth Unemployment at the End of the Weimar Republic', in Richard J. Evans and Dick Geary (eds.), *The German Unemployed: Experiences and Consequences of Mass Unemployment from the Weimar Republic to the Third Reich* (London, 1987).

[31] The following research on women workers in the Weimar Republic, while not specifically focusing on the younger age-groups, is clearly relevant to the subject of young women: Karen Hagemann, *Frauenalltag und Männerpolitik: Alltagsleben und gesellschaftliches Handeln von Arbeiterfrauen in der Weimarer Republik* (Bonn, 1990); Gabriele Wellner, 'Industriearbeiterinnen in der Weimarer Republik: Arbeitsmarkt, Arbeit und Privatleben 1919–1933', *GG* 7 (1981), 534–54; Ute Frevert, 'Vom Klavier zur Schreibmaschine—weiblicher Arbeitsmarkt am Beispiel der weiblichen Angestellten in der Weimarer Republik', in Annette Kuhn and Gerhard Schneider (eds.), *Frauen in der Geschichte* (Düsseldorf, 1979); Ingrid Wittmann, ' "Echte Weiblichkeit ist ein Dienen"—Die Hausgehilfin der Weimarer Republik und im Nationalsozialismus', in Frauengruppe Faschismusforschung (ed.), *Mutterkreuz und Arbeitsbuch: Zur Geschichte der Frauen in der Weimarer Republik und im Nationalsozialismus* (Berlin, 1981); Renate Bridenthal, 'Class Struggle around the Hearth: Women and Domestic Service in the Weimar Republic', in M. Dobkowski and I. Wallimann (eds.), *Towards the Holocaust: The Social and Economic Collapse of the Weimar Republic* (Westport, Conn., 1983).

employment offering social mobility to young working-class women, and the rise of new forms of mass consumption, entertainment, and sports available to or targeted at young women.[32]

A further body of work has focused on the political role of youth and the impact of generational tensions on Weimar politics.[33] Important insights into political developments, particularly in the final Weimar years, have been gained by looking at how the category of youth was turned into a weapon of political struggle against the Republic. The 'generation in revolt' in the late Weimar period was divided and fragmented along class, confessional, and ideological lines; however, the existence of generation-specific factors in determining responses to the economic and political crisis cannot be overlooked. The youthful profiles of the anti-republican parties of the Left and the Right became increasingly marked, and efforts to mobilize youth for the centre ground of Republican politics came to little.[34] Recent research on young people's alienation from the Republic has included work analysing the social and ideological factors which created a generation of organized bourgeois youth in the late Weimar Republic susceptible to the appeal of Nazism,[35] while other historians have examined the circumstances under which a 'lost generation' of young unemployed male workers in the Depression became a prime constituency for the paramilitary organizations of both the NSDAP and the KPD.[36] For the present study, the work on the Republic's

[32] Helgard Kramer, 'Veränderungen der Frauenrolle in der Weimarer Republik', *Beiträge zur feministischen Theorie und Praxis*, 5 (1981), 17-25; Gisela Wysocki, 'Der Aufbruch der Frauen: verordnete Träume, Bubikopf und "sachliches Leben" ', in Dieter Prokop (ed.), *Massenkommunikationsforschung* iii. *Produktanalysen* (Frankfurt am Main, 1977); Atina Grossmann, 'The "New Woman", the New Family and the Rationalization of Sexuality', Ph.D., Rutgers University, 1983.
[33] See the works cited above in n. 4.
[34] Larry Eugene Jones, 'German Liberalism and the Alienation of the Younger Generation in the Weimar Republic', in Konrad H. Jarausch and Larry Eugene Jones (eds.), *In Search of a Liberal Germany: Studies in the History of German Liberalism from 1789 to the Present* (Oxford, 1990).
[35] Irmtraud Götz von Olenhusen, *Jugendreich, Gottesreich, Deutsches Reich: Junge Generation, Religion und Politik 1928–1933* (Cologne, 1987).
[36] Rosenhaft, 'Organising the "Lumpenproletariat" '; Dick Geary, 'Jugend, Arbeitslosigkeit und politischer Radikalismus am Ende der Weimarer Republik', *Gewerkschaftliche Monatshefte*, 5 (1983), 304–9; Richard Bessel, *Political Violence and the Rise of Nazism: The Storm Troopers in Eastern Germany 1925–1934* (New Haven, Conn., and London, 1984), 44–53; Mathilde Jamin, *Zwischen den Klassen: Zur Sozialstruktur der SA-Führerschaft* (Wuppertal, 1984), 77–89; Conan Fischer, *The German Communists and the Rise of Nazism* (London, 1991), 139–45.

inability to mobilize the support of youth poses the problem of assessing how social and economic conditions in Weimar Germany and experiences of the Republic's policies may have shaped young workers' attitudes to the Republic's institutions and contributed to a process of alienation from the Weimar state.

The different perspectives on the history of the Weimar welfare state and the questions raised above about the social history of working-class youth in Weimar Germany thus dictate the approach of the present study. Using this framework, it seeks to explore questions not fully answered by previous work on youth policy. It is only recently that historians have begun to turn their attention to the development of state policies towards youth. Previously, such studies tended to be written by specialists in social policy and welfare whose aim was to illuminate the background to contemporary institutions and policies relating to vocational schooling, reformatory education, juvenile justice, and social work.[37] However, such studies tend to portray the history of youth policy as a succession of increasingly enlightened measures designed to alleviate social problems, the existence and nature of such problems being taken as read. Only since the 1970s have German historians been tackling the history of youth policy in late nineteenth- and early twentieth-century Germany in a way which avoids these pitfalls.[38] Here, the work of Detlev Peukert is of fundamental importance, whose history of youth welfare (*Jugendfürsorge*) in the period 1878 to 1932 analyses a central strand in policies towards working-class male youth. Peukert challenges accounts which make the history of the welfare state into a success story, part of a process of modernization which has seen a steady progress towards enlightenment and rationality in the organization of industrial society. While acknowledging the real gains in material well-being and security which the welfare state provided, he also stresses the price which had to be paid for the extension of the pedagogic

---

[37] Hans Scherpner, *Geschichte der Jugendfürsorge* (Göttingen, 1966); Peter Dittmer, 'Zur Geschichte der Zwangs- und Fürsorgeerziehung', Diss. jur. (Hamburg, 1960); Christa Hasenclever, *Jugendhilfe und Jugendgesetzgebung seit 1900* (Göttingen, 1978); Olaf Miehe and Friedrich Schaffstein (eds.), *Weg und Aufgabe des Jugendstrafrechts* (Darmstadt, 1968).

[38] See e.g. Klaus Saul, 'Der Kampf um die Jugend zwischen Volksschule und Kaserne: Ein Beitrag zur "Jugendpflege" im Wilhelminischen Reich', *MM* 9/1 (1971), 98–144; Jürgen Reulecke, 'Bürgerliche Sozialreformer und Arbeiterjugend im Kaiserreich', *AfS* 22 (1982), 299–329.

sphere: its invasive impact on working-class life—in the case of youth welfare, on the culture of the unskilled working-class adolescent. However, he argues, social disciplining also had its limits. These were partly set by the financial constraints which limited the expansion and reform of the youth welfare apparatus, but they were also inherent in the educational reformers' project: their all-encompassing pedagogical ambitions presupposed a universal receptiveness to their educational efforts which in practice did not exist.[39]

More recently, works have also appeared in English on the history of policies towards youth in Wilhelmine and Weimar Germany. In contrast to Detlev Peukert's study, Derek Linton's analysis of the campaign to save young workers in Imperial Germany focuses less on *Jugendfürsorge* than on vocational schooling and the diverse forms of youth work (*Jugendpflege*, translated by Linton as 'youth cultivation') carried out by the Churches and other organizations under the aegis of the Prussian state. Linton stresses the disciplinary intentions of the bourgeois social-reforming associations, the churches, municipalities, and the Prussian state authorities, who sought to impose on young workers norms of orderly adolescent behaviour and—in an effort to combat the rise of Social Democracy—political conformity.[40] Looking ahead to the Weimar period, Linton stresses the continuities in youth policy between Imperial Germany and the Weimar Republic, seeing a 'lack of major innovations' in youth policy during the Republic.[41] By contrast, Peter Stachura argues that in the field of youth policy the Weimar Republic marked a clear break, with social welfare inspired by humanitarian motives superseding the repressive practices of the Wilhelmine state. In his study of youth policies during the Weimar Republic, covering the areas of labour market policies, vocational training, youth welfare, and youth work, Stachura takes issue with interpretations which, like Peukert's, emphasize the social disciplining dimension of Weimar youth policies, and argues that the policies of the Weimar state towards the young up to the onset of the Depression in 1929 'are best

---

[39] Detlev J. K. Peukert, *Grenzen der Sozialdisziplinierung: Aufstieg und Krise der deutschen Jugendfürsorge 1878–1932* (Cologne, 1986), 15–26, 292–317.
[40] Derek S. Linton, *'Who Has the Youth, Has the Future': The Campaign to Save Young Workers in Imperial Germany* (Cambridge, 1991).
[41] Linton, *'Who Has the Youth'*, 219–25, 225.

understood as expressions of a genuine concern to further social justice with no strings attached: a fundamental humanitarianism sought to bring about material and broadly spiritual amelioration in the situation of the young'.[42] Only in the Depression, he argues, did policies towards young workers take a disciplinary and repressive turn.

The works mentioned above leave a number of questions unresolved. One central problem is to assess where the balance lay between, on the one hand, the benefits and protection given to young workers by Weimar social and welfare policies and, on the other, the controls and sanctions imposed in the name of education. Other issues include the problems of continuity and discontinuity, both between the Kaiserreich and the Weimar Republic and between Weimar and the Third Reich; the specific place of young women workers in policies towards youth; and the role of local government in formulating and implementing policy.

To shed light on these issues, it was clearly important to look not only at declarations of intent by the policy-makers but also at how policies were put into practice, both at central and local level. It also seemed appropriate to look at a broader spectrum of public policies towards young workers than that covered by Detlev Peukert's study of *Jugendfürsorge*. This book accordingly covers policies aimed at young workers generally (labour market policies, vocational training, measures to train and occupy the young unemployed) as well as youth welfare and juvenile justice policies aimed at adolescents who were defined as being at risk or delinquent. While the scope of policies covered in this study is wide, it is not comprehensive: in particular, it does not attempt to cover the area of cultural policy towards youth, which involved censorship of books, films and other entertainments seen as liable to corrupt and deprave the working-class adolescent.[43] Nor does it examine in detail the area of policy known as *Jugendpflege* which entailed state authorities subsidizing and promoting the recreational

---

[42] Peter D. Stachura, *The Weimar Republic and the Younger Proletariat: An Economic and Social Analysis* (London, 1989), 3.

[43] On the so-called *Schund- und Schmutzkampf*, see Peukert, *Sozialdisziplinierung*, 175–91; Margaret F. Stieg, 'The 1926 Law to Protect Youth against Trash and Dirt: Moral Protectionism in a Democracy', *Central European History*, 23/1 (1990), 22–56.

activities for young people organized by private voluntary organizations and clubs.[44]

The different strands of policy explored in the present study did not all have an identical target group. For instance, some young offenders dealt with by the juvenile courts came from middle-class backgrounds and were still in full-time education beyond the age of 14. However, it remains true that the majority of the young people aged over 14 who came into contact with the juvenile courts and the public youth welfare apparatus belonged to the category of young workers from working-class or lower-middle-class family backgrounds, where household budgets dictated that children should leave school and begin earning as early as possible, even if they obtained only an apprentice's wage.

While 'young workers over 14' were thus for policy-makers a recognizable social category, the upper age-limit of this group remained difficult to define. In Weimar Germany, the transition from adolescence to adulthood was marked by a number of different socio-economic and legal stages. These included the break in working life at the age of 17–18 years, marked, for those entering skilled manual trades by the completion of apprenticeship and the beginning of journeyman (*Geselle*) status. In the working life of juveniles in non-manual or unskilled occupations, however, there was less of a clear-cut break. The upper age-limit of 'youth' for the purposes of criminal justice was 18: persons over 18 years of age were treated as adults in criminal law. Political maturity came at 20 years, the minimum voting age, while full legal rights as an adult in civil law were granted only at 21 years, which was the formal age of majority. The upper limits of the phase designated as 'youth' were therefore unclear to contemporaries, and it is for this reason that no hard-and-fast upper age-limit can be set for the category of young workers who are the object of this study: while the 14–18-year-olds are the relevant group where juvenile justice and vocational schooling are concerned, in other contexts the 18–21-year-olds (or, when talking about unemployment, even the 18–25-year-olds) have to be considered as well. However, it is made clear at each stage in the study which age-group is being discussed.

[44] On *Jugendpflege* in the Weimar Republic, see Hermann Giesecke, *Vom Wandervogel bis zur Hitlerjugend: Jugendarbeit zwischen Politik und Pädagogik* (Munich, 1981), 140–68; Franz Josef Krafeld, *Geschichte der Jugendarbeit: Von den Anfängen bis zur Gegenwart* (Weinheim and Basle, 1984), 102–10.

To shed light on the degree of continuity between the Kaiserreich and the Weimar Republic and the question of what, if anything, was new and distinctive about Weimar policies, the book begins with a survey of developments in Imperial Germany. It argues that policies towards working-class youth during the Kaiserreich were characterized by the desire on the part of bourgeois reformers, politicians, and administrators to discipline and 'improve' young workers, particularly the unskilled. Many of these arguments were to be repeated virtually unchanged in the Weimar period; however, a number of initiatives aimed at expanding and reforming public education and welfare for young workers did not get beyond the stage of discussion or draft legislation. In this respect, the collapse of the monarchy and the founding of the Weimar Republic did herald a decisive change: public social and welfare policies towards youth were given added impetus as the central state authorities committed themselves to the expansion of state social policy, public welfare, and intervention in the economy.

Moreover, the founding of the Republic was accompanied by a noticeable shift towards implementing pedagogical approaches to social welfare and the control of deviant behaviour, the young inevitably being prime targets for such educational efforts. The German child's right to education became for the first time codified in national legislation. Education for work was one fundamental concept underpinning Weimar policies towards youth: reliable workers committed to their jobs would make responsible citizens for the new democracy. 'Education not punishment' was another key slogan: guiding the delinquent juvenile back on to the straight and narrow—and into proper work habits—was to take precedence over imposing punishments as retribution and a deterrent to others. From the point of view of the policy-makers, the development of such measures was of relevance not only to the adolescents who were their immediate targets. The young represented a testing-ground for educational techniques which could later be applied to adult recipients of welfare and to adult criminals: policies towards youth were a laboratory for developing future policies towards the population as a whole. Targeting the young also provided a gateway for the welfare authorities to gain access to the working-class family: under the pretext of promoting the welfare of the adolescent, the public authorities could place his or her entire home environment under scrutiny.

Young workers benefited from Weimar policies in a number of respects. The social rights they gained in the Weimar period included the right to organize in trade unions and, in principle, the entitlement to unemployment benefit. Apprentices increasingly had their wages laid down in collective agreements rather than in individually negotiated contracts with their employers. Young workers entering the labour market enjoyed access to public vocational guidance and referral to jobs and places to train. Public vocational schooling expanded, providing education and theoretical back-up to vocational training for young people who had left the *Volksschule* at 14. In some cities, young people could benefit from recreational and counselling services offered by their local youth welfare departments. However, the security and rights gained by young workers were limited by the crises which affected the Weimar economy and by the sharpening of conflicts between the opposing camps of labour and employers over social policy.

The story of Weimar youth policies is thus on one level that of Weimar social and welfare policies generally: social reform hindered by economic crisis and employer opposition. However, the status of young workers *as* youth meant that even where they gained entitlements to benefits and protection these were hedged around by discriminatory conditions and disciplinary mechanisms. This was clear, for example, in relation to unemployment benefits. In contrast to the core workforce of adult male breadwinners, young workers were assumed to be in some sense dependent on their families and thus less in need of financial benefits. At the same time, they were assumed to be more in need of education to enhance their employability, and disciplinary measures to reinforce their motivation to work.

Pedagogical zeal permeated the whole spectrum of policies towards working-class youth, from those aimed at the mass of young workers to those targeted at juvenile delinquents. Such educational efforts, it was argued, should not just modify the behaviour but rather mould the entire personality of the young person. The prime targets of these efforts in the Weimar period remained, as in Imperial Germany, the 'high risk' category of unskilled young workers, whose precocity and independence contravened what had come to be regarded as healthy norms for adolescence. In defining the lifestyle and outlook of unskilled youth as a problem, a consensus justifying pedagogical intervention emerged which united the paternalism and moralism of pre-war bourgeois 'youth savers' with the ethos of health, self-discipline, and self-improvement of Weimar Social Democrats and educational reformers from the bourgeois youth movement. The Right and the moderate Left were also united by broader social and political fears. Beneath the concern to rescue the most deprived section of the youthful proletariat from social degradation was an undertow of anxieties about a depraved residuum of the proletariat dragging the nation down into degeneracy, and fears concerning the volatility of the young unemployed from the unskilled working class in periods of political instability.

While the target of educational efforts was a matter of broad consensus, educational goals and methods proved in the Weimar period to be intensely controversial. No unitary statement of the state's educational goals could be agreed upon beyond the empty formula of the National Youth Welfare Law which proclaimed the child's right to education for physical, mental and social fitness. Where methods of education were concerned, the conservative establishment, which remained strongly represented in Weimar's social policy and welfare apparatus, tended to advocate penalties and compulsion in measures targeted at young workers and the young unemployed, to regard probation as an alternative to the reformatory with suspicion, and to embrace only with reluctance demands for liberalizing reformatory regimes. By contrast, the educational reform lobby, encompassing Social Democrats, left-liberals, and ex-youth-movement activists, sought to minimize coercion and to advocate solidarity and mutual respect between educator and educated as the route to pedagogical success. The educational reform lobby therefore favoured the principle of voluntary participation in schemes for unemployed youth and preferred where possible to work with delinquents in their own environment rather than removing them from their families. In so far, as referring juveniles into residential care was unavoidable, they argued, the reformatories needed to be transformed on more enlightened pedagogical lines.

Histories of youth policy have hitherto tended to focus on male youth. While this bias has recently begun to be remedied,[45] little has

---

[45] Gillis, *Youth and History*, p. xii; Angela McRobbie and Mica Nava (eds.), *Gender and Generation* (London, 1984); Maureen Cain (ed.), *Growing Up Good: Policing the Behaviour of Girls in Europe* (London, 1989).

been undertaken as far as policies towards young people in early twentieth-century Germany are concerned. Of the studies mentioned above, Peukert explicitly focuses on the male unskilled and Stachura's emphasis is also mainly on male youth;[46] only Linton devotes a chapter to policies towards young women workers in Imperial Germany. Public policies towards young women workers in Weimar Germany have remained almost entirely unexplored. The existing literature includes studies of the Nazi labour service for women which also cover the voluntary labour service for women in the final phase of the Weimar Republic,[47] and works which either focus on an aspect of girls' vocational schooling during the Weimar period[48] or cover it in a general history of vocational schooling for girls.[49] The present study accordingly tries as far as possible to bring a gendered perspective to bear on the history of Weimar social and welfare policies towards youth, assessing how far and in what manner young women figured in the perceptions and plans of Weimar policy-makers, and exploring the aims and impact of policies towards female youth. Education for work, it argues, was as fundamental to policies towards young working-class women as it was to those aimed at male youth. However, it was education for two sorts of work, paid employment and domestic labour in the family. Teaching young women workers the principles of hygiene and rational household management would, it was argued, enhance the quality of family life and the health of the nation. In stressing that girls had to be prepared for both aspects of their dual role at the workplace and in the family, Social Democrats and bourgeois feminists were in agreement with conservatives; at most, there were disagreements over where the emphasis should be placed, resulting in a confused and contradictory policy on vocational schooling for

[46] Peukert, *Sozialdisziplinierung*, 29; Stachura, *Weimar Republic and the Younger Proletariat*, 5.
[47] Dagmar Morgan, *Weiblicher Arbeitsdienst in Deutschland* (Darmstadt, 1978); Lore Kleiber, ' "Wo ihr seid, da soll die Sonne scheinen!"—Der Frauenarbeitsdienst am Ende der Weimarer Republik und im Nationalsozialismus', in Frauengruppe Faschismusforschung (ed.), *Mutterkreuz und Arbeitsbuch*.
[48] Wiltrud Ulrike Drechsel, 'Ausbildung für zwei Berufe: Zur Geschichte der Hauswirtschaftlichen Pflichtfortbildungsschule für Mädchen in Bremen 1920–1933', in Jutta Dalhoff, Uschi Frey, and Ingrid Schöll (eds.), *Frauenmacht in der Geschichte: Beiträge des Historikerinnentreffens 1985 zur Frauengeschichtsforschung* (Düsseldorf, 1986).
[49] Ellen Schulz, *Die Mädchenbildung in den Schulen für die berufstätige Jugend* (Hamburg, 1963).

girls. Overall, policy discussions on young women workers saw little in the way of a radical socialist or feminist agenda challenging established gender roles in the household and in the labour market. In practice, girls leaving the *Volksschule*, assisted by public vocational counselling, were channelled into a narrow range of low-status, low-paid occupations in a labour market segregated horizontally and vertically on gender lines. When young women found themselves unemployed, they received lower rates of unemployment benefit than their male peers, and were seen by politicians and administrators as 'less unemployed than men'. The assumptions that young women workers were destined for motherhood and family responsibilities also shaped the perceptions and aims of educationalists and social workers concerned with girls defined as delinquent. If the spectre haunting the 'youth savers' where boys were concerned was that of crime and political anarchy, where girls were concerned it was prostitution. Adolescent girls committed far fewer crimes than boys, but they were nearly as likely as boys to end up in correctional education, usually having contravened norms of sexual behaviour which condemned precocious sex and promiscuity in girls. Some youth welfare administrators admitted that the moral ground on which they were standing was shifting, given that sexual mores in the Weimar Republic were becoming generally more liberal; this did not, on the whole, deter practitioners of youth welfare.

Local authorities were a key structural element in the Weimar welfare state. However, it is only recently that policies towards young workers have begun to be examined in the context of particular localities.[50] The present study combines its survey of policies at national level, together with illustrative examples from different parts of the Reich, with a case study of the city-state of

---

[50] Elizabeth Harvey, 'Sozialdemokratische Jugendhilfereform in der Praxis: Walter Friedländer und das Bezirksjugendamt Berlin Prenzlauer Berg in der Weimarer Republik', *Theorie und Praxis der sozialen Arbeit* 36/6 (1985), 218–29; Frank Zadach-Buchmeier, 'Staatliche Jugendpflege in der kommunalen Praxis: Das Beispiel Hannover', in Adelheid von Saldern (ed.), *Stadt und Moderne: Hannover in der Weimarer Republik* (Hamburg, 1989); Axel Schildt, ' "Gesunde Jugend"—"Gesunde Stadt": Zur Förderung von Erholung und Freizeit der großstädtischen Jugend in den 1920er Jahren—am Beispiel von Hamburg', in Jürgen Reulecke and Adelheid Gräfin zu Castell Rüdenhausen (eds.), *Stadt und Gesundheit: Zum Wandel von 'Volksgesundheit' und kommunaler Gesundheitspolitik im 19. und frühen 20. Jahrhundert* (Stuttgart, 1991).

Hamburg. Local records are important in themselves for the clues they give to young people's responses to public policy measures. Moreover, a local case study can shed light on how national and local government interacted in the formulation and implementation of social and welfare policies. In some areas of policy (for instance vocational schooling), the Reich government merely set broad guidelines and delegated the responsibility for detailed policy to the *Länder* and local authorities; in other cases (for instance support for the long-term unemployed under the 1927 unemployment insurance law) the central government imposed new obligations on the localities—with major financial consequences for local governments, the Erzberger tax reform of 1920 having taken from local authorities much of their financial autonomy.[51] The case study of Hamburg also enables one to make an assessment of Social Democratic policies and practices at local level in the Weimar period: Hamburg has been described as 'in some respects a typical example of what the SPD could achieve in the field of local government (*Kommunalpolitik*)'.[52]

Hamburg—which combined the status of federal state (*Land*) with that of commune or local authority (*Gemeinde*)—was the second largest city in the Reich during the Weimar period; it was a major commercial and industrial centre and Germany's biggest port. Hamburg's city authorities, as those of other cities, were faced with the task of managing the social effects of rapid urbanization: these were particularly evident in the city's notorious dockland slums.[53] Before the First World War, Hamburg's long tradition of oligarchic government by a small circle of merchant families, whose interests lay in creating a favourable climate for commerce, had proved an obstacle to local programmes of social reform and social hygiene. After an ambitious but short-lived attempt in the late eighteenth century to eradicate poverty by means of public action

[51] Von Saldern (ed.), *Stadt und Moderne*, 14–16.
[52] Winkler, *Schein der Normalität*, 408.
[53] Michael Grüttner, 'Soziale Hygiene und Soziale Kontrolle. Die Sanierung der Hamburger Gängeviertel 1892–1936', in Arno Herzig, Dieter Langewiesche, and Arnold Sywottek (eds.), *Arbeiter in Hamburg: Unterschichten, Arbeiter und Arbeiterbewegung seit dem ausgehenden 18. Jahrhundert* (Hamburg, 1983); id., *Arbeitswelt an der Wasserkante: Sozialgeschichte der Hamburger Hafenarbeiter 1886–1914* (Göttingen, 1985); Richard J. Evans, ' "Red Wednesday" in Hamburg: Social Democrats, Police and Lumpenproletariat in the Suffrage Disturbances of 17 January 1906', *Social History*, 4 (1979), 1–31, repr. in id. *Rethinking German History* (London, 1987).

(the *Allgemeine Armenanstalt* of 1788), the city fathers reverted in the nineteenth century to a policy of non-intervention in the workings of the economy.[54] Only towards the end of the century, galvanized by the cholera epidemic which swept through the city in 1892 and by the dock strike of 1896, did the city-state authorities belatedly begin municipal programmes of economic intervention and social reform.[55] Public involvement in 'child saving', however, had been something of an exception to Hamburg's tradition of non-interventionist local government, and Hamburg's public youth welfare services had by the First World War developed to the point where they were seen as a model for the rest of the Reich.[56]

With the advent in the new Republic of democratic local government, Social Democracy, the former enemy within—now shorn of its left wing—became the dominant force in Hamburg politics.[57] While never regaining the absolute majority of votes it won in the March 1919 elections, the SPD continued to attract the largest number of votes of any party in the elections to the city-state assembly (*Bürgerschaft*) throughout the period until 1932.[58] The city-state government (*Senat*) was initially formed by an alliance between reformist Social Democracy and left liberalism; after 1925, the DVP became part of the ruling coalition.[59] As in other Social Democratic strongholds in the Weimar Republic, Social Democrats were able to secure a decisive influence over departments concerned with education and welfare matters: Social Democratic Senators held responsibility for the welfare department, the youth welfare department, the health department and the vocational schooling department.[60] During the Weimar period, Social Democrats, together with their bourgeois allies, sought to construct a prestigious

---

[54] On the treatment of paupers in Hamburg in the late 18th and early 19th centuries, see Mary Lindemann, 'Unterschichten und Sozialpolitik in Hamburg 1799–1814', in Herzig et al. (eds.), *Arbeiter in Hamburg*.

[55] On the cholera epidemic and its consequences, see Richard J. Evans, *Death in Hamburg: Society and Politics in the Cholera Years 1830–1910* (Oxford, 1987).

[56] Heinz Schröder, 'Die Geschichte der hamburgischen öffentlichen Jugendfürsorge 1863–1924', Diss. jur. (Hamburg, 1966).

[57] Richard Comfort, *Revolutionary Hamburg: Labor Politics in the Early Weimar Republic* (Stanford, Calif., 1966), 152, 159–63.

[58] J. Falter, Th. Lindenberger and S. Schumann, *Wahlen und Abstimmungen in der Weimarer Republik* (Munich, 1986), 94.

[59] Ursula Büttner, *Hamburg in der Staats- und Wirtschaftskrise 1928-31* (Hamburg, 1982), 28–9.

[60] Ibid. 29, 664.

civic image for Hamburg focusing on its modern public housing and social welfare provision.[61]

At one level, the city-state authorities' policies towards working-class youth demonstrate the scope for the reforming drive of the SPD and its allies. Despite the financial constraints on local authorities, the Hamburg city-state government expanded public provision of vocational schooling, youth welfare, and health and recreational services for youth substantially beyond the minimum prescribed by Reich legislation. In its work with juvenile offenders and delinquents, Hamburg's increasingly professionalized youth welfare service followed the principle of 'education rather than punishment' and sought to apply the latest scientific insights of psychology and psychiatry together with the pedagogical ideas of the youth movement. However, Hamburg's role as a pioneer of modern welfare also had its less benign side.[62] The expansion of public welfare and the growing numbers of professional social workers enabled the state authorities to gain greater access to working-class households and neighbourhoods—and with it the opportunity both for closer policing and for the gathering of information upon which supposedly more scientific solutions to welfare problems could be based. Confronted with the seemingly depraved and degenerate slum proletariat of the *Gängeviertel*, leading welfare and youth welfare officials debated the problem of the 'ineducable' and the incurably 'asocial' and explored the most systematic and cost-efficient methods of controlling them.

Both Detlev Peukert and Peter Stachura have stressed the Depression as a key phase and a turning point in the development of youth policies. High youth unemployment, the political mobilization of working-class youths and their growing involvement in political violence, gave policies towards youth a new urgency for

---

[61] Ibid. 180-1; Axel Schildt, 'Hanseatische Vernunft kontra Extremismus? Zum antifaschistischen Kampf der Hamburger Sozialdemokratie 1929–1933', in Jörg Berlin (ed.), *Das andere Hamburg* (Cologne, 1981), 263–4.

[62] Ebbinghaus et al. (eds.), *Heilen und Vernichten*; Gaby Zürn, ' "A. ist Prostituiertentyp": Zur Ausgrenzung und Vernichtung von Prostituierten und moralisch nicht-angepaßten Frauen im nationalsozialistischen Hamburg', in Projektgruppe für die vergessenen Opfer des NS-Regimes (ed.), *'Verachtet, verfolgt, vernichtet'* (Hamburg, 1986). See also Evelyn Glensk and Christiane Rothmaler (eds.), *Kehrseiten der Wohlfahrt: Die Fürsorge Hamburger auf ihrem Wege von der Weimarer Republik in den Nationalsozialismus* (Hamburg, 1992).

Reich governments; at the same time, cuts in public spending and a right-wing reaction against the 'wasteful' welfare state changed the nature of Weimar social and welfare provision. Focusing on the Depression as a turning-point furthermore raises the question of continuities between policy developments in the late Weimar Republic and those under the National Socialist regime, a problem examined in a number of works on youth welfare.[63] In the present study, the importance of the final years of the Weimar Republic for youth policies is reflected in the focus of several of its chapters: Chapter 4, dealing with the problem of youth unemployment, concentrates on the Depression; Chapter 6, on juvenile justice, also focuses on the latter half of the Weimar period, while Chapter 7, on probation and correctional education, includes a detailed analysis of the background to the 1932 reform of correctional education. Chapter 8 summarizes trends in youth policy in the final months of the Republic before surveying developments under National Socialism in order to investigate the problem of continuities and discontinuities between Weimar and the Third Reich.

Although the Republic's policies towards young people had, during the Weimar period, consistently emphasized the disciplinary aspects of welfare, the final Weimar governments pushed this trend to new extremes in their attempts to organize and control youth. The possibility that there might exist an irredeemable residuum of working-class youngsters resistant to the educational efforts of social welfare had been banished to the margins of debate in the optimistic atmosphere of the early years of the Weimar Republic; now, in the Depression, a debate on the 'ineducables' gathered momentum. However, even the application of tougher, simpler, less welfare-oriented measures to control and discipline the 'ineducable', the 'undeserving', and the 'unfit' cost money, and the comprehensive implementation of such policies would have cost more than the governments of the Depression were prepared to pay.

The Depression also brought new departures in policies towards

---

[63] Rüdeger Baron, ' "Ballastexistenzen"—Sparmaßnahmen in der Krise: Fürsorgeerziehung im Übergang zum Dritten Reich', in Georg Vobruba (ed.), *'Wir sitzen alle in einem Boot': Gemeinschaftsrhetorik in der Krise* (Frankfurt am Main and New York, 1983); Martin Guse and Andreas Kohrs, 'Zur Entpädagogisierung der Jugendfürsorge in den Jahren 1922–1945', in Hans-Uwe Otto and Heinz Sünker (eds.), *Soziale Arbeit und Faschismus* (Frankfurt am Main, 1989); Carola Kuhlmann, *Erbkrank oder erziehbar? Jugendhilfe als Vorsorge und Aussonderung in der Fürsorgeerziehung in Westfalen von 1933-1945* (Weinheim and Munich, 1989).

working-class youth, and a shift in the balance between central and locally-based initiatives. While facilities funded and controlled locally were cut back, the Reich governments under Brüning, Papen, and Schleicher launched schemes such as the voluntary labour service and the *Notwerk der deutschen Jugend* to get unemployed youth off the streets and occupied 'usefully' at minimum public cost. For the purposes of propaganda they were presented as achieving all the aims of public youth policy at a stroke, allegedly transforming demoralized, delinquent, and politically rebellious unemployed youngsters into models of moral and physical fitness, imbued with team spirit, a passion for work, and loyalty to the state; but without comprehensive and effective means of coercion, such schemes could not impose discipline on those seen as most in need of it.

Continuities between the Weimar Republic and the Third Reich in the field of youth policy can be identified at different levels. At one level, continuities can be perceived in the fact that the apparatus of modern public health and welfare and the labour market planning bureaucracy were taken over and instrumentalized by the National Socialists for their pathological ends. These structures were not products of the Depression but central features of the Weimar welfare state after 1918, and they formed part of the apparatus needed by the Nazis to run a modern industrialized state efficiently. However, much more immediate continuities can be seen when one looks at the final phase of the Republic, when the growing stress on selection and exclusion in welfare policies, the mass schemes to organize the unemployed, and the search for a grand strategy to 'integrate youth into the state' directly anticipated policies towards youth under National Socialist rule. Nevertheless, the discontinuities are clear. In 1933 there was a major purge of personnel who had been involved in the administration of Weimar social welfare, a massive increase in the use of coercion to discipline the unemployed, the swift introduction of sterilization legislation based on the principles of negative eugenics, and rapid moves towards the creation of a state youth organization. There was no seamless transition between Weimar, even in its final phase, and the Third Reich.

While this book does not aim to provide a social history of working-class youth in Weimar Germany, it does suggest how public policies may have affected young workers and shaped their perceptions of the Republic. It raises in particular the question of possible connections between the impact, or lack of impact, of public policies towards young workers, and the phenomenon of a 'generation in revolt' in the final years of the Republic. Clearly, one cannot assert a simple connection between young people's reactions to the policies of the Weimar state authorities during the Depression and the mobilization of young male workers by the Communists or by the National Socialists against the Republic. However, two possible sorts of links suggest themselves. First, it has been argued that disappointed expectations of the welfare state amplified in the Depression a negative reaction against the Republic and its institutions.[64] This idea of frustration at a 'pledge unredeemed' would certainly appear to be plausible where young workers are concerned: the present study stresses the negative dimension of young people's experience of public policies and of the state authorities in the Depression, whether this involved cuts in unemployment benefit, pressure to 'volunteer' for the voluntary labour service, or prosecutions in the juvenile court for busking or begging. A growing number of young workers experienced long-term unemployment and a process of de-skilling, neither of which the state authorities managed to combat. By 1932, young workers might well have wondered what had happened to the Republic's promises to protect youth.

Secondly, public policies may have influenced the conditions under which the radical anti-Republican parties could appeal specifically to youth *as* youth. Dick Geary has argued that the experience of unemployment in the Depression fragmented the German working class along generational lines, playing off older workers against younger in the struggle to keep or find a job.[65] The state's policies on unemployment benefit, in discriminating against the young worker, may have exacerbated such inter-generational tensions and highlighted to young people their subaltern position in the family and society. At the same time, by bringing unemployed youngsters together with their peers in day centres or in residential work schemes, youth policies in the Depression may have strength-

[64] Richard Bessel, 'Why Did the Weimar Republic Collapse?', in Kershaw (ed.), *Weimar: Why Did German Democracy Fail?*, 135–6; Dan P. Silverman, 'A Pledge Unredeemed: The Housing Crisis in Weimar Germany', *Central European History*, 3/1–2 (1970), 112–39.
[65] Geary, 'Jugend, Arbeitslosigkeit und politischer Radikalismus am Ende der Weimarer Republik', *Gewerkschaftliche Monatshefte*, 5 (1983), 304–9.

ened in unemployed young workers a sense that they were a category apart from the older generation. The young unemployed, from their socially marginalized position, may have felt themselves to constitute a 'lost generation'.[66] Adopting a different perspective, however, they might also have seen themselves as the potential vanguard of a new order.

[66] Peukert, 'The Lost Generation', in Evans and Geary (eds.), *The German Unemployed*.

2
Public Policies and the Young Worker in Imperial Germany

In Germany, young workers were from the last decades of the nineteenth century emerging as a distinct target of public policy. This chapter discusses the reasons for working-class youth becoming constructed as a social problem requiring state action, and assesses the consequences of this development, examining the extent to which a basis was laid in Imperial Germany at national and local level for the policies pursued subsequently during the Weimar Republic.

The Construction of a Social Problem: The Discovery of the Working-Class Adolescent

The discovery in Germany of working-class youth as a phenomenon and as a social problem took place, it has been argued, during the last decade and a half of the nineteenth century.[1] At one level, a growing interest in working-class adolescents has been related to the growth of concern with adolescence generally as a phase in the life-cycle. Not only in Germany but also in other industrialized countries at this time, adolescence was coming to be seen as a phase in life between childhood and adulthood with distinctive biological, psychological, and social characteristics.[2] Prescriptive norms arose for this newly defined phase of life; adolescence was seen as a phase of sexual, emotional, and social disorientation and ferment requiring

---

[1] D. Peukert, *Grenzen der Sozialdisziplinierung: Aufstieg und Krise der deutschen Jugendfürsorge 1878–1932* (Cologne, 1986), 59.
[2] John Gillis, *Youth and History: Tradition and Change in European Age Relations, 1770–Present*, 2nd edn. (London, 1981), 98–105; Elisabeth Domansky, 'Politische Dimensionen von Jugendprotest und Generationenkonflikt in der Zwischenkriegszeit in Deutschland', in Dieter Dowe (ed.), *Jugendprotest und Generationenkonflikt in Europa im 20. Jahrhundert* (Bonn, 1986), 115.

guidance, protection, and control. This entailed a period of prolonged economic dependence, sexual and political abstinence, and subjection to the authority of parents, teachers, Church, and state.[3]

Both socio-economic and ideological factors have been adduced to explain the emergence of adolescence as a concept. A growing readiness on the part of the middle and upper classes in the industrial societies of the nineteenth century to invest in educating and training their children coincided with a need for an increasingly educated and specialized workforce. As a result, ever larger numbers of middle-class children experienced a prolonged period of economic dependence and protectedness as a transition between childhood and adulthood. Other explanations of the 'discovery of adolescence' have been put forward in terms of the psychological need on the part of the middle classes in industrial society for a cult of youth to set against fears of the decadence and decline of civilization. Adolescence was constructed as a phase of life embodying naturalness and spontaneity and was mythologized as a world apart, an idyll unsullied by the realities of the production process and of social and political conflict.[4]

In Wilhelmine Germany, the discovery of adolescence acquired particular significance as young people themselves added their own self-definitions and ideas to the emerging cult of youth. The German youth movement arose as middle-class youth began to define itself in opposition to the dominant culture of the German bourgeoisie, developing a distinctive ethos of self-discipline, sincerity, comradeship, and group loyalty to a freely chosen leader.[5] Many youth movement activists subsequently sought to apply the experiences they gained within the select community of the *Wandervogel* to the task of shaping mass society through youth welfare, social work, and education.[6]

---

[3] Philip Cohen, 'Historical Perspectives on the Youth Question especially in Britain', in Dowe (ed.), *Jugendprotest*, 241–59.

[4] Frank Trommler, 'Mission ohne Ziel: Über den Kult der Jugend im modernen Deutschland', in T. Koebner et al. (eds.), *'Mit uns zieht die neue Zeit': Der Mythos Jugend* (Frankfurt am Main, 1985), 14–49; Gillis, *Youth and History*, 182.

[5] On the history of the youth movement, see Walter Laqueur, *Young Germany: A History of the German Youth Movement* (London, 1962), and Werner Kindt (ed.), *Grundschriften der deutschen Jugendbewegung* (Düsseldorf and Cologne, 1963).

[6] See Ch. 5.

The idea of adolescence was associated with the specific experience of middle-class youth and was not obviously of any relevance to the lives of working-class youngsters. However, adolescence soon came to be defined as a universal human condition and a necessary phase of life. The fact that working-class children left school and went into jobs at the age of 14 meant that, in middle-class eyes, they grew up too quickly. Adolescence became one more of the bourgeois norms and values which middle-class legislators, social reformers, educationalists and social workers in Germany and elsewhere attempted, with varying degrees of success, to propagate among the working classes.[7]

While a growing concern with adolescence in general among the German middle classes may provide part of the explanation of the discovery of the working-class adolescent, other factors such as the age-structure of the population and the size of the youthful workforce may have played a role.[8] It has been suggested that a particularly high proportion of adolescents and young adults in the population of Germany's fast-growing towns and cities played a role in the formulation of a 'youth problem' around the turn of the century.[9] People of working age were flooding to the urban areas, with the result that the age-profiles of the cities became more 'youthful' than those of rural areas. Between 1870 and 1890 the age-profile of big-city populations was characterized by disproportionate numbers of people aged 20–40 years; this in turn resulted from 1900 onwards in a particularly large proportion of babies being born in cities.[10] In certain cities, moreover, there were, after 1900, particularly large concentrations of adolescents. These were industrial cities as opposed to commercial or administrative centres, and included cities such as Bochum and Dortmund, Barmen and Elberfeld.[11]

The economic developments which affected demographic change in Germany in the late nineteenth century brought a rapid increase in the number of young people in the workforce. Between 1895 and

---

[7] Gillis, *Youth and History*, 134–5; Domansky, 'Politische Dimensionen', 115–16.
[8] Derek S. Linton, *'Who Has the Youth, Has the Future': The Campaign to Save Young Workers in Imperial Germany* (Cambridge, 1991), 19–22.
[9] Klaus Tenfelde, 'Großstadtjugend in Deutschland vor 1914. Eine historisch-demographische Annäherung', *VSWG* 69/2 (1982), 182–218.
[10] Ibid. 198–200.
[11] Ibid. 203.

1907, the size of the youthful workforce aged between 14 and 18 years rose from 2.5 million to nearly 3.2 million. In 1895, 60 per cent of the resident population in the 14–18 age group had been economically active; in 1907, this had risen to 66 per cent. Broken down according to sex, 82 per cent of males and 50 per cent of females aged 14–18 years were economically active in 1907.[12] The distribution of juvenile labour outside the agricultural sector was also changing. While juvenile workers continued to be employed widely in industry and in the craft trades, they were also increasingly drawn into the growing retail, commercial, and service sectors, which absorbed large numbers of girls and boys in low-paid jobs, for example as servants, messengers, or delivery boys.[13]

A heightened awareness of the young worker on the part of politicians and middle-class reformers was in part a response to the visibly growing army of juvenile workers in the factories, workshops, stores, and streets of Germany's cities. However, the middle-class image of the working-class adolescent did not simply reflect changes in social structure.[14] The German middle classes' fear of the growing political power of organized labour expressed itself in the image of the young working-class male seduced by unscrupulous political agitators.[15] Growing up in a proletarian milieu where the church exerted little authority, no longer under the control of the *Volksschule* (elementary school), and still awaiting the disciplining influence of the army, working-class male adolescents were seen as liable to fall prey to Social Democratic propaganda.[16]

At the same time, middle-class unease about urbanization and the fear of the slum and its inhabitants expressed itself in the image of the shiftless, insolent youngster corrupted by a world of the big city and tempted into a life of disorder, shiftlessness, and crime.[17] A

[12] Figures taken from Linton, 'Who Has the Youth', 24.
[13] Ibid. 23–30; Toni Pierenkemper, 'Jugendliche im Arbeitsmarkt: Deutschland seit dem Ende des 19. Jahrhunderts', in Dowe (ed.), *Jugendprotest*, 56–8.
[14] Domansky, 'Politische Dimensionen', 117.
[15] Deutsche Zentrale fur Jugendfürsorge (ed.), *Der Kampf der Parteien um die Jugend* (Berlin, 1912); Linton, 'Who Has the Youth', 118 ff.
[16] There was much concern over the 'gap' of 3 or 4 years between the end of compulsory schooling at 13 or 14 and conscription into the army at 18 or 19 years: see Klaus Saul, 'Der Kampf um die Jugend zwischen Volksschule und Kaserne: Ein Beitrag zur "Jugendpflege" im Wilhelminischen Reich', *MM* 9/1 (1971), 98–144.
[17] Kaup, in *Verhandlungen der 5. Generalversammlung der Gesellschaft für Soziale Reform am 12. und 13. Mai 1911 in Berlin* [= Gesellschaft für Soziale Reform (ed.), *Die jugendlichen Arbeiter in Deutschland*, 5/6] (Jena, 1911), 89; Lutz

rising trend in the juvenile crime statistics prompted a contemporary observer to comment on the effects of hectic urban life in whipping up the nerves of the young, the degrading influence of mass entertainments, the erosion of working-class family life and the temptations open to youngsters with excessive freedom and unchannelled energies.[18] The unskilled were singled out by this commentator and by other contemporaries as being particularly prone to drift into disreputable activities.[19] Unskilled male youngsters were thought to be disproportionately involved in crime, even 'predestined' to become delinquent.[20] However, it was not merely criminal behaviour, but a whole range of forms of behaviour in unskilled working-class adolescents which affronted middle-class respectability and were diagnosed as symptoms of delinquency (*Verwahrlosung*).[21] The unskilled were not subject to the patriarchal authority of the master craftsman; not being bound by an apprenticeship contract, they had no need to bow to the whims of employers, and they could and did throw up their jobs and move on from one day to the next. They could earn in their unskilled jobs relatively high wages compared to the nominal sum (at best) paid to apprentices, and as a result enjoyed a status that enabled them to indulge in 'adult' leisure activities and to ignore parental discipline and other forms of authority alike.

Germany's economic prosperity and political stability appeared to depend on working-class boys being properly socialized into their roles as disciplined workers and loyal subjects of the Kaiser. Her military potential and racial future, it was argued, depended on the reproduction of a healthy population, this in turn being based on sound family life. The problem of the deteriorating fitness of the population (revealed in statistics on army recruits), the fear of racial degeneration, and the concern about the falling birth rate were recurrent themes in debates among bourgeois politicians, social reformers and educationalists in the decade before the First World

---

Niethammer, 'Some Elements of the Housing Reform Debate in Nineteenth-Century Europe', in Bruce M. Stave (ed.), *Modern Industrial Cities: History, Policy, Survival* (Beverly Hills, Calif., and London, 1981), 129–64.

[18] Paul Köhne, *Kriminalität und sittliches Verhalten der Jugendlichen* [= Gesellschaft für soziale Reform (ed.), *Die jugendlichen Arbeiter in Deutschland*, 2] (Jena, 1910), 10–15.

[19] Peukert, *Sozialdisziplinierung*, 62.

[20] Köhne, *Kriminalität*, 12.

[21] Peukert, *Sozialdisziplinierung*, 55.

War on the health, education, and morals of youth.²² They particularly figured in debates about the education of working-class girls: the future of the race required the successful transformation of the working-class girl into a thrifty housewife, conscientious mother, and custodian of the health and morals of future generations.²³ Using stereotypical images of working-class life, middle-class commentators portrayed the working-class family in a state of crisis and city life fraught with sexual risks. Dangers were alleged to stem from the increasing prevalence of lodgers in the working-class household;²⁴ outside the home, the factory floor was seen as a potential den of vice;²⁵ shop work and domestic service were seen as confronting girls with a world of wealth and privilege which would incite envy together with tastes and aspirations beyond their station.²⁶ Young women who indulged their tastes for fashion and entertainments such as the cinema or dance-halls were regarded as already on the slippery slope towards immorality and away from marriage and family life.²⁷ It seemed that every independent young working woman out on the streets of the cities was liable to arouse in the middle-class mind the spectre of the prostitute.²⁸

In Hamburg, with its harbour, its slums, its crime, and its prostitution, the complex of political and social circumstances which inspired middle-class concern with the problem of working-class youth was much in evidence. Hamburg's population grew in

²² Max von Gruber, 'Der Berufsschutz der Jugendlichen', in *Verhandlungen der 5. Generalversammlung der Gesellschaft für Soziale Reform am 12. und 13. Mai 1911 in Berlin* [= Gesellschaft für Soziale Reform (ed.), *Die jugendlichen Arbeiter in Deutschland*, 5/6] (Jena, 1911), 12–50; Paul Weindling, *Health, Race and German Politics between National Unification and Nazism 1870–1945* (Cambridge, 1989), 81–2, 210–11.
²³ Von Gruber, 'Berufsschutz', 31, 41, 45; Derek Linton, 'Between School and Marriage, Workshop and Household: Young Working Women in Late Imperial Germany', *European History Quarterly*, 18 (1988), 387–408, 390–1; id., '*Who Has the Youth*', 166–7.
²⁴ Von Gruber, 'Berufsschutz', 42.
²⁵ Oberbürgermeister Cuno, 'Die Fortbildungsschule', in *Verhandlungen der 5. Generalversammlung der Gesellschaft für Soziale Reform*, 139.
²⁶ Hans Weicker, *Bildung und Erziehung außerhalb der Schule (Jugendpflege)* [= Gesellschaft für soziale Reform (ed.), *Die jugendlichen Arbeiter in Deutschland*, 4] (Jena 1911), 16–18, 20–1.
²⁷ Cuno, 'Die Fortbildungsschule', 140.
²⁸ Karin Walser, 'Prostitutionsverdacht und Geschlechterforschung: Das Beispiel der Dienstmädchen um 1900', *GG* 11, (1985), 99–111, 104; Lynn Abrams, 'Prostitutes in Imperial Germany 1870–1918: Working Girls or Social Outcasts?', in Richard J. Evans (ed.), *The German Underworld: Deviants and Outcasts in German History* (London, 1988), 189.

size from a quarter of a million in 1867 to one million in 1913, nearly two-thirds of this increase being due to migration.[29] The structure of the population in 1905 showed an above-average proportion of the population being between the ages of 20 and 30,[30] reflecting among other things the number of young, single migrants coming to the city from rural areas to work in the docks, the shipyards, the factories, and workshops of the city. In so far as their work did not entail living-in, many of these incomers boarded with Hamburg families. In Hamburg, as in other cities, this phenomenon aroused middle-class concern over the impact of overcrowding and the presence of non-family members on working-class family life, in particular on the health, welfare, and morals of children and adolescents growing up in such an overcrowded and apparently disorderly milieu.[31]

Significantly, the classic description of unskilled male urban youth in pre-war Germany derived from observations made in Hamburg by the Lutheran pastor, Clemens Schultz. His portrait of Hamburg's youthful 'toughs' (*Halbstarke*) was based on his experiences attempting to organize and 'improve' the working-class boys of the parish of St Pauli in the first decade of this century. His memorable description brings together a range of characteristic motifs used by middle-class reformers of the time, as this extract shows:[32]

Most of all, he [the *Halbstarker*] likes standing around idly in market-places . . . he is the sworn enemy of order . . . For this reason he hates regularity, he hates all things of beauty and above all he hates work, the orderly, regular fulfilment of duty. As a consequence he has no feeling for that which for other people makes life worth living: home, family, friendship, not to mention enthusiasm, or the desire to get on in life.[33]

---

[29] Clemens Wischermann, 'Wohnquartiere und Lebensverhältnisse in der Urbanisierung', in Arno Herzig et al. (eds.), *Arbeiter in Hamburg: Unterschichten, Arbeiter und Arbeiterbewegung seit dem ausgehenden 18. Jahrhundert* (Hamburg, 1983), 343.

[30] Tenfelde, 'Großstadtjugend', 203.

[31] Wischermann, 'Wohnquartiere', 347. A programme of slum clearance following the cholera epidemic of 1892 and the dock strike of 1896 increased the number of families in the *Gängeviertel* taking in lodgers. See Grüttner, 'Soziale Hygiene und soziale Kontrolle', in Herzig et al. (eds.), *Arbeiter in Hamburg*, 359.

[32] Peukert, *Sozialdisziplinierung*, 63–6; id., 'Clemens Schultens "Naturgeschichte des Halbstarken" ', in Deutscher Werkbund (ed.), *Schock und Schöpfung* (Darmstadt and Neuwied, 1986), 391–3.

[33] Clemens Schultz, *Die Halbstarken* (Leipzig, 1912), 8.

The Hamburg *Halbstarker*, characteristically employed in the docks and living in the slums of the inner city, featured notably in the records of political and social disturbances in the city in the years before the First World War such as the disturbances following the dock strike of 1896,[34] and the riots following the suffrage demonstration organized by the SPD ('Red Wednesday') of 1906.[35] For Hamburg's ruling classes, such youths embodied both the political and social aspects of the threatened subversion of the existing order.[36] The sense of threat obscured from the bourgeoisie the fact that the reformist leaders of Hamburg's Social Democracy actually shared many of the respectable values of the middle classes and had little patience with the undisciplined lifestyle of unskilled youth.[37]

In the decade following the turn of the century, a consensus emerged among middle-class social reformers and politicians in Germany that the working-class adolescent presented a set of problems requiring action.[38] Underlying their prescriptions was a concept of adolescence as a norm for young people of all classes, which entailed dependence on adult protection and subordination to adult authority. Such a phase, defined in terms of biology and psychology, took little account of the economic status of youngsters out at work after leaving school at 14.

There were some differences of emphasis among those who expressed concern about working-class adolescents. Some argued in terms of the problems suffered by working-class youth: exposed to neglect, stress, and danger at a vulnerable period of their lives, such youngsters were in need of protection by society and the state to safeguard their health and well-being as individuals—a strategy which would also promote the future health of the nation. Other commentators emphasized the degree to which the behaviour of working-class adolescents caused problems for society. Here already were to be found the twin strands which were to characterize many of the policies towards young people adopted in

---

[34] Grüttner, 'Soziale Hygiene und soziale Kontrolle', 360–3; Evans, *Death in Hamburg*; *Society and Politics in the Cholera Years 1830–1910* (Oxford, 1987), 512.
[35] Richard J. Evans, ' "Red Wednesday" in Hamburg: Social Democrats, Police and *Lumpenproletariat* in the Suffrage Disturbances of 17 January 1906', in id.. *Rethinking German History* (London, 1987), 279–80.
[36] Evans, *Death in Hamburg*, 78–108.
[37] Evans, ' "Red Wednesday" ', 279.
[38] Linton, '*Who Has the Youth*', 1–5.

Imperial Germany and subsequently: on the one hand, the impulse to protect and provide; on the other, the impulse to discipline and control.

Social Policy and Social Reform in Imperial Germany

Faced with the political challenge of the growing industrial working class, the state authorities in Imperial Germany were quick to resort to political repression. As part of the resistance by Reich governments to any moves towards full parliamentary democracy, restrictions were imposed on the Press, on the freedom of association, and the rights of trade unions. Even after the lifting of Bismarck's anti-socialist legislation, Social Democrats continued to be harassed by the public authorities, while the Reichstag as a whole was subject to government manipulation and intimidation. Within the government's campaign against political opponents in general, working-class adolescents were a target of specific measures of state repression, as we shall see below. However, in this period measures of political repression were increasingly accompanied by new strategies promising to bring political and social stability in the longer term. Social policy and reform represented one such strategy.

In terms of state social policy Germany was a pioneer: its schemes of workers' insurance are often seen as a turning-point in the history of the modern welfare state. Some historians have seen German social insurance in terms of its function as a means of investing in and consolidating the industrial labour force at a key point in economic development.[39] The immediate motive behind the introduction of social insurance, however, was political. Social insurance was part of the socially conservative, protectionist policy pursued by Bismarck from the end of the 1870s onwards; it was a policy designed to confound the National Liberals and take the wind out of the sails of the SPD.[40]

[39] Gaston V. Rimlinger, 'Welfare Policy and Economic Development: A Comparative Historical Perspective', *JEH* 26 (1966), 556–71; F. Tennstedt, *Sozialgeschichte der Sozialpolitik in Deutschland vom 18. Jahrhundert bis zum Ersten Weltkrieg* (Göttingen, 1981), 142–7; Hans-Peter Ullmann, 'German Industry and Bismarck's Social Security System', in Wolfgang J. Mommsen and W. Mock (eds.), *The Emergence of the Welfare State in Britain and Germany 1850–1950* (London, 1981), 133–49.

[40] Hans-Ulrich Wehler, *Das deutsche Kaiserreich 1871–1918* (Göttingen, 1973), 136; Detlev Zöllner, 'Germany', in Peter Köhler, F. Zacher, and Martin Partington (eds.), *The Evolution of Social Insurance 1881–1981* (London, 1982), 1–92, 12–17.

The introduction of state social insurance did not achieve its aim of eradicating support for Social Democracy among the working class, nor did it silence the calls for social reform in other spheres. Bourgeois social reforming groups in the Kaiserreich ranged from the academic social reformers represented in the Verein für Sozialpolitik (Association for Social Policy), founded in 1872, and the Gesellschaft für Soziale Reform (Society for Social Reform), founded in 1901, to specific organizations concerned with single issues like housing reform and health education, and Catholic and Protestant organizations for social welfare and social reform: the Caritas, the Innere Mission and the Evangelisch-Sozialer Kongreß.[41] On the whole, these social reformers welcomed Bismarck's social insurance schemes, but saw them as a mere beginning. From the 1870s onwards, middle-class social reformers' efforts extended beyond the area of social insurance and they became involved in campaigns to reform the poor law, housing, public health provision, and factory legislation. It was within the framework of these campaigns that the question of policies towards children and adolescents arose.

Bourgeois social reformers in the Kaiserreich sought, in the short term, speedy and effective measures to relieve the poor, cure the sick, and reform the criminal; in the long term, the goal of their campaigns was social stability and the improvement of the condition of the working class through the prevention of poverty, disease, and crime. The stress on preventive policies led logically to a focus on the younger sections of the population. Working-class adults might be doomed to live in misery and to hate the social order, but their children might be saved to form a future population of industrious and healthy citizens. Social reformers thus saw children and young people as a priority in the context of general social reforms; at the same time, they sought to bring together disparate areas of policy to form a single integrated strategy of social reform targeted at children and young people. These efforts found their expression in the youth welfare movement, which emerged around the turn of the century with the unifying concept of the child's right to education and the state's obligation towards the child.

[41] Rüdiger vom Bruch, 'Bürgerliche Sozialreform im deutschen Kaiserreich', in id. (ed.), *Weder Kommunismus noch Kapitalismus: Bürgerliche Sozialreform in Deutschland vom Vormärz bis zur Ära Adenauer* (Munich, 1985), 61–179.

The Young Worker in the Economy

One context in which working-class adolescents became the focus of public policy in this period was that of the economy and of economic policy. Juvenile labour came to be seen as a problem distinct from that of child labour. Child labour was coming to be seen as a social evil and detrimental to the health of the future workforce, and children were the object of legislation designed to curb their employment.[42] Juvenile labour, on the other hand, was not regarded as a problem in itself; it was the type of work, the nature of the working environment, and the relationship between employer and juvenile employee which aroused concern.

Educationalists and social reformers were chiefly concerned about two issues. The first was the growing number of youngsters going into 'dead-end' jobs after leaving school. Such youngsters, it was feared, would later swell the ranks of the casually employed poor. Social reformers therefore looked for methods to encourage youngsters to learn a trade and set up voluntary advisory centres for vocational counselling. The second issue giving rise to concern was the qualitative changes in the institution of apprenticeship itself.[43] The traditional form of apprenticeship in the artisan trades, where the apprentice lived in his master's household and was subject to his authority, not only inside the workshop but also in moral and social matters, was in decline. It was not only educationalists who were concerned about these developments; the master craftsmen themselves campaigned to uphold the traditional system of apprenticeship, this campaign being part of the efforts by *Handwerk* organizations generally to shore up the position of craft trades in an industrial economy.[44] From the 1880s onwards, under pressure from the craft organizations and in the context of a general retreat from the era of economic liberalism of the 1860s and 1870s, the governments of the Reich gradually restored some of the powers of

---

[42] On the *Kinderschutzgesetz* of 30 Mar. 1903, see Christa Hasenclever, *Jugendhilfe und Jugendgesetzgebung seit 1900* (Göttingen, 1978), 26–37.

[43] Linton, '*Who Has the Youth*', 30–7.

[44] David Blackbourn, 'Between Resignation and Volatility: The German Petite Bourgeoisie in the 19th Century', in Geoffrey Crossick and Hans-Georg Haupt (eds.), *Shopkeepers and Master Artisans in 19th-Century Europe* (London, 1984), 35–61, 47; Shulamit Volkov, *The Rise of Popular Antimodernism in Germany* (Princeton, NJ, 1978), 109–11.

the guilds. Of most significance for the question of apprenticeship was the legislation of 1908, which laid down that only qualified master craftsmen were entitled to train apprentices in the artisan trades. This measure went some way towards satisfying the interests of the *Handwerk* lobby. However, it did nothing to halt the economic developments—such as the beginning of industry-based vocational training—which were threatening the craft trades' monopoly of training and the master's traditional authority over the apprentice.[45]

Regulations to maintain the traditional system of apprenticeship were one way in which the state authorities intervened in the area of vocational training. Another way was by promoting vocational schooling.[46] Public vocational schooling had developed in the German federal states (*Länder*) since the 1850s on a local basis.[47] To offset the possible decline in the standards of craft training brought about by the deregulation of the craft trades in the 1850s and 1860s, the *Gewerbeordnung* (Industrial Code) of 1871 empowered local authorities, in agreement with the guilds, to make it obligatory for certain categories of apprentice to attend classes at vocational school, or, as it was more commonly known before the First World War, 'continuation school' (*Fortbildungsschule*).

Continuation schools in this period were largely geared to the training of skilled workers and were part of a 'dual system' of vocational training: practical training on the job was supplemented by theoretical instruction and technical drawing in continuation school classes in the evenings and on Sundays. The schools were often run by the local guilds on a private basis, but state-run continuation schools were also beginning to be set up. Local legislation on compulsory attendance became quite common by the First World War. Hamburg was an exception in this respect. In 1865, the city state authorities had taken over from a private philanthropic association the running of Hamburg's 'trade schools'

---

[45] Heinrich A. Winkler, *Mittelstand, Demokratie und Nationalsozialismus: Die politische Entwicklung von Handwerk und Kleinhandel in der Weimarer Republik* (Cologne, 1972), 45–6; Volkov, *Popular Antimodernism*, 344; Blackbourn, 'Between Resignation and Volatility', 51.

[46] On vocational schooling in Imperial Germany, see Linton, 'Who Has the Youth', 73–97.

[47] Wolfdietrich Jost, *Gewerbliche Schulen und politische Macht: Zur Entwicklung des gewerblichen Schulwesens in Preußen in der Zeit von 1850–1880* (Weinheim and Basle, 1982).

(*Gewerbeschulen*), which corresponded to the continuation schools elsewhere in Germany. The curriculum of the schools was developed in line with the wishes of the craft organizations and Hamburg's Chamber of Commerce; meanwhile, a number of private vocational schools continued to exist alongside the public ones. Individual employers and craft associations began to include clauses on compulsory attendance at the trade schools in apprenticeship contracts; however, it was only in 1913 that a law was passed by the city authorities to enforce vocational schooling for apprentices.[48] The fact that this legislation was so belated reflected the long-standing reluctance of the city fathers to interfere in the workings of Hamburg's economy—moreover, due to the outbreak of war, its implementation was delayed until the post-war period.[49]

The state authorities in Imperial Germany promoted vocational schooling partly to improve skilled workers' training; from the 1890s onwards, however, a new dimension of vocational school policy was becoming evident. In Prussia, continuation schools were increasingly regarded as instruments in the campaign to stop the spread of Social Democracy: the schools were to inculcate patriotic values and obedience to state authority into their working-class pupils. In line with this new goal, the attendance of unskilled youngsters as well as apprentices began to be enforced.[50] In Hamburg, too, discussions took place on extending the scope of the vocational school so that it would become an instrument of moral and political education as well as of training, and would extend to young unskilled male and female workers as well as apprentices. Accordingly, Hamburg's law of 1913 laid down compulsory attendance at vocational school not just for apprentices, but for all young male workers.[51]

Organizing Leisure: The State and Jugendpflege

The additional new role envisaged for the vocational school—as an institution to educate as well as to train working-class youth

---

[48] Jürgen Brühns, 'Der Schülerstreik an den Gewerbeschulen in Hamburg 1918/19', in Hans-Peter de Lorent and Volker Ullrich (eds.), *Der Traum von der freien Schule: Schule und Schulpolitik in Hamburg während der Weimarer Republik* (Hamburg, 1988), 41. [49] Evans, *Death in Hamburg*, 38–44.
[50] Saul, 'Kampf um die Jugend', 108.
[51] Brühns, 'Der Schülerstreik', 42–3.

beyond the elementary school—points to the concern on the part of the state authorities in Imperial Germany with the potential political threat posed by working-class adolescents. These fears were fuelled by the emergence of socialist youth organizations in various parts of the Reich from 1904 onwards.[52] It was working-class male youth who were primarily of concern in this context. The socialist youth organizations were mixed, but girls remained a small minority of members, and it was male youngsters, the soldiers and the voters of the future, who were thought to be the major problem.[53]

The state authorities' reaction to the signs of radical political activity among working-class youth was twofold. On the one hand the Reich authorities adopted a strategy of repression, culminating in the clause in the Imperial Law on Associations (*Reichsvereinsgesetz*) of 19 April 1908, which banned persons under 18 years from belonging to political associations, participating in the meetings of such associations, or attending public political meetings. All Social Democratic youth organizations were declared to be political associations for the purposes of this law.[54] From 1908 onwards, Social Democratic youth organizations were forced to restrict their activities to educational and cultural work under the supervision of the party executive—a development not unwelcome to the SPD leadership.[55]

The other aspect of the authorities' attempts to counteract the influence of Social Democracy on working-class youth lay in state attempts to promote 'positive' measures designed to weaken the attraction of the socialist youth organizations. Leisure activities under adult supervision were seen as appropriate 'positive' measures of this kind. Such activities were known as *Jugendpflege* ('cultivation of youth', or 'youth work'), as distinct from *Jugendfürsorge*

---

[52] Karl-Heinz Jahnke et al., *Geschichte der Arbeiterjugendbewegung 1904–1945* (Berlin, 1973), 11–58; Erich Eberts, *Arbeiterjugend 1904–1945: Sozialistische Erziehungsgemeinschaft—politische Organisation* (Frankfurt am Main, 1979), 25–8; Heinrich Eppe, *Selbsthilfe und Interessenvertretung: Die sozial- und jugendpolitischen Bestrebungen der sozialdemokratischen Arbeiterjugendorganisation 1904–1933* (Bonn, 1983), 15–23.

[53] Martina Naujoks, *Mädchen in der Arbeiterjugendbewegung in der Weimarer Republik* (Hamburg, 1984), 24; however, see Linton, 'Between School and Marriage', 395, for references to Prussian officials' fears of Social Democracy extending its influence over young women.

[54] Saul, 'Kampf um die Jugend', 104–6.

[55] Eberts, *Arbeiterjugend*, 29.

('youth welfare'): the latter term covered welfare measures directed at specific categories of 'problem' or deviant adolescents rather than at 'normal' youth generally. The aim of *Jugendpflege* was to steer a mass of potentially if not actually delinquent working-class adolescents away from various forms of undesirable behaviour, while the more coercive measures of youth welfare were employed to deal with those adolescents whose delinquency or deviance took acute forms.[56]

There was already a tradition of *Jugendpflege* in Germany dating from the mid-nineteenth century, but until the turn of the century such attempts to organize young people's leisure had been dominated by the Churches and had not succeeded in reaching the mass of urban working-class adolescents.[57] From the turn of the century onwards, such forms of youth work came to be challenged. Young people were starting to take a greater part in organizing their own activities, and middle-class social reformers and educationalists pointed out that the stuffy piety of the traditional boys' clubs and girls' circles was a deterrent to the mass of youngsters. Seeing new fields to conquer, the reformers attempted to expand and enliven youth work by organizing 'modern' activities such as sports, hikes, excursions, and discussions. Two Hamburg practitioners were notable pioneers of the new youth work, both known for their work with working-class boys: the pastor Clemens Schultz (author of the study on *Halbstarke*), and Walter Classen, founder of the Hammerbrook *Volksheim* (settlement house) and initiator of apprentices' clubs in various working-class districts of the city.[58]

The first decade of the century saw a boom in *Jugendpflege*. Public authorities were not initially involved: the development took place on the basis of private and philanthropic organizations and activities throughout Germany. However, in the years preceding the outbreak of war the state authorities in Prussia sought to move into this network of activities with the aim of harnessing youth work to their own 'national' and anti-socialist ends.[59] On the basis of a series of decrees from 1901 onwards which culminated in the decree on *Jugendpflege* of 18 January 1911 (the provisions of which were extended to youth work for girls in 1913),[60] the Prussian state

[56] Peukert, *Sozialdisziplinierung*, 109–13.   [57] Ibid. 107.
[58] Jürgen Reulecke, 'Bürgerliche Sozialreformer und Arbeiterjugend im Kaiserreich', *AfS* 22 (1982), 321–3.
[59] Linton, '*Who Has the Youth*', 139–64.
[60] Linton, 'Between School and Marriage', 387–8, 395–8.

authorities provided funding for approved *Jugendpflege* organizations: these did not include Social Democratic organizations. Closely linked with these efforts to promote the state's ideas of patriotic youth work was the founding in 1911 of the Young Germany League (Jungdeutschlandbund). This was an explicitly nationalist organization personally backed by the Kaiser, which was set up on a nationwide basis and offered facilities for physical and paramilitary training as an incentive for existing youth organizations to affiliate to the League.[61] The success of the Young Germany League was impressive on paper, and by 1914 it claimed a membership of three-quarters of a million via its affiliated organizations; however, such affiliations were in many cases merely nominal, and a more realistic estimate of its membership put it at 67,000.[62] Sceptics pointed out how unsuccessful the League was in reaching its real target group, working-class male youth over the age of 14.[63] In the event, the experiment of a directly state-sponsored youth organization was soon abandoned and was not to be revived until the very end of the Weimar period, when once again direct attempts were made to mobilize young men for national ends through the promotion of paramilitary training.

Saving the Child and Disciplining the Adolescent: The Youth Welfare Movement in the Kaiserreich

Private philanthropic institutions and the Churches had long been concerned with providing care and education for neglected, orphaned, and destitute children. Publicly organized and financed measures emerged in the eighteenth century, when absolutist rulers saw the state as being responsible for training its subjects in the virtues of industry, piety, and obedience; workhouses and orphanages were founded to take in delinquent and vagrant children as well as orphans and foundlings and set them to work in manufacture. During the upsurge of economic liberalism in the nineteenth century, a reaction took place against such institutions.[64] In the later

[61] Saul, 'Kampf um die Jugend', 119–23.
[62] 'Who Has the Youth', 157.
[63] Saul, 'Kampf um die Jugend', 124.
[64] Lindemann, 'Unterschichten und Sozialpolitik in Hamburg, 1799–1814', in Herzig et al. (eds.), *Arbeiter in Hamburg*, 61–70, 66–8; Peukert, *Sozialdisziplinierung*, 44–6.

nineteenth century, however, child and youth welfare moved into a new phase. In the context of campaigns for social reform and the growing concern with working-class adolescence as a problem, child and youth welfare increasingly became a definable area for public intervention and regulation.

Jugendfürsorge was targeted at children and young people who could be categorized according to definable social, educational, or physical deficiencies. The measures required to remedy these deficiencies involved a number of disparate areas of policy; the decades before the First World War saw the emergence of a movement which sought to unify these diverse strands of policy. A youth welfare lobby emerged, comprising not only the general social-reforming groups already mentioned, but also specialized pressure groups such as the Archiv deutscher Berufsvormünder (German Professional Guardians' Association), the Deutsche Zentrale für Jugendfürsorge (German Central Association for Youth Welfare), the Deutsche Vereinigung für Jugendgerichte und Jugendgerichtshilfen (Juvenile Courts Association), and the Allgemeiner Fürsorgeerziehungstag (Conference on Correctional Education). The administrators, doctors, lawyers, clergy, teachers, and educationalists organized in these groups set out to make education and health care central planks of a scientific and systematic policy of public youth welfare catering for the young from infancy to maturity.

CHILD AND YOUTH WELFARE, THE POOR LAW AND PUBLIC HEALTH

The state's responsibility for the health and education of the young was most easily invoked where children were already under the supervision of the public authorities. These included orphans and destitute children and juveniles, the care of whom was until 1918 the responsibility of the municipal and parish poor-law authorities.[65] Other categories of children under public supervision included the children fostered privately, many of whom were illegitimate. Social reformers called for a greater degree of intervention by the state to supervise the welfare of this large category of children, who were known to be disproportionately at risk from neglect and disease, and a movement arose for the establishment of public guardianship

[65] Hasenclever, *Jugendhilfe*, 23–7.

for illegitimate and other foster children. However, by 1918 the legislative basis and the administrative apparatus for such an institution on a national scale were still lacking.[66]

The principle behind the demands for the reform of welfare for orphans, the illegitimate, and the children of the poor was the emancipation of such provision from the stigmas and restrictions of the traditional poor-law system. While the thorough overhaul of the entire poor law remained the main goal of organizations such as the Deutscher Verein für Armenpflege und Wohltätigkeit (German Association for Poor Relief and Welfare), the youth welfare lobby worked for the short-term goal of separating or 'liberating' child and youth welfare from the rest of the poor law. This involved not only creating an administrative distinction between child welfare and the rest of the poor law, but in bringing together all the fragmented powers and obligations regarding children and juveniles in a single authority—powers which were scattered between the local poor-relief authorities, the guardianship courts, the orphans' board (Gemeindewaisenrat), and the correctional education authorities. Administrative reforms taken in several large cities before the First World War went some way towards achieving this by setting up special children's departments of the poor-law authorities to deal with orphans and destitute children.[67]

One goal underlying the campaign for children's departments was pedagogical. The departments were to become guarantors of the 'child's right to education', a concept propagated in the first decade of the twentieth century above all by Wilhelm Polligkeit, a prominent social reformer and leading member (later chairman) of the German Association for Poor Relief and Welfare.[68] There was, however, an additional driving force behind welfare reforms directed at children: the concern with public health. To social hygienists, child and youth welfare was part of a comprehensive programme to counteract the threat of national physical degeneration.[69] Social hygiene, a strategy for public health which sought explanations for the occurrence of disease in the physical and social environment of individuals and social groups, arose as a school of

[66] Ibid. 25; Walter Friedländer and Earl Myers, *Child Welfare before and after Nazism* (Chicago, 1940), 75–8.
[67] Hasenclever, *Jugendhilfe*, 31–3.
[68] Peukert, *Sozialdisziplinierung*, 131–3.
[69] On the movement for child health and youth welfare in the context of the social hygiene movement, see Weindling, *Health, Race and German Politics*, 188–214.

thought around the turn of the century in reaction both to the older environmental hygiene and to the more recent theories based on bacteriology.[70] Social hygienists called for public action which went beyond the improvement of sanitation on the one hand and the isolation of infectious individuals on the other. They focused on social groups which were particularly at risk from disease—such as infants and young children—and undertook efforts to improve their environment and living standards as well as their habits and attitudes to health.

Concern for preventive health and education came to prevail in marginal areas such as child and youth welfare more quickly than in the core areas of poor relief for adults, where public welfare continued to be determined primarily by the drive to keep costs down and deter 'scrounging'.[71] In the years before the First World War, public facilities such as infant welfare clinics and school medical services expanded in the larger urban centres such as Hamburg and Berlin. Meanwhile, public subsidies were made available to private organizations providing school meals, excursions, and holidays for children.[72]

In Hamburg, a basic separation of child and youth welfare from general poor relief was achieved in conjunction with the general reform of the city-state's poor law in 1892–3 which introduced the 'Elberfeld system', enabling an intensified supervision of the poor by honorary middle-class officials.[73] A separate law of July 1892 laid down that the care of pauper children was the responsibility of the Orphanage Board (Waisenhauskollegium).[74] These reforms reflected the growing concern of the Hamburg middle classes with the need to control and supervise the poor, together with the view that pauper children had specific health and educational needs which were most effectively catered for separately from the general system of poor relief. Just as the city-state authorities were

[70] Weindling, *Health, Race and German Politics*, 168–73.
[71] Tennstedt, *Sozialgeschichte der Sozialpolitik*, 215.
[72] Adelheid Gräfin zu Castell Rüdenhausen, 'Die Überwindung der Armenschule: Schülerhygiene an den Hamburger öffentlichen Volksschulen im Zweiten Kaiserreich', *AfS* 22 (1982), 201–77.
[73] Evans, *Death in Hamburg*, 99–100, 104–5; Heinz Schröder, *Die Geschichte der hamburgischen öffentlichen Jugendfürsorge 1863–1924* (Hamburg, 1966), 81–6. On the Elberfeld system of poor relief generally, see Sachße and Tennstedt, *Geschichte der Armenfürsorge*, i. 214–22.
[74] Schröder, *Geschichte der hamburgischen öffentlichen Jugendfürsorge*, 72–80.

implementing the reforms, a public health catastrophe hit Hamburg which stretched the city's public health and welfare provision, including its child welfare system, to the limit. Hamburg's cholera epidemic of August–September 1892 accelerated the creation of a more highly professionalized city administration, gave new impetus to public health reforms in the city, and strengthened—at least temporarily—the will of the public authorities to tackle the problems of poverty and disease.[75] The reform of public child welfare continued apace after 1892: further administrative reforms, transferring further responsibilities to the Orphanage Board, gradually brought all welfare and educational measures for children and juveniles apart from normal schooling under a single public authority. The Orphanage Board, which in 1910 was renamed the Public Youth Welfare Board (Behörde für öffentliche Jugendfürsorge), had as its director from 1900 to 1913 Johannes Petersen, a prominent figure in the youth welfare movement, a vigorous campaigner for the 'child's right to education', and a driving force behind the centralization and rationalization of child and youth welfare services in Hamburg.[76]

By 1910, Hamburg's Youth Welfare Board was caring for orphans, supervising children fostered privately, and exercising official guardianship over all illegitimate children in the city-state of Hamburg; in addition, it administered correctional education, put children and juveniles judged at risk on probation (Erziehungsaufsicht, later renamed Schutzaufsicht) and carried out investigations for the newly established Juvenile Court (see below). By the outbreak of the First World War, Hamburg was one of the cities which had gone furthest down the road of public intervention to prevent and remedy educational problems, and its youth welfare department was the first in Germany to encompass a comprehensive range of youth welfare services.[77] The youth welfare movement saw Hamburg's youth welfare institutions as a model for the future nation-wide regulation of youth welfare.[78]

Welfare for orphans, the illegitimate, abandoned, and otherwise destitute children was the longest-established area of state child and

---

[75] Evans, *Death in Hamburg*, 508–22.
[76] On Johannes Petersen, see Schröder, *Geschichte der hamburgischen öffentlichen Jugendfürsorge*, 249–52.
[77] Hasenclever, *Jugendhilfe*, 31; Peukert, *Sozialdisziplinierung*, 102–3.
[78] Paul Felisch, *Ein deutsches Jugendgesetz* (Berlin, 1917), 34.

youth welfare, and it retained its importance as public youth welfare institutions developed and became more specialized. At the same time, however, reformers' attention was becoming increasingly focused on another area of youth welfare: the task of reforming and educating the delinquent adolescent.

YOUTH WELFARE AND THE TREATMENT OF DEVIANCE AND CRIME

The impulse behind the development of public child and youth welfare was the concern both for the physical and the moral health of the future adult population: youth welfare was to educate the child as well as to provide for its bodily needs. While the emphasis in welfare measures for infants and young children tended to be on physical health, the emphasis where older children and adolescents were concerned was on controlling and reforming their behaviour.

Juvenile crime represented the most readily measurable criterion of the extent of juvenile delinquency, and juvenile crime statistics were quoted by experts to demonstrate a rise in juvenile delinquency before and during the First World War.[79] However, as we have already seen, a whole range of forms of behaviour associated with the lifestyle of urban working-class youth became part of a perceived problem of growing *Verwahrlosung* among youth. This led criminologists, social reformers, and psychologists to undertake a search for convincing explanations of delinquent behaviour and for effective methods of dealing with individual adolescents 'at risk' or in trouble. This search generated new explanatory models placing various degrees of emphasis on the influence of hereditary and environmental factors on juvenile behaviour. Attention shifted away from individual sin, wickedness and guilt towards an approach focusing on the wider context of deviance. Crime, like disease, began to be seen as a social disorder, to be tackled in a wider context as well as at the individual level.

Within the search for the underlying general causes of individual deviance there were a number of different approaches. First, there was the school of thought influenced by Social Darwinism, which used medical and pseudo-scientific terminology in arguments purporting to demonstrate that asocial behaviour was caused

[79] G. Erich, 'Die Kriminalität der 12–14jährigen im Deutschen Reiche', *ZGS* 35/21 (1914), 21–5.

wholly or partly by hereditary factors.[80] One extreme version of this was the concept of the physically distinctive 'born criminal' put forward by the Italian criminologist Cesare Lombroso in the 1870s and 1880s.[81] The new science of 'criminal biology' (*Kriminalbiologie*) encouraged assumptions that young working-class delinquents were products of a degenerate residuum of the working class, a genetically inferior stratum passing on its defects from one generation to the next. Such assumptions represented in their biological determinism a dismissal of deviants and young criminals as mere human refuse, destined to perish in the struggle of the fittest to survive. The deprived social environment of this stratum of society was seen as a sign of their inferiority or inability to cope rather than a cause of it.

The emphasis placed by adherents of criminal biology on hereditary factors resulted in their taking a pessimistic view of the possibilities for reforming the individual delinquent. Taken to its logical extreme, it could imply that the only way of dealing with criminal and deviant individuals was to incarcerate them. Lombroso's theories about the 'criminal type' were, however, challenged by the sociologically-oriented 'modern' school of criminologists, who emphasized social environment as a contributory factor to criminal behaviour.[82] Advocates of a reform of juvenile justice adopted an approach to juvenile delinquency which was analagous to the efforts of social hygienists to tackle physical disease both at the level of the individual and at the level of the physical and social environment: they called for education for individual delinquents, to be backed up by reforms to improve the social milieu.[83]

The pre-war period thus saw the emergence of distinct schools of thought on the causes of and cures for delinquency, a debate which was to continue and intensify in the Weimar period. Meanwhile, policies towards delinquent adolescents were becoming an increasingly important part of public child and youth welfare provision. Youth welfare reformers campaigned with some success for the extension of state powers and obligations regarding children and

---

[80] Weindling, *Health, Race and German Politics*, 80–4.
[81] Ibid. 82–3; Robert Nye, *Crime, Madness and Politics in Modern France: The Medical Concept of National Decline* (Princeton, NJ, 1984), 99–101.
[82] Friedrich Kitzinger, *Die Internationale Kriminalistische Vereinigung: Betrachtungen über ihr Wesen und ihre bisherige Wirksamkeit* (Munich, 1905), 20–4.
[83] Ibid. 54–65.

adolescents seen as either threatened by their environment or as actively posing a threat to society. From the 1870s onwards, legislation was passed by the Reich and by the *Länder* which amounted to a new departure in state attitudes to the problem of delinquency.[84] The significance of this legislation lay, firstly, in the recognition of the problem of juvenile delinquency and children 'at risk' as a problem requiring state intervention; secondly, in the readiness to provide education in foster-families or in reformatories at public expense for the juveniles whose families were unable to contribute to the costs of such education; and, thirdly, in the state's readiness to intervene if necessary without the permission and against the will of parents.

The legislation passed between 1870 and 1900 relating to the education and treatment of deviant, neglected, and delinquent juveniles arose out of the system of criminal justice.[85] The new Imperial Criminal Code of 1871 dealt in its paragraphs 55–7 with various categories of juvenile offender. The age of criminal responsibility was fixed at 12 years (Criminal Code, paragraph 55). Juveniles between 12 and 18 years of age were regarded in limited respects as a category distinct from adult offenders: if they were judged to possess an understanding of the criminal nature of their actions, they were tried in ordinary courts and could be sent to prison.[86] However, in cases where young offenders aged 12–18 were judged not to be fully aware of the criminal nature of their offence, they were to be acquitted: the court could then decide whether to send them to a reformatory (Criminal Code, paragraph 56).

The treatment of children under 12 who had committed an offence was laid down in the law revising the criminal code (*Strafrechtsnovelle*) of 26 February 1876 (Criminal Code, paragraph 55, section 2).[87] The *Länder* were given powers to pass legislation on suitable measures, including correctional education (Zwangserziehung, later termed Fürsorgeerziehung) for dealing with offenders under 12 years.[88] On the basis of this new clause, a number of states passed laws dealing with child offenders. Prussia, for instance,

[84] Peukert, *Sozialdisziplinierung*, 68–72.
[85] Hasenclever, *Jugendhilfe*, 22.
[86] Peter Dittmer, 'Zur Geschichte der Zwangs- und Fürsorgeerziehung', Diss. jur. (Hamburg, 1960), 51.
[87] Peukert, *Sozialdisziplinierung*, 69–71.
[88] Hans Scherpner, *Geschichte der Jugendfürsorge* (Göttingen, 1966), 162; Dittmer, 'Zwangserziehung', 69.

passed a law in 1878 providing for correctional education (in foster families or in reformatories) for children under 12 who had committed a criminal offence.[89] Hamburg was among the states which went further and passed legislation which allowed for correctional education not only for child offenders but also for juveniles who, while not being criminal, were judged to be *verwahrlost* (delinquent or neglected).[90] Hamburg's law of 1887 enabled correctional education to be ordered not only in the cases envisaged by the Imperial Criminal Code in its revised version of 1876, but also for young criminals who had already been judged accountable for their actions and had been sentenced by the courts; and, furthermore, for children and juveniles under 16 in cases where the 'normal methods of education in home and school have proved inadequate to protect them from moral decay'.[91]

One consequence of the expansion of correctional education from the 1870s onwards was a shortage of reformatory places for those the state authorities chose to place in residential care rather than have fostered. In Prussia between 1900 and the outbreak of the First World War, there was a fivefold increase in the number of children and young people in correctional education; by 1913, the numbers stood at nearly 50,000; 40 per cent of these juveniles were in reformatories as opposed to foster care.[92] State reformatory provision was expanded, but financial constraints on such expansion meant that the correctional education authorities fell back on the confessional welfare organizations to provide reformatory places for the new influx of state referrals.[93] Confessionally-based reformatories were private charitable institutions, many of which dated from the mid-nineteenth century.[94] The beginnings of state-regulated correctional education brought the private reformatories into a new relationship with the state authorities and gradually into a position of financial dependence on the fees paid by the state for state-referred pupils.

Another consequence of the growth of state correctional education were disputes over which public authorities should bear its

[89] Dittmer, 'Zwangserziehung', 70.
[90] Scherpner, *Jugendfürsorge*, 162–3.
[91] Gesetz vom 6. Apr. 1887 betreffend die Zwangserziehung verwahrloster jugendlicher Personen, in *Gesetzsammlung der freien und Hansestadt Hamburg 1887*, 67–71.
[92] Dittmer, 'Zwangserziehung', 123.   [93] Ibid. 122.
[94] Peukert, *Sozialdisziplinierung*, 46–9; Scherpner, *Jugendfürsorge*, 126, 149, 155.

costs. These took place particularly in Prussia, where regional as opposed to local authorities bore a substantial part of the costs of correctional education. The Prussian state in turn subsidized the regional authorities for this purpose.[95] However, the Prussian law on correctional education of 1900 left a loophole which enabled the courts to declare that the removal of a juvenile from his or her home on the grounds of moral risk was not in itself sufficient grounds for the ordering of correctional education: instead, the courts decided, the child should simply be fostered at the expense of the local poor-law authorities. A Prussian law of 1915 reversed this ruling and laid down that if the removal of a child from its family and its transfer to other accommodation involved public costs—in other words if the child's parents were too poor to be made to pay for such accommodation—this did constitute sufficient grounds to order correctional education. This new law was intended to relieve local authorities of the burdens of financing substitute care for children 'at risk' and to encourage earlier, 'preventive' referrals to correctional education.[96] Behind these legal and financial twists and turns—which were to be of significance in the Weimar period—lay the issue of whether state intervention to remove children 'at risk' from their families as a supposedly preventive measure should be facilitated or not.

Further disputes arose over the principle of the supremacy of parental rights and obligations as compared to the rights and duties of the state. This emerged as a major issue in the debates on the new Civil Code of 1900. Representatives of the youth welfare movement criticized the provisions of the Civil Code for what they saw as its over-emphasis on the principle of parental rights. The Civil Code limited the powers of the state to intervene in order to take a juvenile into public care to those cases where the parents could be shown to be actually guilty of negligence or cruelty (Civil Code, paragraph 1666).[97] The law passed in 1902 to introduce the Civil Code made a concession on this point to the youth welfare lobby: it was left to the competence of the *Länder* to pass legislation enabling the public authorities to take children into care, not only in cases where the child had committed an offence or where the parents

---

[95] Hasenclever, *Jugendhilfe*, 23.
[96] Dittmer, 'Zwangserziehung', 126–8.
[97] Hasenclever, *Jugendhilfe*, 22.

could be proved guilty of neglect, where public care could be ordered anyway, but also where it was considered necessary to prevent their 'complete moral ruin'.[98]

In Hamburg in the decades before the First World War, the education of young delinquents and children and adolescents 'at risk' quickly developed into one of the chief tasks of the new centralized youth welfare authority.[99] One unusual feature marked out Hamburg's system of correctional education from that of other states. This was the system whereby parents could apply on their own initiative for their 'difficult' or delinquent children to be taken into public care at public expense, the decision on whether to grant such applications for so-called 'voluntary correctional education' (Freiwillige Fürsorgeerziehung) resting with the public authorities.[100] This system contributed to a rise in the number of children and young people referred to state correctional education in Hamburg in the years before the First World War, a rising proportion of these being adolescents aged 14 and above.[101] As a result of the increased referrals, there was a growing shortage of reformatory places.[102] The main confessionally-based institution in Hamburg was the famous Rauhes Haus, a Protestant boys' reformatory founded by Johannes Heinrich Wichern in 1833; however, by the 1880s the city-state authorities had already opted to expand their own provision for delinquent juveniles. A purpose-built reformatory was opened in 1884 in Ohlsdorf (on the outskirts of Hamburg) and a new public reformatory for girls was opened in 1911.[103] At the same time, alternatives to correctional education were also being explored. In 1912, the Youth Welfare Board's director Petersen explained in a lecture to the honorary officials of the Board that supervising youngsters 'at risk' in their own environment rather than referring them to a reformatory had a number of advantages: economic rationality (the youngsters involved would not be

---

[98] Scherpner, *Jugendfürsorge*, 163.
[99] Schröder, *Geschichte der hamburgischen öffentlichen Jugendfürsorge*, 53–61; Johannes Petersen, 'Erfahrungen über die Erziehungsaufsicht', *Blätter für die hamburgische öffentliche Jugendfürsorge*, 11/8 (1912), 35–8.
[100] Schröder, *Geschichte der hamburgischen öffentlichen Jugendfürsorge*, 57.
[101] Johannes Petersen, *Die hamburgische öffentliche Jugendfürsorge* (Hamburg, 1911), 89. [102] Ibid. 36.
[103] Schröder, *Geschichte der hamburgischen öffentlichen Jugendfürsorge*, 52; 'Die Erziehungsanstalt für schulentlassene Mädchen in Alsterdorf', *Blätter für die hamburgische öffentliche Jugendfürsorge*, 10/6 (1911), 29–33.

removed from their jobs) and the preservation (under the supervision of middle-class honorary officials) of the working-class family unit.[104] He assured his audience that such supervision was not an over-lenient treatment and affirmed that 'nothing is more damaging then cloying tenderness in face of the fearful horror of delinquency'.[105]

Meanwhile, at national level, debates were continuing regarding the situation of juvenile offenders. As we have seen above, the Imperial Criminal Code of 1871 fixed the age of criminal responsibility at 12 years. Young offenders aged between 12 and 18 years, unless they were judged to be incapable of understanding the criminal nature of their actions, were treated like adults, apart from certain modifications regarding sentencing—for instance, it was possible merely to issue a caution (*Verweis*) in cases of trivial offences or misdemeanours (*Vergehen* or *Übertretungen*).[106] The state of affairs whereby juvenile offenders could be tried in ordinary courts and sent to prison along with adults was seen by youth welfare reformers and criminologists as both harsh and ineffective. Alternative models were sought: the model which gained the most support was that of a special system of juvenile justice.

The campaign to reform the treatment of juvenile offenders which arose in Germany in the 1890s constituted a part of the general campaign for youth welfare, but it was at the same time a product of new trends in criminology and was associated with a movement for the reform of criminal justice as a whole.[107] According to the 'modern school' of criminology, punishment conceived as retribution and as a general deterrent to the community at large failed to prevent crime effectively. Instead, punishment should be determined by the goal of preventing crime at the individual level by educating and reforming the individual offender. This implied a flexible sentencing policy where the punishment should be designed to fit the criminal rather than the crime. Judicial reformers argued that the problem of young offenders was a

---

[104] Petersen, 'Erfahrungen über die Erziehungsaufsicht', 36–8.
[105] Ibid. 38.
[106] Wilhelm Ramcke, 'Die Jugendstrafgerichtsbarkeit in Hamburg während der Zeit 1909–1923', Diss. jur. (Hamburg, 1959), 1.
[107] On the development of juvenile courts in Germany generally, see Herbert Ruscheweyh, *Die Entwicklung des deutschen Jugendgerichts* (Weimar, 1918), 49–165.

particularly appropriate field for implementing the new approach. Juvenile offenders were considered 'suitable cases for treatment' in that they were regarded as not having reached the point of no return in a criminal career. At the same time, crime figures appeared to justify a focus on the juvenile criminal. Statistics for the Reich as a whole from 1882 onwards showed a rise in juvenile crime as a proportion of total crime, and above all a rising rate of reoffending among juveniles.[108] This, declared Franz von Liszt, a leading figure in the juvenile justice movement, demonstrated the bankruptcy of the existing criminal justice system.[109]

The German juvenile justice movement took its inspiration partly from the development of juvenile courts in the United States at the end of the nineteenth century, most notably in Massachusetts, Denver (Colorado), and Chicago.[110] Meanwhile, similar moves were taking place in Europe towards a special system of juvenile justice: in England, for instance, the Children Act of 1908 prescribed that separate juvenile courts be set up throughout the country.[111] In Germany, the reformers' programme included plans to raise the age of limited criminal responsibility from 12 to 14 years and to relax the principle of compulsory prosecution (*Legalitätsprinzip*) in order to allow trivial offences to be kept out of court. Together, these reforms would reduce the number of youngsters appearing in court in the first place. For those who were required to appear in court, the reformers advocated a reform of court proceedings in imitation of American juvenile courts, so that a specialized judge would preside together with lay assessors in a special courtroom from which the public would be excluded.

German juvenile justice reformers were concerned to turn the court into an educational institution in which the judge would have the freedom to operate a flexible system of educational measures and punishments according to the personality and diagnosed needs of the individual offender. To carry out this task, the juvenile court

---

[108] Peukert, *Sozialdisziplinierung*, 73, 82–3.
[109] Olaf Miehe, 'Die Anfänge der Diskussion über eine strafrechtliche Sonderbehandlung junger Täter', in Olaf Miehe and Friedrich Schaffstein (eds.), *Weg und Aufgabe des Jugendstrafrechts* (Darmstadt, 1968), 1–30, 2.
[110] Anthony M. Platt, *The Child Savers: The Invention of Delinquency*, 2nd edn. (Chicago and London, 1977), 9–10. For an early German-language account of American juvenile courts, see J. M. Baernreiter, *Jugendfürsorge und Strafrecht in den Vereinigten Staaten von Amerika* (Leipzig, 1905), 159–98.
[111] W. Clarke Hall, *Children's Courts* (London, 1926), 55.

judge would need an extensive back-up service of staff undertaking investigations into the background of the individual prior to the trial and subsequently carrying out supervisory tasks under probation orders. The juvenile justice movement therefore pressed for the expansion of such auxiliary services and for close liaison with the existing state youth welfare authorities.

From 1908 onwards, the Reich authorities were preparing legislation to put some of the demands of the juvenile justice movement into practice. However, neither the draft of 1908 nor that of 1912 reached the statute book.[112] In view of the delay in Reich legislation, the advocates of juvenile justice reform urged local authorities to implement some of their demands. Suspended sentences had already been introduced from 1895 onwards in several *Länder* and were increasingly linked to a system of probation, and, from 1907–8 onwards, juvenile courts were set up in a number of large cities.[113]

Hamburg was not the first city to set up a juvenile court, but followed the example of other cities without much delay; those campaigning in Hamburg for the introduction of juvenile courts sought to bring pressure on the city state government by playing on the fact that Hamburg was lagging behind cities like Frankfurt am Main, Berlin, and Munich.[114] In October 1908, the judicial administration was reorganized so that all cases involving young people under 18 would be dealt with by a single court.[115] The new court came into operation in January 1909 under the direction of Wilhelm Hertz. From 1915, the powers of the juvenile court judge were extended so that he could also function as a guardianship court judge (*Vormundschaftsrichter*), with the powers to order correctional education where appropriate.[116]

In the years before the First World War, the juvenile justice movement appears to have had a more dramatic appeal than other campaigns for infant and child welfare. Its experiments in setting up juvenile courts and its debates on legislative reform captured the attention of a middle-class public, and the juvenile justice movement began to assume a leading role in the youth welfare movement as a whole.

[112] Ruscheweyh, *Entwicklung des deutschen Jugendgerichts*, 132–49.
[113] Peukert, *Sozialdisziplinierung*, 86–91.
[114] Ramcke, *Jugendstrafgerichtsbarkeit*, 11.
[115] Ibid. 42.
[116] Ibid. 145.

The First World War and its Impact on Policies towards Adolescents

The war broke down obstacles to state intervention in a number of vital areas of economic activity and social life.[117] Increasingly, and particularly from 1916 onwards, state authorities supervised industrial production, controlled the labour market, and organized food supplies.[118] Economic mobilization for a 'total war' was matched by efforts at political mobilization. This entailed more than propaganda: the Reich government saw itself compelled to cement the new national unity and social peace declared by the Kaiser with a degree of social welfare.

The poverty of the families of soldiers in the field and those left bereaved after husbands, sons, fathers, and brothers were killed presented one acute set of problems for the state authorities. In response to the problem of poverty directly caused by the war, the Reich government provided financial assistance which for the first time was outside the framework of poor relief and financed by central and local government funds.[119] The absence or death of breadwinners meant a sudden increase in the number of children taken into care as their families became unable to look after them. In Hamburg, 3,500 children were taken into residential care by the city authorities in the course of the war.[120] Poverty and food shortages also had an immediate impact on health. The physical health of infants and children was observed to be deteriorating in the war and the post-war period as a result of malnutrition, a deterioration which appeared all the more alarming in the light of the sharp fall in the birth rate.[121] The social hygiene movement and advocates of an

---

[117] Preller, *Sozialpolitik*, 85; Hentschel, *Geschichte der deutschen Sozialpolitik*, 55; Paul Weindling, 'The Medical Profession, Social Hygiene and the Birth Rate in Germany, 1914–1918', in Richard Wall and Jay Winter (eds.), *The Upheaval of War: Family, Work and Welfare in Europe, 1914–1918* (Cambridge, 1988), 417, 432–3.

[118] Gerald Feldman, *Army, Industry and Labor in Germany 1914–1918* (Princeton, NJ, 1966), 197–291.

[119] Rolf Landwehr, 'Funktionswandel der Fürsorge bis zum Ende der Weimarer Republik', in Rolf Landwehr und Rüdeger Baron (eds.), *Geschichte der Sozialarbeit: Hauptlinien ihrer Entwicklung im 19. und 20. Jahrhundert* (Weinheim and Basle, 1983), 73.

[120] Landesjugendamt und Jugendamt Hamburg, *Jahresbericht 1925* (Hamburg, 1926), 1.

[121] 'Der Massenmord an deutschen Kindern', *SP* 28/43 (1918/19), cols. 749–50.

active population policy drew attention to these problems and found more support than hitherto from state authorities.[122] The Reich Department of the Interior declared in March 1918 that, in view of the losses of human life and the fall in the birth rate during the war, the tasks of youth welfare were 'gaining a new significance for the future of our nation due to considerations of population policy and military planning'.[123]

Unemployment was an acute problem in the early months of the war before the economy had been adapted to the needs of war production. In response to the sharp rise in the numbers of young unemployed as a result of this dislocation, local authorities set up schemes to occupy unemployed youth and to keep them off the streets; in order to enforce this measure, the payment of unemployment benefits was made conditional upon attendance at these courses.[124] This so-called 'Barmbek system' was a Hamburg invention later copied elsewhere.[125] Wartime unemployment was short-lived, quickly giving way to a shortage of labour as the war industries expanded and adult male workers were conscripted. The development of the war economy drew women and young workers out of other sectors of the economy into industry: women and young people were recruited on a large scale for jobs as clerical staff and as manual workers in the war industries.[126] The total number of boys in the labour force between the ages of 14 and 18 increased by 10 per cent between 1913 and 1918, and the percentage increases were much higher in certain sectors like coalmining.[127]

The significance for youth policies of the wartime development of the labour market was twofold. First, it brought some important steps towards state control over the labour market to ensure that workers vital for war production were not called up.[128] Secondly, it focused attention on vocational training issues: the public authorities

---

[122] Weindling, 'Social Hygiene and the Birth Rate', 424–33.

[123] Reichsamt des Innern an das Preußische Ministerium des Innern, 7 Mar. 1918. ZStA Merseburg, Rep. 191, 2376.

[124] Wilhelm Kießling and Emma Ender, *Hamburgische Jugendpflege in und nach dem Krieg* (Hamburg, 1919), 9.

[125] Karl Christian Führer, *Arbeitslosigkeit und die Entstehung der Arbeitslosenversicherung in Deutschland 1902–1927* (Berlin, 1990), 502.

[126] Pierenkemper, 'Jugendliche im Arbeitsmarkt', in Dowe (ed.), *Jugendprotest*, 58–9.

[127] Domansky, 'Politische Dimensionen', in Dowe (ed.), *Jugendprotest*, 118; Linton, '*Who Has the Youth*', 197–203.

[128] Feldman, *Army, Industry and Labor*, 301–16, 409–20.

were already becoming concerned during the war that the recruitment of young workers into semi-skilled work in the munitions industry meant an interruption of skilled training and the prospect of a skill shortage after the war.[129]

Another area where demands for state intervention increased during the war was the problem of working-class adolescent behaviour. In contrast to the images of young war heroes on the battlefield, young workers on the home front had a bad press, being portrayed as earning lavish wages in the war industries (this has been shown to be a myth),[130] refusing to defer to authority in the family and the workplace, and contributing to crime and public disorder. Criminal statistics appeared to confirm the widespread view that delinquency was increasing: in Hamburg, there was a rise of 80 per cent in the number of juveniles convicted by the juvenile court between 1913 and 1917.[131] Young workers participated in bread riots, anti-war demonstrations, and strikes that were growing in the second half of the war, and there were signs that it was specifically young people who protested earlier and more strongly against the war.[132]

One response on the part of the state to the phenomenon of 'uncontrollable' working-class youth lay in repressive measures. Such measures were partly in response to young people's political activities. In Hamburg, for instance, the radical left-wing socialist youth group, set up in March 1916 in defiance of the local Social Democratic leadership, was banned after it organized an anti-war demonstration in August 1916.[133] However, a number of measures were intended to prevent 'delinquency' more generally: these included the abortive efforts by the military authorities to recruit male youth into paramilitary training schemes and the attempts to impose by military decree compulsory savings schemes to reduce the amount of money young workers had to spend.[134] In Hamburg,

[129] Preußisches Landesgewerbeamt an den Verein deutscher Maschinenbau-Anstalten, 22.10.1917. StAH, BSB I, B239.
[130] Linton, 'Who Has the Youth', 200–2.
[131] A. Heskel, 'Aus der Kriegsarbeit der Behörde für öffentliche Jugendfürsorge', Blätter für die hamburgische öffentliche Jugendfürsorge, 17/2 (1918), 12–15 and 17/3 (1918), 14.
[132] Domansky, 'Politische Dimensionen', in Dowe (ed.), Jugendprotest, 121–2.
[133] Ullrich, Kriegsalltag, 37–8.
[134] Gudrun Fiedler, Jugend im Krieg: Bürgerliche Jugendbewegung, Erster Weltkrieg und sozialer Wandel 1914–1923 (Cologne, 1989), 76–80; Domansky, 'Politische Dimensionen', 121.

attempts to control leisure activities included bans on young people attending popular shows and entertainments and even on smoking in public, measures which some state officials sought to retain into the post-war period.[135]

The end of the war and the revolutionary upheavals of 1918/19 brought a new focus on the politically threatening aspects of working-class adolescents' perceived disregard for authority. Conservative commentators in the public administration and in the churches expressed fears that the politically troubled times were bringing a breakdown of authority, unleashing youthful insubordination and indiscipline. According to an alarmed contemporary observer, a civil servant from Oppeln in Prussia, the erosion of traditional structures of authority was wreaking moral havoc in the younger generation: 'The revolution and its consequences have been particularly harmful for the psyche of many people, particularly of youth. . . . The foundations have been shattered. State institutions have almost completely lost their authority, as has the Church. The educational influence of parents has often been reduced to nil.'[136] The image of depraved youngsters running wild proved useful not only to those attempting to step up repressive measures; it also proved convenient for those seeking to develop social and welfare policies as an alternative to repression. In the course of the war, the idea of a comprehensive youth policy and a codification of all laws affecting the welfare of children and young people into a single 'Youth Law' gained currency within youth welfare circles.[137] In September 1918, a special conference was convened in Berlin by a large number of bourgeois social reform organizations, penal reform groups, and youth welfare agencies, which was attended by state officials.[138] Its theme was the need for the reorganization and

[135] Auszug aus dem Protokoll der Behörde für öffentliche Jugendfürsorge vom 5.1.1918. StAH, JB I, 333; Protokoll der Sitzung der Fachkommission der Zentralstelle für Volkswohlfahrt, 13 Dec. 1917. ZStA Potsdam, 30.01, 6083.

[136] Dr Lemke, Regierungsrat, Oppeln, an das Preußische Volkswohlfahrtsministerium, 20 Oct. 1920. ZStA Merseburg, Rep. 191, 2431.

[137] Helene Simon, 'Das Jugendrecht', *Schmollers Jahrbuch*, 39/1 (1915), 227–81; Paul Felisch, *Ein deutsches Jugendgesetz* (Berlin, 1917); Jacques Stern, *Der Weg zum deutschen Jugendgesetz* (Berlin, 1918).

[138] Deutscher Verein für öffentliche und private Fürsorge (ed.), *Jugendämter als Träger der öffentlichen Jugendfürsorge im Reich: Bericht über die Verhandlungen des deutschen Jugendfürsorgetags am 20. und 21. September 1918 in Berlin* (Berlin, 1919). The organizations convening the conference were the Deutscher Verein für Armenpflege und Wohltätigkeit (subsequently renamed the Deutscher Verein für

expansion of public child and youth welfare facilities and for better co-ordination between voluntary and public provision: a central demand of the reformers was the creation of a network of public youth welfare departments throughout the Reich. The war, they argued, had shown the urgency of effective measures of child and youth welfare, and had broken down resistance to state intervention in economic and social matters. Bourgeois social reformers and state officials alike agreed at this conference that one of the first tasks of the peace would be to build up educational and welfare provision for the young.

Armenpflege und Wohltätigkeit (subsequently renamed the Deutscher Verein für öffentliche und private Fürsorge), the Archiv Deutscher Berufsvormünder, the Zentrale für Volkswohlfahrt, the Deutsche Zentrale für Jugendfürsorge and the Deutscher Kinderschutzverband.

3
Public Policies towards Apprentices and Young Workers, 1918–1933

The Weimar Republic saw the debate on the young worker widen and intensify under the changed political and economic circumstances of the post-war period. In the wake of the social compromise between organized labour and employers, struck as the old order was collapsing, discussions of the young worker problem became bound up with the controversy over the new Republic's social policy and acquired an additional political charge. Young workers and apprentices were directly affected by reforms ranging from the legal recognition of collective agreements to the introduction of unemployment benefits and a shorter working day. In turn, they were hit by employers' efforts to erode the gains won by labour, as the balance of class forces shifted and the room for political compromise, determined by the faltering performance of the Weimar economy, shrank.[1] Where central legislation left discretionary powers to the *Länder* and local authorities, the impact of social policy reforms was in addition determined by the local balance of political forces. The development of government policies towards young workers therefore paralleled that of social policy generally; however, Weimar's social policy reforms did not affect all workers equally. As this and the next chapter seek to show, the status of young workers and apprentices as 'youth' was to affect the extent to which they participated in the gains made in the Weimar Republic by labour.

There was also a new sense of economic urgency in state officials' efforts to develop vocational training policies. Their concern arose from the difficulties afflicting the Weimar economy and from the hopes and fears aroused by the rationalization movement of the 1920s—the drive to modernize German industry through techno-

[1] Volker Hentschel, *Geschichte der deutschen Sozialpolitik 1880–1980* (Frankfurt am Main, 1983), 55–135; D. Peukert, *Die Weimarer Republik 1918–1933: Krisenjahre der klassischen Moderne* (Frankfurt am Main, 1987), 112–16.

logical and organizational innovation.² The implications of rationalization for the labour market were complex: an increase in mass mechanized production meant an increased demand for semi-skilled and unskilled labour, but also a growing need for highly-trained technical specialists and managerial staff.³ The strategy of the Reich authorities in the Weimar Republic to shape Germany's workforce in line with its future needs entailed focusing on the rising generation, in order to promote recruitment into skilled training and to upgrade training provision in industry and commerce alongside craft apprenticeships. Meanwhile, policies targeted at unskilled juveniles were to instil into them the attitudes and the basic skills equipping them to cope with a fast-changing and crisis-prone labour market. The unifying technocratic concept beyond all these plans was the efficient use of human resources (*Menschenökonomie*).⁴

New developments also characterized Weimar discussions on the education and welfare of the young worker. Before the First World War bourgeois social reformers, educationalists and eugenicists had already seen working-class youth as an accessible, legitimate, and necessary target for preventive social reform. Now, however, fears sparked off by modern mass urban society in post-war Germany created new priorities for such reform. Increasing attention was focused on the problem of alienation from work which, it was feared, would result from conditions in the modern rationalized plant and the increasing specialization and division of labour.⁵ Health issues gained a new urgency in the aftermath of wartime population losses and a perceived crisis in infant and child health.⁶ Meanwhile, new voices began to be heard in discussions of the young worker alongside those of the bourgeois social reforming establishment. Youth organizations themselves, above all those of

---

² Joan Campbell, *Joy in Work, German Work: The National Debate, 1800–1945* (Princeton, 1989), 131–57; Peukert, *Weimarer Republik*, 116–22; H. James, 'Economic Reasons for the Collapse of the Weimar Republic', in I. Kershaw (ed.), *Weimar: Why Did German Democracy Fail?* (London, 1990), 36–7.
³ Käthe Gaebel, in *Verhandlungen des 33. Evangelisch-Sozialen Kongresses in Saarbrücken am 25.–27. Mai 1926* (Göttingen, 1926), 151–2.
⁴ Wolfgang Muth, *Berufsausbildung in der Weimarer Republik* (Stuttgart 1985), 94–9. ⁵ Campbell, *Joy in Work*, 131–5.
⁶ Paul Weindling, *Health, Race and German Politics between National Unification and Nazism 1870–1945* (Cambridge, 1989), 338–44; Christoph Sachße and Florian Tennstedt, *Geschichte der Armenfürsorge in Deutschland*, i. *Vom Spätmittelalter bis zum Ersten Weltkrieg* (Stuttgart, 1980), 114–21.

the Left, demanded policies to protect a particularly vulnerable section of the workforce.[7] A new generation of social reformers and educationalists from the bourgeois youth movement, who after 1918 moved into careers in welfare administration and social work, stressed their solidarity with working-class youth.[8] Bourgeois feminists and socialist women attempted to promote the interests of young women workers.[9] While the stereotypical images characteristic of the pre-war period, focusing on the unskilled (male) juvenile, politically volatile and prone to drift into crime, continued to be prominent in Weimar debates, more differentiated perceptions of young workers began to gain currency as well, assisted by a boom in the academic study of adolescence: the Weimar period saw an upsurge in empirical social research into the condition and mentality of the working-class juvenile.[10] Discussions on educating the young workers and promoting their health and welfare thus, in the Weimar period, came to be informed by a variety of perceptions young workers and promoting their health and welfare thus, in consensus, however, was the perception of young workers *as* youth, with age-related problems requiring specific forms of pedagogical intervention, care, and protection.

Apprenticeship Training and Unskilled Juvenile Labour: Issues and Debates

The perspectives outlined above on the young worker problem shaped the discussion of a range of policies concerning skilled

[7] Heinrich Eppe, *Selbsthilfe und Interessenvertretung: Die sozial- und jugendpolitischen Bestrebungen der sozialdemokratischen Arbeiterjugendorganisation 1904–1933* (Bonn, 1983), 15–23; Manfred Zwerschke, *Jugendverbände und Sozialpolitik. Zur Geschichte der deutschen Jugendverbände* (Munich, 1963); Cornelius Schley, 'Die jugendpolitischen Vorstellungen und Aktivitäten des "Reichsausschusses der deutschen Jugendverbände" in den letzten Jahren der Weimarer Republik', Diplomarbeit (Göttingen, 1980); Detlef Prinz and Manfred Rexin, *Gewerkschaftsjugend im Weimarer Staat* (Cologne, 1983); Horst Pietschmann, 'Probleme der Massenarbeit des KJVD: Zur Einführung der "neuen Arbeitsmethoden" 1926–1928', *Wissenschaftliche Zeitschrift der Wilhelm-Pieck-Universität Rostock*, 31/1–2 (1982), Gesellschaftswissenschaftliche Reihe, 19–25.
[8] On the influence of the youth movement on post-war social welfare and social work, see below, Ch. 5.
[9] Martina Naujoks, *Mädchen in der Arbeiterjugendbewegung* (Hamburg, 1984), 53; Ute Frevert, *Women in German History: From Bourgeois Emancipation to Sexual Liberation* (Oxford, 1989), 199–203.
[10] D. Peukert, *Jugend zwischen Krieg und Krise: Lebenswelten von Arbeiterjungen in der Weimarer Republik* (Cologne, 1987), 22–8.

training and the employment of the young worker. One area of debate was by what means and to what extent the state should intervene in the labour market to regulate the supply of labour in the different sectors of the economy and to combat specific skills shortages.

The youthful workforce expanded between 1907 and 1925: the number of 14–20-year-olds who were economically active (*Erwerbspersonen*) rose from 4.9 million to 5.95 million.[11] In 1925, 76 per cent of the resident population in the age group 14 to 20 were on the labour market.[12] Although the economic activity rate among the youthful male population changed little between 1907 and 1925, there was a clear increase in economic participation on the part of young women: whereas in 1907 50.2 per cent of 14–18-year-old girls and 56.5 per cent of 18–20-year-old girls had been on the labour market, by 1925 the rate of economic participation among 14–20-year-old females overall had risen to 67 per cent. This was still a substantially lower proportion than that for youthful males—85 per cent of male 14–20-year-olds were economically active in 1925. However, the gap between economic participation rates for girls and boys was narrowing, and it narrowed further by a slight margin between 1925 and 1933: in 1933, 68.3 per cent of female 14–20-year-olds were economically active compared to 82.6 per cent of males.[13] Within the 14–20-year-old group, economic activity rates increased with age. In 1925, out of the 14–16 age group, 72.4 per cent of boys and 52 per cent of girls were on the labour market; these rates compared with those for 18–20-year-olds of 93.6 per cent (for males) and 77.4 per cent (for females). The lower rates of economic participation in the younger age group are partly accounted for by the numbers of young people staying on at school after the minimum school-leaving age of 14: in 1931, 18 per cent of boys and 12 per cent of girls aged 14–16 were still in full-time schooling.[14]

[11] Derek S. Linton, 'Who Has the Youth, Has the Future': The Campaign to Save Young Workers in Imperial Germany (Cambridge, 1991), 24; Hertha Siemering, *Deutschlands Jugend in Bevölkerung und Wirtschaft* (Berlin, 1937), 141. The 'economically active' population (*Erwerbspersonen*) included both the employed (*Erwerbstätige*) and the unemployed (*Erwerbslose*).
[12] Johanna Ernst, 'Die wirtschaftliche und berufliche Lage der weiblichen Jugend im Winter 1931/2', *Arbeit und Beruf*, 7/8 (1932), 93.
[13] See Table 3. For 1933 figures, see Siemering, *Deutschlands Jugend*, 122–3. On this trend in male and female economic activity rates, see also Peukert, *Jugend*, 43.
[14] Peter Lundgreen, *Sozialgeschichte der deutschen Schule im Überblick* ii. *1918–1980* (Göttingen, 1981), 118.

Where girls were concerned, the relatively low economic participation rates among 14–16-year-olds also reflected the continuing practice of daughters staying at home for a while after they left the *Volksschule* to help in the household before entering paid employment: the phenomenon of the so-called *Haustochter*. Nevertheless, even if they did not look for a job immediately, young women in the Weimar period increasingly took it for granted that they would go out to work after leaving school.[15]

The size of the youthful workforce peaked in 1925; this was followed by a sharp decrease in the absolute numbers of young people coming on the labour market during the Depression due to the low birth rate during the First World War. While the economically active population as a whole grew between 1925 and 1933 from 32 million to 32.3 million, the economically active population aged between 14 and 20 declined from 5.95 million to 3.82 million.[16] The public authorities were thus faced, in the Weimar period, with the short-term problem of a crowded youthful labour market, but at the same time the possibility of a skills shortage.

In response to the threat of skills shortages, the Reich Labour and Economics Ministries set out to promote vocational guidance for the young, which would counsel them to take up skilled training as far as possible and guide them into occupations where shortages threatened and away from overcrowded trades. In pursuing such policies, state officials were potentially at odds with both the free trade unions and employers. While the trade unions advocated the expansion of vocational counselling and the introduction of a grants system to encourage school-leavers to train as apprentices,[17] they were not in favour of promoting skilled training at all costs. Such a policy was likely to increase the number of young people unable to find skilled jobs after finishing an apprenticeship, to promote the dependence of craft firms on apprentice labour, and to depress the wages of adult workers.[18] Organized employers, meanwhile, opposed any plans on the part of the state authorities to designate as

---

[15] Ute Frevert, 'Traditionale Weiblichkeit und moderne Interessenorganisation: Frauen im Angestelltenberuf 1918–1933', *GG* 7 (1981), 507–33, 515.
[16] See Table 1.
[17] 'Ein Jugendschutz- und Jugenderziehungsprogramm', *CB* 29 (1919), 266–7; J. Sassenbach, 'Vorschläge zur Regelung der Lehrlingsfrage', *CB* 29 (1919), 287–9.
[18] *Bericht des Ortsausschusses Hamburg des ADGB über das Geschäftsjahr 1925* (Hamburg, 1926), 80.

overcrowded certain trades or occupations or to restrict recruitment of apprentices into those sectors.

Further debates arose concerning the status of apprentices and the conditions under which they were employed. Training in the skilled manual trades in the Weimar period continued to be dominated by craft traditions. Of the 986,000 apprentices of both sexes counted by the census in 1925, 540,000 were craft apprentices.[19] Craft apprenticeships generally lasted three to four years (apprenticeships in commerce and retailing were often shorter)[20] and were subject to contracts entered into by the employer, the juvenile, and the juvenile's parents. The form of apprenticeship contracts was laid down by the *Gewerbeordnung*; in return for their obligation to the employer for the duration of the agreed training period, apprentices enjoyed a degree of protection from dismissal. However, they could be dismissed before the end of their training period if they committed a criminal offence or if the firm employing them closed down.[21]

The traditional craft apprenticeship had the benefit of security, but the disadvantage, in the eyes of trade unions and socialist youth organizations, of giving the apprentices little protection against exploitation. Before the First World War, socialist youth groups in North Germany had waged a press campaign exposing scandalous cases of ill-treatment and calling for the reform of the 'decayed and rotten' system of craft apprenticeship.[22] After the revolution, restrictions on the rights of apprentices to organize were abolished; the free trade unions now began to recruit apprentices and to take up apprenticeship questions more energetically.[23] The general congress of the free trade unions in Nuremberg in June–July 1919 laid down guidelines, drawn up by Johannes Sassenbach, for the reform of the apprenticeship system: these envisaged transferring the administration of apprenticeship (the detailed regulation of

[19] Results of national census quoted in *Bericht des Ortsausschusses Groß-Hamburg des ADGB über das Geschäftsjahr 1929* (Hamburg, 1930), 74.
[20] A survey conducted in 1929 found that 12% of male and 34% of female white-collar trainees were undergoing a training lasting under 3 years. *Die kommende Angestelltengeneration: Eine sozialstatistische Untersuchung des GDA über Herkunft und Arbeitsverhältnisse und Berufsausbildung der Lehrlinge in Angestelltenberufen* (Berlin, 1933), 98.
[21] Hildegard Böhme, 'Die Entwicklung des gewerblichen Lehrlingswesens in Preußen während und nach dem Krieg', Diss. jur. (Hamburg, 1923), 16.
[22] Eppe, *Selbsthilfe und Interessenvertretung*, 43.
[23] Böhme, 'Entwicklung des gewerblichen Lehrlingswesens', 194.

training in each trade, the number of trainees, the setting of exams) from the guilds to joint central and local committees of employer and employee representatives.[24] Apprentices' wages should, argued the trade unions, be regulated by collective agreements rather than by the individual apprenticeship contract, and state legislation should be introduced laying down basic rights for all apprentices, in particular the 8-hour day (48-hour week) including attendance at vocational school.

Employers were reluctant to meet these demands. The employers' case hinged on drawing a strict distinction between the apprentice and the wage labourer and rejecting the trade union claims that apprentices performed useful work for their employer during the greater part of their training. The view of the organized employers was that apprenticeship involved a relationship between employer and employee which was educational in nature (*Erziehungsverhältnis*) rather than being based on work (*Arbeitsverhältnis*): payment made to the apprentice was a contribution to living costs, not a wage in the normal sense.[25] If the apprentice were to be regarded as a wage labourer and his pay regulated through collective agreements, it was argued, 'the apprentice would be oriented towards class struggle. He would march in step with organized workers ... The inevitable consequence would be the exacerbation of social conflict.'[26] This dispute over the status of apprentices was fundamental to the conflicts over working hours and vocational school attendance examined below.

A further area of debate concerned the relationship of craft apprenticeship to industrial and other kinds of training. While craft traditions continued to exert a strong influence on training in the manual trades in the Weimar period, important developments were also taking place in industrial training. Increasingly, large industrial firms were setting up training workshops (the number of firms with such facilities rose from 39 in 1919 to 175 in 1926, falling again to 167 in 1933) and works schools, the former providing practical, the latter theoretical instruction.[27] DATSCH (Deutscher Ausschuß für

---

[24] 'Konferenz der Vertreter der Verbandsvorstände', *CB* 29 (1919), 221–3, 222; 'Vorschläge zur Regelung der Lehrlingsfrage', ibid. 287–9.

[25] Otto Leibrock, 'Zur Neuregelung des Lehrlingswesens', *Der Arbeitgeber*, 3 (1921), 37–8, 37.

[26] Dr Lübbering, 'Kampf um den Lehrling', *Deutsche Arbeitgeber-Zeitung*, 20/23 (5 June 1921).

[27] Muth, *Berufsausbildung*, 336, 551–9.

technisches Schulwesen), an organization formed by industrialists in 1908 on the initiative of the Prussian government, was active in the Weimar period developing standard curricula and examinations for apprentices in different branches of industry.[28] From 1925 onwards, the efforts of DATSCH to promote industrial training were joined by those of DINTA (Deutsches Institut für technische Arbeitsschulung), which, backed by the resources of Ruhr heavy industry, energetically sought to persuade firms across Germany to adopt its totalizing, 'hearts and minds' approach to industrial training.[29] What remained unresolved was the degree to which craft employers would recognize qualifications gained in industry as equivalent to craft qualifications, and the extent to which commercial training and even training for domestic service could develop a formal structure and accredited qualifications.[30]

Disputes concerning the unskilled worker focused on the aspirations of the state authorities to include the unskilled within some form of educational or training framework. The free trade unions backed such plans;[31] employers were less enthusiastic. While employers were ready to join in the condemnations of the hedonistic lifestyle of the unskilled and to weigh in during the period of hyperinflation with implausible anecdotes about overpaid adolescents living on fresh salmon,[32] they were against any attempts to restrict the supply of juvenile unskilled labour or to lay down compulsory vocational school attendance for the young unskilled worker during working hours.[33]

Many of the negative perceptions of the unskilled juvenile were related to the behaviour of boys, but most young unskilled workers

[28] Erwin Runge, 'Industrielle Lehrlingsausbildung und Leistungssteigerung mit besonderer Würdigung Hamburger Verhältnisse', Diss. phil. (Hamburg, 1941), 8–13.

[29] Rolf Seubert, *Berufserziehung und Nationalsozialismus. Das berufspädagogische Erbe und seine Betreuer* (Weinheim, 1977), 70–109.

[30] Muth, *Berufsausbildung*, 340–7, 406–7; *Die kommende Angestelltengeneration*, 9–10; Renate Bridenthal, ' "Professional" Housewives: Stepsisters of the Women's Movement', in Renate Bridenthal, Atina Grossmann, and Marion Kaplan (eds.), *When Biology Became Destiny: Women in Weimar and Nazi Germany* (New York, 1984), 158, 162.

[31] 'Die Handwerksmeister zum Lehrlingsmangel', *CB* 29 (1919), 35; *Jahrbuch des ADGB 1924* (Berlin, 1925), 191; 'Gewerbliche Arbeit der Jugendlichen', *CB* 30 (1920), 196–7, 197.

[32] 'Jugendliche Arbeiter im Bergrevier: Die Folgen des Lohn-Wahnsinns', *Deutsche Arbeitgeber-Zeitung*, 21/33 (13 Aug. 1922); 'Die hohen Löhne der Jugendlichen', *Deutsche Arbeitgeber-Zeitung* 21/42 (15 Oct. 1922)

[33] Hans Braetsch, 'Das Berufsausbildungsgesetz', *Der Arbeitgeber*, 8 (1929), 213–21.

were in fact female. While the participation of female youth in the workforce was rising, female school-leavers were much less likely to go into skilled training than boys.[34] The problem of the imbalance in vocational qualifications between the sexes was brought to public attention by Social Democrats, trade-unionists and bourgeois feminists, who sought to increase the number of girls entering vocational training, improve the standards of that training and of their education in the vocational school, and—against the opposition of employers—promote equal pay for female workers.[35] There was a conflict, however, between such efforts to promote equality for young women in training and at work, and the efforts of housewives' organizations to have working-class girls prepared systematically for their future domestic duties as wives and mothers—thereby improving the housekeeping knowhow of recruits to domestic service.[36] In the Weimar period this debate was to echo through discussion of public policies towards young women workers, but without reaching a resolution.

'The Right Person for the Right Job': Vocational Guidance, Labour Exchanges, and the Young Worker

Public vocational guidance was above all part of the state's labour market strategy. In theory, the interests of the individual juvenile client and the interests of the economy were to be reconciled: in practice, this balancing act was harder to achieve. Apart from its economic function, vocational guidance also had a social and moral

---

[34] Renate Bridenthal and Claudia Koonz, 'Beyond *Kinder, Küche, Kirche*: Weimar Women in Politics and Work', in Renate Bridenthal, Atina Grossmann, and Marion Kaplan (eds.), *When Biology Became Destiny*, 50, 55.
[35] Clara Bohm-Schuch, *Willst Du mich hören? Weckruf an unsere Mädel* (Berlin, 1922), 6–8; Erna Barschak, *Die Schülerin der Berufsschule und ihre Umwelt* (Berlin, 1926), 6–11; A. Scheibert, 'Die weibliche Jugend im Handelsgewerbe', in Lehrkörper der Allgemeinen Berufsschulen für die weibliche Jugend et al. (eds.), *Frauenarbeit und öffentliche Berufserziehung in Hamburg* (Hamburg, 1929), 40–7; Agnes Karbe, 'Die Entwicklung der Frauenlöhne, insbesondere für Jugendliche', ibid. 13; Anne Schlüter, *Neue Hüte—alte Hüte? Gewerbliche Berufsbildung für Mädchen zu Beginn des 20. Jahrhunderts: Zur Geschichte ihrer Institutionalisierung* (Düsseldorf, 1987), 175–88; Frevert, 'Traditionale Weiblichkeit', 521–9.
[36] E. Krukenberg-Conze, 'Die Lebens- und Arbeitsverhältnisse der erwerbstätigen weiblichen Jugend', in *Verhandlungen des 33. Evangelisch-Sozialen Kongresses in Saarbrücken am 25.–27. Mai 1926* (Göttingen, 1926), 132–48, 144–5.

purpose: its advocates argued that matching the right worker to the right job would promote job satisfaction and social integration. Friedrich Syrup, president of the national labour administration (Reichsarbeitsverwaltung), saw the wrong choice of job leading to a lack of job commitment, frequent changes of job, unemployment, and juvenile crime; fulfilment in work (*Freude am Beruf*), he argued, was 'the best antidote to the perilous temptations of the street'.[37]

National legislation provided the framework during the Weimar Republic for the development of public facilities designed to direct young people into appropriate training or jobs.[38] The Reich demobilization authorities issued a decree in December 1918 giving powers to the *Land* authorities to set up facilities for comprehensive, non-commercial vocational guidance and for referral to apprenticeships, normally to be affiliated to the public labour exchanges.[39] In Hamburg, non-commercial vocational guidance and referral facilities dated back to a philanthropic initiative in 1905.[40] When the Hamburg city government set up a public labour exchange in December 1918, the private agency for vocational guidance became part of the labour exchange; it was taken over fully by the city-state authorities in 1920. Further steps towards creating a national network of vocational guidance facilities came with the Reich law on labour exchanges of 1922: the federal state authorities were empowered to pass binding legislation on the setting up of local facilities, and as a consequence Prussia, Württemberg and Thuringia passed legislation in 1923/4 setting up vocational guidance offices throughout their respective territories.[41] Finally, the law on labour exchanges and unemployment insurance of 16 July 1927 (Gesetz über Arbeitsvermittlung und Arbeitslosenversicherung or AVAVG) declared that the new national employment administration was responsible for the tasks of vocational guidance and

[37] Friedrich Syrup, 'Die Ziele der Berufsberatung', in Reichsarbeitsverwaltung (ed.), *Berufsberatung, Berufsauslese, Berufsausbildung* (Berlin, 1925), 7–11, 8.
[38] On vocational guidance in the Weimar period, see Muth, *Berufsausbildung*, 78–246.
[39] Anordnung über Arbeitsnachweise, 9 Dec. 1918, *RGBl* (1918), 1421–2.
[40] 'Die Kommission der patriotischen Gesellschaft zur Förderung der schulentlassenen Jugend', *Blätter für die hamburgische Waisenpflege und Jugendfürsorge*, 4/2 (1905), 7–8.
[41] Arbeitsnachweisgesetz, 22 July 1922, *RGBl* 1922, i. 657–71; Gaebel, 'Die rechtliche Grundlage der Berufsberatung und Lehrstellenvermittlung', in Reichsarbeitsverwaltung (ed.), *Berufsberatung*, 12–20.

apprenticeship referral.[42] The 1922 law on labour exchanges had laid down that commercial vocational guidance was to be completely phased out over a ten-year period and replaced by public facilities; as a result of the AVAVG, the provision of public facilities nationwide was speeded up.[43]

The public vocational guidance service succeeded in reaching a growing proportion of school-leavers. In the Reich as a whole, the number of clients of both sexes rose steadily until 1927/8, and the decline thereafter in the number of school-leavers did not produce a corresponding decline in the number of clients.[44] However, the growing clientele was not matched by an increasing number of training places available, and the proportion of successful referrals declined. The ratio of clients to training places rose from 1.5 to 1 in 1922/3 to 1.7 to 1 in 1926/7 in the case of boys, and from 2 to 1 in 1922/3 to 2.7 to 1 in 1926/7 in the case of girls. In 1922/3, 45 per cent of male and 33 per cent of female clients were referred to training places, rates which fell to 41 per cent (for boys) and 29 per cent (for girls) in 1926/7.[45]

Precise figures on the proportion of 14–18-year-olds who were by the mid-1920s in skilled training as opposed to unskilled work are lacking, but what are probably reasonable estimates can be derived from a survey of 200,000 vocational school pupils carried out in 1927. Of the sample, 72 per cent (84 per cent of the boys and 50 per cent of the girls) were apprenticed, undergoing other training, or already qualified; 28 per cent of the sample (16 per cent of the boys and 50 per cent of the girls) were in unskilled occupations.[46] Insofar as the aim of Reich government policy was to promote skilled training, there would seem—at least by 1927—to have been little cause for alarm where male youth was concerned. Those concerned about the training of young women workers would have been less reassured: of the total of 986,567 apprentices in industry and crafts counted by the census of 1925, about 850,000

---

[42] Abschnitt 2, Gesetz über Arbeitsvermittlung und Arbeitslosenversicherung, 16 July 1927, *RGBl* (1927), i. 187–220.
[43] 'Vierter Bericht der RAVAV für die Zeit vom 1.1.1931 bis zum 31.3.1932', Beilage zum *RABl* 7 (1933), *RABl* NS (1933), ii. 23–31.
[44] 'Vierter Bericht der RAVAV', 23.
[45] Ibid.
[46] Bernhard Mewes, *Die erwerbstätige Jugend: Eine statistische Untersuchung* (Berlin and Leipzig, 1929), 37–49; see also Peukert, *Jugend*, 110–11.

were male.[47] More precise figures on the proportion of female to male apprentices emerged from later surveys: in 1928, female apprentices made up 8.4 per cent and in 1929 9.2 per cent of the total number of craft apprentices.[48] These figures reflected the limited number of skilled manual trades in which girls could obtain apprenticeships, the main ones being tailoring and hairdressing.[49] There were growing training opportunities for girls leaving the *Volksschule* in the commercial and retail sector, but still not enough to satisfy demand.[50] Vocational counselling was supposed to advise youngsters against going into the popular but overcrowded trades—frustrated would-be motor mechanics could be steered in the direction of, say, boiler-making. However, suggesting alternatives to those girls who wanted to train in the most popular occupations of tailoring, hairdressing, or clerical work was less easy.[51] The proposal made in the employers' press in 1927 by an official of the Reich labour administration that the anticipated shortfall in skilled labour be combated—as it had been during the First World War—by recruiting girls into 'male' trades appears to have had minimal impact.[52] In the metal-working industry, for instance, there were in 1930 only 706 female apprentices, representing 1.9 per cent of all apprentices in the industry.[53]

In Hamburg, the opportunities open to school-leavers from the *Volksschule* were determined by the city-state's particular economic structure. Shipbuilding was the biggest single industry training male apprentices in Hamburg, with 1,104 apprentices—in a wide range of trades—employed by nine shipbuilding firms in 1929; the largest shipbuilders, Blohm und Voß, trained its apprentices from 1917

[47] Results of national census quoted in *Bericht des Ortsausschusses Groß-Hamburg des ADGB über das Geschäftsjahr 1929* (Hamburg, 1930), 74; Muth, *Berufsausbildung*, 280.
[48] Muth, *Berufsausbildung*, 316.
[49] On training for women in the craft trades, see Schlüter, *Neue Hüte—alte Hüte?*, 175–86.
[50] Ernst, 'Die wirtschaftliche und berufliche Lage der weiblichen Jugend', 93–101; Frevert, 'Traditionale Weiblichkeit', 517.
[51] Walter Stets, 'Mittel und Wege zur Behebung des in den nächsten Jahren durch den Geburtenausfall zu erwartenden Facharbeitermangels', *Der Arbeitgeber*, 12 (1928), 284–8.
[52] Ibid. 286.
[53] Anne Schlüter (ed.), *Quellen und Dokumente zur Geschichte der gewerblichen Berufsbildung von Mädchen* (Cologne and Vienna, 1987), 274–5. Out of 706 female apprentices, 579 were apprentice gold- and silversmiths.

onwards in the only private works school in the city.⁵⁴ However, the characteristic feature of Hamburg's economy was the dominance of its commercial sector. In 1933, 42 per cent of the city's economically active population aged 14–20 were classified as belonging to the sector of commerce and transport, compared to 11.5 per cent of *Erwerbspersonen* aged 14–20 in the Reich as a whole.⁵⁵

In Hamburg, as in the Reich as a whole, an increasing number of clients sought out vocational advice, and demand for training places exceeded supply.⁵⁶ A survey of young male workers in the Hamburg area confirmed that the public authorities, in promoting the idea of skilled training, were pushing against an open door. Most of the unskilled in the survey said they had gone into their jobs as factory workers or messenger boys due to material circumstances or the inability to obtain a place to train, rather than out of lack of interest in skilled training.⁵⁷ Where girls were concerned, the mismatch between demand for and availability of training was exacerbated as girls' expectations increased. Surveys of girls from Hamburg in their final year of the *Volksschule* demonstrated this trend: compared with the pre-war period, the vocational plans of girls were in the course of the 1920s becoming both more definite and more ambitious: a declining proportion wanted to go into domestic service, an increasing proportion sought qualified work in the craft trades and commerce.⁵⁸

Figures on vocational school pupils in Hamburg in 1926 show a slightly lower overall rate of participation by girls in training and a larger discrepancy between participation rates between boys and girls than in the 1927 nationwide survey of vocational school pupils.⁵⁹ According to the Hamburg vocational school figures of

---

⁵⁴ Arbeitsamt Hamburg an die Vertrauenslehrer für Berufsberatung an den Hamburger Schulen, Oct. 1930. StAH, Oberschulbehörde v, 123r; on the Blohm und Voß *Werkschule*, see *Jahresbericht des Hamburger Gewerbeaufsichtsamtes 1929*, 39.   ⁵⁵ See Tables 1 and 2.

⁵⁶ *StJB Hamburg* (1925), 18; (1928/9), 308; (1930/1), 291; (1934/5), 159. See also K. Hagemann, *Frauenalltag und Männerpolitik: Alltagsleben und Gesellschaftliches Handeln von Arbeiterfrauen in der Weimarer Republik* (Bonn, 1990), 381.

⁵⁷ Hermann Bues, *Die Stellung der Jugendlichen zum Beruf und zur Arbeit* (Bernau, 1926), 269–97; extracts reproduced in Peukert, *Jugend*, 140–8.

⁵⁸ Hagemann, *Frauenalltag*, 376–7.

⁵⁹ *Jahresbericht des Ortsausschusses Hamburg des ADGB*, 30. Geschäftsjahr (1926), 98–101. See Table 4.

1926, 85.5 per cent of the boys and 37.8 per cent of the girls were in some form of skilled training. Of the apprentices and trainees, around two-thirds of the boys and a third of the girls were in skilled manual trades. Of the 14,185 male apprentices in crafts and industry, 2,900 were in mechanical engineering and metal-working; of the 2,639 female craft apprentices, 1,281 were in tailoring. Of those undergoing training, about a third of the boys and just under two-thirds of the girls were commercial trainees—reflecting the growth in female 'white-blouse' labour in offices and shops. Of the 4,421 girls in commercial training, about half were in clerical work (of whom many actually received little systematic training) and half in retail sales. Of the boys, 14.5 per cent were in unskilled occupations or out of work; 62.2 per cent of the girls were either in unskilled occupations in factories or domestic service, unemployed, or 'without occupation'—which usually meant they were at home helping with housekeeping.[60] Girls' rising aspirations were not adequately matched by growing opportunities in the Hamburg labour market.

Young people's preferences were in potential conflict not only with the reality of the labour market but also with the interest of employers in recruiting the best-qualified candidates. The pressure on vocational guidance to serve employers' interests was evident in the debate on how to assess young people's suitability for the trade of their choice. The much-hailed, though controversial innovation in this area was the application of 'psychotechnics', a branch of industrial psychology developed in pre-war Germany but enjoying a boom in the Weimar period.[61] Scientific assessment was to replace chance: the application of a rational method of vocational testing would guide school-leavers into the trade where they would perform best, benefiting both them and the economy.[62] The advocates of psychotechnical testing (which typically combined tests of manual dexterity and of intelligence) argued that it gave working-class children a fairer chance than an assessment on the basis of their academic performance at school.[63] Its critics warned

[60] Ibid.
[61] On the origins of psychotechnics, see Campbell, *Joy in Work*, Ch. 5.
[62] Peter Dehen, *Die deutschen Industriewerkschulen in wohlfahrts-, wirtschafts- und bildungsgeschichtlicher Beleuchtung* (Munich, 1928), 225–36; Muth, *Berufsausbildung*, 201–46; Campbell, *Joy in Work*, 135–45.
[63] Jahresbericht der Jugendabteilung der Behörde für das Arbeitsamt Hamburg, 1922/23. StAH, JB I, 325.

that psychotechnic tests were liable to become a tool of business interests, assisting employers to select recruits rather than offering guidance to the individual juvenile.[64] One apprentices' instructor from a works school condemned the tests as being of an unrealistically high standard, declaring that he himself would have difficulty passing them.[65] Such criticisms did not stem the enthusiasm for psychotechnics: psychotechnic tests came to be widely carried out by the public authorities and in some towns all school-leavers were subjected to testing.[66] In Hamburg, such aptitude tests were soon established as a method of assessing clients' capabilities, and many employers came to expect that young people referred by the public authorities to an apprenticeship would have a favourable test result to support their application.[67]

The vocational guidance system was thrown into turmoil by the Depression. The earlier assumptions that after 1928 employers would be searching for young people to take on as apprentices were overturned: employers were in many cases trying to get rid of the apprentices they already had. Young people revised their expectations and became less choosy about which trade they went into: in Hamburg in 1930, it was reported that young people were prepared to take any apprenticeship that came up.[68] During the 1920s girls had become increasingly unwilling to go into domestic service if there were alternative jobs available; now they were prepared to take jobs as domestic servants, but found that for inexperienced school-leavers there were few opportunities.[69] Meanwhile the metal-working industry and the building industry—major recruiters of male apprentices—were among the sectors of the economy worst hit by the crisis. In Hamburg, no apprentice bricklayers and joiners were taken on at all in 1932, while the number of apprenticeships available in the metal-working industries was estimated in 1932 to have fallen by 70 per cent in comparison with the years before the

[64] Maria Kratz, 'Das Für und Wider der Eignungsprüfungen', in *Frauenarbeit und öffentliche Berufserziehung in Hamburg*, 122–3.
[65] Dehen, *Industriewerkschulen*, 236.
[66] Die behördlichen psychotechnischen Einrichtungen in Deutschland: Ergebnisse einer Umfrage des Deutschen Städtetags, 17 Aug. 1929. StAH, AB I, 38. See also Muth, *Berufsausbildung*, 206.
[67] Jahresbericht der Jugendabteilung der Behörde für das Arbeitsamt Hamburg 1922/3, 6; Jahresbericht des Hamburgischen Arbeitsamtes 1925, 28–9. StAH, JB I, 325.
[68] Berufsberatung und Lehrstellenvermittlung Hamburg, monthly report for Oct. 1930. StAH, AB I, 37.
[69] Hagemann, *Frauenalltag*, 376.

Depression.[70] The total number of training places reported to the Hamburg vocational guidance office declined between 1927/8 and 1932/3 by 38 per cent (for boys) and 53 per cent (for girls), while the number of clients fell over the same period by only 14 per cent and 13 per cent respectively.[71]

Employers during the Depression tended to revert to unofficial channels of recruitment.[72] A loophole in the 1927 law on unemployment insurance and labour exchanges allowed political organizations to undertake referrals for their members, and job agencies of this kind quickly spread. It was reported in Hamburg in 1930 that a Stahlhelm agency known as 'Deutsche Hilfe' was successfully referring around thirty 'patriotic workers' per month to Hamburg employers.[73] Employers could pick and choose more than before: for school-leavers who had not successfully completed their final year of elementary school, it was now virtually impossible to find an apprenticeship.[74] Where young people did find a place to train, they often found that the training was inadequate. Some employers in the Depression were running their businesses using only apprentice labour, while others had too few contracts on their books to train their apprentices effectively.[75]

Vocational guidance in this situation faced a series of dilemmas. No one could know how long the crisis would last, and whether unemployment in certain trades reflected a passing crisis or long-term structural change due to technological development.[76] New guidelines for vocational advice in the economic crisis were issued by the Reich employment administration in February 1932 to replace those of 1927.[77] In 1927, vocational advisers had been instructed to take into account the inclinations and the circumstances of the client as well as their aptitudes and the labour market

[70] Niederschrift über die 3. Sitzung des Unterausschusses für Berufsberatung des Arbeitsamtes Hamburg, 11 Mar. 1932. StAH, Oberschulbehörde V, 123g, vol. 3.
[71] StJB Hamburg (1931/2), 277; (1934/5), 159.
[72] Walter Maschke, 'Jugend ohne Beschäftigung und ohne Ausbildungsmöglichkeit', Die Arbeit, 9/4 (1932), 246–51, 247.
[73] Bericht über die 'Deutsche Hilfe', Jan. 1930. StAH, AB I, 34.
[74] Berufsberatung und Lehrstellenvermittlung Hamburg, monthly report Apr. 1930. StAH, AB I, 37.
[75] Rudolf Wiedwald, 'Vom Lehrlingswesen nach den Jahresberichten 1930 der Gewerbeaufsichtsbeamten', Das junge Deutschland 25/12 (1931), 600–4, 601–2.
[76] Otto Uhlig, 'Berufsberatung in der Krise', Arbeit und Beruf, 6/6 (1931), 73–8.
[77] RAVAV an die Landesarbeitsämter, betr. Gesichtspunkte für Berufsberatung in der Krise, 15 Feb. 1932, in Beilage zum Reichs-Arbeitsmarkt-Anzeiger (22 Mar. 1932).

situation.[78] In 1932, young people were to take what they were given: the emphasis was to be on their suitability for a trade.[79] The guidelines of the RAVAV prescribed furthermore that efforts should continue to be made to encourage youngsters to go into skilled training, regardless of the prospect of unemployment at the end of it.

By 1933, the fall in the number of school-leavers together with the impact of the Depression had combined to reduce the total number of apprentices in the Reich by 38 per cent compared with 1925: in June 1933, there were 607,245 apprentices in industry and crafts, of whom 535,000 were male.[80] In Hamburg, despite the efforts of the vocational guidance officials, about 40 per cent of the boys and over half the girls who left the elementary schools in the city in 1932 had no apprenticeship or job to go to.[81] Even where they were successful in placing school-leavers, vocational guidance officials had to ask themselves if this was at the expense of young adults' chances on the labour market. The institution of vocational guidance had sought to prevent unemployment at an individual level: it was powerless to hold up the tide of mass unemployment.

Vocational Schooling

Article 145 of the Weimar Constitution included a pledge to introduce compulsory vocational (or 'continuation') schooling for all young people between the ages of 14 and 18 no longer in full-time education.[82] At a stroke, a commitment to uniform nationwide provision seemed to have made the uneven and haphazard growth which had characterized the development of vocational schooling before 1918 a thing of the past.

In 1920, the Reich Ministry of the Interior under the DDP minister Koch began to draft legislation to translate Article 145 of the constitution into practice. This followed a decree issued by the

[78] AVAVG, para. 58, sect. 2.
[79] RAVAV, Gesichtspunkte für Berufsberatung in der Krise.
[80] Muth, *Berufsausbildung*, 280, 315; Peukert, *Jugend*, 110.
[81] Niederschrift über die 3. Sitzung des Unterausschusses für Berufsberatung des Arbeitsamtes Hamburg. StAH, Oberschulbehörde v, 123g, vol. 3.
[82] Die Verfassung des Deutschs Reichs, 11. Aug. 1919, Article 145, *RGBl* 1919, 1383–1418, 1410.

demobilization authorities in March 1919 allowing local authorities to introduce compulsory vocational schooling for the under-16s.[83] Now, more comprehensive legislation was planned. The Social Democratic secretary of state in the department of culture and education in the Interior Ministry, Heinrich Schulz, drafted a law on the basis of guidelines laid down by the Reich School Conference early in 1920: these called for three years of compulsory vocational schooling for both sexes to follow the *Volksschule*. Schulz's draft, completed in July 1920, soon ran into difficulties over its financial provisions.[84] In December 1921 the Reich Ministry of the Interior announced that the draft law on national compulsory schooling had foundered.[85] Later attempts to revive the draft national legislation, such as the SPD initiative in the Reichstag in February 1925, came to nothing.[86] Each *Land* accordingly went its own way, which led to considerable variations between the different federal states in the number of hours of attendance per week laid down for the various groups of pupils: above all in Prussia, provision in small towns and rural areas remained patchy.[87]

The city state of Hamburg had been slow in comparison with other federal states before 1918 in moving towards compulsory vocational school attendance; in 1918/19, however, the strong Social Democratic presence in the city government ensured that Hamburg was one of the first federal states to prescribe compulsory vocational school attendance in full for all categories of young workers, male and female, skilled and unskilled alike. Hamburg's law of October 1919 laid down eight hours of classes as the weekly norm, plus two hours of sport. Attendance was to be for three years, or until the end of the young person's apprenticeship, whichever was the longer.[88]

The failure of plans for national legislation hampered attempts to

[83] Verordnung über Erweiterung der Fortbildung für die Zeit der wirtschaftlichen Demobilmachung, 28 Mar. 1919, *RGBl* 1919, 354–5.
[84] RMdI an die Landesregierungen betr. Reichsberufsschulgesetz, 20 July 1920. BA Koblenz, R36, 2293.
[85] RMdI an die Landesregierungen (außer Preußen), 12 Dec. 1921. StAH, BSB II, FI a. 1b.
[86] Reichstagsdrucksache 515, *Verhandlungen des Reichstags*, 3. Wahlperiode 1924–1928, vol. 398.
[87] Kornemann, 'Gesetzliche Grundlage der Berufsschule', in A. Barth, G. Bode, H. Erben (eds.), *Die Beschulung der Ungelernten* (Wittenberg, 1928), 81–91.
[88] Gesetz über die Fortbildungsschulpflicht, 20 Oct. 1919, *Amtsblatt der freien und Hansestadt Hamburg*, 259 (22. Oct. 1919), 1802–4.

consolidate vocational schooling as an institution. Throughout the Weimar period, its advocates—typically Social Democrats, educationalists, social hygienists, and feminists—argued the case for state vocational schooling against the sceptics in the employers' camp who complained about the burden on the public budget and the inconvenience caused to employers.

The principle of compulsory vocational schooling was relatively well established for apprentices in crafts and industry and commercial trainees. Employers generally accepted the necessity for compulsory theoretical instruction through vocational school classes to back up training on the job. However, they criticized the hours prescribed by local authorities for school attendance, the alleged over-emphasis on general subjects seen as irrelevant to the young workers' training, and the rising costs incurred in the expansion of vocational schooling: this was a sore point particularly in Prussia, where employers were required to contribute directly to the costs of vocational schooling.[89] While most employers continued, in the absence of alternatives, to send their apprentices and trainees to public vocational classes, an increasing number of larger industrial firms chose to set up their own private works schools, which could obtain recognition as equivalent alternatives to state vocational schools. By 1927, 146 such works schools were in operation, with 23,000 pupils.[90] Among the benefits to the firms concerned, which DINTA propaganda was particularly energetic in publicizing, were convenience, the high training standards which could be reached through specialized instruction, the close match between training and the specific requirements of the firm, and the opportunity for educating young employees in the corporate ethos—the latter being a major reason why trade unions opposed the works schools.[91]

Where the unskilled juveniles were concerned, employers attacked not just the methods and the costs of vocational schooling, but the very principle of compulsory attendance. Defending schooling for the unskilled, its advocates presented a number of arguments in its

---

[89] Kurt Roß, 'Die Kosten und die Finanzierung der Berufsschulen in Preußen', *Der Arbeitgeber*, 24 (1928), 623–4; 'Sitzung des Bildungsausschusses des DIHT in Berlin, 9.12.1926', *Verhandlungen des Deutschen Industrie- und Handelstags*, 16 (Berlin, 1926), 28–9.

[90] Dehen, *Industriewerkschulen*, 189, 264–70.

[91] Ibid. 260–1; Muth, *Berufsausbildung*, 360–9, 551–8.

favour. Spokesmen for the Reich Ministry of Labour and the Prussian Ministry of Trade declared that an economy in the process of rapid technological transformation required a semi-skilled and unskilled workforce more flexible, alert, and disciplined than before.[92] Moreover, schooling the unskilled could, it was argued, increase the attractions of skilled training: a leading official in the Hamburg vocational school authority thought that the inconvenience of part-time school attendance would actively deter young people from going into unskilled work.[93]

However, the case for the vocational school for the unskilled had to stand and fall with its role in educating a category of working-class adolescents commonly considered to be in need of assistance, guidance, and discipline. One official of the Hamburg vocational school authorities portrayed the vocational school for young unskilled workers as a measure that would keep their wages down (since they lost wages for the time spent at school), underline their dependent status as juveniles, and generally reduce them to size.[94] More characteristic arguments used by educationalists, welfare politicians and doctors were couched in terms of the deprivation of unskilled youth and the potential of the vocational school as an instrument of welfare.[95] From this perspective, the vocational school was presented as a refuge from and a counterweight to the stresses of the workplace, the unhealthy environment of the proletarian neighbourhood, and the chaos of the working-class household.[96] In vocational school classes, pupils would enter a more wholesome milieu and come under the influence of a set of values centred on regular work and a rationally-organized lifestyle.[97] Apart from their moral welfare, their physical well-being would be

---

[92] Ministerialrat Kühne, in Niederschrift über die Sitzung am 20.5.1925 im Preußischen Handelsministerium betr. Stellungnahme zum Reichsberufsschulgesetz. ZStA Potsdam, 49.01, 7501.
[93] Schulrat Thomae, Bericht zu dem Äußerungsersuchen des Herrn Senatsreferenten vom 11.5.1921, betr. Anrechnung des gewerblichen Fortbildungsschulunterrichts auf die Arbeitszeit, 17 May 1921. StAH, BSB II, FI a. 5.
[94] Ibid.
[95] 'Gesellschaft der Freunde des vaterländischen Schul- und Erziehungswesens', Hamburger Echo, 10 Mar. 1918.
[96] E. Geilen, 'Sozialhygiene in der Berufsschule', Die Arbeit, 7/7 (1930), 465–70, 470; Barschak, Die Schülerin der Berufsschule, 38.
[97] Maria Lusch, Fürsorge an Mädchenberufsschulen und Wege zu ihrer Durchführung (Cologne, 1930), 39–40.

catered for through medical inspections, health education, and compulsory sports.[98]

In their eagerness to prove the indispensability of compulsory vocational schooling to the national good, its advocates ran the risk of assigning to the institution an impossible burden of different and even conflicting functions. This was nowhere clearer than in the debate on the education of young female workers. Social Democrats, bourgeois feminists, and organized housewives were in agreement that a key task for girls' vocational classes should be to prepare pupils for their future role as housewives and mothers.[99] However, it was unclear how this was to be reconciled in practice with preparing young women adequately for their paid employment, which bourgeois feminists and Social Democrats, in contrast to the housewives' organizations, tended to see as ultimately taking priority over training for housework.[100] A range of solutions to this dilemma were proposed and tried, including the Bremen experiment of full-time one-year courses in home economics for all female school-leavers from the *Volksschule* before they embarked on work or vocational training.[101] However, the basic conflict of goals

---

[98] Antrag des Arbeiterrats an die Bürgerschaft betr. Erweiterung des Tätigkeitsgebiets der Schulärzte auf die Gewerbe- und Fortbildungsschulen, 2 July 1919. StAH, BSB II, FII g. 1; Preußisches Ministerium für Handel und Gewerbe an die Regierungspräsidenten und das Provinzialschulkollegium Berlin, betr. Unterricht über Gesundheitspflege in den gewerblichen und kaufmännischen Fach- und Berufsschulen, 10 Dec. 1927. ZStA Merseburg, Rep. 120, E Abt. I, 44, vol. 2; Lusch, *Fürsorge an Mädchenberufsschulen*, 8; Geilen, 'Sozialhygiene in der Berufsschule'; Theodor Lewald, 'Die Deutsche Wirtschaft und der Volkssport', *Der Arbeitgeber*, 6 (1925), 129–30.

[99] On home economics in vocational schools in the Weimar period, see Ellen Schulz, *Die Mädchenbildung in den Schulen für die berufstätige Jugend* (Hamburg, 1963), 109–20; Wiltrud Ulrike Drechsel, 'Ausbildung für zwei Berufe: Zur Geschichte der Hauswirtschaftlichen Pflichtfortbildungsschule für Mädchen in Bremen 1920–1933', in Jutta Dalhoff, Uschi Frey, and Ingrid Schöll (eds.), *Frauenmacht in der Geschichte* (Düsseldorf, 1986), 105; Karen Hagemann, 'Hauswirtschaftsunterricht für Mädchen an Volks- und Berufsschulen' in Hans-Peter de Lorent and Volker Ullrich (eds.), *Der Traum von der freien Schule: Schule und Schulpolitik in Hamburg während der Weimarer Republik* (Hamburg, 1988). On the organized housewives' campaign for home economics for all 14-year-old female school-leavers, see Bridenthal, 'Class Struggle around the Hearth: Women and Domestic Service in the Weimar Republic', in M. Dobkowski and I. Wallimann (eds.), *Towards the Holocaust: The Social and Economic Collapse of the Weimar Republic* (Westport, Conn., 1983), 254–5.

[100] Else Ulich-Beil (ed.), *10. Jahrbuch des BDF 1927 (1921–1927)* (Mannheim, 1927), 69–71; Olga Essig, quoted in Schulz, *Mädchenbildung*, 111.

[101] On the Bremen experiment, see Drechsel, 'Ausbildung für zwei Berufe'.

remained unresolved and the purpose of girls' vocational schooling continued to be disputed.[102] The debates on the merits and purpose of universal compulsory vocational schooling continued at national level as local authorities went ahead with expanding their vocational schooling provision (the extent of the expansion depending on the relevant *Land* legislation) and developing curricula for the various categories of pupils involved. In Hamburg, the specialized vocational content of the curriculum for apprentices and trainees in various trades and occupations continued to be taught in the Weimar period along much the same lines as before 1918. However, the teaching of civics (*Staatsbürgerkunde*) to all vocational school pupils had to be updated to fit the new democratic political context. Before 1918, civics had sought to promote loyalty to the authoritarian institutions of the Kaiserreich; now, under Article 148 of the Weimar constitution, it had the task of upholding democratic values.[103] Moreover, it was now targeted at girls as well as boys: girls' political education had gained a new significance now that women had the vote.[104] In Hamburg's general vocational school for girls, special efforts were made to adopt an approach to political education which did not simply depend on learning facts about the Weimar constitution: the election of school councils and participation in Constitution Day ceremonies were intended to give the pupils a more immediate and stimulating experience of political practice and political ritual.[105]

In Hamburg, from 1920 onwards, the unskilled of both sexes were obliged to attend vocational school. Classes for young male workers focused on the key idea of job satisfaction (*Arbeitsfreude* or *Berufsfreude*).[106] If a boy could be encouraged to cultivate a

[102] Schulz, *Mädchenbildung*, 109–20.
[103] Heribert Weber, 'Ratlosigkeit und Rebellion: Jugend und politische Erziehung', Diss. phil. (Tübingen, 1972), 16; Johannes Kempkens, 'Hemmungen in der Staatsbürgerkunde, Prinzip oder Fach', *Die deutsche Berufsschule*, 39/16 (1930), 483–92, 485.
[104] Allgemeine Fortbildungsschule für Mädchen, 3.3.1921 an die Behörde für Gewerbe-und Fortbildungsschulwesen, betr. Entwurf eines Lehrplans für Bürgerkunde. StAH, BSB II, FXI b. 1.
[105] Käthe Wiese, 'Die Schülervertretung an den allgemeinen Berufsschulen für die weibliche Jugend', in *Frauenarbeit und öffentliche Berufserziehung*, 81–8; Gertrud Pardo, 'Unsere Pflichtberufsschulen', ibid. 103.
[106] Johannes Schult, 'Lebens- und Bildungsziele der Ungelernten im Rahmen des Volksganzen', *Erziehung*, 4 (1929), 369–81, 372–3.

positive identification with his job as a van-driver's mate, for instance, in the same way as a carpenter saw himself as a carpenter, he would, it was argued, become a happier, steadier, and more efficient worker.[107] In practice, the Hamburg authorities' attempts to group the boys according to their jobs in order to promote a sense of vocational identity tended to founder on the practical difficulties of timetabling: the boys in the same job category could not get time off work at the same time. Even where classes were made up on an occupational basis, an extraordinary level of fluctuation prevailed: yesterday's delivery boy could be tomorrow's packer. 'There is generally no particular vocational interest to be found amongst the pupils', commented an official report resignedly.[108]

Where the curriculum for the unskilled girls was concerned—who formed the majority of female vocational school pupils, whereas unskilled boys formed a minority of male pupils[109]—home economics dominated: the classes were taken up with cooking, sewing, laundering, infant care, and hygiene, with an hour a week of 'cultural affairs' in the first year and an hour a week of civics in the third and final year.[110] This was in contrast to the curriculum for female apprentices and commercial trainees, where the argument prevailed—supported by, among others, a prominent local pioneer of girls' education—that girls in skilled training should concentrate on their specialized vocational programmes and not be distracted by classes on infant care and cookery.[111] Some effort was made to group the unskilled girls in classes according to their jobs (for instance according to the type of factory they worked in) and thereby to promote some form of vocational identification, as was the practice initially in the boys' classes.[112] However, the guiding principle of the unskilled girls' vocational schooling was to be the

---

[107] *Jahresberichte der Berufsschulbehörde 1915–1924* (Hamburg, n.d.), 7.
[108] Ibid. 7.
[109] Jahresbericht der Berufsschulbehörde (1925), 28. StAH, BSB I, B 703; Staatliche Allgemeine Gewerbeschulen für das weibliche Geschlecht an die Berufsschulbehörde, 10 Sept. 1925. StAH, BSB II, FV b. 1/2; *StJB Hamburg* (1930/1), 385.
[110] *Jahresberichte der Berufsschulbehörde 1915–1924*, 4–5.
[111] Frl. Düsedau and Emmy Beckmann, in Protokoll der Sitzung der Kommission für die Allgemeine Fortbildungsschule für Mädchen, 5 Nov. 1919. StAH, BSB I, B639; Dora Auras, 'Berufslehre und Arbeitspraxis der weiblichen Jugend in der Hauswirtschaft', in *Frauenarbeit und öffentliche Berufserziehung*, 64.
[112] Gertrud Pardo, 'Unsere Pflichtberufsschulen', in *Frauenarbeit und öffentliche Berufserziehung*, 102.

learning of rationalized housework techniques. The poverty and illhealth of working-class families and the exhaustion of working-class mothers would be combated by the application of logical household planning.[113] A new generation of housewives would emerge with energies spare to devote to tasks outside the home: home economics would liberate the working-class housewife for active citizenship.[114]

If the new vocational school curricula were to achieve their hoped-for impact, attendance had to be enforced effectively. Here, local vocational school authorities were to run into major problems. The Reich government's failure to establish the vocational school firmly in national legislation meant that conflicts over matters such as the hours of compulsory attendance and the categories of youngsters obliged to attend were fought out at local level. One such issue was the timing of vocational school classes, and in particular whether vocational school attendance fell within the eight-hour day decreed by the revolutionary government in November 1918. The trade union view was that the eight-hour day should apply to workers and apprentices alike and that vocational school should be counted as working time.[115] Employers took the contrary view.[116] The compromise proposed by the Labour Ministry in 1922 was to allow up to six hours per week of classes to be held outside working hours, thus permitting 'as an exception only' a working week of up to 54 hours for young people under 18.[117] This solution was written into the new decree on working hours of 21 December 1923.[118] The decree did not, however, settle the issue once and for all, but once again left the initiative in the hands of the *Länder* and local authorities (paragraph 5, decree on working hours), some of whom—like Hamburg—continued to order that all vocational classes be held within working hours.

[113] Mary Nolan, ' "Housework Made Easy": The Taylorized Housewife in Weimar Germany's Rationalized Economy', *Feminist Studies*, 16 (Autumn 1990), 549–78.
[114] Pardo, 'Unsere Pflichtberufsschulen', in *Frauenarbeit und öffentliche Berufserziehung*, 101–2.
[115] 'Vorschläge zur Regelung der Lehrlingsfrage', *CB* 29 (1919), 287–9.
[116] C. Lieberich, 'Lehrling und Fortbildungsschule', *Der Arbeitgeber*, 8 (1922), 130–1.
[117] RAM an Preußisches Ministerium für Handel und Gewerbe, 18 June 1921. ZStA Potsdam, 49.01, 7520; RAM an die Sozialministerien der Länder, 12 Aug. 1922. Handelskammer Hamburg 67.K.4.2.
[118] Arbeitszeitverordnung vom 21. Dez. 1923, *RGBl* (1923), i. 1249–51.

Where local authorities did override employers' opposition over the timing of classes, another problem immediately arose: young people who took time off work to attend vocational school had deductions made from their pay.[119] The group who most commonly suffered such deductions from their pay were the unskilled workers, who tended to be paid piece-rates or by the hour, unlike apprentices, who were paid weekly or monthly.[120] Again, the lack of national legislation banning such deductions made itself acutely felt.[121]

In Hamburg, the Social Democrats' influence in the city government meant that its commitment to public vocational schooling was strong in comparison with the rest of the Reich.[122] However, the city authorities were to have great difficulties implementing the expansion pledged by the 1919 law. In the face of employer opposition and funding shortages, neither the planned two hours per week of physical education nor the other eight hours a week envisaged as the compulsory standard for all vocational school pupils were fully enforced. From 1922 onwards, commercial apprentices and the unskilled boys had their third-year classes cut from eight to four hours per week (from 1926 these hours were restored for the commercial trainees only).[123] The unskilled girls had never been required to attend for more than four hours a week in the third year anyway, and domestic servants, due to the fierce opposition from their employers, had never been required to attend for more than four hours in any of the three years.[124]

Hamburg's legislation of 1919 laid down that classes should fall within normal working hours. This ruling had come about partly due to direct pressure from the pupils themselves: in December

---

[119] Regierungsrätin Käthe Gaebel, in Besprechung des Entwurfs eines Gesetzes über die berufliche Ausbildung Jugendlicher im Reichsarbeitsministerium, 12 Dec. 1922. ZStA Potsdam, 39.01, 1923.
[120] Regierungspräsident Düsseldorf an Preußisches Min. für Handel und Gewerbe, 8 Oct. 1919. ZStA Potsdam, 49.01, 7520.
[121] Preußisches Min. für Handel und Gewerbe an Preußisches Min. für Landwirtschaft, Domänen und Forsten, 13 Aug. 1924. ZStA Potsdam, 49.01, 7520.
[122] Protokoll der 17. Sitzung der Kommission für die Allgemeine Fortbildungsschule für Mädchen, 6 Sept. 1921. StAH, BSB I, B639.
[123] Senatsverfügung vom 31.3.1922. StAH, BSB II, FIII e. 3 vol. 2; Aktenvermerk der Handelskammer über Besprechung in der Berufsschulbehörde am 9.12.26. Handelskammer Hamburg, 67.K.4.2.
[124] 20. Sitzung der Kommission für die allgemeine Fortbildungsschule für Mädchen, 30 Mar. 1922. StAH, BSB I, B639.

1918, and again in May and June 1919, socialist youth groups had organized a boycott by apprentices of vocational school classes held in the evenings and on Sundays.[125] After 1919, the Hamburg authorities held to their new policy of holding classes during working hours despite the decree of December 1923 allowing classes to be held outside the working day. Local employers, particularly in the retail trade, continued to pressure the authorities on this issue and attempted to evade the legislation where possible: cases were quoted of young people being made to work from 5.30 a.m. till 2 p.m. and then being sent by their employers to vocational school.[126] Employers in hotels were reported by the union of hotel and catering employees to be making their young employees take their day off on the day they had to attend school.[127] Blohm und Voß sought a more long-term solution to the inconvenience to the firm caused by young employees going to classes during the working day: their works school for shipyard apprentices, set up in 1917, held its classes after working hours.[128] Rudolf Blohm remarked in 1922 that the investment in the school was paying off simply in terms of the trouble it saved his firm.[129]

While truancy tended to decline after the mid-1920s, throughout the Weimar period it remained at a level that was embarrassing to the vocational school authorities throughout the Reich.[130] In Hamburg, it was unskilled male youths who were most frequently absent from classes; the staff of the general vocational school for boys observed in 1921 that it was generally accepted that apprentices

---

[125] Sozialistischer Jugendbund, leaflet, 7 Dec. 1918; A. Kasten an die Behörde für das Gewerbe- und Fortbildungsschulwesen, 10 Dec. 1918; J. Schult an Senator Krause, 31 May 1919; Leaflet of 4 June 1919. StAH, BSB I, B58; Gesetz über die Fortbildungsschulpflicht, 20 Oct. 1919, *Amtsblatt der freien und Hansestadt Hamburg*, 259 (1919), 1802.
[126] Auszug aus dem Protokoll der Berufsschulbehörde, 4 June 1926. StAH, BSB II, FII f. 1; Niederschrift über die Sitzung des Verwaltungskörpers der Allgemeinen Gewerbeschulen für das männliche Geschlecht, 28 Apr. 1925. StAH, BSB II, FIII e. 3 vol. 2.
[127] Zentralverband der Hotel-, Restaurant- und Cafeangestellten Hamburgs an die Berufsschulbehörde, 23 June 1926. StAH, BSB II, FII f. 1.
[128] 'Die erste Werftschule in Hamburg', *Hamburgische Schulzeitung*, 26/2 (1918), 7–8.
[129] Rudolf Blohm an Syndikus Reymann, Handelskammer Hamburg, 29 May 1922. Handelskammer Hamburg 67.K.2.2.
[130] Fränkel, 'Fortbildungsschulversäumnisse und deren Behandlung', *ZBl*, 17/4 (1925/26), 85–7; 'Der Schulbesuch der ungelernten Arbeiter in der Berufsschule', *Gewerkschaftszeitung*, 38/32 (1928), 508–9.

attend vocational school, but that 'most parents and employers find it completely incomprehensible and unjustified that messenger-boys, labourers or van-drivers' mates should be compelled to attend'.[131] Apart from deducting wages, employers could also stop their employees from attending by threatening to dismiss them.[132] One domestic servant fined in 1932 for missing classes claimed: 'I had no time to go to vocational school as I would have lost my job otherwise'.[133] The Hamburg employment office also confirmed that young people were losing their jobs because of vocational school.[134]

The Hamburg city government's methods of dealing with truancy combined efforts to put pressure on employers and parents with punitive measures against the pupils themselves. Occasionally the city authorities brought a court case against an uncooperative employer: however, the vocational school authorities had the impression that the sympathy of the courts was with the employers.[135] Attendance officials sent on home visits by the vocational school often encountered hostile reactions from the families of truants. The welfare officials undertook in such cases to persuade parents that the vocational school was doing a useful job and would benefit their children. However, one official reported that it was hard not to agree with the parents in some cases: in one case, parents pointed out that their daughter was losing 15 marks in wages for three hours at school which she spent waiting for a sewing machine.[136]

Truancy was most commonly dealt with by punishing the pupils themselves. Fines imposed by the police were, however, seldom paid, since the young people soon found out that the Hamburg authorities were helpless in cases of non-payment.[137] The Hamburg

---

[131] Allgemeine Fortbildungsschule für Knaben an die Behörde für das Gewerbe- und Fortbildungsschulwesen, 18 Jan. 1921. StAH, BSB II, FII a. 3.
[132] 20. Sitzung der Kommission für die Allgemeine Fortbildungsschule für Mädchen, 30 Mar. 1922. StAH, BSB I, B639.
[133] Hilde R. LGH A15128/1934.
[134] Louis Korell, Hamburger Arbeitsamt, an die Behörde für das Gewerbe- und Fortbildungsschulwesen, 19 June 1920. StAH, BSB II FII c. 2.
[135] Case against H. Lindemann, shipowner: Landgericht proceedings 30 May 1923. StAH, BSB II, FII e. 2.
[136] Erster Bericht über die Schulpflegearbeit, in Bericht über die 19. Sitzung der Kommission für die Allgemeine Fortbildungsschule für Mädchen, 17 Jan. 1922. StAH, BSB I, B639.
[137] Allgemeine Fortbildungsschule für Knaben an die Behörde für das Gewerbe- und Fortbildungsschulwesen, 18 Jan 1921. StAH, BSB II, FII a. 3.

authorities, unlike those in Prussia, were unable to have fines imposed on truants transmuted into prison sentences.[138] One sanction that the Hamburg authorities did possess against truants was a system whereby the police could use force to bring pupils to school.[139] However, in March 1922, at a heated discussion a police inspector declared, in response to criticism from the school authorities, that the law on vocational schooling was so unpopular that in an area such as the *Gängeviertel* the police were neither willing nor able to implement it.[140]

The schools faced considerable disciplinary problems in view of the fact that, particularly in the schools for unskilled boys, many pupils were there only under duress. The teachers at the general vocational school for boys in Fuhlentwiete wrote to the school authorities in March 1921 asking for help with discipline. They described the situation in vivid terms:

> The mass of our pupils see the school as . . . a tiresome burden and a hateful duty which they seek to evade at all costs. . . . Once they have realised that it is useless to rebel against the law, a substantial number of pupils seek to revenge themselves on the hated institution by disrupting school routine in every way possible. These pupils constantly arrive late for classes, they destroy, damage and deface the buildings, the equipment and the teaching materials, they disrupt classes with inappropriate comments, laughter and whistling, they deliberately show off with their uncouth behaviour and by breaking school rules they try to spark off conflicts and provoke the teacher.[141]

The unskilled of both sexes represented a key target for state efforts to reach, to organize and discipline young people; however, the vocational school as an institution made little headway in this task. This failure may be largely attributed to the inadequacy of legislation which placed new obligations on a whole age-group without providing the conditions whereby those obligations could be fulfilled. Young unskilled workers, who had often gone into

---

[138] Fränkel, 'Fortbildungsschulversäumnisse und deren Behandlung', 85–7.
[139] J. Schult an den Arbeiterrat Groß-Hamburg, 26 May 1925. StAH, BSB II, FII e. 1.
[140] Niederschrift über eine Sitzung über die Durchführung der Strafmaßnahmen aus dem Fortbildungsschulgesetz, 7 Mar. 1922. StAH, BSB II, FII e. 1.
[141] Die Lehrer der Allgemeinen Fortbildungsschule (Knaben) an die Behörde für das Gewerbe- und Fortbildungsschulwesen, Hamburg, 15 Mar. 1921. StAH, BSB II, FII a. 3.

unskilled work precisely because of hardship in the family, seemed to be being penalized for not having been able to afford or obtain the security of an apprenticeship.

In the Depression, vocational schooling for the unskilled came under a fresh barrage of attacks. The Deutscher Städtetag, faced with the crisis in local government finance, in 1931 called for reductions in compulsory attendance; organized employers, who were keen to preserve the specialized instruction provided for apprentices and trainees, pressed the state authorities to cut schooling for the unskilled of both sexes in view of the costs and inconvenience it caused.[142] The Prussian state government responded with a round of cuts in vocational schooling in autumn 1931 which increased class sizes, abolished PE, reduced the hours of compulsory attendance for both skilled and unskilled workers, and allowed, in exceptional circumstances, the abolition of compulsory schooling for domestic servants.[143] In December 1932, the Prussian authorities circulated more far-reaching proposals for reductions in provision, including the abolition of compulsory attendance for all unskilled workers.[144] In Hamburg in November 1932 the city authorities were also on the point of adopting cuts in vocational schooling.[145]

The targeting of proposed cuts during the Depression at vocational schooling for the unskilled, in particular schooling for unskilled girls, shows that as an institution schooling for the unskilled continued to be perceived by many employers as a waste of resources. Some of the state authorities, notably the reactionary Prussian government installed in July 1932 by Papen, appeared to share this view. On the other hand, the state authorities were in a dilemma. In the circumstances of the Depression the case had never been stronger for promoting vocational schooling as an agency for disciplining the unruly, teaching political responsibility, getting across the principles of housekeeping to girls from families hit by

---

[142] Muth, *Berufsausbildung*, 523–30; 'Abbau in der Berufsschule', *Hamburger Industrie- und Gewerbe-Zeitung*, 20 (1931), 268.
[143] Erlaß des Preußischen Ministeriums für Handel und Gewerbe über die Einschränkung der Berufsschulpflicht, 25 Sept. 1931. ZStA Merseburg, Rep. 120, E I, Fach 1, 79 vol. 4.
[144] Erlaß des Preußischen Ministeriums für Wirtschaft und Arbeit betr. zeitgemäße Einschränkung der Berufsschulpflicht, 27 Dec. 1932, ibid.
[145] 'Alarmmeldungen aus der Landesschulbehörde', *Hamburger Tageblatt*, 265, (22 Nov. 1932). StAH, Staatliche Pressestelle I–IV, 5462.

unemployment, and providing welfare for youngsters at risk.[146] These arguments seem to have prevailed in the winter of 1932: the negative response by the Prussian regional governments and the Prussian Städtetag to the Prussian state's proposals of December 1932 apparently caused the cuts to be shelved.[147]

Meanwhile, the impact of the political and economic climate on the vocational schools and their pupils was increasingly evident. In 1928 the communist youth organization, the Kommunistischer Jugendverband Deutschlands (KJVD) had begun a nation-wide campaign of agitation and propaganda in vocational schools. Communist demands included the holding of vocational school classes during working hours, the ban on deductions from pay for time spent at classes, a greater degree of pupil participation in the running of vocational schools, a ban on corporal punishment, fines, and detention, and the abolition of religious education.[148] In Hamburg in 1928, a member of the local KJVD executive was expelled from vocational school for distributing copies of a newspaper called *Der Weckruf* ('Reveille'), which carried allegations of floggings in Hamburg's vocational schools; the school authorities also persuaded the boy's employer to dismiss him.[149] In the Depression, political activism in vocational schools spread, despite repeated bans on political agitation and the wearing of political insignia.[150] In Hamburg, the school authorities now reported that

[146] Stadtverband Bochum für Frauenbestrebungen (u.a.) an den Preuß. Min. für Handel und Gewerbe, 14 Apr. 1932. ZStA Potsdam, 49.01, 8978; Marie Kröhne, 'Das Schicksal der Mädchenberufsschule', *Die Frau*, 40/2 (1932–3), 104–10.

[147] 'Gegen die Verelendung der nachschulpflichtigen Jugend', *Vossische Zeitung*, 18 Jan. 1933; Preußischer Städtetag an den Preuß. Min. für Wirtschaft und Arbeit betr. Einschränkungen im Berufsschulwesen, 28 Jan. 1933; Reichsverband des dt. Handwerks an den Preuß. Min. für Wirtschaft und Arbeit, 26 Mar. 1933; Preuß. Min. für Wirtschaft und Arbeit an den Reichsverband des Dt. Handwerks, 12 Apr. 1933. ZStA Merseburg, Rep. 120, E I Fach 1, 79 vol. 4.

[148] 'Forderungen des KJVD für die Berufsschule', *Rote Schüler-Stimme: Kampforgan der Krefelder Berufsschüler*, 2/3 (1929).

[149] Arnold an die Berufsschulbehörde, 18 Aug. 1928; Urteil des Landesarbeitsgerichtes Hamburg, 21 Aug. 1928; Urteil des Arbeitsgerichts Hamburg, 18 Aug. 1928. StAH, BSB II, FE II e. 2.

[150] Regierungspräsident Erfurt an den Preuß. Min. für Handel und Gewerbe betr. Zugehörigkeit von Schülern staatlicher Fachschulen zur kommunistischen oder nationalsozialistischen Partei, 16 Dec. 1930; RMdI an die Unterrichtsministerien der Länder betr. Ausschuß für das Unterrichtswesen, 8 May 1931. ZStA Merseburg, Rep. 76, VII (neu), Sekt. 1b I, 53 vol. 3; Erlaß des Preuß. Ministeriums für Handel und Gewerbe betr. Pflege der Staatsgesinnung in den Berufs- und Fachschulen, 24 Feb. 1931. ZStA Merseburg, Rep. 120, E I, 48 vol. 1; Landesschulbehörde Hamburg an die

members of both the communist youth organization and the Nazi 'Vocational and Works School League' were distributing leaflets and organizing political meetings during breaks between vocational school classes.[151] Truancy, on the other hand, was paradoxically becoming less of a problem. It was reported in 1931/2 from Berlin and elsewhere that attendance at vocational school was improving; this was due to mass youth unemployment: the unemployed had less to lose by attending vocational school than had those in jobs.[152] Unemployment may have reduced truancy and given the vocational school for the unskilled a new *raison d'être*; however, the usefulness of such schooling for the unemployed remained obscure.[153] Now that the chances of actually finding a job were so poor, there was a certain irony in working-class youngsters undertaking courses in handicrafts to cultivate dexterity, neatness, and conscientiousness or in learning about the virtues and value of work.

Employment Conditions and Wages

The eight-hour day was one of the cornerstones of the Weimar Republic's social policy, and its erosion was indicative of a general process in which the social policy gains won by organized labour in and after November 1918 were dismantled.[154] Employers challenged and sought to undermine the eight-hour day from the outset. Craft employers denied that the legislation on the eight-hour day applied to apprentices at all.[155] The situation for young workers was

Direktoren der öffentlichen Fachschulen, betr. politische Betätigung der Studierenden und Schüler der öffentlichen Schulen, 7 Mar. 1932. StAH, Oberschulbehörde I, D2 vol. 16.

[151] Landesschulbehörde an die Direktoren der öffentlichen Fachschulen, betr. politische Betätigung der Studierenden und Schüler der öffentlichen Schulen, 7 Mar. 1932; Protokollauszug, Landesschulbehörde, 20 Oct. 1932. StAH, Oberschulbehörde I, D2 vol. 16.

[152] Kammergerichtspräsident an Preußisches Justizministerium, 20 Oct. 1932. ZStA Potsdam, 30.01, 5569; Gottfried Drescher, 'Jugend und Berufsschule', *Der Zwiespruch*, 13/26 (1931), 308; Kröhne, 'Das Schicksal der Mädchenberufsschule', 105.

[153] On the role of vocational schools in running courses for the unemployed in the Depression, see Ch. 4.

[154] L. Preller, *Sozialpolitik in der Weimarer Republik* (Düsseldorf, 1978), 269; Bernd Weisbrod, *Schwerindustrie in der Weimarer Republik* (Wuppertal, 1978), 301.

[155] Böhme, 'Entwicklung des gewerblichen Lehrlingswesens', 93.

exacerbated, moreover, as has been outlined above, by the amendments to the legislation on working hours made as a concession to employers in 1923 allowing up to six hours of vocational school per week to be held outside working hours. Young people's working hours were also discussed in the context of protective legislation. The proclamation of the Council of People's Delegates on 12 November 1918 that promised the introduction of the eight-hour day also pledged to restore protective legislation for women and juvenile workers that had been suspended for the duration of the war.[156] This legislation, clauses 135 and 136 of the *Gewerbeordnung*, covered women and young persons under 16 who worked in factories and workshops. It provided a general ban on young persons working at night (between 8 p.m. and 6 a.m.) and laid down statutory rest periods and working breaks. Beyond the restoration of this pre-war legislation, the Weimar period was to bring no change in protective legislation to benefit young workers. Trade unions and youth organizations campaigned energetically for the extension of protective legislation to young workers up to the age of 18 and to young workers in sectors of the economy hitherto excluded, such as domestic service and agriculture. They called for the 48-hour week including vocational school attendance and for the introduction of at least two weeks' annual paid holiday for young workers under 18.[157] None of these demands made any headway against the opposition of the organized employers, who were reported in 1924 to be trying to evade existing protective legislation.[158] A draft of 1926 envisaged extending protective legislation to all workers under 18 and including, for instance, a ban on night work for 16–18-year-old male workers for the first time. However, the law never got past its first reading in the Reichstag. After being introduced into the Reichstag in January 1929 by the new Social Democratic Labour Minister Rudolf Wissell, it was referred to the social policy committee of the Reichstag and never re-emerged after Brüning's takeover in March 1930.[159]

---

[156] Ernst Francke, 'Erfüllung sozialpolitischer Forderungen', *SP* 28/8 (1918/19), col. 113–16, 114–15.
[157] 'Programm für die gewerkschaftliche Jugendarbeit', *CB* 32 (1922), 49–51; Eppe, *Selbsthilfe*, 190–211.
[158] RAM an die Sozialministerien der Länder betr. Arbeiterinnen- und Jugendlichenschutz, 12 June 1924. ZStA Merseburg, Rep. 120, BB VII, Fach 3, 20 vol. 3.
[159] Preller, *Sozialpolitik*, 352–8.

Calls for a reduction in working hours and an increase in paid holidays for young workers and apprentices continued to be a rallying-point for trade union youth sections, socialist youth organizations, and the Youth Organizations Council (Ausschuß der deutschen Jugendverbände, from 1926 known as the Reichsausschuß der deutschen Jugendverbände or RddJ). Wide publicity was given to the findings of the survey of 200,000 vocational school pupils carried out for the major exhibition on German youth mounted by the RddJ in 1927, '*Das junge Deutschland*'. This survey showed that an average working day for a young worker under 18 in large cities, including clearing-up time and travel to work, was 11 hours 15 minutes, while in communities of under 5,000 inhabitants it was even longer, averaging 12 hours 25 minutes.[160] It also showed that nearly half the young people surveyed had only 5 or fewer days' paid holiday per year.[161]

The free trade unions held that matters such as the eight-hour day and paid holidays were basic rights for young workers which should be enacted in state legislation; however, in the absence of such legislation, collective agreements offered an alternative method of obtaining improved conditions for young workers. The problem was that the validity of collective agreements where applied to apprentices was not firmly established in law. The decree issued by the Council of People's Delegates on 23 December 1918 had laid down that collective agreements had binding force and could be declared by the state authorities to apply to all employers and employees in the particular industry or region for which the agreement was concluded.[162] Deviations from the provisions of such agreements were permissible only if they favoured the employee. However, apprentices were not specifically included in the category of employees (*Arbeitnehmer*). It appears that the civil servant in the new Reich Labour Ministry who was responsible for drafting the decree 'forgot' about apprentices at the time of the drafting.[163] It was an omission that was to bring forth a flood of contradictory interpretations and court decisions. The unions

[160] Eppe, *Selbsthilfe*, 192; Peukert, *Jugend*, 113.
[161] Eppe, *Selbsthilfe*, 194; Carmen Klement, 'Freizeit ist Not: Eine Ausstellung und Zeugnisse über "Das junge Deutschland" 1927', in Deutscher Werkbund (ed.), *Schock und Schöpfung: Jugendästhetik im 20.Jahrhundert* (Darmstadt and Neuwied, 1986), 332–7.
[162] Preller, *Sozialpolitik*, 231; Hentschel, *Geschichte der deutschen Sozialpolitik*, 71–2.   [163] Böhme, 'Entwicklung des gewerblichen Lehrlingswesens', 217.

claimed that apprentices counted as employees; the employers, above all the employers in craft trades as opposed to industry, held that the apprentice's remuneration was a matter only for the individual contract signed between master and apprentice.[164] The Reich authorities were divided over this issue. The Reich Labour Ministry was responsible for matters pertaining to apprentices except those in craft trades, while craft trades were the responsibility of the Economics Ministry. The Labour Ministry tended to back the unions' position: it took the view that the regulations concerning the employment of apprentices could be laid down in collective agreements, except where this infringed the responsibilities of other bodies. Where apprentices in craft trades were concerned, the *Gewerbeordnung* assigned certain rights to the guilds (*Innungen*) and Chambers of Crafts (*Handwerkskammern*).[165] Matters of pay, however, the Labour Ministry went on to state specifically, were not the responsibility of the guilds and Chambers of Crafts. This view was rejected by the Economics Ministry, which was more sympathetic than the Labour Ministry to the employers' arguments, and employers' organizations protested at what they saw as the meddling of the Labour Ministry.[166] Overall, the decisions of courts and arbitration committees were split approximately evenly for and against the inclusion of apprentices' wages in collective wage agreements.[167]

A full picture of how far apprentices' wages came to be included in collective agreements is hard to reconstruct. By 1928 the president of the Reich employment administration reported that the practice of regulating apprentices' employment in collective agreements was spreading year by year.[168] While apprentices' wages did increasingly get covered by collective agreements, the gap between their wages and those of the unskilled remained striking. In 1927, Mewes found that, while apprentices' wages varied considerably according to the trade, the sex of the apprentice, and the place of training, apprentices earned on average around 4 marks in their first

[164] Handwerkervereinigung Mecklenburgs an den Reichskanzler, 21 May 1921. ZStA Potsdam, 39.01, 1922.
[165] Brauns an Gewerkschaftskartell Chemnitz, 30 Nov. 1920. ZStA Potsdam, 39.01, 1921.
[166] Deutscher Verband für das kaufmännische Bildungswesen an das Reichsarbeitsministerium, Mar. 1921. ZStA Potsdam, 39.01, 1921.
[167] Böhme, 'Entwicklung des gewerblichen Lehrlingswesens', 219–22.
[168] Ibid. 227; Präsident der RAVAV an das RAM, 17 Sept. 1928. ZStA Potsdam, 49.01, 7320.

year of training, and between 5 and 10 marks in their third and fourth years.[169] In Hamburg in 1930, apprentice metalworkers earned 3 marks in their first year, 4.50 marks in their second year, 6 marks in their third year, and 8 marks in their fourth year of training; an apprentice girl hairdresser would earn 3 marks in her first year, 4 marks in her second year, and 5 marks in her third (and last) year of training.[170] Unskilled juveniles almost invariably took home more than trainees. Delivery boys and factory workers commonly earned 10–15 marks per week; some unskilled juveniles could earn over 15 marks per week before they were 18. The gap between boys' and girls' wages was more marked among the unskilled than among apprentices; unskilled girls were reported to earn 4–7 marks per week on average.[171]

Relatively high wages were seen by the young unskilled as a major source of satisfaction with their work and a compensation for the more negative aspects of what were often dead-end jobs.[172] However, to labour market planners wanting to deter school-leavers from entering unskilled work, the gap between the pay of the unskilled and the apprentice was a source of concern. They hoped that market forces would push up apprentices' pay as the supply of school-leavers dwindled; the Depression, however, put paid to such prospects.[173]

The Abortive Reform of Vocational Training

In April 1927, after years of discussion and preliminary drafting, the Reich government finally published a draft law prepared jointly by the Labour Ministry and the Economics Ministry on the vocational training of youth—the Gesetz über die Berufsausbildung Jugendlicher or Berufsausbildungsgesetz (BAG).[174] Although this law failed to reach the statute book, the debates surrounding it throw light on the conflicting vocational training strategies pursued in the

[169] Mewes, *Die erwerbstätige Jugend*, 74–9.
[170] Arbeitsamt Hamburg, Mitteilungen an die Vertrauenslehrer für Berufsberatung an den Hamburgischen Schulen, Oct. 1930. StAH, Oberschulbehörde V, 123r.
[171] Bues, *Stellung der Jugendlichen zum Beruf*, 76–8; Mewes, *Die erwerbstätige Jugend*, 78–9.   [172] Bues, *Stellung der Jugendlichen zum Beruf*, 76–8.
[173] Stets, 'Mittel und Wege', 285.
[174] Reichsarbeitsverwaltung (ed.), *Entwurf eines Berufsausbildungsgesetzes nebst amtlicher Begründung* (*Reichsarbeitsblatt*, Sonderheft 39) (Berlin, 1927).

Weimar period by the state authorities, the employers, and the trade unions.[175]

The goals which the Reich government sought to achieve through its law on vocational training were set out in the statement accompanying the published draft.[176] The German economy, it was argued, would benefit from a rationalized, systematic, and comprehensive training structure for the entire future workforce. New powers would enable the state authorities to plan and regulate the structure of the workforce by promoting the employment and training of juveniles in scarce trades and restricting or even banning it temporarily in overcrowded branches of the economy.[177] The distinction between the highly-regulated craft apprenticeship and the usually more informal types of industrial and commercial training was to be abolished. Instead, a system of regulatory institutions controlled jointly by employers and organized labour was to create a unitary framework for skilled training and raise standards across the board by formalizing training in industry and commerce in a manner comparable to the regulation of craft apprenticeships.[178] At the same time, the draft sought to erode the rigid distinction between those in the various forms of skilled training on the one hand and unskilled or semi-skilled young workers on the other: all young workers up to the age of 18, including the unskilled, were to be classed as trainees.[179]

Apart from providing economic benefits, the law was presented as serving social goals. It would safeguard the health and well-being of young workers by laying down conditions and duties which the employer of any juvenile was to fulfil—such as the obligation to protect juvenile workers from physical or mental abuse at the workplace.[180] At the same time, the law sought to create a new form of pedagogical control over the unskilled section of the youthful workforce. It was a common lament among social reformers that the unskilled juvenile was not subject to the discipline imposed on apprentices by their employers. Now, the employers of all juveniles, whether in formal training or not, were to supervise the morals, working habits, and behaviour of their young employees.[181]

[175] For a detailed account of the evolution and failure of the Berufsausbildungsgesetz, see Muth, *Berufsausbildung*, 444–82.
[176] *Entwurf eines Berufsausbildungsgesetzes*, Begründung, 30–59.
[177] Ibid. para. 8. [178] Ibid. para. 13–35, 69–80.
[179] Ibid. para. 1–12 and Begründung, 30–4. [180] Ibid. para. 11.
[181] Ibid. para. 11.

At a more general level, the government claimed that the law would promote social harmony: good workers made better citizens, went the familiar argument, investment in training and education was investment in the stability of the social order.[182]

As in the case of all Weimar's social legislation, the draft law on vocational training was a battleground for institutionalized class conflict. The government draft of 1927 was a fragile compromise which emerged from a lengthy process of consultation and negotiation between the state authorities, the trade unions, and organized employers. Early drafts produced by the Reich Economics Ministry in 1922/3 were based on proposals launched by the free trade unions at their conference in Nuremberg in July 1919 and modified in negotiation with the employers within the forum of the *Zentralarbeitsgemeinschaft* in 1920/21.[183] From the earliest stages of the debate over the drafting of the law, serious clashes between employers, trade unions, and the state authorities obstructed the law's progress.[184] One basic sticking-point was the scope of the legislation. The state authorities (backed by the trade unions) insisted on the inclusion of white-collar trainees and the unskilled, but agreed (against trade union protests) to exempt agriculture from the law's provisions.[185] The organized employers, by contrast,

[182] *Entwurf eines Berufsausbildungsgesetzes*, Begründung, 33–4; for similar arguments, see Rudolf Wissell, Reichstagsrede, 2 Dec. 1929, *Stenographische Berichte der Verhandlungen des Reichstags*, 4. Wahlperiode 1928, vol. 426, p. 3393, and Walter Stets, 'Der Entwurf eines Berufsausbildungsgesetzes', *Kölner Sozialpolitische Vierteljahresschrift*, 7/1 (1928), 5–32, 6.

[183] Grundsätze für die reichsgesetzliche Regelung des Lehrlingswesens, angenommen in der Sitzung des sozialpolitischen Ausschusses der ZAG, 11 Feb. 1921. ZStA Potsdam, 39.01, 1921; Ergebnisse einer Besprechung des Referentenentwurfs eines Gesetzes über die berufliche Ausbildung Jugendlicher mit Vertretern der beteiligten Berufe und mit Schul- und Jugendvertretern, 18, 21, and 26 Sept. 1923. StAH, BSB II, FI a. 2.

[184] On employers' reactions to the proposals for the law, see Muth, *Berufsausbildung*, 464–72; Gertrud Tollkühn, 'Die Stellungnahme von Industrie und Handwerk zum Regierungsentwurf eines Berufsausbildungsgesetzes', *SP*, 36 (1927), cols. 1089, 1129; Hans Braetsch, 'Das Berufsausbildungs-Gesetz', *Der Arbeitgeber*, 8 (1929), 213–17; 'Protokoll der Sitzung des Bildungsausschusses in Berlin am 9.12.1926', *Verhandlungen des Deutschen Industrie- und Handelstags*, 16 (Berlin, 1926). On the free trade unions' reactions, see Muth, *Berufsausbildung*, 472–6; Gertrud Hanna, 'Zum Entwurf eines Berufsausbildungsgesetzes', *AW*, 2/14 (1927), 417–21; Clemens Nörpel, 'Grundsätzliches zum Entwurf eines Berufsausbildungsgesetzes', *Gewerkschaftszeitung*, 37/32 (1927), 437–9.

[185] Early drafts had included agricultural workers; the 1927 draft omitted them as a consequence of the protest of the Reich Ministry of Agriculture. Der Reichsminister für Ernährung und Landwirtschaft an den Staatssekretär in der Reichskanzlei, 12 Sept. 1926. BA Koblenz, R43 I, 2013a. See also Muth, *Berufsausbildung*, 459–61.

wanted the law—in so far as they were prepared to accept any law on vocational training—restricted to apprentices in crafts and industry only.

Further debate arose over the planned machinery of joint committees of employer and labour representatives, which were to be attached to the chambers of crafts, of industry, and of commerce. Employers resented the threatened erosion of the chambers' autonomy and feared the growth of union influence, while the trade unions pressed for more far-reaching union participation in the implementation of the law than envisaged under the system of joint committees. The role of collective agreements in relation to the regulations to be set up by the new legislation was another point of contention: the trade unions sought to uphold the role of collective agreements as a means of regulating the working conditions and pay of apprentices, while the employers and the state authorities preferred to see issues concerning young workers' pay and conditions dealt with by the new joint committees and removed from the sphere of collective bargaining. The employers strongly resisted the idea of state intervention in the labour market to determine the number of trainees or young unskilled workers in a particular trade or firm, while such intervention was fundamental to the Reich government's vision of economic planning and went hand-in-hand with the concept of labour market management embodied in the Law on Labour Exchanges and Unemployment Insurance of 1927.[186] Finally, employers rejected the trade unions' call for the draft law to include a ban on wage deductions for time spent by young workers at vocational school, a demand long backed by the state authorities concerned with truancy from vocational school by the unskilled.[187]

These conflicts were played out in the debates in the Reichsrat and in the Provisional National Economic Council (*Vorläufiger Reichswirtschaftsrat*)[188] which lasted from 1927 until 1929.[189] The deliberations were given additional impetus by the advent in 1928 of

[186] On this law, see Ch. 4.
[187] Besprechung des Entwurfs eines Gesetzes über die berufliche Ausbildung Jugendlicher im Reichsarbeitsministerium, 12 Dec. 1922. ZStA Potsdam, 39.01, 1923.
[188] On the role of the Vorläufiger Reichswirtschaftsrat, see Preller, *Sozialpolitik*, 481.
[189] Bericht des Arbeitsausschusses zur Beratung des Entwurfs eines BAG, Vorläufiger RWR, 20 Dec. 1928. StAH, BSB II, FI a. 2; Gutachten des sozialpolitischen Ausschusses des Vorläufigen RWR zu dem Entwurf eines BAG, 9 Feb. 1929.

a Grand Coalition government with a new Labour Minister, Rudolf Wissell (SPD), who succeeded the Centre Party politician Heinrich Brauns. In July 1928, the new government promised to bring in the law on vocational training at the earliest opportunity.[190] In summer 1929, a revised draft was submitted to the Reichstag, concessions having been made to both the employers and the trade unions, though leaving neither side satisfied.[191] The amended draft was finally debated in the Reichstag in December 1929, when it was referred to the social policy committee. The organized employers stepped up their offensive and in February 1930 presented to the social policy committee their own counter-draft to the government's proposals.[192] Employer hostility, the fall of the Grand Coalition, and a deteriorating economic climate combined to seal the fate of the law, which never emerged from the Reichstag committee stage.[193]

Partial Reform and its Consequences: The Impact of Public Policies towards Young Workers and Apprentices

The failure of the law on vocational training to reach the statute book spelled the end of the plans developed by the Reich Ministries of Labour and Economics to control the labour market and to impose a consistent set of regulations on the apprenticeship system. In the absence of the planned reform, the other strands of state policy towards young workers and apprentices remained half-measures. Vocational advice officials might advise youngsters

---

[190] Vermerk der Reichskanzlei, 9 July 1928. BA Koblenz, R43 I, 2013a.

[191] 'Entwurf eines Berufsausbildungsgesetzes', Drucksache des Reichstags, 1303, *Verhandlungen des Reichstags*, 4. Wahlperiode 1928–1930, vol. 437. Concessions to the trade unions included the addition of a clause banning wage deductions for vocational school attendance; concessions to employers included giving chambers of industry and of commerce the right, but no longer the obligation, to hold examinations for industrial and commercial trainees, and the deletion of the clause which would have allowed the state to impose a temporary ban on all recruitment to overcrowded trades.

[192] 'An den Reichstag: Bemerkungen zum Entwurf eines Berufsausbildungsgesetzes, überreicht von dem Deutschen Handwerks- und Gewerbekammertag, dem Deutschen Industrie- und Handelstag, dem Reichsverband des Deutschen Handwerks, und der Vereinigung der Deutschen Arbeitgeberverbände' (Berlin, 1930). BA Koblenz, R43 I, 2013a.

[193] Wiedwald, 'Vom Lehrlingswesen nach den Jahresberichten der Gewerbeaufsichtsbeamten', 604.

against going into overcrowded trades, but the new law would have given the state and the new vocational training boards powers actually to block entry to such trades. Local authorities might appeal to employers to pay their young labourers for the time spent at vocational school, but the planned law would have made it illegal for employers to make deductions.

The blocking of essential aspects of the Labour Ministry's plans affected young workers and apprentices in a number of ways. The social policy innovations carried through by the first Weimar governments had brought them some gains: unskilled workers benefited from being included in collective agreements, and apprentices gained the right to organize in trade unions. Where apprentices were concerned, however, the traditional control exercised by the craft guilds over apprenticeship created lasting obstacles to trade union efforts to integrate apprentices into the framework of collective labour legislation. The status of apprenticeship brought with it a certain security for the apprentices, but at the same time a lack of rights which tended to put apprentices beyond the pale of state social policy. Unskilled juvenile workers enjoyed greater freedom than apprentices, but it was this very freedom and uncontrollability which state efforts sought to curtail through measures such as vocational schooling. Vocational schooling was more of a burden than a benefit for the unskilled, restricting their chances of employment and handicapping them financially when employers made deductions from their pay for time spent at school. Girls, who were encouraged by public vocational guidance officials to plan their working lives, continued to encounter a labour market rigidly segregated on gender lines, a limited choice of occupations, and wage discrimination; meanwhile, much 'vocational' schooling for girls concentrated on preparing pupils less for the workplace than for their supposed future as homemakers. Overall, the benefits gained by young workers and apprentices from state social and employment policies were limited.

Resistance by employers was one major factor which frustrated the ambitious policies of the Reich authorities towards young workers. Economic developments strengthened the hand of the employers, who used signs of economic crisis to fuel their arguments that state expenditure and social policies which favoured labour hampered the performance of the economy. At the same time, economic downswings undermined the Labour Ministry's strategy. The Ministry's concept of organizing and guiding the supply of labour was based on the assumption that the capitalist economy would function smoothly; that production would be maintained and with it the demand for skilled workers; that effort expended on acquiring qualifications would receive its rewards; and that it would be possible, with only a modest degree of social reform, to move towards an economic order where every member of society would perform useful work according to their own capabilities and in return for an adequate wage. All these assumptions were to be overturned in the world economic crisis.

4
Youth Unemployment and Policies towards Unemployed Youth, 1918–1933

Unemployment was a key issue for Weimar governments in their policies towards youth. Politicians, administrators, and educationalists agreed that the experience of work was essential to a young person's socialization; their perceptions of the young unemployed derived from a complex mixture of economic, moral, and political concerns. It was a commonplace to point out how quickly young people forgot skills already acquired, lost interest in work, became indolent, undisciplined, and apathetic. But youth unemployment appeared to threaten not only the future of the workforce and of the economy. Unemployment was thought to produce in the young—even more than in adults—not only the vices of apathy and sloth, but also a loosening of moral standards, leading to rising levels of crime and prostitution. These concerns about the undermining of moral standards and social norms quickly shaded over, in politicians' perceptions, into concern about law and order and the threat posed by the young unemployed—and here it was the male rather than the female unemployed who were the focus of attention—to the authority of the state.[1]

Youth unemployment reached high levels in 1918/19 and again in

---

A shorter version of this chapter has already appeared elsewhere: see E. Harvey, 'Youth Unemployment and the State: Public Policies towards Unemployed Youth in Hamburg during the World Economic Crisis', in Richard J. Evans and Dick Geary (eds.), *The German Unemployed: Experiences and Consequences of Mass Unemployment from the Weimar Republic to the Third Reich* (London, 1987).

[1] On youth unemployment and public policies towards unemployed youth in Weimar Germany, see D. Peukert, *Jugend zwischen Krieg und Krise: Lebenswelten von Arbeiterjungen in der Weimarer Republik* (Cologne, 1987), 167–88; id., 'The Lost Generation: Youth Unemployment at the End of the Weimar Republic', in Evans and Geary (eds.), *The German Unemployed*; P. D. Stachura, *The Weimar Republic and the Younger Proletariat* (London, 1989), Ch. 6; id., 'The Social and Welfare Implications of Youth Unemployment in Weimar Germany, 1929–1933', in id. (ed.), *Unemployment and the Great Depression in Weimar Germany* (London, 1986).

1923/4; during both these phases, political instability gave added impetus to efforts on the part of the public authorities to deal with the problem. The main focus of this chapter, however, is on the years of the Depression, when all policies and plans regarding the social and political integration of adolescents came to stand or fall with the overcoming of youth unemployment.

Central and local governments in the world economic crisis were in agreement that the problem of youth unemployment required action, but there was less unanimity as to what should be done. A wide range of training, recreational and work schemes was discussed and adopted. Although these initiatives were so varied, a distinct trend emerged in public policies towards unemployed youth in the course of the Depression: overall, the goal of reintegration into production through employment policy gave way to a policy chiefly aimed at controlling the behaviour of the young unemployed. At the same time, all efforts to deal with the problem of youth unemployment were hampered by heavy cutbacks in state spending: the efforts of those politicians who pressed for action to combat the moral and political threat posed by the young unemployed were in conflict with the drive by finance ministers to reduce public expenditure.

The Labour Market and Youth Unemployment

The early years of Weimar saw brief but sharp bouts of unemployment; however, inflation cushioned the labour market for much of the period between 1918 and 1923, and relatively high levels of employment were maintained. Unemployment soared during the months of post-armistice demobilization: in February and March 1919, over a million people were claiming unemployment benefits.[2] However, this had dropped by the summer of 1919 to between 500,000 and 600,000. The reduction of unemployment after 1918 was assisted by the Reich government's use of inflation to stimulate the economy and create jobs, and 1922 saw a situation approaching full employment.[3] In the year 1923, with its overlapping succession

---

[2] Karl Christian Führer, *Arbeitslosigkeit und die Entstehung der Arbeitslosenversicherung in Deutschland 1902–1927* (Berlin, 1990), 147.
[3] Carl-Ludwig Holtfrerich, *Die deutsche Inflation 1914–1923: Ursachen und Folgen in internationaler Perspektive* (Berlin and New York, 1980), 194.

of political and economic crises, unemployment fluctuated sharply. The effects of the Ruhr occupation and a temporary stabilization of the mark brought a rise in unemployment in spring 1923, followed by a further surge in inflation and drop in unemployment; only from August 1923 onwards did hyperinflation begin to have a negative effect on the job market, with jobless figures rising while the political tension in the Reich heightened. The stabilization of the currency in November 1923 brought still higher levels of unemployment. In December 1923, over 1.3 million trade union members were out of work and 1.7 million were on short-time working.[4] This phase of high unemployment lasted until the summer of 1924.

Few statistics on youth unemployment exist for the early Weimar years. Local authorities recorded the numbers of young unemployed claiming unemployment benefit, but such statistics covered only 14–18-year-olds, whereas—as commentators in the later years of the Republic were aware—the problem of youth unemployment could be more usefully analysed if 18–21- or 18–25-year-olds were included. What Hamburg's records do show, however, is that juvenile unemployment in these years rose and fell roughly in line with the general trends in the labour market, the highest levels being reached during the demobilization phase: during the peak of unemployment between January and March 1919 between 5,000 and 7,000 young people in Hamburg aged between 14 and 18 were unemployed.[5] By October 1921 unemployment in this age group had all but vanished. Youth unemployment on a large scale did not recur until summer 1923; in November 1923 in Hamburg 2,230 young people (1,268 boys, 962 girls) were registered as unemployed.[6]

After 1924, there was no return to the relatively full employment of the pre-1923 years. The impact of the currency stabilization led industry to reduce its labour costs, which resulted in immediate redundancies, together with longer-term efforts to cut labour

---

[4] Führer, *Arbeitslosenversicherung*, 148.
[5] Jugendausschuß des Hamburger Arbeitsamtes an die Behörde für Gewerbe- und Fortbildungsschulwesen, 11 Dec. 1918. StAH, BSB I, B111; Auszug aus dem Jahresbericht der Jugendabteilung des Arbeitsamtes Hamburg 1918/1919. StAH, JB I, 327 vol. 2.
[6] Behörde für das Arbeitsamt, Jugendabteilung, an das Jugendamt Hamburg, 14 Feb. 1924. StAH, JB I, 327, vol. 1.

through the introduction of labour-saving technology.[7] At the same time, the labour pool was expanding, and between 1924 and 1928 the last large birth cohorts of the pre-war years were coming onto the labour market.[8] Meanwhile, even in the 'good' years after 1924, fundamental problems continued to plague the German economy. Historians have disagreed in their analysis of these problems. While they concur in seeing a shortage of capital, poor levels of investment, misdirected investment, and a growing concentration and rigidity in the structures of German industry as important weaknesses of the Weimar economy before the Depression, they have disagreed over the role played by state expenditure on public services and welfare and by the increased share of national income going on wages and salaries in hampering economic growth.[9] But, whatever the causes of the poor performance of the economy, it is clear that the economy in the second half of the 1920s was not growing fast enough to prevent conflicts over the distribution of wealth, nor was it able to generate a sufficient number of new jobs to absorb the swelling ranks of those seeking work.

Against the background of growing structural unemployment in the second half of the 1920s, the sharp recession of 1925/6 stands out as a period of high unemployment both for young people and for the workforce as a whole. In February 1926, at the deepest point of the crisis, over 2 million people were claiming unemployment benefits. In July 1926, a national survey showed that 272,137 (17 per cent) out of a total of 1,174,899 unemployed were aged between 14 and 21.[10] Young people were not disproportionately hit by this recession: 14–21-year-olds made up only 17 per cent of the total unemployed, while 14–20-year-olds had made up 18.6 per cent of

---

[7] D. Peukert, *Die Weimarer Republik 1918–1933: Krisenjahre der klassischen Moderne* (Frankfurt am Main, 1987), 116–22.

[8] H. James, 'Economic Reasons for the Collapse of the Weimar Republic', in I. Kershaw (ed.), *Weimar: Why Did German Democracy Fail?* (London, 1990), 34; Peukert, *Jugend*, 37–8.

[9] On the debates over the 'sick' Weimar economy, see Peukert, *Weimarer Republik*, 122–9; H. A. Winkler, *Der Schein der Normalität: Arbeiter und Arbeiterbewegung in der Weimarer Republik 1924–1933* (Berlin and Bonn, 1987), 27–41; James, 'Economic Reasons for the Collapse of the Weimar Republic', and Holtfrerich, 'Economic Policy Options and the End of the Weimar Republic', both in Kershaw (ed.), *Weimar*; and Dietmar Petzina, 'Was There a Crisis before the Crisis? The State of the German Economy in the 1920s', in J. von Kruedener (ed.), *Economic Crisis and Political Collapse: The Weimar Republic 1924–1933* (New York and Oxford, 1990), 1–19.   [10] Peukert, *Jugend*, 168–71.

the economically active population in June 1925.¹¹ However, in absolute terms the numbers of young unemployed appeared sufficient to the public authorities to justify special measures targeted at them.¹²

The world economic crisis which began to affect the German economy from 1928 brought a collapse of industrial production levels and of foreign trade, together with a crisis in government finances. Brüning's efforts to balance the Reich budget by cutting state expenditure and to restore profitability to industry by cutting wages and social policy benefits served only to deepen the crisis, and unemployment rose to unprecedented levels.¹³ By July 1932, 5.39 million unemployed were registered at the labour exchanges. Of these, 1.46 million were aged between 14 and 25.¹⁴

Analysing the development of youth unemployment in the Depression is difficult in the absence of a series of unemployment statistics where the figures are broken down according to age. The best information is that provided by the Reich census statistics of June 1933, which at least give a detailed 'snapshot' of youth unemployment.¹⁵ These statistics enable, firstly, a comparison between the unemployment of young people aged between 14 and 25 and that of the population as a whole.¹⁶ The unemployment rate for the economically active population was higher for the 14–25 age-group than for the total working population, but not dramatically higher: 19.3 per cent of economically active 14–25-year-olds were

[11] Hertha Siemering, *Deutschlands Jugend in Bevölkerung und Wirtschaft* (Berlin, 1937), 132.
[12] Ernst Herrnstadt, *Die Lage der arbeitslosen Jugend in Deutschland* (Berlin, 1927), 5–9, 15–25.
[13] Holtfrerich, 'Economic Policy Options and the End of the Weimar Republic', in Kershaw (ed.), *Weimar*, 65–74.
[14] Sondererhebung über die Zahl der jugendlichen Arbeitslosen am 31.7.1932. ZStA Merseburg, Rep.120, BB VII, 1, 181.
[15] Census data in Siemering, *Deutschlands Jugend*, 241–392; these data also provide the basis for Peukert's analysis in 'The Lost Generation', in Evans and Geary (eds.), *The German Unemployed*, 173–8.
[16] The categories used here, which are those used by the Reich statistical office, require some explanation. The resident population (*Wohnbevölkerung*) was made up of two main categories: *Erwerbspersonen* ('economically active population') and *Berufslose* ('non-working population'). The *Erwerbspersonen* were divided up into those actually in work (*Erwerbstätige*) and those out of a job but seeking work (*Erwerbslose*). The *Berufslose* included *Berufslose Selbständige* (pensioners, those on private incomes, etc.) and *Angehörige ohne Hauptberuf* (dependants: children, non-earning housewives, etc.).

unemployed in 1933 as opposed to 18.1 per cent of the total economically active population.[17] However, the picture of youth unemployment appears more striking when the age-group 14–25 is broken down further. Only 8.2 per cent of economically active 14–18-year-olds were unemployed in June 1933, but the figure was 18.6 per cent for economically active 18–20-year-olds and 23.5 per cent for *Erwerbspersonen* aged 20–25.[18] Although it was becoming more difficult for school-leavers to find apprenticeships, 14–18-year-olds still had a better chance on the labour market than older age-groups: apprentices still represented a form of conveniently cheap labour to employers seeking to cut labour costs, and—unless the firm actually shut down altogether—apprentices could not simply be laid off during their training.[19] Demographic developments also favoured the 14–18-year-olds: during the crisis years 1929–34, those leaving school belonged to the smaller birth cohorts of the war years. The age-groups over 18, and particularly newly-qualified skilled workers, were more vulnerable. It was not unusual before the Depression for the newly-qualified to leave the place where they had trained once they had qualified, but a survey conducted in the Depression showed that dismissal at the end of training was becoming the rule.[20] Young male adult workers were particularly prone to be dismissed from workplaces where older, married men were also employed. In many cases, pressure from the works council was reported to have been a factor in employers' decisions to save the jobs for fathers of families.[21]

Secondly, it is possible to compare unemployment rates for men and women in different age-groups. The unemployment rate was higher in the 14–25 age-group both for men and for women than in

---

[17] See Table 5.   [18] Ibid.
[19] See Ch. 3 on the declining number of apprenticeships available in the Depression.
[20] K. Gaebel, 'Berufsfürsorge für erwerbslose Jugendliche', in Deutscher Verein für öffentliche und private Fürsorge (ed.), *Die Verwertung der Arbeitskraft als Problem der Fürsorge* (Karlsruhe, 1927), 37–76, 45; Hans Eggers, 'Das Berufsschicksal von Handwerkslehrlingen nach Beendigung der Lehre', *RABl* (1932), ii. 483.
[21] E. Niffka, 'Die berufliche Lage der Jugend in der Gegenwart unter besonderer Berücksichtigung der männlichen Jugendlichen im Alter von 14–21 Jahren', in *Handbuch der Jugendpflege* 1/2 (Eberswalde and Berlin, 1932); Ludwig Bregmann, 'Aus dem Problemkreis: Jugend, Beruf, Arbeitslosigkeit', *Archiv für Soziale Hygiene und Demographie* (1932), 423–6, 423; Dick Geary, 'Unemployment and Working-Class Solidarity: The German Experience 1929–1932', in Evans and Geary (eds.) *The German Unemployed*, 274.

the overall working population. Unemployed men aged 14–25 made up 25 per cent of the *Erwerbspersonen* in that age-group, while in the male economically active population overall, 22.6 per cent were unemployed. Unemployed women aged 14–25 made up 11.9 per cent of the economically active population aged 14–25, compared to an unemployment rate of 9.9 per cent in the female economically active population overall. Within the 14–25 age-group, it was 20–25-year-old women as well as 20–25-year-old men who were worst hit by unemployment.[22]

The rate of male unemployment was higher than the rate of female unemployment in the working population as a whole.[23] This was also evident in the youthful age-groups. The gap between the rate of male and female unemployment widened with increasing age within the 14–25 age-group: whereas unemployment hit the under-18s of both sexes almost equally (8.9 per cent of economically active boys under 18 and 7.3 per cent of economically active girls under 18 were unemployed in 1933), this gap widened in the 20–25 age-group, in which 30.8 per cent of male *Erwerbspersonen*, but only 13.6 per cent of economically active women were unemployed. Overall, therefore, young women were less badly hit by unemployment than men of the same age, but were worse hit by unemployment than older women.

Part of the explanation for the discrepancy in the rates of unemployment for women and men lay in the distribution of male and female workers in different sectors of the economy, which were not all equally hit by the economic crisis.[24] For instance, a larger proportion of the total female workforce was occupied in agriculture than the proportion of men who were in the agricultural sector: 40.5 per cent of economically active women, but only 22.5 per cent of economically active men were involved in the agricultural sector in 1933. Agriculture was the sector of the economy with the lowest unemployment rate in 1933: whereas 32.1 per cent of the total *Erwerbspersonen* in the industry and crafts sector were unemployed

---

[22] See Table 5.
[23] Ernst, 'Die wirtschaftliche und berufliche Lage der weiblichen Jugend im Winter 1931/2', *Arbeit und Beruf*, 7/8 (1932), 99; Gaebel, *Die deutsche Wirtschaft und das Berufsschicksal der Frau* (Berlin, 1932), 6; Helgard Kramer, 'Frankfurt's Working Women: Scapegoats or Winners of the Depression?', in Evans and Geary (eds.), *The German Unemployed*, 113–15.
[24] Louise Willmot, 'National Socialist Youth Organisations for Girls: A Contribution to the Social and Political History of the Third Reich', D.Phil. (Oxford, 1980), 58.

in 1933, only 3.3 per cent of the total economically active population in agriculture were out of work. The low rate of unemployment in agriculture had a favourable influence on women's employment chances in the Depression.[25] It was older women in particular who were employed in agriculture, but young women too were more likely to be employed in agriculture than young men and thus to some extent protected against unemployment: 30.1 per cent of female *Erwerbspersonen* under 25 years were involved in the agricultural sector, while only 25.9 per cent of male *Erwerbspersonen* of the same age were in agriculture.[26]

However, it was not only the distribution of male and female workers in the various sectors of the economy that accounted for the discrepancy in unemployment rates. Even within the sector industry and crafts, the unemployment rate for young men was higher than for young women. In industry and crafts, 35.9 per cent of male *Erwerbspersonen*, but only 19.6 per cent of economically active women aged 14–25 were unemployed.[27] This may be explained by the fact that women workers in industry and crafts may have been concentrated in the consumer goods industries that were on the whole less badly hit by the Depression than production goods industries. Another explanation would lie in women's position in the workforce and in the pay structure: the fact that women were concentrated in low-paid unskilled or semi-skilled work may have given them more security of employment.[28] This would shed some light on the fact that the discrepancy between the unemployment rate for 14–18-year-olds and that for 18–25-year-olds was less marked in the female workforce than among male workers: the system whereby newly-qualified *Gesellen* suddenly became eligible for the higher wages paid to skilled workers made for higher unemployment among young adult men than among women of the same age. Figures on the industry and crafts sector appear to bear this out: 12.8 per cent of 14–18-year-old boys were unemployed in June 1933, compared with unemployment rates of 35.3 per cent in the age-group 18–20 and 44.4 per cent in the age-group 20–25 in the same sector. At the same time, the proportion of the labour force in the sector fell with increasing age, that is, after

---

[25] Ernst, 'Wirtschaftliche Lage', 100; Gaebel, *Die deutsche Wirtschaft und das Berufsschicksal der Frau*, 6–7.   [26] See Table 7.   [27] Ibid.
[28] Gaebel, *Die deutsche Wirtschaft und das Berufsschicksal der Frau*, 9.

completing an apprenticeship many 18-year-old youths became unemployed and some were forced into other sectors. Meanwhile, the unemployment rate for young women in industry and crafts also rose with increasing age within the age-group 14–25, but the difference between the unemployment rates of the 14–18-year-olds and that of the young women aged 18–25 was not so marked.[29]

Hamburg, like other major cities, was particularly badly affected by the economic crisis.[30] Its big shipbuilding industry and its large commercial sector were hard hit by the shrinking of world trade. Youth unemployment rates were higher in Hamburg than in the Reich as a whole, and slightly higher than the unemployment rate of the overall population in Hamburg.[31] Of the *Erwerbspersonen* aged between 14 and 25, 32.6 per cent were unemployed in June 1933 in Hamburg compared with 19.3 per cent in Germany as a whole.[32] If the Hamburg figure is broken down according to sex, it emerges that 39 per cent of male *Erwerbspersonen* under 25 and 25.2 per cent of female *Erwerbspersonen* in the same age-group were unemployed, confirming the impression given by the Reich figures that young men were worse affected by unemployment than young women. However, in the Hamburg economy, agriculture was too insignificant to play a role in keeping female unemployment down. The discrepancy between unemployment rates for young men and young women must be sought in other factors, such as the difference between the levels of unemployment in major sectors of the city-state's economy. Thus, for instance, in 1933, 26.9 per cent of female garment workers and 22.8 per cent of domestic servants were unemployed, while 54.1 per cent of male workers in the metalworking and engineering sector and 55.1 per cent of male building workers were unemployed.[33]

Young people made up a quarter of the unemployed in Hamburg in 1932 and 1933. In July 1932, the young unemployed aged under 25

---

[29] Siemering, *Deutschlands Jugend*, 266–7.
[30] Birgit Wulff, *Arbeitslosigkeit und Arbeitsbeschaffungsmaßnahmen in Hamburg 1933–1939: Eine Untersuchung zur nationalsozialistischen Wirtschafts- und Sozialpolitik* (Frankfurt am Main, 1987), 96–108; Ursula Büttner, *Hamburg in der Staats- und Wirtschaftskrise 1928–1931* (Hamburg, 1982), 138–40.
[31] On unemployed youth in Hamburg in the Depression, see Wulff, *Arbeitslosigkeit*, 108; Büttner, *Hamburg in der Staats- und Wirtschaftskrise*, 267–71.
[32] See Table 5.
[33] StJB Hamburg, *Nachtrag zum Jahrgang 1933/4*, 28–9.

numbered 34,074 in a total unemployed population of 136,112;[34] by June 1933, the figures had risen to 42,376 in a total of 168,426 unemployed.[35] The young female unemployed made up a larger proportion of the total female unemployed than was the case in the corresponding figures for males: 21.1 per cent of Hamburg's unemployed men were under 25 in July 1932, but 36.7 per cent of the city's unemployed women were under 25. This was because the average age of the female workforce was lower than that of the male workforce: women's working lives (as far as waged work outside the home was concerned) were on the whole shorter than men's.

State officials' perceptions of young workers before the Depression had been based on assumptions about the high risk of unemployment affecting unskilled young workers—with their hand-to-mouth lifestyle and supposed lack of vocational commitment—compared to the greater security of employment and prospects enjoyed by young workers undergoing skilled training. Such assumptions were undermined in the Depression. It became clear that having an unskilled job was as much a consequence as a cause of unemployment: the ranks of the unskilled were swollen in the Depression as more and more youngsters failed in their attempts to find a foothold in a skilled trade. This was confirmed by a survey carried out in autumn 1931 of just over 1,000 unemployed young people aged between 18 and 21.[36] Of these, nearly three-quarters had completed an apprenticeship training; of these skilled workers, 154 had not been able to work in their trade at all since qualifying, and 80 per cent of them had worked in unskilled jobs before becoming unemployed.[37]

Mass unemployment made a mockery of young people's attempts to plan their working lives. Those in a job or training feared being made redundant at any time, while the energies of the young unemployed were focused on the scramble for any job available, unless they had given up the attempt altogether—observers noted a common pattern whereby after a period of intensive searching the unemployed tended to become apathetic and resigned.[38] Meanwhile, while they waited for a job to turn up, the unemployed faced the problem of finding a means of subsistence.

[34] See Table 6. [35] See Table 5.
[36] Peukert, 'The Lost Generation', 182.
[37] Ibid. [38] Ibid. 180–3.

The Young Unemployed and the Unemployment Benefits System

The First World War broke down some of the resistance to the idea that supporting the unemployed was an obligation of the state. During the war, many local authorities supported the unemployed and received financial assistance from the Reich and from some of the *Länder* for this purpose. However, there was no statutory obligation on local authorities to do this, and it was the revolution which finally brought a pledge by the Reich government to ensure the provision of financial assistance to the unemployed.[39] Article 163 of the Weimar Constitution formalized this pledge in its declaration that every German should have the opportunity of earning their living; failing that, they would have the right to public support.[40] This declaration did not, however, clarify how such support was to be provided. Tortuous negotiations followed between the state authorities, trade unions and employers over the relative merits of publicly-funded means-tested benefits as opposed to insured benefits funded by employer and employee contributions, or a mixture of the two systems. The outcome was the 1927 law on labour exchanges and unemployment insurance (AVAVG); this replaced the system of means-tested unemployment assistance set up in 1918 and modified in 1923/4.[41] One of the constant themes running through the debates preceding the AVAVG was the problem of safeguarding the rights of the 'deserving' while preventing abuse of the system by the 'work-shy'. Where the young were concerned, the need to deter the work-shy was seen as being particularly acute, an assumption which influenced legislation and administrative practice with regard to the young unemployed throughout the Weimar period.

The decree of 13 November 1918 which introduced a national system of unemployment benefits was designed as a short-term measure to deal with the problem of unemployment directly caused by the war. The decree was intended to reduce unrest in a period of

---

[39] Führer, *Arbeitslosenversicherung*, 119–43.
[40] Die Verfassung des Deutschen Reichs vom 11. Aug. 1919, *RGBl* 1919, 1383–418, 1414.
[41] Gesetz über Arbeitsvermittlung und Arbeitslosenversicherung vom 16.7.1927, *RGBl* 1927, i, 187 ff. For a detailed analysis of the origins and evolution of the AVAVG, see Führer, *Arbeitslosenversicherung, passim*.

political instability; it was also part of a policy to organize the labour market and discipline the unemployed, who were required to register for work and prove their willingness to work in return for their (means-tested) benefits.[42] The young unemployed—large numbers of whom had been employed in the war industries—were beneficiaries of the decree of November 1918, but at the same time the particular objects of its disciplinary aspects. The decree laid down that 14 was the minimum age for receiving unemployment benefit— thus all young people above school age were in principle eligible— but that young people in particular could be required to attend prescribed courses and activities in return for their benefits.[43] Even with the imposition of these conditions, unemployment benefits for the young were attacked by conservative officials and by employers as cushioning 'work-shy' youngsters.[44] It was not long before entitlements of the young unemployed began to be eroded: in January 1920, the minimum age for claiming benefits was raised from 14 to 16.[45] For those young people who did fulfil the conditions for receiving unemployment assistance, the rates of benefit were—on the grounds of young people's lower rates of pay—fixed at levels generally around 50–60 per cent of the rates paid to adults of the same sex (rates of unemployment assistance for women were—until 1925—set below those for men).[46] Young single unemployed women received the lowest benefits: in 1921/2, unemployed women under 21 received benefits worth about a quarter of those of adult males.[47] The often-repeated cliché that a rise in female unemployment and poverty automatically produced an increase in prostitution—an argument used by, among others, Social Democratic women pressing for higher benefits for the female unemployed[48]—was clearly insufficient to persuade the Reich authorities to raise women's

[42] Preller, *Sozialpolitik*, 236; Merith Niehuss, 'From Welfare Provision to Social Insurance: The Unemployed in Augsburg 1918–1927', in Evans and Geary (eds.), *The German Unemployed*, 44–72, 45–6.
[43] 'Aus der Praxis der Erwerbslosenfürsorge', *SP* 28/14 (1918/19), col. 222.
[44] Gaebel, 'Abbau der Erwerbslosenfürsorge—Schaffung einer Arbeitslosenversicherung', *SP* 28/44 (1918/19), col. 763; Rudolf Blohm to Handelskammer Hamburg, 24 Nov. 1919. Handelskammer Hamburg, 66.A.6.3.
[45] 'Die Verordnung über Erwerbslosenfürsorge von 15.1.20', *SP* 29 (1919/20), col. 411.
[46] Führer, *Arbeitslosenversicherung*, 496.   [47] Ibid. 489–90.
[48] Grete Zabe, in Niederschrift über die 41. Sitzung des Verwaltungsrats der Behörde für das Arbeitsamt Hamburg, 3 Oct. 1919. Handelskammer Hamburg, 66.A.6.3.

unemployment benefit levels. The low rates for women were, in the view of the Reich government, justified in order to prevent undue upward pressure being exercised on women's wages and in view of the need to induce young women to take the jobs which were available in domestic service and agriculture.[49]

Through the emergency decrees on unemployment assistance of 13 October 1923 and 13 February 1924, a hybrid form of semi-insurance was installed: unemployment assistance was now to be funded by contributions from employers and employees, but the unemployed continued to be subject to a means test as a condition of receiving assistance.[50] This reform was accompanied by new regulations on unemployment benefit for young people. Under the decree of 13 February 1924, 14–16-year-olds continued to be excluded as a rule from receiving unemployment benefit, but could now as an exception be allowed to participate in obligatory labour schemes and in return qualify for benefit.[51] A more significant change lay in the new restrictions on the entitlements of 16–18-year-olds to benefit. The decree laid down that 16–18-year-olds were to be eligible for benefit only in case of the job market being designated by the Land authorities as 'unfavourable' and then on condition of performing so-called obligatory labour (*Pflichtarbeit*). These clauses on the conditions for young people claiming benefit were in addition to the general clauses on eligibility: on being willing and able to work, and having worked for 13 weeks in the previous year. A survey undertaken by the Labour Ministry in 1924 revealed that the *Länder* authorities varied in their policy on granting benefit to 16–18-year-olds.[52] Prussia, Bavaria, Württemberg, and Oldenburg did not judge the job market to be sufficiently 'unfavourable', while Hamburg, Sachsen, Baden and Hessen did grant benefits to 16–18-year-olds. By 1927, most *Länder* were granting benefits to this age group.[53]

With the advent of unemployment insurance in 1927, young people's entitlements to unemployment benefit were altered once more.[54] The law on labour exchanges and unemployment insurance

---

[49] Reichsfinanzministerium an das RAM, 2 June 1920. ZStA Potsdam, 39.01, 926.
[50] Führer, *Arbeitslosenversicherung*, 181–3.
[51] RAM an das Arbeitsministerium Baden, 11 June 1924. ZStA Potsdam, 39.01, 1500. [52] Ibid.
[53] Präsident des Reichsamts für Arbeitsvermittlung an das RAM, 3 Aug. 1927. ZStA Potsdam, 39.01, 1501.
[54] Herrnstadt, *Lage der arbeitslosen Jugend*, 9–14.

was passed by the Reichstag on 16 July 1927 and came into force in October 1927. Under its provisions, all workers and employees covered by compulsory sickness insurance (together with those whose earnings were higher than the 'ceiling' for compulsory sickness insurance but lower than 6,000 M per annum), who had worked and paid contributions for 26 weeks in the 52 weeks before becoming unemployed were entitled to receive unemployment benefit (*Arbeitslosenunterstützung*) for 26 weeks. Those remaining unemployed after this time, together with those who had worked for a minimum of 13 weeks but less than 26 weeks, could, after passing a means test, receive 'crisis relief' (*Krisenunterstützung*). Unemployment benefit was funded by contributions from employers and employees which totalled 3 per cent of the wage; crisis relief was financed out of public funds, four-fifths from central government, one-fifth from local authorities. The long-term unemployed whose entitlement to crisis relief was exhausted could then apply for public welfare assistance (*Wohlfahrtsunterstützung*) administered and funded by the local authorities and subject to a means test even more stringent than that applied to applicants for crisis relief.

The law of 1927 linked the new system of unemployment insurance to an expanded and reorganized network of labour exchanges and vocational advice centres. Material support for the unemployed was thus made part of what was intended to be a comprehensive policy to regulate the labour market: job referral and retraining schemes were aimed at preventing and reducing unemployment. To administer the law, a national employment administration was created—Reichsanstalt für Arbeitsvermittlung und Arbeitslosenversicherung, or RAVAV—with employment offices in thirteen new administrative regions.

The law on unemployment insurance of 1927 laid down no minimum age for the entitlement to claim insured unemployment benefit. To that extent the law extended young workers' rights in comparison with the various regulations on unemployment benefit in force since 1918. In principle all young workers were subject to the obligation to pay contributions and in return they were entitled to receive insured benefit at rates related to their earnings before unemployment. However, there were some discriminatory restrictions built into the law. Apprentices were not obliged to pay unemployment insurance contributions until six months before the apprenticeship contract expired—a measure which helped to keep apprentices' pay low and which represented a concession to employers. No benefits were payable if the apprenticeship was terminated before the expiry of the contract.[55] Furthermore, young people were a particular target for the application of paragraph 137 of the AVAVG, which specified that all claimants of unemployment benefit could be required to attend vocational training or retraining courses. More specifically, young people under 21 in receipt of insured unemployment benefit and recipients of crisis relief were singled out as being subject to the imposition of obligatory labour in return for their benefit (AVAVG, paragraph 91). Conditions such as these contradicted the principle of insurance on which the law of 1927 was based, according to which the claim to insured benefits was a right based on previously paid contributions.[56]

The AVAVG had been in operation for just over a year when the effects of the world economic crisis began to make themselves felt on the German labour market. The law had been designed to cope with short-term, cyclical unemployment, not with mass long-term unemployment on the scale experienced by Germany from 1929 onwards. Already in 1928 the financing of unemployment insurance was in crisis, and from 1929 onwards the Reichsanstalt was being substantially subsidized by central government funds. Meanwhile, the AVAVG was constantly amended so that the budget of the Reichsanstalt could be balanced. This process began under Hermann Müller's Grand Coalition government, and the issue of an increase in unemployment insurance contributions (as advocated by the SPD) as opposed to a cut in benefits (as advocated by the DVP) was the occasion for the break-up of the Grand Coalition in March 1930.[57] Brüning and his successors continued with attempts to balance the budget of the Reichsanstalt by raising the level of contributions as well as by cutting the level of benefits.

Within this overall erosion of the unemployment insurance

---

[55] Führer, *Arbeitslosenversicherung*, 342–5. The AVAVG regulations on apprentices were based on an earlier ruling of Nov. 1924 exempting apprentices from paying contributions until 6 months prior to expiry of their contract.
[56] Ibid. 503–5.
[57] L. Preller, *Sozialpolitik in der Weimarer Republik* (Düsseldorf, 1978), 427–8; Bernd Weisbrod, 'The Crisis of Unemployment Insurance in 1928/29 and its Political Repercussions', in Wolfgang J. Mommsen and Wolfgang Mock (eds.), *The Emergence of the Welfare State in Britain and Germany 1850–1950* (London, 1981), 188–197.

system, young people fared particularly badly. Discrimination against the young unemployed in the insurance system had been increased under the Müller government through the exclusion of the under-21s from crisis relief. It was stepped up decisively from 1930 onwards under Brüning: the entitlement of young people to the standard unemployment benefit was made dependent on a means test applied to the income of the young person's relatives. This regulation initially applied to the under-17s, then only to the under-16s, and, finally, under the notorious emergency decree of 5 June 1931, to all under 21.[58] Those under 21 could now only receive insured unemployment benefit if it could be demonstrated that they could not be supported by their family. These provisions rendered void the principle of unemployment insurance where young people were concerned and paved the way for Papen's policy of dismantling insured benefits generally.[59]

The impact of these increasingly restrictive regulations is illustrated by the statistics on the number of claimants of insured unemployment benefit in the city of Hamburg. The number of claimants of the standard benefit aged under 21 years fell from 5,235 in December 1930 to 2,237 in November 1932. Claimants under 21 as a proportion of total claimants of standard benefit fell from 12.9 per cent in July 1930 to 9.7 per cent in December 1931, rising from July 1932 onwards due to the new restrictions on adults' claims.[60] The mass of unemployed youth was forced to rely on means-tested public welfare assistance, the level of which was subject to the discretion of the local authorities.[61] The Hamburg general welfare department (*Wohlfahrtsbehörde*) fixed minimum rates of benefit for the young single unemployed living at home at 5 marks per week

[58] Winkler, *Der Weg in die Katastrophe: Arbeiter und Arbeiterbewegung in der Weimarer Republik 1930–1933* (Berlin and Bonn, 1988), 424–5; Peukert, *Jugend*, 172.

[59] Erlaß des RAM, 29 June 1929, see Preller, *Sozialpolitik*, 421; VO zur Behebung finanzieller, wirtschaftlicher und sozialer Notstände, 26 July 1930, *RGBl* 1930, i. 311; VO zur Sicherung von Wirtschaft und Finanzen, 1 Dec. 1930, *RGBl* 1930, i. 517; Zweite VO zur Sicherung von Wirtschaft und Finanzen, 5 June 1931, *RGBl* 1931, i. 279; VO über Maßnahmen zur Erhaltung der Arbeitslosenhilfe und der Sozialversicherung sowie zur Erleichterung der Wohlfahrtslasten der Gemeinden, 14 June 1932, *RGBl* 1932, i. 273.

[60] Monthly figures in *Arbeitsmarktanzeiger des Landesarbeitsamtes Nordmark* (1930–3).

[61] Heidrun Homburg, 'From Unemployment Insurance to Compulsory Labour: The Transformation of the Benefit System in Germany 1927–1933', in Evans and Geary (eds.), *The German Unemployed*, 79–80.

and for those living away from home at 9 marks per week. The district welfare offices (*Wohlfahrtsstellen*) decided if more than the basic rate was to be paid: some welfare offices added up to 3 marks a week to the minimum rate. The higher rates payable to those living away from home in lodgings offered an opportunity for cutting back on benefits to the young unemployed. This was effected either by reducing the level of benefit payable so as to make it impossible for the young person concerned to carry on paying the rent, or by simply cutting off benefit altogether if the unemployed person was under 21 and refused to move back home.[62]

The Reich government and local authorities justified imposing restrictions on young people's unemployment benefit with the argument that they could and should be supported by their families: state welfare should give way to family self-help. Those working with unemployed youth were, however, quick to point out the tensions which a young person's unemployment set up in the working-class household.[63] Some illustration of this, albeit impressionistic, is given by studies by social investigators during the Depression. One such study, carried out in Berlin, quotes unemployed boys who complained that their parents, particularly their fathers, were constantly nagging them to get work: 'My father's always moaning at me'; 'You sit from 8 o'clock till 12 at the labour office. When you get home that's another disappointment, you just get dirty looks and sarcastic remarks.'[64] According to this study, unemployed girls, since they were given housework to do, were placed under less pressure by their families to get out and find work than boys were.[65] The public authorities, too, tended to regard the integration of young women in the parental household for the duration of their unemployment as unproblematic—in the words of the president of the regional labour office in the Hamburg area in November 1932, young unemployed women are 'not as unemployed as men, because they can be occupied in the

[62] Survey of districts, Oct. 1930. StAH, SB I, AW 00.12; Niederschrift der Leitersitzung der Wohlfahrtsbehörde, 4 Nov. 1931 and 2 Dec. 1931. StAH, SB I, VG 24.31 vol. 3.
[63] Fritz Gräsing, 'Erziehungsarbeit an erwerbslosen Jugendlichen', in Carl Mennicke (ed.), *Erfahrungen der Jungen* (Potsdam, 1930), 43–4; Walter Krafft (= Friedländer), 'Erfahrungen in der deutschen Fürsorge für jugendliche Arbeitslose', *Schweizerische Zeitschrift für Hygiene*, 13 (1933), 430–45, 431.
[64] Gertrud Staewen-Ordemann, *Menschen der Unordnung: Die proletarische Wirklichkeit im Arbeitsschicksal der ungelernten Großstadtjugend* (Berlin, 1933), 84.
[65] Ibid. 87.

household'.[66] However, clearly not all girls found the integration into the household a smooth one. Essays written in the winter of 1932 by unemployed girls from Hamburg on a voluntary labour scheme express a sense of frustration at being at home and financially dependent on their parents. The 15-year-old daughter of a building worker wrote that she wanted 'to get out of the house sometimes, and not to be at home all the time and not to be a burden on one's parents because they don't have any money themselves and they can't afford to keep me ... you go and try and get whatever work is going but it's usually taken'. And in the words of a 17-year-old unemployed sales assistant from Hamburg:

There are a lot of young people out of work at the moment, and many of them have a real urge to work. Every one of us knows what it is like: going for an interview, looking for jobs, waiting for an answer to advertisements. ... When we are at home, we don't know how to pass the day, we just keep rushing to the labour office to sign on and most of us don't even get any money anyway.[67]

State officials, youth welfare workers and teachers warned of the social effects of poverty resulting from youth unemployment, pointing out in particular how poverty fuelled juvenile crime, prostitution and political radicalism.[68] Such warnings notwithstanding, discrimination against the young unemployed with regard to financial provision was a constant throughout the period in question: the welfare system thus helped to divide the unemployed population along generational lines. The assumed ties of young people to their families were used to legitimize either rates of benefit lower than those for adults or the denial of benefit altogether. Moreover, since young people allegedly lacked work morale and discipline, conditions for claiming benefit were hedged around with restrictions to prevent abuse: the fear of the effects of poverty

---

[66] Link, speech to Gemeinnützige Gesellschaft Lübeck, reported in *Lübecker General-Anzeiger*, 18 Nov. 32. StAH, Staatliche Pressestelle I–IV, 3334a.

[67] Essays written by Gretchen S. and Elfriede P. for church authorities running FAD scheme in Malente, Holstein, winter 1932. KAH, KJA, L2/L4/L6.

[68] Preußisches Ministerium für Volkswohlfahrt, Erlaß betr. praktische Maßnahmen für die erwerbslose Jugend, 15 Jan. 1924, repr. in Herrnstadt, *Die Lage der arbeitslosen Jugend*, 45; Justus Ehrhardt, 'Arbeitslosigkeit und Jugendverwahrlosung', *Der Zwiespruch*, 12/20 (1930), 229–30; Verein Hamburgischer Gewerbelehrer, Denkschrift betr. Einschulung des Berufsschuljahrganges 1932. Handelskammer Hamburg, 67.K.4.2; Hans Muser, *Homosexualität und Jugendfürsorge: Eine soziologische und fürsorgerische Untersuchung* (Paderborn, 1933), 75–8.

appeared to be less acute than the fear of encouraging 'work-shy' youth through over-generosity. These arguments—that young people were less in need of income than older workers (in particular fathers of families), but equally if not more in need of occupation—underlay all the measures adopted by Weimar governments towards unemployed youth. Public efforts to combat the 'moral catastrophe' (the words of the Prussian Ministry of Trade and Industry in May 1932)[69] which long-term unemployment would bring upon youth were focused on ways of occupying and disciplining the young unemployed rather than securing their means of subsistence.

Labour Market Strategy in the Depression

One approach to the problem of youth unemployment was the labour market strategy pursued by the Reich Labour Ministry and, from 1927, the newly-set up national employment administration (Reichsanstalt). The Labour Ministry and the employment administration focused their efforts on measures aimed at improving the chances of young workers on the labour market: these ranged from vocational courses for the unemployed to schemes redirecting the unemployed into supposedly less overcrowded sectors of the economy such as agriculture. By channelling central funding to the employment offices (*Arbeitsämter*) and—on certain conditions—to local authority departments, the Labour Ministry and the Reichsanstalt sought to impose a uniform approach throughout the Reich to the problem of unemployment. This policy, spelled out in the autumn and winter of 1930, entailed targeting funds only at measures undertaken primarily from the point of view of labour market considerations.[70] Measures aimed at youth were 'particularly urgent', in the words of the Reichsanstalt, since the young unemployed, after a lengthy period of unemployment 'all too easily lose their will to work regularly; their capacity to work is impaired, and ultimately they end up physically, intellectually and morally at

[69] Preußisches Ministerium für Handel und Gewerbe an das Reichsfinanzministerium, 7 May 1932. BA Koblenz, R2, 18881.
[70] RAVAV an die Landesarbeitsämter und Arbeitsämter, betr. Richtlinien zur Durchführung beruflicher Bildungsmaßnahmen für Arbeitslose, 17 Sept. 1930; RAVAV an die Landesarbeitsämter betr. Mitarbeit bei der Winterhilfe für Arbeitslose und Maßnahmen für jugendliche Arbeitslose, 20 Dec. 1930. StAH, Schulamt Altona, II/7/130/6.

risk'.[71] However, no grants were to be made by the Reichsanstalt for courses designed merely to promote the physical fitness or general education of the unemployed: the emphasis was to be firmly on training for work.[72]

As a result of the Reichsanstalt initiative, local employment offices set up vocationally-oriented training and retraining courses for the young unemployed which provided an average of 10–12 hours of instruction per week over a period of 6–12 weeks.[73] They were initially targeted at recipients of insured unemployment benefit. The participants were placed in courses according to their vocational qualifications. Those who had completed a training in a manual trade or in commercial work were sent on courses to maintain, refresh and extend their specific skills. Unskilled boys were given practical crafts instruction to maintain their dexterity and their work discipline; unskilled girls were taught housekeeping skills in the hope that they would find work in domestic service. The vocational school authorities, which welcomed the additional funding and the chance to prove the indispensability of the vocational schools as institutions, were soon drawn into the programme: in 1931/2, two-thirds of the courses financed by the Reichsanstalt were held on the premises and using the facilities of the vocational schools.[74] The Labour Ministry reported with satisfaction that, in the financial year 1931/2, more than 330,000 young unemployed people had taken part in vocational courses run by the employment offices or subsidized by RAVAV funds; this total rose to 527,354 participants in the financial year 1932/3.[75]

A change of priorities on the part of the Reichsanstalt became

[71] RAVAV an die Landesarbeitsämter betr. Maßnahmen für jugendliche Arbeitslose, 20 Dec. 1930, ibid.
[72] RAVAV an die Landesarbeitsämter und Arbeitsämter betr. Richtlinien zur Durchführung beruflicher Bildungsmaßnahmen für Arbeitslose, 17 Sept. 1930, ibid.
[73] Rudolf Wiedwald, 'Fürsorgemaßnahmen für jugendliche Arbeitslose vom Standpunkt der Arbeitsämter', *AW*, 5/24 (1930), 737–40; id., 'Die Betreuung der arbeitslosen Jugend—Rückschau und Ausblick', *RABl* (1933), ii. 441–2.
[74] RAVAV an den RAM, 23 June 1932. StAH, AB I, 153. On the role of the vocational schools in running schemes for the unemployed, see E. Harvey, 'Weg von der Straße? Die Hamburger Volks- und Berufsschulen und die Jugendarbeitslosigkeit 1918–1933', in H.-P. de Lorent and V. Ullrich (eds.), *Der Traum von der freien Schule* (Hamburg, 1988), 187–93.
[75] RAM an das Reichsfinanzministerium, 21 July 1932. BA Koblenz, R2, 18881; Wiedwald, 'Die Betreuung der arbeitslosen Jugend—Rückschau und Ausblick', 441–2.

evident as its programme for the unemployed developed. While the moral dangers of youth unemployment had been stressed from the outset as a reason for financing vocational courses for the young unemployed, the Reichsanstalt's initiative in the autumn of 1930 had still been based on a concept of labour market planning: the courses were to train and retrain youthful claimants of insured benefit with the aim of quickly getting them into jobs (thereby, apart from anything else, relieving the budget of the Reichsanstalt.[76] This priority shifted increasingly—since skills were, at the height of the Depression, no guarantee of a job—towards stressing the general maintenance of work discipline and morale with a view to the more distant prospect of an economic upturn. A letter from the Labour Minister to the head of the employment administration in March 1931 argued that 'our task . . . must lie not in giving a relatively small number of young people the most thorough vocational knowledge possible, but rather in getting as many youngsters on to the courses as possible, getting them off the streets, maintaining their ability and will to work and protecting them from the physical, intellectual, and moral dangers of unemployment'.[77] The conditions attached to the financing of courses were amended accordingly to include a broader spectrum of activities and of participants. The Labour Ministry and Reichsanstalt issued circulars in autumn 1931 allowing 'recreational measures' (*jugendpflegerische Maßnahmen*) to be financed if organized in conjunction with vocationally-oriented courses—as long as the overall orientation towards training and work remained clear—and making it easier for non-recipients of insured unemployment benefit and crisis relief to participate.[78]

In Hamburg, the courses run by the employment office for the young unemployed in previous periods of high unemployment— 1919–21, 1923/4, and 1926/7—were revived in 1930.[79] In February 1931, 600 young unemployed were attending employment-office

[76] RAVAV an die Landesarbeitsämter und Arbeitsämter betr. Richtlinien zur Durchführung beruflicher Bildungsmaßnahmen für Arbeitslose, 23 Sept. 1930. StAH, Schulamt Altona, II/7/130/6.

[77] RAM an RAVAV, 19 Mar. 1931. ZStA Merseburg, Rep. 120, E I, Fach. 1, 80 vol. 2.

[78] Erlaß der RAVAV betr. Maßnahmen für jugendliche Arbeitslose, 21 Sept. 1931; RAM an die obersten Sozialbehörden der Länder, 15 Oct. 1931; RAVAV an die Präsidenten der Landesarbeitsämter, 26 Oct. 1931. StAH, SB I, AW 00.97.

[79] Bericht der Behörde für das Arbeitsamt Hamburg, 4 Oct. 1926 and 24 Jan. 1927. StAH, Senat, Cl. I, Lit. T, no. 25, vol. 17.

courses; by the winter of 1931/2, the number of participants had risen to 2,330.[80] In November 1931 the employment office also began granting funds to subsidize courses for the unemployed run by the vocational schools.[81] Since February 1931, the school authorities had been empowered by the city-state government to extend compulsory attendance at vocational school for unemployed 14–17-year-olds to 20 hours per week.[82] By October 1931 the vocational school for girls, particularly active in promoting courses for the unemployed, had laid on courses for 1,189 participants. It was claimed that the courses had saved substantial numbers of girls from delinquency and acute 'moral dangers' as well as maintaining their interest in work.[83]

Where the young unemployed received insured benefit, the employment office was able to use the threat of withdrawing their benefit to enforce attendance at its courses. However, some young people tried to get round these rules. One case of this came up in August 1931 before the Hamburg juvenile court. Louise B., a 17-year-old unemployed domestic servant, was convicted of fraud for having forged the signature of the course leader in order to claim her unemployment benefit. The court saw mitigating circumstances in the fact that the girl had missed the courses in order to look for work, since she had seen no prospect of obtaining work through the employment office.[84] Although those who considered the courses a waste of time were penalized for non-attendance, the employment office itself admitted in March 1932 that attendance was enforced largely as a disciplinary measure: in its words, 'while the vocational training courses for the unemployed do have primarily a vocational training function, they also serve to a large degree to test people's willingness to work and to prevent moonlighting'.[85]

Alongside the vocationally oriented courses run by the local employment offices and vocational schools, the Labour Ministry and the employment administration sought other measures to

---

[80] Niederschrift über die 44. Sitzung des Ausschusses zur Förderung der Jugendwohlfahrt, 9 Feb. 1931. StAH, SB I, AW 00.97; 'Junge Erwerbslose auf der Schulbank', *Hamburger Echo*, 15 Jan. 1932.
[81] L. Korell (Arbeitsamt) an die Berufsschulbehörde, 11 Nov. 1931. StAH, AB I, 153. [82] Protokoll des Senats, 20 Feb. 1931. StAH, AB I, 153.
[83] Landesschulbehörde, Wohlfahrtsbehörde und Jugendbehörde Hamburg an die Finanzdeputation, 15 Oct. 1931. StAH, AB I, 53. [84] LGH A3832/1933.
[85] Amtliche Mitteilungen des Arbeitsamtes Hamburg, 19 Mar. 1932. StAH, SB I, AW 90.10.

relieve the pressure on the labour market. Transferring young workers from the cities on to the land and delaying the entry of school-leavers on to the labour market by raising the school-leaving age were measures which had all been attempted in the immediate post-war period with limited success. Despite such unpromising precedents, these ideas were revived in the Depression.

Transferring 'superfluous' young workers from industrial cities into agricultural work was propagated as a solution to the political and social problems caused by youth unemployment and, at least initially, by a shortage of agricultural labour. The plans were even seen by some in the context of a possible re-agrarianization of Germany. The Reich Labour Ministry promoted the policy and after 1926 subsidized the practical efforts of local authorities.[86] In 1930, approximately 18,500 young people under 21 were referred by labour exchanges throughout the Reich to work on the land.[87] However, by this time unemployment in agriculture, though still low in comparison with that in other sectors, was rising as farmers tried to save on labour costs. By the summer of 1932, the employment administration reversed its policy and subsidies for retraining urban youth in agricultural work were stopped.[88] The Hamburg employment office had never been in favour of the transplanting of the young unemployed on to the land, pointing out that young people were as unwilling to adapt to rural life as farmers were intolerant of city youngsters.[89]

Another idea that had been tried out in some places in the immediate post-war years, the extension of obligatory school attendance at the *Volksschule* to nine instead of eight years, was put forward in the economic crisis as a way of relieving the urban labour market for young workers—if only temporarily, since it merely postponed the entry of a cohort of school-leavers on to the labour market by a year.[90] However, when the *Länder* attempted to put

[86] Rundschreiben des RAM an die obersten Landesbehörden für Erwerbslosenfürsorge, 20 Sept. 1926. StAH, Senat, Cl. I, Lit. T. no. 25, vol. 17.

[87] Bernhard Ehmke, 'Die Überführung städtischer Jugendlicher in die Landwirtschaft', *RABl* (1931), ii. 193–6, 194.

[88] Rundschreiben der RAVAV betr. Umschulungsbetriebe Fliegerhorst und Niklasdorf, 29 June 1932. StAH, AB I, 116.

[89] Arbeitsamt Hamburg an die Landherrenschaft, 11 Mar. 1930. StAH, AB I, 116; Oberschulbehörde an die Behörde für das Arbeitsamt Hamburg, 24 Jan. 1931. StAH, AB I, 116.

[90] Rundschreiben des RAM betr. Verlängerung der Schulpflicht, 22 and 29 Nov. 1930. StAH, SB I, AW 34.01.

this plan into practice, the financial obstacles proved insuperable. The largest *Land*, Prussia, abandoned its plans for making a ninth school year compulsory, and introduced it on a voluntary basis only in February 1931.[91] In Hamburg, a compulsory ninth school year had been in operation from 1919 to 1921, and the measure came in for renewed consideration in 1930 as a response to the Prussian proposals; however, the Hamburg school authorities abandoned the idea when Prussia failed to push its plan through. Propaganda efforts were then undertaken to persuade parents to let their children stay on for an extra year. No financial assistance was made available to encourage parents to keep children at school, and the campaign was not a great success: instead of the hoped-for 1,000 that had been expected to stay on at Easter 1932, fewer than 600 opted to stay on out of 5,572 children due to leave school.[92]

Overall, the various measures making up the labour market strategy of the final Weimar governments towards youth unemployment were limited to attempts to regulate the overall supply of juvenile labour on the one hand and to improve the individual chances of young workers on the labour market on the other. Efforts to transfer labour back on to the land and to encourage children to stay on at school failed to achieve either of these aims, while the vocational courses increasingly took place in a vacuum as the labour market deteriorated. As a result, attempts to combat the phenomenon of youth unemployment gave way to attempts to combat at most its political and social effects. The Labour Ministry and the employment administration became more and more concerned with ways of simply keeping the maximum number of young people off the streets and occupied and preventing their 'demoralization'.

Recreation, Therapy, and Education: Youth Welfare and the Young Unemployed

The measures of the Labour Ministry and the Reichsanstalt were criticized by welfare administrators and educationalists on the

[91] Hans-Peter Ehni, *Bollwerk Preußen? Preußen-Regierung, Reich-Länder-Problem und Sozialdemokratie 1928–1932* (Bonn–Bad Godesberg, 1975), 189; Erlaß des Preußischen Kultusministeriums, 18 Feb. 1931. ZStA Potsdam, 49.01, 7544.

[92] Merkblatt der Landesschulbehörde Hamburg für die Eltern der Kinder, die Ostern 1932 die Schule verlassen; Vermerk der Oberschulbehörde, 14 Mar. 1932. StAH, Oberschulbehörde V, 963.

grounds that short courses designed to teach or refresh vocational skills neither enabled the participants to find a job nor equipped them to cope with long-term unemployment.[93] Youth welfare administrators and social workers called instead for measures which would combat more effectively what were perceived as the moral and psychological effects of youth unemployment. A Social Democratic youth welfare spokesman saw the young unemployed as being liable to become 'anti-social, apathetic, work-shy and full of destructive urges'.[94] With only a slightly different slant, a Catholic youth welfare expert emphasized how the 'unorganized' unemployed in particular, whose lifestyle was untouched by the pedagogical influence provided by youth organizations, were exposed to the 'temptations of the cinema, of the dance-hall, flirting, idleness, and in general the danger of moral degeneration'.[95] Furthermore, youth welfare spokesmen emphasized the importance of reaching the long-term unemployed who were not in receipt of unemployment benefit and consequently less likely to be reached by the measures financed by the Reichsanstalt. In the absence of sanctions such as the withdrawal of benefit for non-attendance, this group of young unemployed had to be attracted to public welfare schemes on a voluntary basis.[96]

Focusing accordingly on 'the unemployed person as an individual human being' (in the words of a youth welfare publication[97]), public youth welfare authorities, confessional welfare associations, the Arbeiterwohlfahrt and youth organizations set up a variety of projects targeted at the young unemployed which ranged from organized football, hiking trips, and musical evenings to sewing circles and political discussion groups.[98] Youth welfare workers saw

[93] Richtlinien der Vereinigung großstädtischer Jugendämter für die Fürsorge für jugendliche Arbeitslose, Sept. 1931. StAH, AB I, 153; Walter Friedländer, 'Bildungsmaßnahmen für jugendliche Arbeitslose', *Die Gemeinde*, 7 (1930), 1011–13; Herman Kranold-Steinhaus, 'Die Entwicklung der Wohlfahrtspflege in der Krise', in Hauptausschuß für Arbeiterwohlfahrt (ed.), *Jahrbuch der Arbeiterwohlfahrt 1931* (Berlin, 1932), 149–50.
[94] Walter Friedlander, 'Zur Frage der Tagesheime für jugendliche Erwerbslose', *ZBl* 23 (1931/2), 322–4, 323.
[95] Niffka, 'Unsere Aufgaben den nichtorganisierten Jugendlichen gegenüber', *Der Weckruf*, 7/11 (1931), 9.
[96] Krafft (= Friedländer), 'Erfahrungen in der deutschen Fürsorge für jugendliche Arbeitslose', *Schweizerische Zeitschrift für Hygiene*, 13 (1933), 430–45, 437.
[97] Deutsches Archiv für Jugendwohlfahrt (ed.), *Aus der Praxis der Erwerbslosenhilfe an Jugendlichen* (Eberswalde and Berlin, 1931), 16.
[98] Ibid; Bertha Finck (ed.), *Was können wir für unsere arbeitslose Jugend tun? Bilder aus der Arbeit der evangelischen Liebestätigkeit* (Berlin, 1931); *Jahrbuch der*

such schemes as an opportunity to reach and educate hitherto elusive groups of 'problem' working-class adolescents; youth organizations hoped to extend their influence to a wider circle of young people.[99]

The day centres (*Werkheime* or *Tagesheime*) for unemployed youth represented the most significant innovation by the public youth welfare authorities in response to the problem of youth unemployment.[100] These centres, pioneered by the Social Democratic youth welfare authority and by the district youth welfare departments (*Bezirksjugendämter*) in Berlin from 1926 onwards, combined facilities for practical work and handicrafts instruction with the functions of a drop-in centre for cultural and recreational activities; they also provided meals free of charge or at reduced prices. Participation was free of charge and on a voluntary basis. The aim, in the words of one of their pioneers, was to create for the young unemployed a 'substitute for the family': a community based on the peer group under the pedagogical, 'comradely' leadership of the youth workers.[101] The centres also tried—with some success, it was claimed—to counteract the influence of the 'cliques' or youth gangs, whose presence in working-class districts of Berlin was becoming increasingly noticeable before and during the Depression.[102]

Berlin's day centres were imitated in a number of other cities.[103] In Hamburg, the youth welfare department began to set up day centres in September 1931, albeit in the face of some opposition: an official in the general welfare department alleged that providing cheap meals for young people who could eat at home would 'undermine the family', while a DVP senator considered that

---

Arbeiterwohlfahrt 1931, 17; Josepha Fischer, 'Die Jugendpflege in den Haushaltsplänen der Länder', *Das junge Deutschland*, 26/6 (1932), 188–9.

[99] Gehse, 'Psychologische Betrachtungen über die Arbeitslosigkeit Jugendlicher', *Das junge Deutschland*, 26/3 (1932), 92–4, 92.

[100] Ernst Wauer, 'Die Erwerbslosigkeit der Jugend: Berliner Maßnahmen und Erfahrungen', *Berliner Wohlfahrtsblatt*, 2/7 (1926), 97–101; Bruno Klopfer, *Jugendpflege an erwerbslosen Jugendlichen* (Berlin, 1926); Erna Magnus, *Werkheime für erwerbslose Jugendliche* (Berlin, 1927); Friedländer, 'Zur Frage der Tagesheime für jugendliche Erwerbslose', 322–4.   [101] Friedländer, ibid. 323.

[102] Interview with Ella Kay and Jeanne Bauer, 9 Feb. 1984; Rosenhaft, 'Organising the Lumpenproletariat', in Evans (ed.), *The German Working Class*, 182. On the cliques, see also Ch. 6.

[103] Deutsches Archiv für Jugendwohlfahrt, *Aus der Praxis der Erwerbslosenhilfe*, 24.

'gathering the young unemployed together in a day centre is bound inevitably to produce delinquency'.[104] Such opposition, coupled with the dwindling financial resources of the city government, hindered the expansion of the public day centres: by the end of 1932, the youth welfare department was running only four such centres, while private organizations ranging from the churches to the trade unions were running eleven centres between them, catering primarily for their own members.[105]

The style of the day centres varied. Some of the centres in Berlin prided themselves on their wide-ranging and demanding programme, including vocational facilities and cultural activities, carried through in a 'youth movement' atmosphere with bans on smoking, card games, and 'trash' literature.[106] Others—fearing that such an atmosphere would repel precisely those adolescents whom the centres were trying to attract—avoided such regulations and stressed the need to avoid activities too overtly educational. A youth worker at a centre in Mainz observed that bans on smoking would only have driven people away, that the favourite activity for many of the young clientele was playing cards, and that 'the main thing for most of the young people was to have a heated room where they could spend the day'.[107]

In Hamburg, a report written in January 1933 for the youth welfare authority by the leader of the largest public day centre (with a capacity of 260 people) gives some impression of the work of the centre.[108] Apart from offering subsidized meals and somewhere to escape the cold, the centre—like the Berlin *Werkheime*—provided practical instruction in crafts (sewing for girls and woodwork for boys); it also laid on sports and entertainments. It attracted about three times as many boys as it did girls, confirming the impression from reports elsewhere that girls were more difficult to organize on

[104] Kurt Struve (Wohlfahrtsbehörde) memo, 30 Jan. 1931. StAH, SB I, AW 00.77; Senator Hirsch, in Niederschrift über die 2. Sitzung des Ausschusses zur Fürsorge für jugendliche Erwerbslose, 9 Mar. 1931. StAH, SB I, AW 00.97.
[105] Zusammenstellung der Maßnahmen, die von den Jugendpflegeorganisationen für erwerbslose Jugendliche getroffen sind, 21 Jan. 1933. StAH, AB I, 147.
[106] Verwaltungsbericht des Bezirksjugendamtes Prenzlauer Berg für die Zeit, 1 Apr. 1924–31 Mar. 1928 (Berlin, n.d.), 26; Friedländer, 'Zur Frage der Tagesheime für jugendliche Erwerbslose'.
[107] Deutsches Archiv für Jugendwohlfahrt, *Aus der Praxis der Erwerbslosenhilfe*, 24.
[108] H. Hennings, 'Übersicht über die Tätigkeit des Jugend- und Erwerbslosenheims Nagelsweg', 9 Jan. 1933. StAH, AB I, 147.

this basis than boys. This was ascribed partly to the pattern of working-class girls' leisure, which took less collective and organized forms than that of boys, and partly to the fact that girls had less leisure overall, tending to be kept at home by their families to do housework.[109]

From the point of view of attracting the sort of young unemployed who would otherwise resist official schemes and organized activities, the relative openness of the day centres was an advantage; from the point of view of exerting pedagogical influence, it posed problems. An 'educational' agenda could be negotiated only with some difficulty, as is evident from a report on the Hamburg public day centre:

> Since those that come tend to be the sorts of young people that one sees hanging around the Süderstraße, Idastraße, Lorenzstraße, etc. in Hammerbrook it is clear that one cannot reach them if one sticks strictly to the tenets of the youth movement and of youth work generally. That is why there was from the beginning a smoking room in the centre and on social evenings not folk dancing but 'modern dancing'. These dance evenings (modern) have been a success. The young people initially tried to introduce customs that did not accord with what we were trying to do, but customs have by now been established of a decidedly superior kind. News of this dance evening got round very quickly, so that on the second evening 160–170 young people suddenly appeared and we were not in a position to control the situation. We have now introduced tickets, so that each youth is invited personally with his girlfriend. We are currently attempting to develop these dance evenings into social evenings with a greater intellectual content.[110]

The work of the day centres was restricted by the budget cuts forced upon the municipalities in the Depression by the financial policies of the Reich government. The Berlin municipal government began to cut the funding of the *Werkheime* in 1930, ordering the exclusion of the 18–21-year-olds—a decision which provoked a protest demonstration—and leaving the district youth welfare departments increasingly struggling to keep their centres open.[111]

---

[109] Ruth Weiland, 'The Effects of Unemployment on Children and Young People', in Save the Children International Union (ed.), *Children, Young People and Unemployment* (Geneva, 1933), 14–53, 50.

[110] Hennings, 'Übersicht über die Tätigkeit des Jugend- und Erwerbslosenheims Nagelsweg'.

[111] Ernst Wauer, 'Maßnahmen der Stadt Berlin für die erwerbslose Jugend', *Berliner Wohlfahrtsblatt*, 7/5 (1931), 33–39, 35.

As we have seen above, the Hamburg city government was unable to expand its provision to cope with more than a few hundred out of the thousands of young unemployed in the city in 1932. Meanwhile, central government funding was increasingly channelled into work schemes for unemployed youth less 'therapeutic' than disciplinary in nature and aimed at larger numbers than could be catered for by the day centres and the other schemes run by the youth welfare authorities.

Work Schemes for Unemployed Youth

The scale of work creation for the unemployed generally in the final years of the Weimar Republic was limited by Brüning's rejection of all major public investment plans to stimulate the economy, while his successors in their short period of office did little more than lay the basis for Hitler's initial work-creation schemes.[112] The main forms of work creation—the 'emergency labour' schemes (*Notstandsarbeit*) partly financed by the Reich and aimed after 1927 at the recipients of unemployment benefit, and the 'welfare labour' schemes (*Fürsorgearbeit*) financed by the municipalities and aimed at those on municipal welfare assistance—were generally reserved for older, married male workers. Though paid at below normal wage rates, such work was based on a normal work contract and was subject to the payment of social insurance contributions.[113] Work schemes set up for young people, on the other hand, rarely provided anything approaching normal work at normal wages, nor were they set up with this objective in mind.

Two types of work scheme run in the final years of the Weimar Republic were aimed exclusively or to a large degree at the young, unmarried unemployed: the municipal obligatory labour schemes, and the voluntary labour service. Most of this work was unskilled manual labour and could only have a de-skilling effect. Moreover, the work was defined as being outside the bounds of normal work contracts and outside labour law. The remuneration for such

---

[112] On work creation in the final phase of the Weimar Republic, see Helmut Marcon, *Arbeitsbeschaffungspolitik der Regierungen Papen und Schleicher* (Frankfurt am Main, 1974).
[113] Notstandsarbeit, regulated in AVAVG, paras. 139–41; Fürsorgearbeit, regulated in Verordnung über die Fürsorgepflicht, 13 Feb. 1924, *RGBl* 1924, i. 100–7, para. 19.

work—in the form of a bonus on top of a minimal unemployment benefit or of 'pocketmoney'—was set at a level below legal wage rates. A by-product of this policy was that the schemes could function as a source of cheap labour for local authorities. The schemes also shared an overall disciplinary function: they aimed to keep the young unemployed off the streets and to control their behaviour.

MUNICIPAL WORK SCHEMES

Of the various forms of municipal work schemes developed in the Weimar Republic, obligatory labour (*Pflichtarbeit*) was the form most commonly foreseen for the young, single unemployed. Obligatory labour was of two kinds: it could be imposed on claimants of welfare assistance or on claimants of insured unemployment benefit under 21.[114]

Municipal interests and the pursuit of efficiency in managing the long-term unemployed led the Hamburg welfare department under its conservative director Martini (DVP) to expand work schemes for claimants of welfare assistance during the world economic crisis.[115] *Fürsorgearbeit* was a method of enabling the 'deserving' unemployed (above all those on high rates of benefit, such as married men with families) to regain their entitlement to insured unemployment benefit.[116] Obligatory labour schemes, on the other hand, were used to deter claimants and to provide a pretext for stopping benefits to those judged 'undeserving'. The work was officially defined as being performed as a condition for receiving welfare assistance. Those identified by the welfare department as most likely to be defrauding the state and thus as a primary target for obligatory labour were the 'younger, single men, who are supported by the district welfare offices, who have only worked very irregularly and with regard to whom considerable doubts about their willingness to work are justified'.[117] State officials also alleged

[114] VO über die Fürsorgepflicht, 13 Feb. 1924, para. 19; AVAVG, para. 91.
[115] On municipal labour schemes generally, see Homburg, 'From Unemployment Insurance to Compulsory Labour', in Evans and Geary (eds.), *The German Unemployed*, 92–100.
[116] Senator Neumann, in welfare department discussion, 7 Jan. 1930. StAH, SB I, AW C0.64; Regierungsrat Marx, memo 30 Sept. 1930. StAH, SB I, AW 00.62.
[117] Oskar Martini, Denkschrift über die Belastung der Fürsorge durch Wohlfahrtserwerbslose, 16 Nov. 1929. StAH, SB I, AW 00.21.

that large numbers of fraudulent claims came from unemployed women with 'a certain irregularity of life-style'.[118] Obligatory labour was not only imposed on those considered to be abusing the system: it was also part of a strategy for dealing with 'troublemakers'. Officials labelled those who dared to complain or protest about the handling of their claims as 'mentally defective and asocial elements' incited by 'political subversives'.[119] The welfare department justified its treatment of the unemployed by portraying itself as being in the front line in the battle for law and order. The department worked closely with the police, who sent reinforcements on critical days such as Monday, 29 June 1931, the day on which the provisions of the emergency decree of 5 June 1931 came into force, and supplied 61 rubber truncheons from police stocks for the use of the welfare officials who requested them; other cities adopted similar precautions.[120]

Fear of the unemployed could lead the welfare department to take steps to relieve the pressure on its district offices and to give the impression that practical initiatives to tackle financial need were being taken. In June 1931, the department spent some time discussing recent disturbances in the welfare offices: 'One district office reports that it has observed that the troublemakers are mostly youths. The new emergency decree will result in the welfare offices having to deal with a vast new influx of youths: thus the trouble is bound to get worse. Martini remarks that plans have already been made to set up new work sites for young people.'[121]

A breakdown by age of the workers on two obligatory labour schemes in December 1932 showed that young people under 25 made up 40–45 per cent of the workers.[122] There were also sites set aside for young people under 21, where, by the summer of 1932, 240 young people were occupied. The total number of obligatory

[118] Wohlfahrtsstelle I, report Nov. 1929. StAH, SB I, AW 00.21.
[119] Report of discussion between Martini and police president, 18 Dec. 1929. StAH, SB I, VG 74.12.
[120] Chef der Ordnungspolizei to Wohlfahrtsbehörde, 26 June 1931; Vermerk, betr. Anfrage des Abgeordneten Westphal im Haushaltsausschuß der Bürgerschaft, Wohlfahrtsbehörde, 17 Aug. 1932. StAH, SB I, VG 74.12; Stadt Frankfurt am Main an den Deutschen Städtetag, 4 Aug. 1930, betr. Schutz der Beamten der Wohnungs- und Wohlfahrtsämter. BA Koblenz, R36, 1080.
[121] Niederschrift über die Leitersitzung der Wohlfahrtsbehörde, 13 June 1931. StAH, SB I, VG, 74.12.
[122] Sozialer Querschnitt der Unterstützungsarbeiterbelegschaften Langenhorn-Süd, 15 Dec. 1932, und Maienweg, 31 Dec. 1932. StAH, SB I, AW 60.11, vol. 1.

labourers reached a maximum of 5,582 in August 1932 before falling to 2,288 in January 1933, so the number of workers under 25 is unlikely to have exceeded 2,500 at the most.[123] This made the welfare department's comprehensive plan for disciplining the unemployed a hopeless enterprise. The argument for the use of coercion—that it enabled the authorities to exert control across the board over the 'hard cases'—was undermined by the fact that the exercise of such control could only be partial and arbitrary. Moreover, the deterrent effect of obligatory labour became weaker as the crisis deepened. In 1929, the district welfare offices in the 'problem' districts of St Pauli and the Altstadt, who were the first to impose obligatory labour on young unemployed claimants, had reported a marked deterrent effect: prospective claimants tended to evade the measure by moving to the district of St Georg.[124] However, by the autumn of 1930, all the district welfare offices reported that the deterrent effect had worn off. Some of the unemployed were even volunteering for work for the sake of the small bonus of 75 pfennigs paid on top of the normal rate of welfare assistance for each of the three days worked per week.

Although fewer people dared to refuse to undertake obligatory labour as the economic crisis worsened, the implementation of the work schemes on the basis of coercion remained a problem. Passive resistance to the work was reflected in low productivity. Active tactics of evasion and opposition emerged more sporadically. Collective opposition was most common on the outdoor sites where unemployed men were made to chop wood, clear scrub, dig drainage ditches, and the like, and it was on several such sites in October 1930 that the longest strike occurred. The strike, which lasted from 14 to 29 October 1930, was led by KPD activists and coordinated with similar action in other cities.[125] It was supported at its height by three-quarters of those employed on the sites concerned—a total of around 470 strikers. The strikers demanded wages at the rate fixed by collective agreement for municipal

[123] Kurt Struve, 'Und wer schafft Arbeit für Männer und Frauen?' *JV*, 8/3 (1932), 84–91; Hamburger Staatsamt (ed.), *Hamburgs Fürsorgewesen im Kampf gegen die Arbeitslosigkeit* (Hamburg, 1935, 21.
[124] Niederschrift über die Leitersitzung der Wohlfahrtsbehörde, 21 Oct. 1929. StAH, SB I, AW 00.92.
[125] 'Das Verhalten der Fürsorgeverbände bei Streiks von Pflichtarbeitern und Fürsorgearbeitern', *Nachrichtendienst*, 11/10 (1930); Edith Rasche, 'Die Entwicklung des FAD in den Jahren der Weltwirtschaftskrise und der Kampf des KJVD gegen den FAD 1930–1933', Diss. phil. (Dresden, 1967), 59.

employees for the days worked on the sites, a demand which was above all in the interests of the unmarried, who were on lower rates of welfare assistance. 80 per cent of the workers on the site were unmarried, and it was reported that among those who carried on working, the married men predominated. This may have been to do with the fact that the married men with children received a benefit which with the bonus for the days worked was as high as or higher than the wage would have been which was being demanded for the three days worked.[126] The strike ended in failure with the strikers losing their entitlement to welfare assistance.[127] A second strike wave in June 1932, which was coordinated by the communist-led committee of the unemployed, was sparked off by the news that the working day for those on the work schemes was to be lengthened. This time the department responded by closing all the men's sites (the women were judged unlikely to strike) for a period of weeks.[128]

Although there were no recorded strikes by women on work schemes, the welfare department nevertheless met with determined opposition on an individual basis from unemployed young women. This was particularly evident in the case of a residential scheme run by the department in premises in Fleestedt, outside Hamburg, owned by the Protestant welfare organization, the Innere Mission. The scheme was set up in October 1932 with the dual goals of depriving the 'undeserving' of benefits and of retraining the industrious and compliant for domestic service. The girls were required to live in and perform housework, with the occasional free Sunday, in return for board and lodging and pocketmoney of 50 pfennigs per week instead of their usual welfare assistance. The girls rebelled against this deprivation of liberty: some simply left, and as a result lost their right to benefits, while others sought the support of their parents in finding reasons to leave. The parents generally backed their daughters against the welfare department on the grounds that if their daughters were going to do unpaid housework, they could do it at home.[129] Those who planned the scheme had

[126] 'Ein Bärendienst', *Hamburger Echo*, 16 Oct. 1930; 'Familienstand der Unterstützungsarbeiter', 16 Oct. 1930 and Niederschrift der Leitersitzung der Wohlfahrtsbehörde, 20 Nov. 1930. StAH, SB I, AW 00.93.
[127] Martini to Wilhelm Polligkeit, 21 Oct. 1930. StAH, SB I, AW 00.93.
[128] 'Zwangsarbeit', *Hamburger Volkszeitung*, 1 June 1932; 'An alle Pflichtarbeiter Hamburgs' (leaflet of strike committee), June 1932; Becker, report to Martini, 9 June 1932. StAH, SB I, AW 00.92.
[129] Leiterin E. Ostermann to Wohlfahrtsbehörde, 8 Dec. 1932 and report on Luise S. and Mariechen H., Oct. 1932. StAH, AB I, AW 92.10, vol. 1.

underestimated the difficulties involved in reducing the expectations of unemployed girls so radically: the scheme succeeded only in stopping a number of girls from receiving further welfare payments.

By 1932 at the latest, it was apparent that the conflicting goals pursued by the welfare department in its obligatory labour schemes policy could not be reconciled. A policy of coercing the 'hard cases' and selecting those perceived as 'asocial' for the schemes made for low productivity on the sites and attracted unwelcome adverse publicity. The strikers failed in their aim of obtaining the wage rate they demanded, but they helped to push the welfare department into altering its policy. From the point of view both of projecting a positive image of the city government's welfare provision, and of getting work done for the municipality efficiently, the use of voluntary rather than conscripted labour began to appear a better alternative. Therefore, by the autumn of 1932, officials in the welfare department were looking at the voluntary labour service as an alternative model for occupying the unemployed.

THE VOLUNTARY LABOUR SERVICE

Introduced in June 1931, the voluntary labour service (Freiwilliger Arbeitsdienst, or FAD) was the Brüning government's main initiative to deal with mass youth unemployment.[130] It was run by the national employment administration, which by offering central funding at a time when local municipal initiatives were drying up for lack of funds could ensure that measures for the young unemployed at local level would increasingly take the form of voluntary labour service schemes. National subsidies under the voluntary labour service were provided for labour-intensive projects of land improvement and the like which were judged to be in the public interest. Regulations regarding work contracts and social insurance payments did not apply to the work, which was to be carried out by young unemployed volunteers. Private organizations were encouraged to become involved in organizing voluntary

[130] Henning Köhler, *Arbeitsdienst in Deutschland: Pläne und Verwirklichungsformen bis zur Einführung der Arbeitsdienstpflicht im Jahre 1935* (Berlin, 1967); Wolfgang Schlicker, 'Arbeitsdienstbestrebungen des deutschen Monopolkapitalismus in der Weimarer Republik', *Jahrbuch für Wirtschaftsgeschichte*, pt. 3 (Berlin, 1971); VO über die Förderung des FAD, 23 July 1931, *RGBl* 1931, i. 398; Peter Dudek, *Erziehung durch Arbeit: Arbeitslagerbewegung und Freiwilliger Arbeitsdienst 1920–1935* (Opladen, 1988).

labour service projects. The regulations regarding the eligibility of volunteers for public funding were initially restrictive: recipients of insured unemployment benefit were eligible for Reich funding for a period of 20 weeks: those who would have qualified for insured benefit but were under 21 could only be subsidized at the discretion of the local authorities.

The motives for the introduction of the voluntary labour service were diverse. While a compulsory labour service was regarded by the Brüning cabinet as neither financially nor politically feasible in the short term, the voluntary labour service was intended as a sop to right-wing advocates of labour conscription for youth: this had been canvassed in right-wing circles since the First World War and was increasingly proposed in the Depression (by, among others, the Jungdeutscher Orden, the Stahlhelm, the NSDAP, and DINTA) as a panacea for Germany's ills.[131] The voluntary labour service was also envisaged as a cheap alternative to substantial programmes of public works and as such was hoped to have some propaganda effect.[132] Labour service volunteers would be temporarily removed from the labour market; in the longer term, it was hoped that an élite of volunteers would be recruited for agricultural settlement.[133]

The whole concept of the voluntary labour service was a quasi-militaristic one in which girls were marginal.[134] The right-wing nationalists who wanted to see the scheme paving the way for the introduction of general labour conscription for all young men saw the labour service acting as a substitute army, a 'school for the nation'. Although the Brüning government did not fully share the ambitions of such propagandists, its motives for launching a major national initiative on youth unemployment were influenced by the desire to impose some control over the politically threatening mass of the male unemployed: this phenomenon, which Brüning declared on the eve of his fall to be a problem 'concerning us day and night',[135] inevitably preyed on the minds of the government

---

[131] Köhler, *Arbeitsdienst*, 15–38; Dudek, *Erziehung durch Arbeit*, 60–87; Klaus Hornung, *Der Jungdeutsche Orden* (Düsseldorf, 1958), 108–19.

[132] Gutachten zur Arbeitslosenfrage, erstattet von der Gutachterkommission zur Arbeitslosenfrage (Brauns-Kommission) (Berlin, 1931), pt. 2, 7–8.

[133] VO über die Förderung des FAD, para. 18.

[134] Dagmar Morgan, *Weiblicher Arbeitsdienst in Deutschland* (Darmstadt, 1978), 26–52.

[135] Brüning, Rede vor dem Verein der ausländischen Presse, 28 May 1932. *Frankfurter Zeitung*, Reichsausgabe 29 May 1932, quoted by Manfred Hermanns,

politicians more than considerations about the alleged moral risks of unemployment for girls.

Voluntary labour service schemes were either 'open' daytime work sites or 'closed' residential work camps: the Reich authorities preferred the latter form and increasingly promoted it in the course of 1932.[136] The residential work camp had a number of precursors, notably the work camps run by groups in the *bündische Jugend* since the mid-1920s, the most well-known of which were the camps for 'workers, peasants, and students' organized by the Schlesische Jungmannschaft from 1928 onwards.[137] Youth movement activists tried to present the voluntary labour service as having been inspired by the work-camp movement and they sought to play a role in its development, both through formulating proposals for its amendment and through organizing their own voluntary labour service schemes within government guidelines.[138] In the end, however, the youth movement's direct influence on the Reich government's decision to introduce the voluntary labour service and on its subsequent development appears to have been limited.[139]

While the youth movement's work camps represented experiments in learning through work, recreation, and collective living in a self-chosen peer group, 'education through work' meant, to the right-wing Reich governments in the final phase of the Republic, above all a process of disciplining. They preferred the form of the residential camp because it enabled a more effective supervision of the urban recruits in an environment away from the pernicious influence of the city. This removed from the city a source of political unrest, as the Prussian Ministry of the Interior pointed out in the autumn of 1932. The Ministry considered that transplanting the young unemployed out of the industrial cities and areas with high unemployment, even for a short period of time, would

Jugendarbeitslosigkeit 1926–1988: Ein sozialgeschichtlicher und zeitgeschichtlicher Vergleich (Opladen, 1983), 5.

[136] Der Reichskommissar für den FAD an die Bezirkskommissare, 3 Sept. 1932 betr. Durchführung des Dienstes bei offenen Arbeitslagern, in *Beilage zum Reichs-Arbeitsmarkt-Anzeiger*, 17, 7 Sept. 1932.

[137] Dudek, *Erziehung durch Arbeit*, 118–68.

[138] Friedrich Uhde, 'Wann endlich handelt die Regierung? Stimmen zum freiwilligen Arbeitsdienst', *Der Zwiespruch*, 14/15 (1932), 169–70; 'Richtlinien zum freiwilligen Arbeitsdienst', ibid. 173.

[139] Dudek, *Erziehung durch Arbeit*, 165–7; Helmuth Croon, 'Jugendbewegung und Arbeitsdienst', *Jahrbuch des Archivs der Jugendbewegung* 5 (1973), 66–84, 74–6.

'facilitate very substantially the police's task of maintaining the peace and upholding law and order'.[140]

The educational and social goals of the labour service were stressed in the decree on the FAD issued by the Papen government in July 1932: 'The voluntary labour service gives young Germans an opportunity to perform significant work for the public good on a voluntary basis and at the same time to undergo training for physical, mental and moral fitness'.[141] The broad ideological and educational purpose of the voluntary labour service was a feature which contrasted with the municipal work schemes, the latter leaving those engaged on such schemes to their own devices in their free time—which helped the organization of opposition to the schemes. Other features which contrasted with the municipal schemes were the principle of voluntary participation and the role of private organizations. The labour service was set up on a voluntary basis in order to avoid the low productivity and disciplinary problems of work schemes based on coercion. However, its critics argued that most volunteers were motivated by the material reward, however marginal, and were forced by their desperate economic situation to participate.[142] In addition, cases were quoted where, towards the end of 1932, local authorities illegally threatened to withdraw benefits unless unemployed youths 'volunteered'.[143]

A nationwide survey conducted in January 1932 showed that public authorities ran (as *Träger der Arbeit*, i.e. with responsibility for administering the finances and ensuring that the works planned were carried out) less than a third of all schemes.[144] By allowing private organizations such as youth groups, sports clubs, political organizations, and the churches to run schemes (both as *Träger der Arbeit* and as *Träger des Dienstes*—the latter role involving the recruitment, accommodation, and welfare of volunteers), the Reich government sought to mobilize the resources of the private sector within a framework set by the state. The state's aim in relying on

---

[140] Preußisches Ministerium des Innern an die RAVAV, 20 Oct. 1932. ZStA Merseburg, Rep. 120, BB VII, 1, 181.
[141] VO über den FAD, 16 July 1932, *RGBl* 1932, i. 352.
[142] Ernst Schellenberg, *Der Freiwillige Arbeitsdienst auf Grund der bisherigen Erfahrungen* (Berlin, 1932), 12.
[143] 'Niemand darf gezwungen werden!', *Hamburger Anzeiger*, 16 Jan. 1933.
[144] Schellenberg, *Der Freiwillige Arbeitsdienst*, 24.

private initiative to such an extent was partly financial—the private organizations often used their own assets to subsidize the schemes—and partly political: Brüning's ministers Stegerwald and Treviranus argued that involving the paramilitary organizations in the 'constructive' task of the voluntary labour service would tame them and counteract their 'political dilettantism'.[145]

After Brüning's fall, the voluntary labour service underwent a major expansion on the basis of new regulations by the Papen government on 16 July 1932.[146] This created a new administrative structure for the FAD, under Friedrich Syrup, head of the Reichsanstalt. The decree extended the potential duration of labour service schemes from 20 to 40 weeks by extending the subsidies payable to projects judged to be 'economically valuable'. It also expanded the pool of eligible participants: where formerly the Reich subsidy paid per volunteer was in principle restricted to recipients of insured unemployment benefit, the subsidy was now to be made available to all volunteers below the age of 25 regardless of their entitlements to unemployment benefit. The FAD was thus now open to the young unemployed on public welfare assistance and to those receiving no benefit payments at all. By the autumn of 1932, it was clear that these two categories had come to predominate among FAD volunteers. In Essen at the end of October 1932, a survey of FAD projects at the time revealed that 11 per cent of volunteers had been receiving insured unemployment benefit, 17 per cent crisis relief, 35 per cent welfare assistance, and 37 per cent of the volunteers had been receiving no benefits at all.[147]

Even before the expansion brought about by the July 1932 decree, the voluntary labour service had become a seemingly unstoppable bandwagon, attracting much publicity in the Press and attracting attention from many who had hitherto opposed or ignored it. The Social Democratic labour movement had been wrestling with the issue of the voluntary labour service since the summer of 1931. Its advocates (particularly members of the Reichsbanner) saw certain merits in the FAD as an emergency form of social welfare and education for the young unemployed, while its

---

[145] Vermerk über Chefbesprechung im Reichsinnenministerium über den FAD, 30 Apr. 1931. ZStA Potsdam, Reichsministerium des Innern, 25372.
[146] Köhler, *Arbeitsdienst*, 116–18.
[147] Reichskommissar für den FAD an den Deutschen Städtetag, 24 Nov. 1932. BA Koblenz, R36, 1940.

opponents warned that it would undermine wages and pave the way for labour conscription.[148] By the summer of 1932, the advocates of participation gained the upper hand with their argument that backing the voluntary labour service and setting up FAD schemes of their own was preferable to staying on the sidelines, proclaiming a boycott, and allowing right-wing organizations to take over; the voluntary labour service was gaining momentum, and young socialists were reported to be volunteering for labour service schemes anyway.[149] By the end of 1932, the Social Democratic coordinating organization Sozialer Dienst had established itself as one of the major agencies running labour service schemes: at the end of 1932, a total of around 30,000 volunteers were taking part in schemes run by the Sozialer Dienst and 10,000 by the Reichsbanner.[150] The rapid growth of 'red', 'Marxist' voluntary labour service schemes from the summer of 1932 onwards was a thorn in the flesh of right-wing FAD organizers accustomed hitherto, as 'national' organizations, to having the field to themselves. The chairman of the right-wing Reichsbund für Arbeitsdienst wrote indignantly to Papen at the end of October 1932 that it was high time that the government decided whether the labour service 'is to be a training-school educating our male youth in discipline and patriotric values, or whether the work camps are going to be allowed to train auxiliary troops for trade unions or even become breeding-grounds for Bolshevism'.[151]

Youth welfare administrators, social workers, and feminist organizations also became convinced in the course of 1932 that the voluntary labour service, given that it was there to stay, could be harnessed to useful ends. Youth welfare practitioners began to argue that the voluntary labour service could be a suitable environment for resocializing young offenders and ex-inmates of reformatories, as well as providing material assistance and educational supervision for the mass of unemployed and uncontrolled adolescents on a scale beyond that which could be financed by youth welfare

---

[148] Winkler, *Weg in die Katastrophe*, 410; Dudek, *Erziehung durch Arbeit*, 214–25.
[149] Bundesvorstand des Allgemeinen Deutschen Gewerkschaftsbundes (ed.), *Hilfe für die erwerbslose Jugend. Die Stellung der Gewerkschaften zum FAD* (Berlin, 1932); Winkler, *Weg in die Katastrophe*, 604; Dudek, *Erziehung durch Arbeit*, 216–17. [150] Dudek, *Erziehung durch Arbeit*, 196.
[151] Faupel to Papen, 31 Oct. 1932. BA Koblenz, R43 I, 2086.

authorities.[152] Meanwhile, bourgeois feminists in the Bund deutscher Frauenvereine and the Allgemeiner Deutscher Lehrerinnenverband were in the summer of 1932 coming to view the voluntary labour service as an important means of educating unemployed young women for their future roles as 'wives, mothers, workers and citizens'.[153] Up to July 1932, only 247 of the total of 5,633 projects that had been approved in the Reich as a whole had been for girls.[154] In September 1932, feminists and youth welfare experts jointly lobbied the FAD administration to give higher priority to the labour service for women.[155] In response to the calls for more positive guidelines, Syrup issued a decree on 10 November 1932 which stressed the need to develop more labour service schemes for women and outlined the range of suitable tasks: cooking and laundering for men's labour service camps, working for the Winterhilfe cultivating land for gardening, and assisting settlers with gardening and housekeeping.[156] The decree came too late to have much impact on the girls' voluntary labour service before the Nazi take-over; while the number of girls in the voluntary labour service rose in the autumn of 1932, they continued to be a small minority of the total participants. The girls' schemes remained, despite feminist hopes, peripheral to the voluntary labour service overall.[157]

The take-off of the voluntary labour service after the summer of 1932 was largely due to the fact that recipients of public welfare

[152] Karl Ruth, 'Der Freiwillige Arbeitsdienst Jugendlicher', *ZBl*, 23/7 (1931/2), 240–4; 'Bericht über die Schulungswoche in Friedrichsroda 1932', *Rundbrief der Gilde 'Soziale Arbeit'*, 23 (July, 1932), 15–16; Paula Oberdörffer, 'Freiwilliger Arbeitsdienst in seiner Bedeutung für das erwerbslose Mädchen', *WRP*, 8/16 (1932), 256–7; Verband der preußischen Provinzen an alle Landeshauptleute, 25 Aug. 1932. BA Koblenz, R36, 1982.

[153] Hilde Lion, 'Die Aufgabe der Frau im freiwilligen Arbeitsdienst', *Frankfurter Zeitung*, 23 Oct. 1932.

[154] Olga Essig, 'Die weibliche Jugend im FAD', *JV* 8 (1932), 80.

[155] Hilde Lion, 'Freiwilliger Arbeitsdienst der Frau', *Die Frau*, 40/1 (1932), 1–9; Syrup an das Preußische Handelsministerium, 15 Sept. 1932. ZStA Merseburg, Rep. 120, E VIII, 1, 62 vol. 1; Friedländer, 'Fachkonferenz für die Ausgestaltung des FAD für Frauen', *AW*, 7/22 (1932), 699–701; 'Der Freiwillige Arbeitsdienst für Mädchen: Eine Denkschrift, bearbeitet vom Deutschen Archiv für Jugendwohlfahrt und der Deutschen Akademie für soziale und pädagogische Frauenarbeit', Sept. 1931. KAH, KJA, M1.

[156] RAVAV an die Bezirkskommissare für den FAD betr. Freiwilliger Arbeitsdienst der weiblichen Jugend, 10 Nov. 1932, *Beilage zum Reichsarbeitsmarkt-Anzeiger*, 22, 22 Nov. 1932.

[157] Morgan, *Weiblicher Arbeitsdienst*, 42.

assistance were now eligible for the Reich subsidy for FAD volunteers. This had a galvanizing effect on local governments, who leapt at the opportunity to reduce the burden of supporting the unemployed on public welfare assistance. Municipally-run FAD projects sprang up and FAD volunteers found themselves clearing city parks, repairing roads, digging drainage ditches, and the like for the local authorities. The organizations who had originally propagated and pioneered the idea of labour service were less than pleased at this development, which they saw degrading their vision of service to the fatherland. A Stahlhelm official from Warburg (near Paderborn) complained to Papen in October 1932 that many local authorities in his area, 'completely failing to recognize the chief purpose of the voluntary labour service', were using central FAD funding to relieve the burden on their welfare budgets.[158]

At the beginning of August 1932, 96,067 volunteers were reported to be currently engaged on voluntary labour service projects in the Reich as a whole. Given that 1,456,854 young people under 25 were registered as unemployed at the end of July 1932, it appears that around 6 or 7 per cent of the total official unemployed under 25 in the Reich were at this time participating in the voluntary labour service. By the beginning of December, the number of participants had trebled to a pre-1933 peak total of 285,000 (no exact youth unemployment figures are available for that month to compare).[159]

At the end of August 1932, 4,037 young people from the Hamburg area (including Harburg, Wandsbek, and Altona) were occupied on voluntary labour service schemes. About 1,000 of these youngsters had gone to schemes outside the area. This was equivalent to 7.4 per cent of the 54,302 unemployed under-25s in the Hamburg area in July 1932. A survey of the 121 projects under way in September 1932 in the Hamburg area revealed the range of organizations and institutions involved in running FAD schemes.[160] The municipal authorities in Altona and Harburg were heavily

---

[158] Graf von Plettenburg to Papen, 19 Oct. 1932. BA Koblenz, R43 I, 2086.
[159] Friedrich Syrup, 'Der FAD für die männliche deutsche Jugend', *RABl* 1932, ii. 381–90; youth unemployment figures for July 1932 in Kurt Richter, 'Maßnahmen zur Betreuung der erwerbslosen Jugend', *Handbuch der Jugendpflege*, 14 (Eberswalde and Berlin, 1933), 18–75, 18; 'FAD und Werkhalbjahr', *SP* 42 (1933), cols. 269–74.
[160] Aufstellung über Maßnahmen im FAD im Bezirk des Arbeitsamts Hamburg. Stand von September/Oktober 1932. StAH, AB I, 95.

involved. Sports clubs also played a major role: the chance of improving club facilities with the aid of public subsidies proved irresistible. The political complexion of the city was reflected in the breakdown of organizations with political affiliations running schemes. Those run by right-wing organizations—the Kyffhäuser-Jugend, the DHV, the Turnverein Jahn and the Stahlhelm—were outnumbered by schemes run by Social Democratic organizations ranging from the Reichsbanner to the Arbeiterradfahrerbund.[161] For its part, the Stahlhelm alleged it was being discriminated against by the Hamburg employment office, whose approval was necessary for setting up projects.[162]

Recruiting volunteers does not appear to have been a problem in the Hamburg area up until the winter of 1932/3, except for particularly unpleasant work.[163] Records of two schemes in the Hamburg area confirm that the labour service recruited from among those unemployed who were financially most desperate. Of 70 youths engaged on the Oejendorf scheme, run from October 1932 by the Hamburg welfare department, 34 had been dependent on welfare assistance and 16 had been receiving no benefits at all. Of the 160 youths, mainly from Hamburg, on a church-run project in Süderdeich in Holstein, 60 had been receiving welfare assistance and 67 no benefits at all. Only 29 per cent of the Oejendorf volunteers and 21 per cent of the Süderdeich volunteers had been receiving insured benefits.[164] Of the Süderdeich volunteers, 48 per cent had been out of work for more than a year.

Some further light is thrown on the organization of the voluntary labour service and on the recruitment and motivation of volunteers by looking in some detail at one scheme for which relatively detailed records exist.[165] While it cannot be representative, this example may serve to illustrate one type of project and a certain type of participant. The voluntary labour service scheme for girls in Malente (Holstein) was run by the welfare bureau of the Lutheran

[161] Aufstellung über Maßnahmen im FAD im Bezirk des Arbeitsamts Hamburg.
[162] Niederschrift über die Sitzung des Heimatwerkes, 29 Dec. 1932. KAH, KJA, Heimatwerk.
[163] G. Donndorf, in Ausschuß zur Förderung der Jugendwohlfahrt, 11 Feb. 1932. KAH, KJA, G12; Baubehörde Hamburg to Wohlfahrtsbehörde, 11 Jan. 1932. StAH, SB I, AW 49.10, vol. 1.
[164] Zusammensetzung der Arbeitsdienstwilligen des FAD Oejendorf. StAH, SB I, AW 49.11; Mitgliederliste, FAD Süderdeich. KAH, KJA, 6.
[165] Records of the Malente girls' FAD: KAH, KJA, L2/L4/L6.

church in Hamburg from October 1932 to March 1933. The twenty-eight volunteers were accommodated in a church holiday home: the possession of such premises gave the churches a great advantage in setting up projects. The majority of the volunteers were already involved in church youth clubs and girls' circles. The scheme was run on clearly confessional lines, its organizer observing that 'the voluntary labour service offers opportunities for pastoral work that no pastor can expect to find today in his parish'.[166] The slow development of the labour service for girls was sometimes ascribed to the low degree to which girls were organized as members of youth groups:[167] projects were most easily set up where, as in this case, there was a basis in already existing clubs and organizations.

The work in Malente consisted of sewing and repairing clothes for the church welfare, plus housework and gardening on the premises. The girls received board and lodging and 30 pfennigs pocket-money per working day. The list of participants and the essays they wrote while on the scheme (which have to be read with the consideration that they were written for the organizers) provide some information about the volunteers. They were aged between 14 and 23; thirteen had been domestic servants, one a laundress, three had been shop assistants and five clerical workers; six had never been employed. Eight of the twenty-eight had been out of work continuously for over 18 months. Only four participants had been receiving welfare benefits; none of the rest had been receiving any sort of benefit. Five of the girls had fathers who were unemployed.[168]

Regarding the girls' motives for volunteering, not all emphasized material need. Some gave as their motive 'getting away from it all' and 'being with other girls'. Others wrote that the voluntary labour service was an opportunity to learn useful skills, and that later on employers would be likely to prefer those who had been in the voluntary labour service. Several, however, emphasized the poverty in their family as a reason for volunteering.

---

[166] Donndorf, in Sitzungsbericht über die Zusammenkunft der evangelischen Dienstträger für FAD in der Nordmark am 19 Nov. 1932 in Lübeck. KAH, KJA, 12.
[167] Margarete Ehlert, 'Der freiwillige Arbeitsdienst der weiblichen Jugend', *RABl* (1932), ii. 480–3, 480.
[168] Records of Malente girls' FAD. KAH, KJA, L2/L4/L6.

I am here because I got nothing from the welfare office and my mother cannot support me either, my brother is unemployed and doesn't get anything either, neither of us can live at home because my sister earns so little, and my mother only gets her pension. (Gertrud R., b. 1911.)

To say this is voluntary . . . for many people it is out of need and if one of you can live away from home and have work that is a great relief for parents. (Frieda L., b. 1916.)

The difficulties of organizing the voluntary labour service grew with its expansion. A report submitted to the Reichsanstalt by an official of the regional employment office of Brandenburg was critical of many aspects of FAD schemes currently in operation.[169] The non-residential camps were according to this report neglecting the task of 'training for physical, mental and moral fitness'; political organizations were running schemes that threatened to degenerate into indoctrination camps; accommodation in residential camps was almost without exception unsatisfactory. Overall, the report concluded, the recent expansion of the FAD had taken place so fast that the resources of the institutions and organizations involved were severely overstretched. By the winter, it was also apparent that volunteers were becoming scarce. Private organizations involved in running the voluntary labour service in Hamburg reported in January 1933 that the youth organizations were having problems recruiting for measures currently in progress and that the voluntary labour service in its present form had reached its limits.[170]

Disciplinary problems also increased as the labour service grew, and it was these problems as much as financial or economic considerations that were seen in November 1932 by Friedrich Syrup, head of the Reichsanstalt and director of the voluntary labour service, as the chief obstacle to the introduction of compulsory labour service.[171] The Reich government was well aware that conscript armies were liable to subversion.

Collective action against the voluntary labour service was difficult, though not wholly impossible, to organize. In its campaign against the voluntary labour service, the communist

---

[169] Oberregierungsrat Gerlach, 'Bericht über die Besichtigung von Lagern des FAD im Bereich der Bezirkskommissare Hessen, Westfalen, Rheinland, Mitteldeutschland und Bayern', 15 Nov. 1932. BA Koblenz, R43 I, 2086.
[170] Dulk, in Niederschrift der Mitgliederversammlung des Heimatwerkes Groß-Hamburg, 23 Jan. 1933. KAH, KJA, Heimatwerk.
[171] Syrup, 'Der FAD für die männliche deutsche Jugend', 382.

youth organization had initially urged for a boycott of any such schemes.[172] The emphasis of the KJVD campaign shifted in the summer of 1932 to strike action. In the Hamburg area, the campaign made most impact in Altona, where in October 1932 the schemes organized by the town authorities were almost paralysed by a strike.[173] The strike, which affected 12 municipally-run sites with a total of 1,200 volunteers, was sparked off in mid-October by the announcement by the town authorities that the imposition of new national regulations meant that the pay on voluntary labour service projects had to be cut. The strike failed to reverse this cut and a partial boycott continued. By the beginning of November, the SPD newspaper reported that only 250 of the original 1,200 workers were prepared to work for the lower rate.[174] The large number of volunteers in Altona, the fact that the sites were non-residential, and the ease of coordination between the different sites helped to make the strike relatively long and well-supported. Where volunteers were isolated in the countryside on a residential scheme, without political support from the neighbourhood or the means of making their protest visible, the chances of success were even slighter: this was, after all, one reason why the Reich government preferred residential schemes.

Policies at a Dead End: The Notwerk der deutschen Jugend

A further problem connected with the expansion of the voluntary labour service in the summer and autumn of 1932 was that a growing number of young people were returning, after six months' 'service', to further unemployment and the street. Schleicher's 'Emergency Aid for German Youth' (*Notwerk der deutschen Jugend*) was aimed at, among others, this group of unemployed youth. Although the real development of the scheme, such as it was, took place after January 1933, it deserves outlining as an attempt by Weimar's last government to launch a major initiative to tackle youth unemployment.

[172] Ernst Bertram, 'Der Kampf der proletarischen Jugend gegen die Arbeitsdienstpflicht in Deutschland', *Internationale Pressekorrespondenz* (23 Jan. 1931), 177.
[173] Meldungen des Reichskommissars für die Überwachung der öffentlichen Ordnung, 6 Jan. 1933 betr. KPD, Kampf gegen Arbeitsdienstpflicht. BA Koblenz, Bestand R134, microfiche 385, frame 35–42a.
[174] 'Was die Rechte zerschlug', *Hamburger Echo*, 1 Nov. 1932.

The *Notwerk* programme was hastily worked out in December 1932 by the Reich Labour Ministry in discussions with the Reich Defence Ministry and representatives of the ADGB and the DHV; it was announced, for maximum propaganda effect, on Christmas Eve 1932.[175] With the aid of 9–10 million marks from Reich funds (to be spread as thinly as possible) a minimalized version of the day centres described above was to be subsidized. The young unemployed were to form 'comrade groups' (*Kameradschaften*) of up to 25 members each, which would meet for four hours per day, six days per week, for a daily programme including vocational tuition, recreational activities and a hot meal. The aim was to organize a total of 500,000 unemployed young people up to the age of 25.[176]

It was intended that the *Notwerk* would impose a uniform pattern on the diverse and fragmented initiatives at local level targeted at the young unemployed; it would also link up with the voluntary labour service in that it would cater for ex-FAD volunteers. The programme was designed to fit with the policy already adopted in the context of the voluntary labour service of mobilizing organized youth for state goals: the state was to promote the self-help activities of youth groups and organizations.[177] At the same time, the *Notwerk* also aimed to reach those young unemployed who received no benefit, had not hitherto participated in any work or training schemes, and who were not members of youth organizations.[178]

The spectacular numerical expansion of the emergency youth programme—after a month approximately 110,000 participants were reported—was possible only by means of an optical illusion. The organizers of existing courses and activities, including all the courses run by the employment offices, applied for subsidies of up to 25 pfennigs per person per day and laid on a meal for participants as prescribed in the regulations for the programme.[179] Such courses

---

[175] Aufzeichnung des Finanzministeriums betr. Notwerk der dt. Jugend. BA Koblenz, R2, 18537.
[176] Aufzeichnungen des RFM betr. Notwerk der deutschen Jugend, 16 Dec. 1932. BA Koblenz, R2, 18537; Erlaß des RAM und der RAVAV betr. Notwerk der deutschen Jugend, 24 Dec. 1932. StAH, AB I, 120; R. Wiedwald, 'Das Notwerk der deutschen Jugend', *ZBl* 24/1 (1932/3), 354–7.
[177] Reichswehrminister an den Reichskanzler, 17 Oct. 1932. BA Koblenz, R43 II, 519.
[178] Reichszentrale für Heimatdienst, Richtlinie Nr. 233 (Feb. 1933), 'Das Hilfswerk für die deutsche Jugend', 4; RAVAV an das RAM, 12 Feb. 1933. StAH, AB I, 120.
[179] OB der Stadt Berlin an den Dt. Städtetag, 3 Feb. 1933. BA Koblenz, R36, 2031.

were thereby transformed into schemes under the programme and appeared as such in the statistics.

In addition, the emergency programme was dependent on the financial participation of private organizations and relied on youth organizations running activities for their members and using the subsidy to offset some of the costs. In Berlin, for example, a third of the 129 *Notwerk* schemes in operation at the beginning of February 1933 were run by private organizations, including youth organizations, sports groups, and trade unions.[180] From February 1933 onwards, the *Notwerk* in Berlin and elsewhere became increasingly taken over by the SA.[181]

Organizing the 'unorganized' proved difficult: the mayor of Hildesheim pointed out in January 1933 that the *Notwerk* represented an 'over-organization' of those young people who were already organized in groups and schemes of one sort or another.[182] An official of the RAVAV, commenting on the 'extraordinary difficulty' of getting 'unorganized' youth into the programme, observed that the material incentive to participate in the *Notwerk* was too slight to compensate for the major change in daily routine required of the participants.[183] Girls were a minority of participants: of 6,775 in Berlin at the start of February 1933, only 1,789 were girls.[184]

In Hamburg, the emergency youth programme was set up on 10 January 1933 with the assistance of a grant from the city government, which saw the scheme as an opportunity to double the capacity of the municipal soup kitchens with the aid of a central government subsidy. Even though the existing courses run by the vocational schools, the employment office, and the day centres turned themselves into emergency youth programme projects, the number of participants failed by February 1933 to reach Hamburg's target of 15,000, which in itself would only have represented around half of the unemployed under-25s registered in Hamburg in January 1933.[185] Hamburg's experience appears to have been shared by

[180] Ibid.
[181] Vermerk des RAM, undated (end of June 1933). BA Koblenz, R2, 18537.
[182] Oberbürgermeister Ehrlicher an den Dt. Städtetag, 19 Jan. 1933. BA Koblenz, R36, 2031.
[183] RAVAV to RAM, 13 Feb. 1933. BA Koblenz, R36, 2031.
[184] OB der Stadt Berlin an den Dt. Städtetag, 3 Feb. 1933. BA Koblenz, R36, 2031.
[185] Auszug aus dem Protokoll des Senats, 9 Jan. 1933. StAH, Senat, Cl. VII, Lit. Bd Nr. 68, Vol. 7, Fasc. 3; Niederschrift der Leitersitzung des Wohlfahrtsamtes, 25 Jan. 1933. StAH, SB I, VG 24.33 vol. 1.

other cities: in April 1933 the Deutscher Städtetag commented critically that only about 10 per cent of the young unemployed had been reached by the *Notwerk* and that the scheme had not fulfilled the expectations placed in it by the public.[186]

Neither the *Notwerk*, nor any of the other policies discussed above had a substantial quantitative impact on youth unemployment. Precise figures are lacking, but an estimate may be made for the summer of 1932: compared with the official youth unemployment figures for July 1932, the vocational courses run by the employment office and the obligatory labour schemes each reached about 7 per cent of the city's unemployed under the age of 25, and the voluntary labour service reached about 7 per cent of the young unemployed in the Hamburg area. Taking other miscellaneous measures into account, it still appears that in the summer of 1932 at least three-quarters of Hamburg's young unemployed were not reached by any of the schemes run or subsidized by the public authorities. How far Hamburg was typical of German cities in the Depression could only be said with certainty if studies of other cities were available, but it seems that Hamburg was not a notable exception to the rest of the Reich: all local governments were reducing their spending on non-statutory measures. This had two consequences: firstly, an increasing share of the task of supervising the unemployed was taken over by private organizations—this was true of Hamburg as for the Reich as a whole. Secondly, Reich subsidies administered via the local employment offices played an increasing role in determining policy.

Financial constraints and the opposition of the young unemployed themselves limited the effectiveness of the state's attempts to extend its control over the young unemployed. The development of 'obligatory labour' in Hamburg during the Depression undoubtedly intensified the punitive treatment of the young unemployed at the hands of the general welfare department; however, it was only after the political transformation of 1933 that the welfare department could proceed unhindered with its measures to discipline the young unemployed.[187] The policies that came to prevail in the final eighteen months of the Weimar Republic took into account the

[186] Vermerk des Dt. Städtetags, 5 Apr. 1933. BA Koblenz, R36, 2031.
[187] Angelika Ebbinghaus, Heidrun Kaupen-Haas and Karl Heinz Roth (eds.), *Heilen und Vernichten im Mustergau Hamburg: Bevölkerungs- und Gesundheitspolitik im Dritten Reich* (Hamburg, 1984), 10–14.

difficulties involved in coercion. These initiatives at national level—above all the voluntary labour service, but also the Emergency Aid for German Youth programme—abandoned the aim of controlling specific categories of unemployed adolescents classified as particularly 'asocial' or 'at risk'. Instead, these schemes set out to organize at low cost on a formally voluntary basis the largest possible number of the young unemployed. Such policies were, apart from anything else, an attempt on the part of the final Weimar governments to achieve a degree of propaganda success. From their impact both at national and local level, it is clear that youth unemployment was one of the problems that these regimes most signally failed even to disguise, still less to solve.

Young workers had always been marginal when it came to state benefits and protection, which were provided by the Weimar welfare state above all for a privileged adult male 'core' of the workforce. However, in more prosperous times they could hope to proceed through this stage of marginality. In the Depression it must have seemed to many young unemployed, barred from the world of employment and with it from the achievement of the normal goals associated with attaining adulthood, that the periphery of the economy and of society was where they would stay.

5
New Approaches to the Problem Adolescent? The Reform of Youth Welfare and Juvenile Justice in the Post-War Period

The problem of the deprived and delinquent adolescent was by no means a discovery of the Weimar period; however, the Republic brought about a number of major changes in the way young people defined as 'at risk' or delinquent were perceived and treated by the state authorities. 'Education instead of punishment' and the right of the child to education had already been slogans of the youth welfare movement in the Kaiserreich. Under the Republic, a more favourable context arose for reforming the youth welfare and juvenile justice system in line with these principles. The pedagogical zeal which characterized the policies of the Weimar state authorities towards young workers and the young unemployed was to be applied particularly intensively to those youngsters classed as *verwahrlost*.

Increasing child neglect and juvenile delinquency were, in the eyes of contemporaries, a sign of the social dislocation which the war and its aftermath had produced. Family ties, it was argued, had been weakened by the war; patriarchal authority had been eroded as a result.[1] The collapse of state authority in November 1918 was seen as having encouraged (male) youngsters to kick over the traces.[2] A prominent medical expert in the Prussian welfare ministry was one of those who saw the revolution itself as a product of collective delinquency, ascribing the acts of rebellion to youthful 'psychopaths'[3] at the forefront of politically extreme movements.[4]

[1] Landesjugendamt und Jugendamt Hamburg, *Jahresbericht 1925* (Hamburg, 1926), 8, 11.
[2] Richard Bessel, 'State and Society in Germany in the Aftermath of the First World War', in W. R. Lee and Eve Rosenhaft (eds.), *The State and Social Change in Germany 1880–1980* (New York, Oxford, and Munich, 1990), 200–2.
[3] The terms *Psychopath*, *psychopathisch* were used in the Weimar period to describe a general condition of mental instability bordering on mental illness.
[4] Dr A. Gottstein, Preußisches Ministerium für Volkswohlfahrt, an sämtliche

The sense of social crisis assisted the youth welfare lobby in its efforts. That lobby, now a broader alliance whose ranks included Social Democrats and educational reformers with links to the youth movement, was pushing strongly in 1918/19 to realize the demands that it had formulated in the years before the war for the reform and expansion of public child and youth welfare services. Tackling the problem of child deprivation and juvenile deviance, ensuring that state authorities intervened swiftly and expertly where the family failed, could be represented by youth welfare advocates as a priority task within the context of post-war social pacification and reconstruction.

With the labour movement temporarily in the ascendant, the political climate in 1918/19 was favourable to the expansion of public local welfare services, just as social policies to appease the mobilized working class were high on the political agenda. Wartime expansion paved the way for the post-war development of the local welfare services which formed a vital element of the Weimar *Sozialstaat*. Central state planning and legislation which prescribed new tasks for local authorities were one factor in that development, but the local constellation of politics and welfare was also of key importance. Local welfare services, as the 'front line' of defence against social ills, expanded partly as the result of hasty improvisation in response to local needs and political pressures.[5] Another vital factor in the growth of the local welfare state was the expansionist ambitions of the welfare professionals and experts. Their vision was of a comprehensive system of medical and educational surveillance and intervention, extending out from the central state down to the local level, which would improve the physical and moral health of the nation and promote social integration.[6]

In the field of child and youth welfare, while the grander visions of the welfare experts were not realized, some substantial developments did take place in the early years of the Weimar Republic. This process was driven forward in part by major central government legislation: the Juvenile Courts Law and the National Youth

Regierungspräsidenten und Oberpräsidenten, 2 Sept. 1920. ZStA Merseburg, Rep. 191, 2431.

[5] Harold James, 'Municipal Finance in the Weimar Republic', in Lee and Rosenhaft (eds.), *State and Social Change*, 230.

[6] Paul Weindling, 'Eugenics and the Welfare State during the Weimar Republic', in Lee and Rosenhaft (eds.), *State and Social Change*, 131–7.

Welfare Law. The phase of reform and expansion was short-lived, however; in the later years of the Republic, the reforming lobby was to be driven on to the defensive as pessimistic views on the 'limits of welfare' and the 'limits of educability' swung into the centre of debate.

This chapter focuses on youth welfare and juvenile justice in the early years of the Weimar Republic, examining the factors favouring and hindering the process of reform and expansion. Chapters 6 and 7 examine the practice of 'educating the delinquent' in more detail, looking first at juvenile courts and then at those aspects of youth welfare which were targeted at the delinquent or problem adolescent: probation and correctional education.

The Changing Constellation of Youth Welfare

In Imperial Germany, the youth welfare and juvenile justice lobby had been dominated by middle-class social reforming groups of professional experts and committed campaigners. Together with the welfare organizations of the churches, these groups, including the German Association for Poor Relief and Welfare (later renamed the German Association for Public and Private Welfare[7]), the German Professional Guardians' Association, the German Central Association for Youth Welfare,[8] and the Conference on Correctional Education, remained active and influential in the youth welfare field in the Weimar period. They produced specialist journals and monographs on the theory and practice of youth welfare and lobbied politicians intensively during the debates over the National Youth Welfare Law. However, the monopoly of expertise held by these established groupings began to be challenged in the post-war period, and new voices began to be heard on youth welfare issues. One new factor in the world of youth welfare was the radical educational reform movement associated with the youth movement.[9] The pre-war youth movement had been among other things

[7] Deutscher Verein für öffentliche und private Fürsorge.

[8] The Deutsche Zentrale für Jugendfürsorge was renamed the Deutsche Zentrale für freie Jugendwohlfahrt in 1923.

[9] On the youth movement, educational reform and social work in the Weimar period, see Gertrud Herrmann, *Die sozialpädagogische Bewegung der zwanziger Jahre* (Weinheim and Berlin, 1956); Peter Dudek, *Leitbild: Kamerad und Helfer: Sozialpädagogische Bewegung in der Weimarer Republik am Beispiel der 'Gilde Soziale Arbeit'* (Frankfurt am Main, 1988).

New Approaches to the Problem Adolescent 155

an experiment in self-education. Its sense of educational mission was to carry through into youth welfare and social work in the Weimar period in a number of ways. The sense of group identity and solidarity cultivated in the youth movement encouraged some members of it, as they embarked on their professional lives, to re-create elements of this experience in schools, reformatories, juvenile prisons, and other group work with problem adolescents. In the early years of the Weimar Republic, individual reformers such as Karl Wilker, Curt Bondy, Walter Herrmann, and Otto Zirker carried through radical educational experiments with delinquent and criminal youngsters and publicized their work energetically in an effort to spark off reforms throughout the apparatus of custodial care.[10] In the course of the 1920s, increasing numbers of young men and women from the youth movement trained as professional social workers, focusing particularly on the field of youth welfare; in 1925, they constituted, in the Gilde Soziale Arbeit, a forum to discuss and promote a distinctive 'youth movement' position on educational and welfare issues.[11] Meanwhile, social work projects were undertaken by youth groups on a voluntary basis with deprived children and the elderly.[12] On another level, the educational and cultural reform efforts of the pre-war youth movement fed into other forms of youth work. The aims and values of the pre-war youth movement were taken up by youth organizations in the Weimar period and harnessed, with the support of the state authorities, to the prevention of delinquency. Through the Youth Organizations Council, youth organizations campaigned for social reforms and exposed the poor living and working conditions suffered by working-class youngsters.[13] At the same time, they projected themselves as a force for cultural, moral, and physical

[10] Karl Wilker, 'Erziehungsheim Lindenhof: Ein Stück Tat gewordene Jugendbewegung', *Internationale Erziehungsrundschau* 11 (Nov. 1920), 91–104; id., *Fürsorgeerziehung als Lebensschulung: Ein Aufruf zur Tat* (Berlin, 1921); Walter Herrmann, *Hahnöfersand: Der Versuch einer Verwirklichung des Erziehungsgedankens im Strafvollzug an Jugendlichen* (Hamburg, 1923); on Otto Zirker, see Franz Hammer, *Traum und Wirklichkeit: Die Geschichte einer Jugend* (E. Berlin, 1982), 98–110.   [11] Dudek, *Leitbild: Kamerad und Helfer*, 71–5.

[12] Ibid. 48–9. For an account of a Berlin youth group engaged in social work, see F. G. Lennhoff, *Die Zugscharen: Eine Jugendhilfe-Organisation* (Munich, 1983).

[13] See Ch. 3. See also Manfred Zwerschke, *Jugendverbände und Sozialpolitik* (München, 1963); Cornelius Schley, 'Die jugendpolitischen Vorstellungen und Aktivitäten des "Reichsausschusses der deutschen Jugendverbände" in den letzten Jahren der Weimarer Republik', Diplomarbeit (Göttingen, 1980); H. Giesecke, *Vom Wandervogel bis zur Hitlerjugend* (Munich, 1981), 157–66.

renewal. Whether 'genuine' youth *movement* groups run by youth for youth (*bündische Jugend*), or organizations of the *Jugendpflege* type run by adults and providing recreational activities for the young, youth organizations in the Weimar period presented themselves as a means of encouraging working-class children to resist the degrading habits of the big city, to reject stimulants such as nicotine and alcohol, to renounce commercial entertainment, and to pursue healthier relations between the sexes.[14]

Youth movement and ex-youth movement activists contributed to debates on youth welfare most noticeably with regard to educational methods and recreational work; they paid, at least in the early years of the Weimar Republic, less attention to questions of administrative and legal reform, which were of central importance to the development of youth welfare in the immediate post-war years. In debates on these issues, it was the reformist Left who represented the new presence in the youth welfare 'establishment'.

Youth welfare was an area in which the SPD, apart from its women's organization, had taken little interest before the First World War. Social Democratic women had set up local children's protection committees (Kinderschutzkommissionen) to oversee the implementation of the 1903 law on the protection of child labour, and these committees had given some impetus to the development of Social Democratic demands, relating not only to protective labour legislation, but also to child health and welfare more generally. Social Democratic women had also organized excursions and holidays for working-class city children.[15] Where Social Democrats had won seats in municipal assemblies, they supported such youth welfare reforms as could be put through at the local level, for example, the setting up of separate children's departments independent of the rest of the poor-law administration; in the Reichstag, Social Democrats supported the setting up of juvenile courts. During the First World War, the SPD was drawn into the practical administration of the war effort. Moving towards greater cooperation with bourgeois social reformers generally, Social

[14] Giesecke, *Vom Wandervogel bis zur Hitlerjugend*, 140–57.
[15] On the welfare work of SPD women before the First World War, see Anneliese Monat, *Sozialdemokratie und Wohlfahrtspflege: Ein Beitrag zur Entstehungsgeschichte der Arbeiterwohlfahrt* (Stuttgart, 1961), 38; Richard J. Evans, *Sozialdemokratie und Frauenemanzipation im deutschen Kaiserreich* (Berlin and Bonn, 1979), 260–1; Christoph Sachße, *Mütterlichkeit als Beruf: Sozialarbeit, Sozialreform und Frauenbewegung 1871–1929* (Frankfurt am Main, 1986), 181–2.

Democrats had taken up the demands put forward by Felisch and Helene Simon for a codification and reform of legislation affecting children and youth.[16] The new broadened alliance for youth welfare reform across the political spectrum was in evidence at the German Conference on Youth and Welfare (Deutscher Jugendfürsorgetag) in September 1918. At this conference, which was intended to send a clear signal to the Reich government regarding the need for the creation of a network of youth welfare offices throughout the Reich, Heinrich Schulz and Rudolf Wissell spoke on behalf of the Social Democrats in favour of such a reform.[17]

On its advent to positions of power at national, *Land*, and local level in 1918/19, the SPD was confronted with the need to develop further its strategy on youth welfare. A number of Social Democratic politicians, lawyers, and administrators experienced in youth welfare work formed a working party within the Arbeiterwohlfahrt, the SPD welfare organization founded by Marie Juchacz in December 1919, to formulate policy on youth welfare issues.[18]

In many respects, Social Democratic welfare policy differed little from that of the bourgeois reformers.[19] The central idea of Social Democratic youth welfare policy was the child's right to educational and material assistance, a long-standing slogan of the bourgeois youth welfare lobby.[20] In their ideas on both the causes

[16] Heinrich Schulz, speech of 8 June 1918 in Reichstag, *Verhandlungen des Reichstages*, vol. 312, 5318–19. See Ch. 2 on Paul Felisch and Helene Simon.

[17] Deutscher Verein für öffentliche und private Fürsorge (ed.), *Jugendämter als Träger der öffentlichen Jugendfürsorge im Reich: Bericht über die Verhandlungen des Deutschen Jugendfürsorgetages am 20. und 21. September 1918 in Berlin* (Berlin, 1919), 47–9, 178. See also Ch. 2.

[18] Helene Simon, Hans Caspari, Toni Pfülf, Gottlob Binder, and Walter Friedländer were among those particularly involved in formulating youth welfare policy within the Arbeiterwohlfahrt. On Helene Simon, see Walter Friedländer, *Helene Simon: Ein Leben für soziale Gerechtigkeit* (Bonn, 1962); on Friedländer, see Elizabeth Harvey, 'Sozialdemokratische Jugendhilfereform in der Praxis', *Theorie und Praxis der sozialen Arbeit*, 36/6 (1985), 218–29. On the Arbeiterwohlfahrt generally, see Monat, *Sozialdemokratie und Wohlfahrtspflege*; Fritzmichael Röhl, *Marie Juchacz und die Arbeiterwohlfahrt* (Hanover, 1961); Cordula Tollmien, *Die Geschichte der Arbeiterwohlfahrt in Hann. Münden* (Hann. Münden, 1983).

[19] Sachße, *Mütterlichkeit*, 181; see also S. Zeller, *Volksmütter: Frauen im Wohlfahrtswesen der zwanziger Jahre* (Düsseldorf, 1987), 104. For an account which by contrast stresses the innovative aspects of the SPD's approach to welfare reform in the post-war period, see David F. Crew, 'German Socialism, the State and Family Policy, 1918–1933', *Continuity and Change*, 1/2 (1986), 2, 256–63, 238–40.

[20] Hans Caspari, speech on 'Wohlfahrtspflege und Jugendwohlfahrt', in 'Bericht über die Frauenkonferenz der SPD, abgehalten am 9. und 10. Oktober 1920 in Kassel', in *Protokoll über die Verhandlungen des Parteitags der SPD in Kassel 10–16*

of and the cure for delinquency, Social Democrats shared many of the assumptions of the bourgeois welfare establishment of experts and administrators.

Nevertheless, party-political differences were not entirely irrelevant to youth welfare debates. Firstly, SPD policy on youth welfare was to stress unequivocally the primacy of public (and non-denominational) youth welfare provision over the work of private welfare agencies.[21] This was in contrast to the politicians of the Centre Party and of the DNVP who were concerned to anchor the role of the private welfare organizations firmly in any codification of youth welfare provision and to preserve confessionally-based fostering and correctional education. Secondly, Social Democrats attempted to bring a class perspective to youth welfare. Criticizing the work of both public authorities and private agencies as being marked by the traditions of bourgeois charity and discriminatory poor relief, they called for a democratization of youth welfare.[22] Given that the clientele of youth welfare was overwhelmingly working-class, Social Democrats argued, professional social workers should be recruited from the working class to carry out the educational tasks of youth welfare. Working-class volunteers, too, should offer their services via the Arbeiterwohlfahrt to the public youth welfare offices. The recruitment of working-class women in particular was seen as a priority.[23] Such a change, it was assumed, would help to overcome the problem of the cultural and social gulf between the social worker and the problem working-class adolescent.

Juvenile Deviance and Delinquency: Definitions, Explanations, and Proposed Remedies

Despite the increased influence of Social Democracy and the ideas of the youth movement on youth welfare, there was much

Oktober 1920 (Berlin, 1920), 363; Walter Friedländer, 'Neue Wege der Gesetzgebung', in G. Danziger and S. Kawerau (eds.), *Jugendnot* (Dresden, 1923), 40–1.

[21] Caspari, 'Wohlfahrtspflege und Jugendwohlfahrt', 364; Friedländer, 'Die Reichsausführungsbestimmungen zum RJWG', *Die Gleichheit*, 33/4 (1923), 25; ibid. 29; Hedwig Wachenheim, 'Der Vorrang der öffentlichen Wohlfahrtspflege: Grundsätzliches zur Krise in der rheinischen Wohlfahrtspflege', *AW*, 1/3 (1926), 65–71.

[22] Caspari, 'Wohlfahrtspflege und Jugendwohlfahrt', 364.

[23] Ibid. 370; Gottlob Binder, 'Das RJWG und seine praktische Durchführung in den Ländern', *Die Gemeinde*, 1 (1924), 449–60, 457.

continuity between the ideas on delinquency formulated during the Kaiserreich and prevailing opinion during the Weimar Republic.[24] Only on the radical fringes of the Left and of the educational reform movement did a fundamental critique emerge of the process whereby young people became diagnosed as at risk or delinquent.

As the professional bureaucracy dealing with 'delinquent' and 'deviant' adolescents grew, so did the efforts of these social workers, youth welfare administrators, doctors, psychiatrists and psychologists to find a satisfactory, 'scientific' definition of deviant and delinquent behaviour. Some proffered neutral, 'open' definitions which defined *Verwahrlosung* in terms of educational deficiency or dissocial behaviour. These tended to be all-encompassing and tautological, seeing *Verwahrlosung* in terms of a lack of adequate education,[25] of a faulty relationship between the individual and the community,[26] or of risk to the individual or society.[27] In 1929, the Kammergericht in Berlin offered the following formula: *Verwahrlosung* 'is to be understood as any substantial deterioration of a person's physical, mental or moral condition below the state of a normal person'.[28]

Closely related to these concepts of behavioural deviance from a norm was the 'medical model' of deviance, which saw *Verwahrlosung* in terms of a disease or disorder to be diagnosed and treated. As a psychiatrist put it in an article for the Social Democratic newspaper *Vorwärts*, *Verwahrlosung* was 'a genuine illness of the mind, encompassing the entire faculties'.[29] Across the political spectrum, those involved with youth welfare presented the application of medical and psychiatric insights to youth welfare as progressive, value-free, and above all modern. One sign of the growing influence of psychiatry on youth welfare was the founding

[24] Peukert, *Sozialdisziplinierung*, 151–62.
[25] Hildegard von Heimann, *Studien zur Erziehungsarbeit an verwahrlosten Mädchen* (Hamburg, 1923), 11.
[26] Henry Jacoby, 'Verwahrlosung und Verbrechen als sozialpathologische Erscheinungen', MS (Berlin, 1930), 24.
[27] Dr Cimbal, quoted in Jacoby, 'Verwahrlosung', 24.
[28] Kammergericht 20 Sept. 1929, quoted in Emmy Hopmann, 'Die Verwahrlosung Minderjähriger', *WRP* 6/22 (1930), 368–70, 368. See also Manfred Heinemann, 'Normprobleme in der Fürsorgeerziehung', in M. Heinemann (ed.), *Sozialisation und Bildungswesen in der Weimarer Republik* (Stuttgart, 1976), 131–50.
[29] 'Eine echte, das ganze Seelenleben umfassende Erkrankung des Geistes'. Dr Cimbal, quoted in H. Becker, 'Ein Amt für seelischen Wiederaufbau', *Vorwärts*, 16 Dec. 1921.

in October 1918 of the 'German Association for the Care of Juvenile Psychopaths' (Deutscher Verein zur Fürsorge jugendlicher Psychopathen).[30] With local groups in Berlin, Hanau, Königsberg, and Breslau, the association held conferences and disseminated literature on the nature and treatment of 'juvenile psychopathy'. It persuaded the state authorities of the Reich and Prussia to support its theoretical work and to fund specialized care facilities.[31] The association quickly established itself as part of the network of specialized youth welfare organizations, and the concept of 'psychopathy' found wide acceptance in the youth welfare field; radical educational reformers such as Herman Nohl and Curt Bondy addressed conferences of the association,[32] while a leading Social Democratic welfare expert quoted uncritically the opinion of a reformatory director that 'the majority of children and young people in correctional education [*Fürsorgezöglinge*] are psychopaths'.[33]

The view of delinquency as a personality disorder went hand in hand with the search for a precise assessment of the relative roles played by 'heredity' and 'milieu' as factors in the formation of the delinquent personality. Many educational practitioners and writers on the subject of delinquency across the political spectrum remained convinced that an important if not a primary role in bringing about delinquent behaviour was played by heredity. The mental and behavioural disorders thought to be inherited included alcoholism, promiscuity, and vagrancy. Psychopathy in particular was seen as an inherited disorder.[34] Seeking to explain the apparent increase in its incidence, welfare experts argued that it could take the

[30] Bericht über einen Lehrgang der Ortsgruppe Berlin des Deutschen Vereins für Psychopathenfürsorge 5–10 Jan. 1920. ZStA Potsdam, 15.01, 9384. On the activities of the Verein, see Weindling, *Health, Race and German Politics between National Unification and Nazism 1870–1945* (Cambridge, 1989), 381–3.
[31] Hedwig Dransfeld an das Reichsinnenministerium, 5 July 1921; RMdI an sämtliche Landesregierungen, betr. Psychopathenfürsorge, 1 July 1921; Vermerk Dr. Wiedel (RMdI), 3 July 1922. ZStA Potsdam, 15.01, 9384; Ruth van der Leyen an das RMdI, Medizinalabteilung, 8 Sept. 1927. ZStA Potsdam, 15.01, 9452; Preußisches Ministerium für Volkswohlfahrt an sämtliche Regierungspräsidenten und Oberpräsidenten, betr. Einrichtungen für Nervenkranke, 2 Sept. 1920. ZStA Merseburg, Rep. 191, 2431.
[32] Bericht über den dritten Kongreß für Psychopathenfürsorge (Heidelberg, 1924), 23–37.
[33] Friedländer, 'Jugendwohlfahrtspflege und Sozialpolitik', Vortragsdisposition der Arbeiterwohlfahrt (Berlin, n.d.), 10.
[34] Friedrich Siegmund–Schultze, at Lehrgang, held by Ortsgruppe Berlin des Deutschen Vereins für Psychopathenfürsorge, Jan. 1920. ZStA Potsdam, 15.01, 9384.

form of a latent predisposition activated by conditions of instability and crisis - the war, the revolution, and inflation were seen as promoting its fully-fledged development in the young.[35]

A belief in the role of heredity as a factor in producing delinquency and a faith in psychiatric diagnoses in classifying and explaining deviant behaviour were to be found among youth welfare professionals of all political affiliations. Where the reformist Left and the radical educational reformers did offer a distinctive perspective on delinquency was in their particular stress on the role of a deprived environment and inadequate education on a child's development.[36] Social Democrats coupled their stress on environmental factors with a denunciation of the class society which perpetuated the deprivation of working-class children.[37] Alongside the explanations relying on a psychiatry heavily coloured by hereditarian thinking, rival insights into juvenile delinquency were derived from the developing disciplines of sociology and psychology. Psychologists at the University of Hamburg, researching on the effects of overcrowded urban dwellings on the mentality and behaviour of young people, came to the conclusion that working-class children lacked 'living-space'. Restricted by their environment, they inevitably sought through dangerous and forbidden activities to satisfy their thirst for sensation and adventure.[38] Further elaborations on the problem of adolescent deviance resulted from the influence of the theories of Freud and Adler. While the Freudian school of psychological theory—popularized among social workers by, among others, Siegfried Bernfeld[39]—saw individual behaviour in terms of conflicts between instinctual drives and the environment, Adlerians saw the delinquent or 'asocial' person as essentially insecure, plagued by an inferiority complex, and compensating for this failure by acts of deviance and destructiveness.[40] Explanations

---

[35] H. Becker, 'Ein Amt für seelischen Wiederaufbau'. *Vorwärts*, 16 Dec. 1921.
[36] Heimann, *Studien zur Erziehungsarbeit*, 18.
[37] e.g. Heinrich Schulz, speaking at the *Deutscher Jugendfürsorgetag* in Sept. 1918, in Deutscher Verein (ed.), *Jugendämter als Träger der öffentlichen Jugendfürsorge*, 47; Friedländer, 'Jugendwohlfahrt', *Die Gleichheit*, 33/4 (1923), 29.
[38] Martha Muchow, 'Grundlinien der seelischen Entwicklung des Kindes im Kindergarten- und Schulalter', *JV* 4/12 (1928), 203–14, 214.
[39] Siegfried Bernfeld, 'Die psychologischen Grundlagen der Gefährdetenfürsorge', *AW* 2/17 (1927), 522–5, 524–5. Bernfeld taught at the social work school at the Deutsche Hochschule für Politik, Berlin. See also Zeller, *Volksmütter*, 85, and Dudek, *Leitbild: Kamerad und Helfer*, 52.
[40] Jacoby, 'Verwahrlosung', 39–40.

of delinquency in terms of unresolved conflicts between the adolescent and a hostile or deprived environment held considerable appeal to the Left; a Social Democratic social worker employed in Berlin in the late 1920s attested when interviewed to the popularity of the ideas of Adler and Freud among her colleagues.[41]

A concern with environmental factors in causing delinquency did not preclude an interest in eugenics. On the contrary, the importance of eugenics—the body of thought dedicated to investigating the methods of improving the quality of the human species— was hailed by many experts in the mainstream of the youth welfare debate.[42] However, different strands of eugenic thinking characterized different camps in the debate on delinquency. Hardcore hereditarians of the Right, who viewed delinquents as an incorrigible residuum predestined to asocial and antisocial behaviour, favoured 'negative eugenics', measures to protect the species from its 'inferior' members by discouraging or preventing the 'unfit' from reproducing.[43] By contrast, youth welfare specialists who stressed environmental factors in delinquency favoured 'welfare eugenics'. Welfare eugenicists, rather than stressing the need to weed out the 'unfit', advocated 'positive' measures by the state to improve the condition of the present and future population.[44] 'Welfare eugenics' pervaded the Weimar welfare establishment, forming common ground between reformist socialists, Naumannite liberals, and Catholic social reformers. Applied to the problem of juvenile delinquency, this school of thinking prescribed social reforms to produce healthy children in healthy families, together with 'social hygiene for the mental functions'[45] or 'mental hygiene', which included, for instance, the deployment of suitable professional experts as counsellors in schools and the setting up of new facilities for advising adolescents and their parents in cases of educational difficulty.[46]

[41] Interview by the author with Ella Kay and Jeanne Bauer on 9 Feb. 1984.
[42] Adalbert Gregor, *Rassehygiene und Jugendfürsorge* (Berlin, 1919); Helene Simon, *Aufgaben und Ziele der neuzeitlichen Wohlfahrtspflege* (Stuttgart and Berlin, 1922), 10; Heinrich Webler, 'Erbbiologie und Eugenik', *ZBl* 20/7 (1928/9), 194.
[43] Helene Friederike Stelzner, *Weibliche Fürsorgezöglinge* (Berlin, 1929), 53; Hildegard Mischke, 'Bedeutung von Anlage und Milieu bei weiblichen Fürsorgezöglingen Mecklenburgs', Diss. phil. (Rostock, 1932), 56–7.
[44] Weindling, *Health, Race and German Politics*, 338–56.
[45] Jacoby, 'Verwahrlosung', 39.
[46] On 'Geistige Hygiene der Großstadt', see Dr Dehio, 'Aufgaben einer sozialen Psychiatrie', *Blätter für die Wohlfahrtspflege, Sachsen*, 2/4 (1922), 137–45, 141; on

Youth welfare experts sought to explain delinquent behaviour in terms of personality disorders derived from complex causes. Their analyses became increasingly sophisticated efforts to penetrate the adolescent psyche. However, these analyses obscured the social and class factors involved in the definition and stigmatization of certain forms of juvenile behaviour as deviant and unacceptable. Behind the scientific definitions and explanations continued to lurk prejudices about the disorderly lifestyle of unskilled working-class adolescents. Some of what came to be analysed in the treatises on delinquency involved contraventions of clear-cut legal norms: this was the case with juvenile crime. However, where no offences had been committed, the norms from which youngsters were perceived by youth welfare professionals to be deviating were much vaguer notions of orderly and healthy behaviour. These norms partly reflected the bourgeois social values of thrift, sobriety, and respectability. They also reflected the youth movement's ideals of self-discipline, self-improvement, and abstinence, as well as the prescriptions of modern medical professionals about rational, reflective behaviour oriented to health and hygiene in the widest sense. Measured against these norms, many aspects of the lifestyle of working-class adolescents, particularly the unskilled, appeared reprehensible or dangerous. An interrupted work record could cause a youngster to be labelled shiftless and work-shy; expenditure on clothes, cigarettes, alcohol, cinema, dance-halls, and 'trash' literature were diagnosed as 'addiction to hedonism' (*Vergnügungssucht*), while staying out too long at night, roaming the streets, or undertaking excursions further afield came under the rubric of a 'pathological urge to roam' (*krankhafter Wandertrieb*).[47]

The difficulty of defining norms of behaviour was particularly obvious where girls were concerned. Delinquency in girls was defined predominantly in terms of sexual behaviour.[48] In the words of Bertha Paulssen, a senior official of the Hamburg youth welfare office and a left-liberal, 'delinquency in girls is almost exclusively of a sexual nature; only seldom does one find true criminality, in

---

'Hygiene der Nerven und des Geisteslebens', see Werner Villinger, in Niederschrift über die 6. Tagung der nordwestdeutschen Vereinigung für praktische Hygiene am 12.5.1928, 30. StAH, Medizinalkollegium, II U 3.

[47] Mischke, 'Anlage und Milieu', 33.
[48] Heimann, *Studien zur Erziehungsarbeit*, 13; Anna Nailis, *Zur Geschichte und Theorie der Verwahrlosung* (Düsseldorf, 1933), 24.

contrast to male youth, whose delinquency is almost always expressed in criminal behaviour'.[49] Where criminal offences were committed by girls, she argued, these were usually linked to the girls' sexual relationships. Paulssen was aware that the norms of sexual behaviour which she upheld in her professional capacity and against which girls' deviance was being measured were challenged by many quarters in society, and she hinted at their class-specific nature: 'One's task is made more difficult by the fact that neither the moral values of the broad masses [*breitester Volksschichten*] nor the law itself give a clear, universally recognized standard to set against these moral misdemeanours and acts of deviance—in contrast to the standards upheld against criminal offences.'[50] However, this awareness did not deter her from her work of pursuing, classifying, and seeking to rescue and cure girls found to be sexual miscreants.

There were few challenges to the definitions and norms by which youngsters from the working class became stigmatized as deviant. Communists, from their position outside the youth welfare establishment, remained isolated in their denunciations of youth welfare as a repressive tool of the bourgeois state.[51] Only occasionally could other voices be heard offering a fundamental criticism of the way the youth welfare establishment sought to impose on working-class adolescents norms of behaviour which bore no relation to the culture in which those adolescents were growing up. A teacher at the Social Democratic social work training school in Berlin warned that the youth welfare system tended to stigmatize working-class children: 'Every proletarian child is at risk in the sense that its background and its development put it at risk of deviating from the bourgeois order.'[52] In 1930, social workers in the Gilde Soziale Arbeit pondered the dangers of superficial categorization and labelling of youngsters as delinquent, and agreed that youth welfare practice left much to be desired in this respect.[53] Writing in 1932, a radical sociologist with *völkisch* sympathies took

---

[49] Bertha Paulssen, 'Erziehungsarbeit an verwahrlosten weiblichen Jugendlichen', in *Bericht über den 3. Kongreß für Psychopathenfürsorge* (Heidelberg, 1924), 38–44, 38.
[50] Ibid. 39.
[51] Adolf Deter, 'Der Fürsorgeskandal Scheuen im Lichte des neuen Beschwerderechts und Prügelverbots und die "Arbeiterwohlfahrt"', *Proletarische Sozialpolitik*, 3/5 (1930), 148–52.
[52] Paula Kurgaß, 'Gefährdetenfürsorge?', *AW* 3/23 (1928), 725–9, 728.
[53] Dudek, *Leitbild: Kamerad und Helfer*, 97–8.

the view that the whole system of youth welfare bore 'the stamp of superiority' resting on class relations: in her view, 'the files of the youth welfare office almost resemble those of the state prosecutor, even when they list no crimes or serious misdemeanours'.[54]

While the occasional dissenting voice was to be heard in the later Weimar years, what is striking about the post-war period is the degree of consensus which existed unchallenged, extending from the political Right to the Social Democratic Left, about what constituted 'unhealthy' and delinquent behaviour in working-class youngsters, and about the need to educate them. The youth welfare lobby was united in pressing for the child's right to education, in stressing the need to educate rather than punish the juvenile offender, and in calling for social reform to prevent delinquency and neglect. That still left room for disagreement over how such education was to be provided, how it was to be financed, over the methods of educational intervention and the role of public versus private institutions. Such debates were to accompany the passage of major national legislation on juvenile justice and youth welfare in the early post-war period.

The National Youth Welfare Law

Youth welfare reformers greeted as a major step forward the inclusion in the Weimar Constitution of August 1919 of clauses laying down the responsibility of central government and other state authorities for matters of youth welfare. Article 120 declared that 'the education of children and young people to physical, mental and social fitness is the prime duty and the natural right of parents; the carrying out of these duties is watched over by the state'.[55] Article 122 stated that 'youth is to be protected from exploitation and from moral, mental, and physical degradation [*Verwahrlosung*]. State and local authorities are to take the measures necessary to achieve this goal.'[56]

However, it was one thing to reach agreement over the necessity of national legislation to create more systematic and comprehensive provision of youth welfare; it was another matter altogether to

---

[54] Lisbeth Franzen-Hellersberg, *Die jugendliche Arbeiterin: ihre Arbeitsweise und Lebensform* (Tübingen, 1932), 79.
[55] Die Verfassung des Deutschen Reichs, 11 Aug. 1919, *RGBl* 1919, ii. 1383–418, 1406.
[56] Ibid.

achieve unanimity on the concrete details of financing and organizing such provision. On some issues there was basic agreement. It was a matter of consensus that such legislation would have a programmatic purpose, namely to establish the rights of the child and to define the role of state youth welfare. Secondly, it would have an organizational aspect: a uniform network of youth welfare departments was to be created to carry out and supervise the administration of youth welfare. Thirdly, it should codify and extend, on a uniform national basis, those core tasks of youth welfare already performed in varying degrees by the state: the care of orphans and destitute children, the public guardianship of foster children, and the care and education of the neglected and delinquent. However, there were some differences of opinion over the wider scope of the law and the extent to which it should prescribe as compulsory tasks for public youth welfare areas such as, for instance, probation work, assistance to the juvenile courts, recreational facilities for young people (*Jugendpflege*), and health care for mothers and children of all ages. Social Democrats, following Helene Simon's lead, argued that the law should be a comprehensive charter providing public aid and services to all children and young people, rather than a measure merely codifying areas of compulsory intervention. The established private welfare agencies, by contrast, sought to limit the degree to which public provision would take over established areas of private agency work such as assistance to the juvenile courts.

The National Youth Welfare Law was the product of political compromise.[57] Nearly five years lay between the first drafts of the National Youth Welfare Law—Reichsjugendwohlfahrtsgesetz, abbreviated in the following as RJWG—and the emergency decree of February 1924 which brought the law into force. These years saw a decline in the electoral fortunes of the SPD and DDP. The SPD was in government at Reich level until June 1920, and again from May 1921 to 1922, but was constrained by the terms of its coalitions, particularly with regard to the Centre Party, the latter ensuring that the influence of Catholic social thinking was clearly felt in the areas of social, welfare and educational policy.[58] Centre

[57] C. Hasenclever, *Jugendhilfe und Jugendgesetzgebung seit 1900* (Göttingen, 1978), 48–77.
[58] H. Winkler, *Von der Revolution zur Stabilisierung* (Berlin and Bonn, 1984), 239–40, 460.

Party politicians were above all concerned to maintain the role of private welfare organizations in any codification of youth welfare provision.[59] The RJWG was also overshadowed by economic difficulties and the collapse of the monetary system. Finance ministers intervened at various stages of the legislative process in an effort to cut back the financial commitments that would be involved in an expansion of state youth welfare provision.

Proposals for national youth welfare legislation were circulated by the Reich Ministry of the Interior on 22 April 1919 and ministerial discussions began in May 1919.[60] Even at this stage, the Finance Ministries of the Reich and of Prussia were warning of major financial obstacles to the realization of such plans.[61] Financial questions were a major issue in the Reichsrat's discussions of the government draft in 1920 and 1921, and the Reichsrat scrapped the provisions for a national youth ministry on financial grounds. The government draft as amended by the Reichsrat was finally presented to the Reichstag in March 1921, after an intervention in January 1921 by women members of the Reichstag calling for proceedings over the law to be speeded up. The draft was then referred to a newly-constituted committee (the 29th Committee) of the Reichstag.[62]

The amendments made by the 29th committee were influenced by the proposals of an independent commission of youth welfare experts, which was convened in April 1921 by the German Association for Public and Private Welfare, the German Central Association for Youth Welfare, and the German Professional Guardians' Association, and which was dominated by the representatives of private welfare organizations. This commission held its deliberations concurrently with the sessions of the 29th Reichstag

[59] Caspari, in 'Bericht über die Frauenkonferenz der SPD in Kassel 9/10.10.1920', 363.
[60] RMdI an das Preuß. Min. Handel und Gewerbe betr. reichsgesetzliche Regelung auf den Gebieten der Jugendwohlfahrt, 22 Apr. 1919; Aufzeichnung über das Ergebnis der kommissarischen Beratung über die reichsgesetzliche Regelung der Jugendwohlfahrt im Reichsministerium des Innern, 5 Mar. 1919. ZStA Merseburg, Rep. 120, BB VII, 1, 124, vol. 1.
[61] Preußisches Finanzministerium an den RMdI, 13 June 1919 and 18 July 1919. ZStA Merseburg, Rep. 191, 2376.
[62] Reichstagsdrucksache Nr. 1666, *Verhandlungen des Reichstages*, 1. Wahlperiode 1920–4, vol. 366, 1220–77. On the passage of the legislation, see also Johannes Münder, '65 Jahre—und kein bißchen weiter?', in Erwin Jordan and Johannes Münder (eds.), *65 Jahre Reichsjugendwohlfahrtsgesetz—ein Gesetz auf dem Weg in den Ruhestand?* (Münster, 1987), 7–11.

committee, and some of its recommendations were adopted by the Reichstag Committee.[63] For example, new clauses were inserted specifying that the local youth welfare boards (Jugendamter) should nominate two-fifths of their members (excluding the ex-officio members) from local private youth welfare organizations and that foster children be cared for by families of the same confession. Moreover, the Social Democrats and those seeking a clear and far-reaching statement of the child's right to education lost the battle over the formulation of the programmatic opening paragraph. The more far-reaching formulation: 'Every German child has a right to physical, intellectual, and spiritual education' ('Jedes deutsche Kind hat ein Recht auf körperliche, geistige und seelische Erziehung') was replaced by the formulation proposed by the Centre and BVP representatives in the 29th committee, so that the opening paragraph read: 'Every German child has a right to education to physical, spiritual, and social fitness' ('Jedes deutsche Kind hat ein Recht auf Erziehung zur leiblichen, seelischen und gesellschaftlichen Tüchtigkeit').[64] However, the private welfare lobby did not prevail on all issues. Although the law did not go as far as Social Democrats wanted in expanding the scope of public youth welfare, the private welfare agencies were not able to establish as a basic principle that public welfare was of a 'subsidiary' nature in relation to private welfare. The principle of 'subsidiarity' was not established in the RJWG of 1922 except with regard to the specific tasks laid down in paragraph 4.

The National Youth Welfare Law was passed by the Reichstag on 13/14 June 1922 and promulgated on 9 July 1922.[65] The preamble to the draft law placed the tasks of youth welfare in the context of national crisis: 'Our German fatherland is in a state of collapse. The unspeakable mental and physical sufferings of the war, the great crisis of the revolution and the harsh peace treaty have sapped the strength of the German people: a dark future with little hope lies before us.'[66] Social reconstruction was to begin by repairing the physical and moral damage upon youth inflicted in the shorter term

[63] Hasenclever, *Jugendhilfe*, 55–6.
[64] RJWG, para. 1, sect. 1.
[65] Reichsgesetz für Jugendwohlfahrt, 9 July 1922, *RGBl* 1922, i. 633–47. The text is reprinted in Jordan and Münder (eds.), *65 Jahre RJWG*, 137–51.
[66] Begründung zum Entwurf eines RJWG, 15 Mar. 1921. Reichstagsdrucksache Nr. 1666, *Verhandlungen des Reichstags*, 1. Wahlperiode 1920–4, vol. 366, 1220–77, 1237.

by the war and in the longer term by industrialization and urbanization.

The programmatic first paragraph of the RJWG defined the rights of the child, the rights and duties of the family, and the role of public welfare, which was required to intervene in the interests of the child where its education was not adequately provided for by its family. Paragraph 2 laid down the form in which public youth welfare was to be organized, and paragraph 3 listed the mandatory tasks of the local youth welfare department (Jugendamt): the supervision of foster children, the care of orphans and the public guardianship of illegitimate children, material assistance to orphans and destitute children, probation work and referrals to correctional education, assistance to the juvenile courts, to the factory inspectorate regarding child labour and the protection of young workers, to the agencies responsible for the care of war orphans, and to the police in providing accommodation for juvenile offenders.

A second category of tasks followed, where the state was not obliged to make provision unless private welfare provision was lacking (paragraph 4). With respect to this category of tasks, but only with regard to this category, the public youth welfare services were to be 'subsidiary' to the private agencies. The tasks in this category comprised counselling and guidance for young people and their families, maternal and infant welfare, health care for pre-school and schoolchildren, and recreational and health facilities for young people of above school age. Details then followed codifying and extending regulations on the obligatory tasks of public youth welfare: fostering, guardianship, and public relief for destitute children and juveniles.

The most important section of the law as far as the treatment of delinquent and deprived adolescents was concerned was the final section, Section 6, which dealt with probation and correctional education. This section partly involved a codification of existing regulations and partly the introduction of new provisions. Paragraphs 56–61 dealt with probation (Schutzaufsicht). Various forms of probation had hitherto existed at local level; now its application was codified for the whole Reich (RJWG, paragraph 56). Probation was defined as a preventive measure to supervise and control a young person 'at risk' (RJWG, paragraph 58) and was to be ordered 'if it appears necessary and sufficient to prevent physical, mental, or moral degradation'. (RJWG, paragraph 56). Probation could be ordered by the guardianship court or by the youth welfare department as long as the juvenile's parents or guardian agreed (RJWG, paragraph 59).

Paragraphs 62–76 went on to deal with correctional education (Fürsorgeerziehung).[67] This section of the RJWG was drafted by an administrator of correctional education from Hanover and was largely based on the existing Prussian regulations regarding correctional education. Paragraph 62 defined the tasks of correctional education: 'Correctional education serves to prevent or remedy delinquency and is carried out at public cost and under the supervision of the public authorities in a suitable foster family or in a reformatory.'

Paragraph 63 laid down the criteria for taking a juvenile into correctional education. First, juveniles could be referred in cases of maltreatment or neglect by their parents or guardian (paragraphs 1666, 1838 BGB). This had been the case since the introduction of the BGB in 1900. However, the RJWG departed in one respect from the existing Prussian regulations: the Prussian law of 7 July 1915 had stated that any removal of a child from its family and a placement in other accommodation, for instance a foster family, was, *if public costs were involved*, a sufficient reason for ordering correctional education.[68] The RJWG restricted this condition by specifying that correctional education could be ordered as a 'preventive' measure to protect juveniles from parental neglect or maltreatment only if no other suitable accommodation elsewhere (*anderweit*) could be found—this included fostering at public expense (RJWG, paragraph 63, section 1). This regulation did not please those with a vested interest in correctional education as an institution, who demanded the restoration of 'preventive' correctional education in the scope afforded by the Prussian ruling of 1915. Eventually, as will be seen below, they were to get their way.[69]

While the grounds for ordering correctional education were thus restricted where it was applied as a 'preventive' measure, its scope was extended where juveniles were judged to be already delinquent and needing correctional education as a 'cure'. Under the terms of the Introductory Law to the Civil Code (*Einführungsgesetz zum*

---

[67] 'Fürsorgeerziehung' ('Fürsorge' = care, welfare) had by now replaced 'Zwangserziehung' ('Zwang' = compulsion) as the official designation.
[68] See Ch. 2, p. 52.   [69] See Ch. 7, p. 250.

BGB), correctional education could be ordered where parents were not at fault only if the juveniles concerned were judged to be on the verge of 'complete moral ruin'. Under the RJWG, a looser formulation was adopted: under paragraph 63, section 2.1, correctional education could be ordered 'if correctional education is necessary to remedy delinquency due to inadequate education'. This extended the number of cases where correctional education was applicable. Another provision widening the application of correctional education was the clause raising the age-limit for referral to correctional education from 18 to 20 years as long as it was thought to have some chance of success (RJWG, paragraph 63, section 2.2). This development was not greeted with unanimous approval by the correctional education establishment.[70] The RJWG made no provision for young people over 18 where correctional education was judged unlikely to succeed. It merely indicated the intended direction of policy in a reference to protective detention (Bewahrung): under paragraph 73, 'incorrigible' youngsters could be released from correctional education if suitable facilities for 'protective detention' were available. However, such facilities were to prove difficult to introduce in practice.[71]

The National Youth Welfare Law was due to come into force in April 1924. However, the autumn and winter of 1922/3 saw a worsening of the economic crisis and the beginning of the occupation of the Ruhr. As public finances slid into chaos, the municipalities, via the Deutscher Städtetag, mounted a rearguard action to stop the implementation of the RJWG. Underlying their protest was resentment of the reform of public finance which had been undertaken by the Reich government in March 1920—the Erzberger tax reform which aimed to consolidate the finances of the Reich by giving central government the sole right to levy income tax. The *Länder* and local governments were to be compensated for their loss of revenue by a system of grants from the Reich out of the revenue from income and corporation tax.[72] From the point of view of local government, the new system was unsatisfactory, bringing both a loss of revenue and a loss of autonomy, and the resistance of local governments to the imposition of new tasks by central

---

[70] Karl Vossen, 'Die Fürsorgeerziehung der über 18jährigen', *Volkswohlfahrt*, 6/6 (1925), 100–4.   [71] See Ch. 7, p. 256.
[72] Karl-Heinrich Hansmeyer (ed.), *Kommunale Finanzpolitik in der Weimarer Republik* (Stuttgart, 1973), 35.

government was all the stronger as a consequence. The National Youth Welfare Law in its original form aroused the municipalities' hostility on both counts, and the Städtetag had succeeded in having the annual central subsidy which was made available to local governments doubled from 50 million RM to 100 million RM per year. However, they continued to be concerned that they would be left bearing the costs of carrying out the new legislation; they also objected to the interference by the Reich authorities in the administrative structure of local authorities entailed in the setting up of a youth welfare department according to a prescribed pattern. In the summer and autumn of 1923, the protests of the Städtetag against the RJWG grew. These protests found support in the Reich and Prussian Finance Ministries, which sought to stop the law being implemented altogether.[73]

The youth welfare lobby mobilized in protest. On 8 December 1923, representatives of the Reich and Länder governments met representatives of the Deutscher Verein and of the municipalities to discuss amendments to the RJWG.[74] As a result, an emergency decree was drafted and passed on 14 February 1924 bringing the National Youth Welfare Law into force.[75] The law was thus rescued from oblivion, but only in a considerably modified form. The emergency decree reduced the law's centralizing and unifying force and weakened some of the binding provisions, in order to allow greater powers of discretion to the federal states and the local authorities. The privileged position of the private welfare organizations in the local youth welfare boards was preserved. Plans for a National Youth Welfare Office were scrapped, and a number of the tasks were made optional, notably the tasks of RJWG paragraph 4 (where the principle of 'subsidiarity' was to apply). One advantage to the Reich of loosening the provisions of the law was that this enabled the cancellation of the central subsidy promised to local governments in the original draft.

In practice, not all the *Länder* were to take advantage of the enabling clauses of the emergency decree. Saxony, for example, laid down in its own legislation to implement the RJWG that the tasks

[73] Preußischer Innenminister an den Preußischen Finanzminister, 4 Dec. 1923. ZStA Merseburg, Rep. 120, BB VII, 1, 124, vol. 2.
[74] Beratung im Wohlfahrtsministerium betr. RJWG, 8 Dec. 1923. ZStA Merseburg, Rep. 191, 223, vol. 4.
[75] Verordnung über das Inkrafttreten des Reichsgesetzes für Jugendwohlfahrt, 14 Feb. 1924, *RGBl* 1924, i. 110.

of paragraph 4 were mandatory after all,[76] and Hamburg implemented the law in its 1922 form in full (see below). However, the emergency decree showed the extent to which the Reich government, now firmly under conservative control, had become reluctant to act as an engine of welfare expansion at local level. The development of youth welfare was to depend all the more on the political will of the *Länder* and local authorities.

'Model' Youth Welfare Institutions? The Hamburg Youth Welfare Department

Hamburg youth welfare officials liked to emphasize Hamburg's pioneer role in shaping the National Youth Welfare Law: Wilhelm Hertz, director of the Hamburg Youth Welfare Department from 1923 to 1933, wrote in retrospect of how Hamburg's practice had been a challenge for the rest of Germany to match up to.[77] The enabling clauses of the emergency decree of February 1924 allowing the *Länder* to delay the implementation of the RJWG or to define certain tasks as optional were therefore of little relevance to Hamburg. Since the provisions of the RJWG did not mean a significant expansion over and above its existing provision, the city-state government opted to go ahead and implement the law as it stood in its 1922 version.[78] The changes entailed by the RJWG were hardly more than minor organizational changes.[79]

Although the National Youth Welfare Law brought little in the way of formal changes to Hamburg, its youth welfare officials saw the spirit of the law as necessitating an expansion and intensification of youth welfare work.[80] This expansion had already been under way thanks to political changes in Hamburg since the collapse of the Kaiserreich. In the newly-constituted youth welfare department

[76] Hans Muthesius, 'Über die "Pflicht"- und "Kann"-Aufgaben des Jugendamtes nach dem RJWG', *ZBl* 25/3 (1933/4), 73–6.
[77] Wilhelm Hertz, 'Zehn Jahre Hamburger Jugendamt 1923–1933', MS (Hamburg, 1934), 8.
[78] Id. 'Zur neuesten Entwicklung der Jugendwohlfahrt in Hamburg', *JV* 1/1 (1925), 2.
[79] From 1924, youth welfare in the state of Hamburg was undertaken by a state youth welfare department (Landesjugendamt Hamburg): two local Jugendämter were set up for the districts of Cuxhaven and Bergedorf, while Hamburg city's youth welfare department was in effect united with the Landesjugendamt.
[80] Hertz, 'Zehn Jahre Hamburger Jugendamt', 5.

headed by a Social Democratic senator, Social Democrats sought to implement some of their key demands. One demand was the democratization of youth welfare work through a greater participation of working-class honorary officials.[81] A second goal was to extend youth welfare work beyond the care of children at risk and the delinquent by expanding, in cooperation with the Arbeiterwohlfahrt, facilities such as crèches, after-school centres, and recuperation centres for 'normal' children and young people.[82] Thirdly, Social Democrats demanded specific reforms in correctional education.[83] Meanwhile, the influence of the youth movement was also making itself felt in the work of the youth welfare department, which set up committees in 1921 to promote the cultural work of youth organizations[84] and a working group to involve volunteers from youth organizations in youth welfare work.[85]

Hamburg's youth welfare department expanded significantly during the Weimar period. The expenditure of the department was 1.56 million marks in 1913; this rose to 6.9 million marks in 1926.[86] During the same period the staff of the youth welfare department grew from 247 civil servants and white-collar employees in 1913 to 665 in 1926.[87] By the late 1920s, under its director, Wilhelm Hertz, a lawyer and former juvenile court judge with left-liberal sympathies, together with his deputy August Hellmann, a former schoolteacher and Social Democrat, and state secretary Bertha Paulssen, a trained psychologist with contacts in the youth movement, a complex administrative structure had evolved. The department was divided into two sections. One section (*offene/ halboffene Fürsorge*) provided assistance to children living with

---

[81] Social Democrats in Hamburg had already pressed for this before the First World War: 'Die öffentliche Jugendfürsorge in Hamburg', *Hamburger Echo*, 13 June 1914 (Erste Beilage).
[82] Karen Hagemann and Ursula Schneider, ' "Einer für alle, alle für einen": Selbsthilfeorganisationen', in Projekt Arbeiterkultur (ed.), *Vorwärts und nicht vergessen: Arbeiterkultur in Hamburg um 1930* (Berlin, 1982), 108–10.
[83] See Ch. 7, pp. 237–9.
[84] Gustav Dahrendorf, 'Der Hamburger Jugendausschuß, seine Organisation und Aufgaben', *JV* 3/1 (1927), 17; Albert Karsten, 'Der Ausschuß zur Förderung der Jugendwohlfahrt und seine Aufgaben', ibid. 1–3.
[85] Herbert Bökel, 'Die Mitwirkung der Jugendbünde in der Jugendfürsorge', ibid. 18–21.
[86] Denkschrift des Präses des Jugendamtes an den Senat, 28 Jan. 1928, 2. StAH, JB I, 3, vol. 1.
[87] Ibid.

their own families. Its remit covered official guardianship for illegitimate children; assistance to the juvenile court; recreational facilities; crèches and kindergartens; and educational welfare, counselling, and probation work. The other section (*vollständige Fürsorge*) dealt with cases where the youth welfare department took on the entire responsibility for a child or juvenile: this covered care for orphans and correctional education for deprived, neglected, and delinquent youngsters.

The Hamburg Jugendamt enjoyed a reputation as one of Germany's leading youth welfare departments, a status reflected, among other ways, by the fact that its director was chairman of the Association of City Youth Welfare Departments (Vereinigung großstädtischer Jugendämter). Its reputation rested not only on the extent of its facilities, but also on its efforts to apply the newest insights of educational theory, psychology, and psychiatry in its practice. The department's emphasis on medical expertise was reflected in 1926 with the appointment of a full-time youth psychiatrist, Werner Villinger.[88] Wilhelm Hertz stressed the need for scientific and systematic analysis and treatment of delinquent and asocial behaviour. The educational tasks of youth welfare, he explained in 1927 to an audience of social workers, demanded 'knowledge . . . familiarity with social phenomena and with individual circumstances, a knowledge of psychology and a basic understanding of people. With the aid of these tools the youth welfare department must make a social and educational [*sozialpädagogische*] diagnosis of the individual case and draw up an educational plan.'[89] This medicalized language of diagnosis and treatment was central to the modern youth welfare work which Hamburg saw itself as representing.[90]

The case of Hamburg is a major example of how public youth welfare institutions developed in a situation where Social Democrats

---

[88] Dienstbesprechung des Jugendamts, 17 Dec. 1931, ibid. On Werner Villinger, see Weindling, *Health, Race and German Politics*, 383; D. Peukert, *Grenzen der Sozialdisziplinierung* (Cologne, 1986), 249; Carola Kuhlmann, *Erbkrank oder erziehbar? Jugendhilfe als Vorsorge und Aussonderung in der Fürsorgeerziehung in Westfalen von 1933–1945* (Weinheim and Munich, 1989), 136. See also Ch. 7, on Villinger's work with criminal and delinquent adolescents.

[89] Hertz, 'Die öffentliche Jugendhilfe als pädagogische Idee und als Gemeinschaftsaufgabe', *JV* 3/8 (1927), 165–6.

[90] Further aspects of the educational practice of the Hamburg youth welfare authorities are examined in Chs. 6 and 7.

strongly committed to social welfare backed the expansionist efforts of welfare professionals who were committed to creating an all-encompassing network of educational facilities and supervision. Hamburg was not unique in its youth welfare services, however. In other cities, too, where the SPD was in a strong position in the local authority administration, notably in Berlin, public youth welfare was substantially expanded and reformed in line with the new teachings of psychiatry, psychology, and scientific pedagogics.[91] Such developments were in contrast to areas of the Reich such as the Rhineland, where the influence of the Centre Party ensured that public youth welfare services did not expand so far as to threaten the entrenched position of the confessional private agencies.[92]

The Juvenile Courts Law

At the same time as the National Youth Welfare Law was being discussed, preparations for a national law on juvenile justice and juvenile courts were under way: together, the two pieces of legislation represented important changes in the state's handling of the juvenile delinquent and criminal.

During the First World War, the juvenile justice movement had continued to press for reform: its representatives presented a memorandum to the Reichstag in December 1917 calling for the revival of the Juvenile Courts Law.[93] The Reich Ministry of Justice rejected the plan, arguing that the rise in juvenile crime was due to the peculiar conditions of wartime and would fall again once the war was over.[94] However, after another two years and under a new minister, Eugen Schiffer (DDP), the Reich Ministry of Justice announced plans for a reform of juvenile justice as part of a comprehensive reform of criminal law.[95]

The draft of a Juvenile Courts Law was submitted by the government to the Reichsrat in February 1920, and by February

---

[91] For a case study of the youth welfare services in the Berlin district of Prenzlauer Berg, see Harvey, 'Sozialdemokratische Jugendhilfereform in der Praxis'.
[92] Hedwig Wachenheim, 'Der Vorrang der öffentlichen Wohlfahrtspflege', in *Geschäftsbericht 1926 des Hauptausschusses für Arbeiterwohlfahrt e.V*, 4.
[93] Vermerk des Reichsjustizamtes, 2 Feb. 1918. ZStA Potsdam, 30.01, 6083.
[94] Ibid.
[95] Reichsjustizministerium an RMdI, 1 Nov. 1919. ZStA Potsdam, Reichsjustizministerium, 5566.

1922 it had completed its discussions. These had been delayed on the one hand by the abandonment of the general plans for a reform of the entire criminal justice system, which meant that the Juvenile Courts Law had to be redrafted as a separate piece of legislation, and on the other hand by the need to coordinate the provisions of the Juvenile Courts Law with those of the National Youth Welfare Law.[96] In October 1922, the Juvenile Courts Law was submitted to the Reichstag.[97] It was passed on 1 February 1923 and came into force on 1 July 1923.[98]

In its preamble, the law sought to justify the approach represented by the slogan 'education instead of punishment' and to counter arguments that a reform of juvenile justice represented excessive lenience towards juvenile delinquents and criminals. Educational measures, it declared, could act as a deterrent just as effectively as punishments.[99] This reflected a consensus across the youth welfare spectrum: Helene Simon, one of the leading Social Democratic youth welfare experts in the Weimar period, had written in 1915 that the 'individualized' educational approach, treating the offender rather than schematically meting out the appropriate punishment for the offence, could under certain circumstances impose stricter measures than the judicial model.[100]

The provisions of the Juvenile Courts Law covered both substantive and procedural aspects of juvenile justice. Firstly, it raised the minimum age of criminal responsibility to 14 and set the upper limit of the age of limited criminal responsibility at 18 years (paragraphs 1 and 2). Young people over 18 years at the time of the offence were to be tried, as hitherto, by the ordinary criminal courts. Secondly, the law reformulated the conditions whereby young offenders' moral and intellectual maturity were to be taken into account. Whereas the National Criminal Code of 1871 had laid down that juvenile offenders could only be punished if they were judged to possess the discernment (*Einsicht*) necessary to recognize the criminal nature of their offence, the Juvenile Courts Law laid down that an offender aged between 14 and 18 years could only be

[96] Kiesow, 'Zum Entwurf eines Jugendgerichtsgesetzes', pt. 1, *ZBl* 14/10 (1922/3), 205–9.
[97] Reichstagsdrucksache 5171, *Verhandlungen des Reichstags*, 1. Wahlperiode 1920–4, vol. 375.
[98] Jugendgerichtsgesetz, 16 Feb. 1923, *RGBl* 1923, i. 135–141.
[99] Begründung zum Entwurf eines Jugendgerichtsgesetzes, Reichstagsdrucksache 5171, 9. [100] Helene Simon, 'Das Jugendrecht', 237.

punished if at the time of the offence he was 'capable on the basis of his intellectual and moral development of recognizing the unlawfulness of the deed and of controlling his will accordingly' (paragraph 3).

Thirdly, the Juvenile Courts Law took a step towards eroding the 'legality principle'—the principle of compulsory prosecution (*Anklagezwang*). The loosening of the 'legality principle' was seen by juvenile justice reformers as a means of preventing the flood of trivial offences by youngsters hitherto brought to court.[101] The Juvenile Courts Law followed the reformers' recommendations and laid down that the state prosecutor could refrain from prosecution if an educational measure had already been prescribed and if further measures were not necessary. Furthermore, the court was empowered to terminate proceedings before judgment with the permission of the state prosecutor (paragraph 32).

One of the most important and controversial aspects of the Juvenile Courts Law was its attempt to create a flexible system of educational and punitive measures. Central to this strategy were the paragraphs allowing the juvenile court judge to refrain from punishing delinquents convicted of an offence if the offence was trivial (paragraph 9, section 4), or if educational measures were deemed necessary and adequate (paragraphs 5 and 6). Hitherto, judges had been compelled to impose some form of punishment— even if it was only a mild form of punishment such as the caution (*Verweis*)—if the young offender had been convicted.

The new law allowed the juvenile court judge not only to prescribe that educational measures were appropriate and necessary, but also actually to order those measures. This was a controversial issue among youth welfare and juvenile justice reformers. Some reformers believed that the juvenile courts should leave the decisions regarding 'educational measures' to the youth welfare authorities, for two reasons. Firstly, they argued, allowing the juvenile courts to order educational measures would create a confusing 'dualism' in the system. This would be the case particularly with regard to correctional education, which could then be ordered both by the guardianship courts upon the application of the youth welfare authorities, and by the juvenile courts. Secondly, they argued that having 'educational' measures ordered by the

[101] Herbert Francke, Denkschrift zum Paragraphen 4 des Jugendgerichtsgesetzes, 1922. StAH, JB I, 487, vol. 1.

criminal courts as well as by the youth welfare authorities would not transform the criminal courts in the eyes of the public at large into benevolent educational institutions. Instead, they argued, the educational measures ordered by the juvenile courts would simply be seen as punishments and discredited even more in popular opinion.[102] The result of the controversy was a compromise which in fact institutionalized the 'dualism' criticised by, among others, Francke and Riebesell. In paragraph 5, section 2, the new law laid down that the court, if it deemed educational measures to be necessary, could either order those measures itself or oblige the guardianship court to order them. The confusion in the law between 'educational' and 'punitive' measures also remained. One example of this confusion was the law's handling of probation. Probation (Schutzaufsicht) was among the range of 'educational measures' laid down in paragraph 7 of the Juvenile Courts Law, but it could also be ordered as part of a punishment, in conjunction with a suspended prison sentence.

As far as procedural law was concerned, the Juvenile Courts Law codified what was already common practice in many areas of Germany. It laid down in its Section 2 how juvenile courts were to be organized, specifying that juvenile courts were to be courts with lay assessors (Schöffengerichte). In normal cases one judge was to preside with two lay assessors (one of whom could be a woman), but in cases of more severe offences an enlarged juvenile court (Großes Jugendgericht) was to be convened, consisting of two judges and three lay assessors (paragraphs 17 and 18). Where a juvenile was to be tried before the larger court, he or she was to have a defence counsel; otherwise, a juvenile was to have a defence lawyer acting on his or her behalf only in exceptional cases (paragraph 29).

Juvenile court judges welcomed the new powers given to them by the law. In a letter sent to a youth welfare journal in October 1923, a Hamburg juvenile court judge wrote:

> In general, we find the new Juvenile Courts Law to be a great step forward in criminal and juvenile justice. We judges now have freedom; gone is the inhibiting and sometimes even humiliating feeling of not having the legal basis to deal as a judge in a humane and sensible way with acts committed

---

[102] P. Riebesell, 'Erziehungsgericht und Erziehungsbehörde', ZBl 12/15–16 (1920/1), 157–8; Francke, Denkschrift zum Paragraphen 4 des JGG. StAH, JB I, 487, vol. 1.

by young people which have often stemmed from the current harsh conditions.[103]

Not all youth welfare experts were as happy with the new law as the judges, however: debates surrounding the juvenile court system continued into the later years of the Weimar Republic. Meanwhile, juvenile courts all over the Reich set about the task of translating the precept 'education instead of punishment' into practice.[104]

The Professionalization of Youth Welfare Work

Discussions on youth welfare reform constantly revolved round the need for more and better-trained paid staff. At the National Conference on Youth Welfare in September 1918, one speaker called for the professionalization of youth welfare work on the grounds that the expansion of welfare work during the war had highlighted the shortcomings of volunteer workers, whose enthusiasm did not make up for their inexperience, lack of training, and unreliability.[105] In 1921, a similar call was made by a prominent advocate of professional welfare work, Marie Baum, who warned against basing decisions on a young person's education and welfare on untrained investigators' reports.[106]

The growing concern about the expertise of youth welfare workers was fuelled by the legislation of the early 1920s. The precepts of individual treatment, education rather than punishment, and of prevention rather than cure, required for their realization a growing number of social workers employed 'at the front' to carry out the work of data-gathering and 'diagnosis' on the one hand and supervision on the other.

The fact that an ever-growing number of young people were to be subjected to scrutiny and surveillance meant an increase in the number of personnel needed to carry out these tasks on behalf of

---

[103] Otto von Bargen an das Zentralblatt für Vormundschaftswesen, Jugendgerichte und Fürsorgeerziehung, 13 Oct. 1923. StAH, JB I, 487, vol. 2.

[104] The further development of the juvenile justice debate and the practice of the juvenile courts in the years following the Juvenile Courts Law are examined in Ch. 6.

[105] Pfarrer Heim, Lennep, in Deutscher Verein (ed.), *Jugendämter als Träger der öffentlichen Jugendfürsorge*, 92.

[106] Marie Baum, 'Wohlfahrtspflege als Familienfürsorge', *Blätter für Wohlfahrtspflege, Sachsen*, 1/1 (1921), 2–16, 3.

New Approaches to the Problem Adolescent 181

the public authorities. One solution to this problem was to use the services of volunteers, and a major issue regarding the organization of the home visits by the juvenile courts and youth welfare services was how far and in what capacity to deploy such unpaid amateur personnel. There were two main kinds of volunteer: on the one hand members of private welfare organizations and on the other unpaid honorary officials nominated by the public authorities to carry out home visits and inspections. In the years before the First World War, some juvenile courts—such as that in Berlin—delegated to private welfare agencies the entire responsibility for assistance to the juvenile court (Jugendgerichtshilfe), which entailed preparing reports on the accused and carrying out probation orders. In Hamburg, by contrast, the public youth welfare authorities were responsible for juvenile court assistance, but they in turn relied on citizens appointed by the city-state authorities as honorary child welfare officials (*Waisenpfleger*).[107]

The National Youth Welfare Law and the Juvenile Courts Law laid down no binding provisions regarding how and by whom the tasks of investigation and supervision were to be undertaken. This meant that the public authorities at local level were still allowed a considerable degree of freedom as to how they organized their investigators and social workers 'in the field'. Although the National Youth Welfare Law allowed public youth welfare authorities to delegate certain tasks wholesale to private welfare organizations, such an arrangement remained an exception. Instead, 'mixed' forms of paid and unpaid personnel became prevalent. During the Weimar period, the back-up services in youth welfare were, as a rule, run by paid public officials who supervised and coordinated the division of labour in home visiting between paid social workers and honorary officials.[108]

The continuing reliance on unpaid personnel did not necessarily reflect a deliberate policy on the part of youth welfare authorities. The problem was partly a continuing lack of specialized and trained personnel. This was despite a relatively rapid increase in the supply of trained social workers. Since the late nineteenth century, growing numbers of middle-class women had been seeking paid and unpaid

---

[107] Wilhelm Ramcke, 'Die Jugendstrafgerichtsbarkeit in Hamburg während der Zeit 1909–1923', Diss. jur. (Hamburg, 1959), 109.
[108] *Verwaltungsbericht der Stadt Berlin für die Zeit 1924–1928*, 12 (Berlin, 1930), 27; Landesjugendamt und Jugendamt Hamburg, *Jahresbericht 1925*, 16.

work in social welfare as a more worthwhile occupation than leading a merely decorative existence or at most indulging in a dilettante fashion in 'good works'. For feminists such as Alice Salomon, social work was a task for which women, if properly instructed, were by virtue of their nature—their 'maternal instinct'—particularly suited. In the decade before the First World War, social work training colleges for women were beginning to be set up.[109] The expansion of state welfare and voluntary welfare activity in the First World War drew both middle-class women and Social Democratic women into war work, which ranged from serving in soup kitchens to supervising the female labour force in munitions factories.[110] In the Weimar period, social work remained overall the preserve of middle-class women. However, the labour movement and the youth movement were additional sources of new recruits to the profession, and men as well as women began to train for social work. The increased demand for social work training led to a diversification of training provision: by the early 1930s, there were half a dozen training schools for men and a school run by the Arbeiterwohlfahrt as well as the more traditional social work schools for women.[111] Male trainees were particularly attracted by youth work: 60 per cent of the male social work graduates in Prussia between 1929 and 1932 specialized in youth welfare.[112] Meanwhile, the state authorities began to regulate social work training and qualifications.[113]

The supply of trained personnel available was thus growing. However, the extent to which professional social workers were appointed to posts in the growing administrative apparatus and in the home visiting service (*Außendienst*) of youth welfare and juvenile justice depended on the attitudes of administrators and the resources available at local level.

[109] On the development of social work training for women in Germany, see Sachße, *Mütterlichkeit*, 116–73; Zeller, *Volksmütter*, 65–7; Rüdeger Baron and Rolf Landwehr, 'Von der Berufung zum Beruf: Zur Entwicklung der Ausbildung für die soziale Arbeit', in Baron (ed.), *Sozialarbeit und Soziale Reform* (Weinheim and Basle, 1983), 1–36; C. Wolfgang Müller, *Wie Helfen zum Beruf wurde: Eine Methodengeschichte der Sozialarbeit* (Weinheim and Basle, 1981), 135–44; Young Sun Hong, 'Femininity as a Vocation: Gender and Class Conflict in the Professionalization of German Social Work', in Konrad Jarausch and Geoffrey Cocks (eds.), *German Professions 1800–1950* (Oxford, 1990).
[110] Sachße, *Mütterlichkeit*, 156–83.
[111] Zeller, *Volksmütter*, 73–9, 90–91.
[112] Ibid. 91.
[113] Baron and Landwehr, 'Von der Berufung zum Beruf', 18–21; Sachße, *Mütterlichkeit*, 250–7; Zeller, *Volksmütter*, 68–71.

In Hamburg, the youth welfare authorities had, from about 1914 onwards, pushed for the deployment of trained professional social workers both in office work and 'in the field'. In the Weimar period, the youth welfare department's goal was to use only qualified professionals for all work involving major intervention and decision-making, restricting the use of volunteers to 'lighter tasks'. In line with this policy, the full-time salaried staff of the youth welfare department engaged on home visits was expanded considerably after the First World War. In 1913 only twenty paid staff had been engaged on home visits; by 1926, this had grown to seventy-six.[114] A number of the new appointments were qualified social workers with a youth movement background, some of whom became involved in the Gilde Soziale Arbeit and sought to bring their youth movement ideals and newly-acquired social work techniques to bear on their casework.[115] Meanwhile, although the number of voluntary honorary officials increased from 1,492 in 1913 to 1,855 in 1925, each was given fewer cases to deal with than before the war.[116] However, financial constraints meant that the use of volunteers continued to a greater extent than the department wished. Hertz, for instance, sought to use only paid officials for juvenile court work. He managed to override the opposition of the honorary officials to this move, but he was forced to retreat in face of the financial cutbacks during and after the hyperinflation of 1923, with the result that the task was partially restored to the honorary officials.[117]

Given that the honorary officials were still an integral part of Hamburg's youth welfare apparatus, the department was conscious of the need to give the institution a more democratic aspect by recruiting the volunteers from a wider political and social spectrum than had been the case before the war. Hertz took a dim view of the way that the task had become the preserve of middle-class, middle-aged men (of the 1,855 honorary officials in 1925, only 354 were women) and that the honorary officials in some districts of Hamburg recruited from among their own kind 'just like a bowling club'.[118] It was in an attempt to remedy this that the department

[114] Denkschrift des Präses des Jugendamts an den Senat, 28 Jan 1928, 3. StAH, JB I, 3, vol. 1.   [115] Interview with Anneliese Ubenauf, 18 Sept. 1984.
[116] Präses des Jugendamts an den Senat, 3.
[117] Waisenpfleger F. Beese to W. Hertz, 15 June 1923; W. Hertz to Waisenpfleger F. Eggers, 8 Aug. 1923. StAH, JB I, 475.
[118] Hertz, 'Zehn Jahre Hamburger Jugendamt', 21–2.

sought to recruit Arbeiterwohlfahrt volunteers as honorary officials and to delegate some of the 'lighter cases' of probation to volunteers from the youth movement.[119]

Overall, in the Reich, the process of professionalization proceeded in fits and starts. By 1928 the personnel of the 1,251 youth welfare departments had grow to 993 senior civil servants (of whom 973 were men), 4,613 other civil servants (of whom 3,073 were men), and 6,099 white-collar public employees (of whom 2,499 were men).[120] The social workers doing the work of visiting clients were in the category of public employees and were mostly women; many of the civil servants were men unqualified for specialist social welfare administration. Among the social workers, as opposed to administrators, in youth welfare departments (*Jugendfürsorger*, *Jugendfürsorgerinnen*), the women were more highly qualified: 67 per cent of the female, but only 14 per cent of the male social workers had social work training.[121] However, this did not speed the promotion of women to administrative posts, despite the exhortation in paragraph 9 of the National Youth Welfare Law that as a rule the personnel of the youth welfare departments should be adequately qualified for and experienced in youth welfare work. A prediction in 1918 that youth welfare departments would to a substantial extent be headed by women[122] was not borne out; in fact, by 1928 there were only two *Jugendamtsleiterinnen*.[123]

The problem of deploying personnel in sufficient numbers and quality continued to hamper the realization of the youth welfare reformers' plans for a smoothly functioning system for investigating, supervising, and controlling problem adolescents. While the statutorily defined tasks of youth welfare and juvenile justice expanded in scope and complexity, and while social work specialists and youth welfare reformers wrote textbooks and specialist articles outlining sophisticated and psychologically-informed methods of 'social diagnosis' and 'social therapy', the expansion and professionalization of youth welfare was in practice an uneven process.

---

[119] Herbert Bökel, 'Die Mitwirkung der Jugendbünde in der Jugendfürsorge', *JV* 3/1 (1927), 18–21.
[120] Peukert, 'Jugend als Beruf', in Deutscher Werkbund (ed.), *Schock und Schöpfung: Jugendästhetik im 20. Jahrhundert* (Darmstadt and Neuwied, 1986), 344.
[121] Zeller, *Volksmütter*, 87.
[122] Friedrich Siegmund-Schultze, in Deutscher Verein (ed.) *Jugendämter als Träger der öffentlichen Jugendfürsorge*, 166.
[123] Zeller, *Volksmütter*, 86.

What actually happened on the ground was rather more haphazard than the laws and textbooks might indicate. Nevertheless, in some of the big cities, among them Hamburg, substantial developments did take place in the post-war period. In such places, encouraged in part by the pledges in the constitution and the new national legislation on youth welfare and juvenile justice, and assisted by the growing numbers of qualified youth welfare workers, welfare experts and politicians at local level were able to build a public youth welfare apparatus along the lines demanded by the youth welfare lobby in the pre-war period. This pedagogically-inspired bureaucracy was in theory equipped to diagnose social and educational difficulties scientifically and to intervene in a timely and effective manner to prevent and cure delinquency in the young. Its educational practices in relation to juvenile offenders and juveniles 'at risk' are the focus of the following two chapters.

6
Juvenile Crime and the Practice of Juvenile Justice

A key area where the Weimar Republic's new approach to the juvenile delinquent was to be tested was the treatment of juvenile crime. Criminal offences represented the most precisely definable and quantifiable form of juvenile deviance and gave the state clear-cut grounds for intervention. Under the new, flexible system of juvenile justice embodied in the Juvenile Courts Law of 1923, such intervention was based on the assumption that a criminal offence was an expression of a defective personality and/or a deficient upbringing. In accordance with this view of juvenile crime, the juvenile courts were to seek as far as possible to scrutinize the individual personality of the offender and prescribe the appropriate mixture of educational and punitive measures.

This chapter examines, first, how juvenile crime in the Weimar Republic developed and how it was affected by the Depression. Secondly, it analyses the practice of the juvenile justice system codified in the Juvenile Courts Law of 1923, examining to what extent and in what manner the principle of 'education instead of punishment' was actually implemented, and what implications this had for the juveniles concerned.

Trends in Juvenile Crime

Any attempt to assess trends in juvenile crime—the frequency with which offences were committed, the types of offence committed, and the type of juveniles involved in criminal offences—confronts the well-known limitations of criminal statistics generally. Statistics on crime have to be read bearing in mind that they reflect the rate of reported and detected crime as opposed to actual crimes committed; the number of unreported cases can vary over time according to the zeal and efficiency of the police and the degree to which the public bothers to report crime. Other factors varying over time which affect the official crime rate are easier to pinpoint: for instance, changes in criminal law can create or abolish categories of criminal offence. Changes in the practice of the judicial administration also have to be taken into account in cases where statistics only record the number of convictions for criminal offences and omit those cases which were dropped before court proceedings took place.

The following account of developments in juvenile crime during the Weimar Republic seeks to portray trends at national and local level and to illustrate some of these trends with evidence from juvenile court records. It does not attempt to provide a full statistical analysis, which would go beyond the limits of this study. The statistics for developments in the Reich as a whole are taken, firstly, from contemporary analyses of the published national criminal statistics.[1] A second source of information on trends in the Reich as a whole are the statistics collected on a number of cities and towns by the German Juvenile Courts Association (Deutsche Vereinigung für Jugendgerichte und Jugendgerichtshilfen).[2] The Hamburg statistics used are those assembled and published by the local Juvenile Court Assistance (Jugendgerichtshilfe).[3] These statistics provide useful information on juvenile offenders and on the type of offences in Hamburg. However, they cover only the period dating from the introduction of the Juvenile Courts Law,

---

[1] 'Die Entwicklung der Kriminalität der Jugendlichen in den Jahren 1930–1933', ZBl 26/4–5 (1934), 124–8; Bruno Gleitze, *Die Konjunkturkriminalität: Eine statistische Untersuchung über die konjunkturellen und demographischen Einflüsse auf die Kriminalitätsentwicklung* (Stuttgart and Berlin, 1941).

[2] Amtsgerichtsrat van Dühren, 'Kriminalstatistik der Jugendlichen 1925 und 1926', ZGS 49 (1929), 255–90; Harald Poelchau, 'Kriminalstatistik der Jugendlichen 1927 und 1928', ZGS 51 (1931), 84–115; Elsa von Liszt, 'Die Kriminalität der Jugendlichen in Berlin in den Jahren 1928, 1929 und 1930', ZGS 52 (1932), 250–71; Heinz Jacoby, 'Der Anteil der 14- und 15jährigen an der Kriminalität der Jugendlichen 1930', ZGS 52 (1932), 35–43; id., 'Die Kriminalität der Jugendlichen in den Jahren 1930 und 1931', ZGS 55 (1935), 85–117; Justus Ehrhardt, 'Die Kriminalität der Jugendlichen in den Jahren 1932 und 1933', ZGS 55 (1935), 665–91; id., 'Die Kriminalität der Jugendlichen in den Jahren 1934 und 1935', ZGS 56 (1936), 577–691.

[3] *StJB Hamburg* (1926/27), 314–15; (1928/29), 318–19; (1929/30), 325–6; (1930/1), 309–10; (1931/2), 182–3; (1932/3), 175–6; (1933/4), 181–2. In the following, references to Hamburg juvenile crime figures are, unless otherwise stated, to these sources. Contemporary analysis of Hamburg statistics in Hans Kruse, 'Bericht der Jugendgerichtshilfe Hamburg für das Jahr 1931', *JV* 8/4 (1932), 112–19; id., 'Die Straffälligkeit der Jugend in Hamburg in den Jahren 1930–1936', *Monatsschrift für Kriminalbiologie und Strafrechtsreform*, 26/11 (1937), 497–516.

and, where some categories of detailed information are concerned, only the period from 1928 onwards. Because of this, and also because the local juvenile court records available cover only the years from 1926 onwards, the following account focuses on the second half of the Weimar period. By this time, the new juvenile justice system codified in the 1923 law was well established, and its workings in practice can be well observed.

The Reich statistics on criminality rates record the number of convictions for offences against Reich laws ('wegen Verbrechen und Vergehen gegen Reichsgesetze ausgesprochene rechtskräftige Verurteilungen') per 100,000 resident population above the minimum age of criminal responsibility. In the first half of the Weimar Republic, the rise in the general crime rate in the immediate postwar years came to an end once the currency had been stabilized at the end of 1923, and the criminality rate remained fairly stable between 1925 and 1927.[4] A comparison between trends in crime generally and trends in juvenile crime over this period must take into account the fact that the age of criminal responsibility was raised from 12 to 14 years under the Juvenile Courts Law of 1923, thereby reducing the absolute number of crimes committed by juveniles appearing in the statistics. However, this change did not affect the juvenile criminality rate, since this was a ratio of convictions measured against the resident population in the age group defined as 'juvenile'. More important for the juvenile criminality rate was the practice, made possible under the 1923 legislation, of dropping cases against juveniles before and during formal court proceedings, which reduced the number of juveniles convicted. The drop in juvenile criminality rates after 1923 therefore reflected at least in part the changing practice of the judicial administration. However, there was general agreement that juvenile crime really did fall after the stabilization of the currency in 1923.[5]

In Hamburg during this period, a similar trend to that in the Reich as a whole could be observed. The number of juveniles convicted fell in the post-war years from the very high levels of wartime: in 1917, 1,568 juveniles between the ages of 12 and 18 were sentenced by the Hamburg juvenile court compared with 775 in 1913. In 1919, 953 juveniles were convicted by the Hamburg

---

[4] *Statistitches Jahrbuch für das Deutsche Reich 1936*, 557; Gleitze, *Die Konjunkturkriminalität*, 2.   [5] Von Liszt, 'Kriminalität', 251.

juvenile court—fewer than in wartime, but still well above 1913 levels.⁶ The number of juveniles sentenced in Hamburg in 1924 still remained at the high level of 708, which reflected the aftermath of the 'crime wave' of 1923. The combined effects of a fall in juvenile crime and of changes in the practice of juvenile justice under the Juvenile Courts Law were only fully evident in 1925, when the number of juveniles convicted of criminal offences in Hamburg fell to 461. A comparison between the juvenile criminality rate in 1925 for the Reich as a whole and for Hamburg shows a higher rate for Hamburg: 642.7 as opposed to 469 in the Reich as a whole.⁷ This rate in the Reich as a whole was markedly below the maximum rate of 1,137 in 1920; comparable figures for Hamburg before 1925 are not available. In 1925 and 1926, the juvenile criminality rate remained, like the criminality rate for the population as a whole, fairly stable.⁸

In the second half of the Weimar period, the overall criminality rate for the population as a whole showed a perhaps surprising downward trend. The total number of criminal convictions did not rise during the Depression, and the overall criminality rate declined from 1,249 in 1927 to 1,187 in 1930 and 1,125 in 1933. Juvenile criminality rates in this period were consistently lower than those for the adult population over 18. This may have reflected the different judicial practice towards the under-18s (the 'legality principle' was applied more strictly to the over-18s)⁹, but according to contemporary commentators crime rates really were higher in the over-18 age group, particularly in the 18–30 age group.¹⁰ However, whereas the overall criminality rate did not rise in the Depression, the juvenile criminality rate did, rising from 469 in 1927 to 566 in 1930, and reaching a peak of 623 in 1932.¹¹ This rise in the juvenile criminality rate was not reflected in the absolute figures for juvenile crime: in fact, there was an absolute fall in the number of juveniles convicted. The latter, however, merely reflected demographic developments which brought a drop in the size of the 14–18-year-old population in the years from 1929 to 1933.

⁶ Oberinspektor Haubenreißer, 'Aus dem Jugendgericht', *Blätter für die hamburgische öffentliche Jugendfürsorge* 18/3 (1919), 17 and 19/3–4 (1920), 15.
⁷ Kruse, 'Straffälligkeit'; *StJB Dt.Reich 1936*, 557.
⁸ Van Dühren, 'Kriminalstatistik', 258–9.
⁹ On the 'legality principle', see Ch. 5, p. 178.
¹⁰ Gleitze, *Die Konjunkturkriminalität*, 14.
¹¹ *StJB Dt.Reich 1936*, 557.

A similar development with respect to juvenile crime took place in Hamburg in the Depression. However, the Hamburg statistics—in contrast to the national criminal statistics—take account of the number of juveniles accused (*Beschuldigte*) as well as the number convicted (*Verurteilte*) and reveal that the number of juveniles accused of an offence rose during the Depression in Hamburg despite the fall in the absolute size of the juvenile resident population. The number of juveniles accused of offences in Hamburg rose from 449 in 1928 to 625 in 1929, 711 in 1930, 732 in 1931, and 989 in 1932, falling again in 1933 to 658. However, the number of juveniles convicted did not rise correspondingly, but instead remained more or less stable (344 in 1928, 400 in 1930, 384 in 1932, 290 in 1933): this meant that proceedings were terminated before a verdict in an ever-larger proportion of juvenile cases. Comparing the juvenile criminality rate in the Depression for Hamburg with that for the Reich as a whole, it emerges that the Hamburg rate remained at a higher level: 757 in 1932 (the national juvenile criminality rate was 623) and increased further in 1933 to 903.[12]

Statistics for the Reich as a whole and for Hamburg can be used to examine trends concerning the types of offence committed by juveniles as opposed to adults and whether these changed over time. Contemporary commentators on trends in crime tended to divide offences into three categories: firstly, offences against the state and against public order; secondly, offences against the person; thirdly, offences against property.

The first category—offences against the state and against public order—included breaches of the peace, resisting arrest, rioting, etc., as well as traffic offences. Figures on these offences overall show that adults were more likely to commit offences in this category than juveniles. In the Reich as a whole in 1928, 34.8 per cent of offences committed by convicted males of all ages were in this category, but only 19 per cent of offences committed by convicted 16–18-year-old boys.[13] In Hamburg, statistics from 1928 onwards enable a breakdown of this category into the numbers of juveniles involved in individual offences. These figures show that, while the number of youngsters accused of traffic offences remained at the

[12] Statistics on resident population in age group from 'Der Altersaufbau der Wohnbevölkerung in der Stadt Hamburg', *Aus Hamburgs Verwaltung und Wirtschaft* 11/4 (1934), 93.   [13] Gleitze, *Die Konjunkturkriminalität*, 55.

same level between 1928 and 1933, the number of juveniles accused of other offences against public order (which were often related to political disturbances) was on the increase—offences like trespass (*Hausfriedensbruch*), obstructing the police (*Widerstand*) and causing a riot (*Aufruhr*). Taking all the offences in this category, the number of juveniles in Hamburg who were accused of offences against the state and public order increased both in absolute terms and in terms of a proportion of the total number of juveniles accused: in 1929, only 2.2 per cent were accused of an offence in this category, compared with 11 per cent in 1932.

The rising number of cases in the juvenile court where young people were involved in clashes with the state authorities reflected the increase of political tensions and of open political conflict during this period. Such clashes came about, for instance, as a result of young people participating in demonstrations involving violent conflicts with the police, or resisting arrest, either after demonstrations or during violent incidents on the streets. One example of a juvenile charged with such an offence was the case of Heinrich J., who appeared before the Hamburg juvenile court in September 1930 on a charge of causing a riot: he was convicted of taking part in a Communist demonstration in January 1930 which led to clashes with police.[14]

The great majority of juveniles charged with offences involving clashes with the state authorities were boys, but girls were involved as well. In September 1931, Dora V. (born 1913) appeared in the Hamburg juvenile court on charges of obstructing the police and insulting an officer (*Widerstand* and *Beamtenbeleidigung*). The charges concerned an incident in August 1931, when a large crowd of the unemployed gathered in front of the employment office in the harbour district: Dora V., who was a factory worker and had been a member of the KPD since she was 16, was one of those arrested for refusing to obey police orders to disperse.[15]

The increase in juvenile court cases involving offences against the state and against public order did not only reflect the real increase in political tension and conflicts in these years: it also reflected the fact that new categories of behaviour had been criminalized. A series of emergency decrees passed by the governments of Brüning and Papen banned various categories of demonstrations and tightened

[14] Jugendgerichtsakte des Landgerichts Hamburg (in the following, LGH) A2469/1931.   [15] LGH A1769/1932.

up other laws relating to public order in order to prohibit the possession of offensive weapons and to outlaw behaviour tending to incite violence.[16] As a result, offences against emergency decrees accounted for much of the increase in the number of juveniles accused of public order offences. One example of a juvenile charged with contravening an emergency decree was Herbert S. (born 1913), who was tried in August 1931 for an offence against the emergency decree of 28 March 1931 banning the distribution of leaflets advertising unofficial demonstrations. Herbert S. had distributed leaflets in May 1931 advertising a banned demonstration on Hamburg's main square, the Rathausmarkt.[17]

'Political' offences committed by juveniles were not restricted to the category of offences against the state and public order. The high political mobilization among young people during the final years of the Republic led to an increase in the number of cases involving incidents in which members of one political grouping threatened and physically attacked members of an opposing group. Many cases of politically motivated crime therefore came under the category of offences against the person, which was the second category of offences recorded in the criminal statistics. The statistics did not isolate 'political crime' as a distinct group of offences: the category of offences against the person covered a wide range of offences. Offences against the person included sexual offences (child molesting, indecency, homosexual offences, etc.) as well as offences involving insulting, intimidating, or threatening behaviour, assault, manslaughter, and murder. According to the 1928 figures for the Reich, 14–18-year-olds were less likely than the population as a whole to commit offences in this category. Of offences committed by convicted males of all ages, 22.4 per cent were offences against

---

[16] e.g. Gesetz zum Schutz der Republik, 25 Mar. 1930, *RGBl* 1930, i. 91–3; Gesetz gegen Waffenmißbrauch, 28 Mar. 1931, *RGBl* 1931, i. 77; Verordnung des Reichspräsidenten zur Bekämpfung politischer Ausschreitungen, 28 Mar. 1931, *RGBl* 1931, i. 79–81; Zweite Verordnung des Reichspräsidenten zur Bekämpfung politischer Ausschreitungen, 18 July 1931, *RGBl* 1931, i. 373; Dritte Verordnung des Reichspräsidenten zur Sicherung von Wirtschaft und Finanzen und zur Bekämpfung politischer Ausschreitungen, 6 Oct. 1931, *RGBl* 1931, i. 537–68; Verordnung des Reichspräsidenten zum Schutze des inneren Friedens, 17 Mar. 1932, *RGBl* 1932, i. 133; Verordnung des Reichspräsidenten zur Sicherung der Staatsautorität, 13 Apr. 1932, *RGBl* 1932, i. 175; Zweite Verordnung des Reichspräsidenten zur Sicherung der Staatsautorität, 3 May 1932, *RGBl* 1932, i. 185; Verordnung des Reichspräsidenten gegen politischen Terror, 9 Aug. 1932, *RGBl* 1932, i. 403–4; Verordnung des Reichspräsidenten zur Sicherung des inneren Friedens, 2 Nov. 1932, *RGBl* 1932, i. 517.   [17] LGH A1132/1932.

the person, but only 18.3 per cent of offences committed by convicted 16–18-year-old boys were in this category.[18] Serious offences against the person such as manslaughter and murder were rarely committed by juveniles, but they were on the increase in the years before 1933.[19]

Despite the difficulty of isolating 'political' offences, an increase in that group of offences which could be linked to political motives could be interpreted as indicating that the crisis of the final years of the Republic produced a rise in political crime among juveniles. The offences of 'coercion' (*Nötigung*) and threatening behaviour (*Bedrohung*) were reported to be on the increase among juveniles during the Depression.[20] These were offences which were often politically motivated. A similar development can be traced in Hamburg over the same period: the number of juveniles accused of coercion and assault (*Körperverletzung*) showed a clear increase in absolute and relative terms over the period 1928–32. Juveniles accused of these two offences made up just under 9.5 per cent of all juveniles accused in Hamburg in 1932 compared with 4.2 per cent in 1928.

Occasionally juveniles were involved in a premeditated political crime, such as the attack by two members of the radical right-wing organization 'Werwolf' on a lawyer known for his newspaper commentaries on the Altona 'bomb trials' (following the bombing campaigns in Schleswig-Holstein). Kurt J. and Walter P. (both born in 1913) were convicted in October 1930 of firing a pistol filled with tear gas at the lawyer in the hallway of his apartment block, and injuring him.[21] More often, political violence was more spontaneous. A fairly typical case with a political motive, which involved not only offences against the person but also criminal damage and obstructing the police, came before the Hamburg juvenile court on 1 February 1933. A Nazi youth, Karl S. (born 1915), an unemployed former delivery boy, was convicted of breaking the window of a Communist pub, threatening a police officer, and resisting arrest, and, in another incident, with threatening a Communist acquaintance in the street. The incidents took place in December 1932 and January 1933.[22] Girls were also occasionally involved in physical attacks on political opponents. Alice S. (born 1912), a member of

[18] Gleitze, *Die Konjunkturkriminalität*, 21.
[19] Jacoby, 'Kriminalität', 109.
[20] Gleitze, *Die Konjunkturkriminalität*, 78.
[21] LGH A913/1933.
[22] LGH A160/1934.

the Communist youth organization, appeared in court in August 1930 on assault charges arising out of an incident at a syndicalist youth meeting in February 1930. In the course of this meeting she had assaulted—apparently out of political motives—another girl, who was an ex-member of the Communist youth.[23]

Political violence may often have been spontaneous, but it often took place according to certain recurrent patterns. Rituals of threat and intimidation developed: a growing practice between rival political youth groups in these years was the use of force to induce political opponents to remove their political badges or insignia.[24] In August 1930, Helmut K. (born 1914), was tried for taking part in an ambush on a right-wing youth group, the Blücherbund Deutscher Jugend. Helmut K., who was a member of the Communist youth, was out on a trip to the countryside with members of the *Falkenberger*, a Hamburg youth gang that adopted some of the pursuits and paraphernalia, if not the values, of the German youth movement. In the course of their hike his group set upon a group from the Blücherbund and forced them to hand over their military-style belts.[25] The Hamburg court records make it appear that it was young Nazis who were predominantly the victims of this kind of political intimidation; however, the records may reflect a greater readiness on the part of Nazis to pursue their opponents, both from the SPD youth organization and from the Communist youth, in the courts.

The eruption of political conflicts into daily life may have served to increase not only the number of crimes committed, but also the readiness to blow up a trivial incident into a case leading to criminal proceedings. Even if the state prosecutor's office endeavoured to keep minor quarrels between neighbours out of the juvenile court, some of these cases did reach the court, such as the case of 17-year-old Helmut F., who was convicted of assault in December 1932 for beating up a 13-year-old neighbour. On 20 July 1932, the day of Papen's coup against the Prussian government, the younger boy had been playing on the street; his taunt that 'the arrows were already crooked', referring to the emblem of the Eiserne Front,[26]

---

[23] LGH A1574/1930.
[24] E. Rosenhaft, *Beating the Fascists?* (Cambridge, 1983), 132–3.
[25] LGH A5172/1933.
[26] The Eiserne Front was the Social Democratic anti-fascist organization founded in December 1931 by the Reichsbanner, the Free Trade Unions, the SPD, the AfA-

provoked a quarrel which ended with Helmut F. assaulting the younger boy.[27]

Not all assaults had a political motive, even in such highly-charged times. A number of cases of assault tried by the Hamburg juvenile courts during these years occurred in the course of drunken brawls in taverns or dance-halls, or, occasionally, in punch-ups initiated by gangs with passers-by as the victims. A case heard in January 1930 involved three youths alleged to be former members of the gang 'The Rats of Rothenburgsort' (Rothenburgsort was a rough working-class district of Hamburg), who were convicted of taking part in a gang attack on a passer-by.[28]

Sexual offences constituted a fairly small group within the category of offences committed by juveniles against the person. Between 1928 and 1932, the number of juveniles accused of sexual offences as a proportion of total juveniles accused in Hamburg remained at a level of between 2 and 4 per cent. The two most common groups of sexual offences were, firstly, offences under paragraph 176 section 3 of the Criminal Code, which usually involved adolescent boys abusing small girls, and, secondly, of male homosexual offences under paragraph 175. Boys who were homeless and without money—many of them reformatory inmates on the run—sometimes resorted to prostitution as a way to get a roof over their heads and some quick money. Johann B. (born 1911), who appeared in court in October 1927 on charges under paragraph 175, described how he was desperate for money and how his friend had given him a tip: 'K. told me that in St. Pauli you can get money for sex with men' and how as a result he had earned 5 marks.[29]

Most juvenile crime fell into the third category of offences, crime against property. This included offences such as theft (*Diebstahl*), burglary (*schwerer Diebstahl*), robbery (*Raub*), embezzlement (*Unterschlagung*) and fraud (*Betrug*). Whereas 42.7 per cent of males of all ages and 43.1 per cent of females of all ages convicted of offences in 1928 were convicted of crimes against property, the corresponding rate for juveniles was much higher. In 1928, between two-thirds and four-fifths of all convicted juveniles had committed

Bund, and the Social Democratic sports organizations. Its emblem was three arrows. See H. Winkler, *Weg in die Katastrophe* (Berlin and Bonn, 1987), 514–16.

[27] LGH A1891/1933.   [28] LGH A125/1934.
[29] LGH A1745/1930.

offences against property, the predominance of property crime being particularly marked where girls were concerned. The convictions of 77 per cent of the boys and 83 per cent of the girls aged 14–16, and 63 per cent of the boys and 71 per cent of the girls aged 16–18, were for property offences.[30]

The predominant form of crime against property committed by juveniles was theft. One very commonly-occurring theft in this period was bicycle theft: dozens of cases of bicycle theft came before the Hamburg juvenile courts in the years for which the records are extant. The sale of a stolen bicycle could bring in a considerable sum in cash. A bicycle was also a means of a quick getaway: for instance, youngsters seeking to escape from their hated employment as farm hands in the depths of rural Mecklenburg would make off back to Hamburg on a stolen bicycle. Others wanting to escape Hamburg in the Depression in search of employment had to steal a bicycle first. Car theft by juveniles was still comparatively rare in Hamburg, but, with the increase in the number of cars on the roads, it was also on the increase.[31]

Theft was the most common offence committed by juveniles of both sexes, though in absolute numbers the boys accused of theft always outnumbered the girls by about 5 to 1. Among the typical thefts committed by girls were thefts from department stores, which tended to offer the greatest opportunities for shoplifting, and, above all, theft from employers, particularly by girls employed as domestic servants.

The phenomenon of gangs of juvenile thieves at work gave rise to some alarm among youth welfare experts in the late 1920s.[32] The concern about criminal youth gangs was part of a more general concern about youth gangs in the big cities in the final years of the Weimar Republic.[33] In Hamburg, the gang 'The Wild Boys' (*Die tollen Jungen*) was rumoured to be a criminal gang. Wilhelm P., a gang member, was tried in Hamburg in September 1928 for burglary. According to the report prepared by the Juvenile Court Assistance, Wilhelm P.

[30] Gleitze, *Die Konjunkturkriminalität*, 21.
[31] Kruse, 'Straffälligkeit', 508, 510; von Liszt, 'Kriminalität', 258.
[32] Curt Bondy, 'Die jugendliche Verbrecherbande als psychologisches und sozialpädagogisches Problem', *Erziehung*, 1 (1926), 146–59; Justus Ehrhardt, 'Cliquenwesen und Jugendverwahrlosung', *ZBl* 21/12 (1929/30), 413–18.
[33] Rosenhaft, 'Die wilden Cliquen', in Deutscher Werkbund (ed.), *Schock und Schöpfung* (Darmstadt and Neuwied, 1986), 345–9.

belongs to the club 'The Wild Boys' where he sees and hears nothing but bad things; what goes on in the club is nothing but thefts and pranks . . . The club consists of groups of youths which have been forming recently in all the districts; they adorn themselves with coloured school caps and with trousers and waistcoats covered with pearl buttons.[34]

Forms of property crime other than theft, such as fraud and embezzlement, were less prevalent in the juvenile age groups than among the adult population. This could be explained by the fact that the access to financial resources which was required in order to commit such offences was more common among older age groups than among juveniles.[35] Nevertheless, the number of juveniles in Hamburg who were accused of embezzlement constituted 14 per cent of the total juveniles accused in 1928, a proportion which fell during the Depression for reasons discussed below.

The fact that juvenile crime was to such a large extent property crime, and that it took above all the form of theft, had implications for the rise in the overall juvenile criminality rate in the Depression. Theft was one of the offences most clearly related to economic conditions: taking the population as a whole, the number of thefts per 100,000 population rose sharply in the Depression.[36] This could lead one to expect that a rise in the juvenile criminality rate in periods of economic crisis would be due to an increase in juvenile crimes against property, and in particular to an increase in thefts. Statistics on the Reich as a whole present a slightly contradictory picture: the number of thefts per 100,000 population committed by boys under 18 increased in the years 1930–2 compared with 1928–9, but the equivalent rate for girls decreased.[37] The incidence of the more serious forms of theft committed by juveniles (burglary and robbery) increased in the years before 1933.[38]

In Hamburg, the absolute number of juveniles accused of theft and burglary increased between 1928 and 1932, though not by a spectacular amount. The number of cases of embezzlement fell: juveniles accused of embezzlement made up 14 per cent of the total accused in 1928, but only 3.7 per cent in 1932. This development was paralleled by the development in the Reich as a whole.[39] It can be accounted for by a decline due to unemployment in the

[34] LGH A152/1934.   [35] Gleitze, *Die Konjunkturkriminalität*, 26.
[36] Ibid. 59–61.   [37] Ibid. 74, 82.
[38] 'Kriminalität der Jugendlichen in den Jahren 1930–1933', 127.
[39] Gleitze, *Die Konjunkturkriminalität*, 80.

opportunities available for embezzlement: this was an offence typically committed by a juvenile at the expense of his or her employer. However, the decline could also be accounted for by a possible change in attitudes among those still employed; in the Depression, juveniles in work may have been more hesitant to commit such an offence and risk losing their jobs over it.

Although the number of juveniles accused of the three most common forms of property crime—theft, burglary, and embezzlement—rose in absolute terms between 1928 and 1932, the proportion of the total juveniles accused in Hamburg who were alleged to have committed property crimes was falling. In 1928, 70 per cent of all accusations against juveniles in Hamburg were for one of these property offences, but by 1932 this proportion had declined to 43 per cent. There was thus a paradox: in the Depression in Hamburg property crime was on the increase in absolute terms, as was juvenile criminality generally, but there was at the same time a shift away from the traditional domination of juvenile crime by property crime. Juvenile crime tended to become more diversified in the years 1928–32, and the rise in juvenile crime in the Depression was only partly due to a rise in juvenile property crime.

The statistics on juvenile crime in the Reich as a whole and in Hamburg also shed some light on various categories of juvenile offender. The first and most obvious fact about juvenile offenders in the courts was that they had nearly all left school and were economically active. In the Reich as a whole in 1925, 86.9 per cent of convicted juveniles were listed as having an occupation; only 4.3 per cent were listed as being full-time school pupils.[40] In Berlin between 1927 and 1930 the proportion of convicted juveniles who were in full-time schooling fluctuated around 4 per cent, while the rest were listed under different occupations.[41] In Hamburg, 8.3 per cent of accused juveniles in 1930 were full-time school pupils; 6 per cent were 'without occupation', the rest were listed according to categories of job.[42]

Secondly, with regard to the ratio of boys to girls, a trend was noticeable both at Reich level and in Hamburg towards an increasing predominance of boys among juvenile offenders. In the Reich in 1925 15.2 per cent of convicted juvenile offenders were

[40] Van Dühren, 'Kriminalstatistik der Jugendlichen 1925 und 1926', 267.
[41] Von Liszt, 'Die Kriminalität der Jugendlichen in Berlin', 255.
[42] Kruse, 'Straffälligkeit', 507.

girls, but only 12.5 per cent in 1932.⁴³ The trend over the same period was even more marked in Hamburg, where girls made up 18 per cent of total juveniles accused in 1925, but only 9.6 per cent in 1932. This shift can be explained at least in part by the tendency mentioned above for juvenile crime to diversify in the years of the Depression. The categories of offences against the person and against the state and public order were even more 'male-dominated' than property crime. This meant that an increase in crimes other than property crime as a proportion of total juvenile crime tended to mean a further increase in the proportion of boys at the expense of the proportion of girls involved in juvenile crime.

In view of the attention paid to the rate of reoffending by juveniles in the debates preceding the introduction of the juvenile courts, statistics on the proportion of juveniles convicted who had received punishments for previous convictions (*vorbestraft*) were of interest to commentators in the 1920s. The first thing which emerges from statistics both for the Reich as a whole and for Hamburg is that the proportion of convicted juveniles who had been punished for previous convictions fell markedly after the introduction of the Juvenile Courts Law. In the Reich as a whole, the proportion of convicted juveniles with previous convictions and punishments fell from 16.7 per cent in 1924 to 10.6 per cent in 1926; in Hamburg, the proportion fell from 43.7 per cent in 1924 to 18.2 per cent in 1926.⁴⁴ This development was only to be expected: under the Juvenile Courts Law, fewer punishments were meted out now that 'educational' measures could be applied as an alternative, resulting in fewer juveniles being punished in the first place. However, the downward trend did not continue after the first 2–3 years after the implementation of the Juvenile Courts Law. In the Reich as a whole, the proportion of convicted juveniles who had been punished for earlier offences rose gradually after 1927, reaching 14.1 per cent in 1932; in Hamburg the rate fluctuated, reaching a peak of 24.7 per cent in 1930 before falling to 15.9 per cent in 1932. The fact that this proportion failed to decline further could be explained in more than one way. On the one hand, it could reflect a growing tendency to drop proceedings against juveniles without previous criminal convictions before they reached court.

[43] *StJB Dt.Reich 1936*, 557.
[44] Hubert Matthias, 'Die Praxis der Jugendgerichte 1924–1933 an Hand der Reichskriminalstatistik', Diss. jur. (Köln, 1937), 52–3; Hamburg JGH statistics.

On the other hand, a commentator on the statistics collected by the German Juvenile Courts Association took a gloomier view; he considered that a rising proportion of juveniles coming to court with previous convictions reflected an increase in the number of 'hardened' juvenile criminals in the Depression, and the breakdown of efforts to educate and reintegrate them.[45]

Occupational patterns were of great interest to contemporary observers of juvenile crime. They sought in juvenile crime statistics confirmation of the assumption that an apprenticeship, and the stability of employment that generally went with it, had a 'character-building' effect on working-class adolescents in the key years after they left school. In 1919, it was reported that six out of seven juvenile male offenders in Hamburg were unskilled.[46] This, however, may have reflected a particularly high percentage of juvenile unskilled labour as a proportion of the total juvenile workforce in 1919–20. From the mid-1920s on, both at national level and in Hamburg, a fairly consistent pattern could be observed: in the larger cities with populations of 200,000 and above, about one third of juvenile offenders of both sexes were apprentices, while apprentices formed between half and three-quarters of the workforce aged 14–18.[47] In Hamburg in 1930, 30 per cent of the juveniles accused were apprentices; in 1931, 33 per cent. Figures showing apprentices to represent the majority of the juvenile workforce but only a third of juvenile offenders in the larger cities confirmed the common assumption that the unskilled juvenile was disproportionately involved in juvenile crime compared to the apprentice. It was, of course, another matter altogether to explain this fact in terms of the character-building effect of the apprenticeship. It was possible to argue, for instance, that the poverty which might drive young people into unskilled work might also drive them to steal. However, this interpretation did not fit so neatly into the prescriptions of those politicians and educationalists who saw regular skilled work in itself as the panacea for all social ills involving working-class adolescents.

By the late 1920s, considerations regarding the links between unskilled work and juvenile crime were being overshadowed by the problem of young people who were without work of any kind. The

---

[45] Jacoby, 'Kriminalität', 105.
[46] JGH Hamburg 1919, quoted in Kruse, 'Bericht 1931', 115.
[47] Van Dühren, 'Kriminalstatistik', 267–9; Jacoby, 'Kriminalität', 100.

link between youth unemployment and juvenile crime was a problem which became evident even before the Depression: statistics were being gathered on the proportion of young offenders who were without work as early as 1925.[48] The survey of juvenile crime statistics for cities with a population of 200,000 and above carried out by the German Juvenile Courts Association showed that the unemployed as a proportion of the total number of juveniles accused of criminal offences rose from 9.4 per cent in 1927 to 11.7 per cent in 1928, to 20.7 per cent in 1930, 27.2 per cent in 1931, 36.6 per cent in 1932, and 31.2 per cent in 1933.[49]

The lack of detailed youth unemployment statistics makes it difficult to assess the full significance of these figures on juvenile crime. They can at most be compared with the figures for June 1933, when in the Reich as a whole 8.2 per cent of the economically active population aged between 14 and 18 were unemployed.[50] Even if this figure represents an underestimate of juvenile unemployment in the preceding period, it would still appear that the juvenile unemployed were disproportionately represented among juvenile offenders. The figures for Hamburg also confirm an over-representation of the young unemployed among juvenile offenders. In 1928, 26.3 per cent of the juveniles accused were out of work at the time of the offence; in 1930, 35.7 per cent; in 1931, 34.9 per cent; in 1932, 43.5 per cent; and in 1933, 36.6 per cent. This can be compared with an unemployment rate for the economically active population in this age group of 14.3 per cent in June 1933.[51] Such figures could give cause for alarm even if the absolute number of unemployed juvenile offenders involved was not vast.

In the records of the cases tried by the Hamburg juvenile court in the years before 1933 involving unemployed juveniles, there were numerous cases where unemployment appeared to social workers to be linked to a juvenile's offence, for instance where youngsters had got into 'bad company' after losing their job, or where unemployed young people had committed thefts out of financial need. A case of desperate financial need was heard in December 1932: Erich J. (born 1915) was an unemployed bricklayer's apprentice who lived at home and received 4 marks per week welfare assistance from the

[48] Poelchau, 'Kriminalstatistik', 97.
[49] Ibid.; Jacoby, 'Kriminalität', 95–7; Ehrhardt, 'Kriminalität 1932 und 1933', 671–4. On the links between unemployment and juvenile crime in the Depression, see also P. Stachura, *The Weimar Republic and the Younger Proletariat* (London, 1989), 138–41. [50] See Table 5. [51] Ibid.

welfare office. According to the social worker's report he was employed by the Hamburg welfare department on one of its compulsory labour schemes.[52] He earned 75 pfennigs per working day, which he had to give to his family for his keep, plus his travel expenses. He wanted to save these expenses, and thereby to gain some pocket-money for himself, by cycling to the site; to put his bicycle in order, he stole a bicycle tyre.[53]

There were also cases where an offence directly arose out of being on the dole, for instance, where young people contravened the regulations on unemployment assistance and made fraudulent claims. One example concerned a youth, also an unemployed bricklayer's apprentice, who was convicted in July 1932 of begging and of defrauding the employment office. Friedrich B. (born 1914) rented a room and had been supplementing his unemployment benefit of 8 marks per week by his earnings from playing the accordion and singing and dancing in courtyards, stairwells, and the street. His takings were alleged to come to 30–40 marks per week.[54]

Commentators interpreted the links between juvenile unemployment and juvenile crime in various ways. Some emphasized how material deprivation could lead directly to crimes such as theft,[55] while the psychiatrist employed by the Hamburg youth welfare department emphasized the degree to which poverty led unemployed youngsters to get mixed up in political violence.[56] However, some commentators thought it less difficult or necessary to explain the links between juvenile unemployment and a rise in juvenile crime than to ask why juvenile crime had not risen more dramatically during the Depression. Comparing the situation of economic crisis with previous crises such as the end of the war and the inflation, when juvenile crime rates had soared, they found it surprising that the juvenile crime wave as it emerged in the Depression was of such modest dimensions.[57] Reining sought an explanation of the unexpectedly small increase in juvenile crime partly in the existence of better welfare measures than previously, cushioning the unemployed

[52] On compulsory labour schemes, see Ch. 4.
[53] LGH A5171/1933.   [54] LGH A1017/1932.
[55] Poelchau, 'Kriminalstatistik', 97.
[56] Werner Villinger, 'Arbeitsscheu, Arbeitslosigkeit und Verstandesschwäche bei jugendlichen Kriminellen', *Mitteilungen der kriminalbiologischen Gesellschaft*, 4 (1933), 147–66, 152–4.
[57] Dr Reining, 'Arbeitslosigkeit und Jugendkriminalität', *Deutsche Richterzeitung*, 24/8–9 (1932), 234–5; Jacoby, 'Kriminalität', 92.

from the full rigours of poverty; Jacoby, too, inclined to the opinion that things might have been worse without the efforts of the youth welfare system. Both authors may have considered it expedient to emphasize such arguments at a time of right-wing onslaughts on the Republic's social and welfare policies. However, they also took other factors into account. Reining was of the opinion that the public was becoming increasingly indifferent to juvenile misdemeanours and not bothering to report offences committed by juveniles to the same extent as before.[58] Jacoby pointed out that crime was perhaps less rewarding in a period of Depression than in the inflation. At most, he argued, unemployed juveniles would steal cash or items for their own use, but getting rid of stolen goods for cash was getting harder and harder.[59] Finally, both Jacoby and Reining suggested that there was the possibility that long-term unemployment did not lead young people into criminal activities—which required a certain amount of initiative and energy—but into a state of passivity and apathy inimical to crime.

The Practice of Juvenile Justice after the Juvenile Courts Law

The Juvenile Courts Law of 1923 aimed to provide a framework within which the young offender could be treated according to his or her individual merits and requirements: education was to take priority over punishment. Using their new discretionary powers, juvenile court judges were to use the criminal offence as the occasion to explore the juvenile's entire life and personality. In the words of Walter Hoffmann, speaking at the Juvenile Courts Conference in Leipzig in 1924:

> Above all, we must never look at the offence as an isolated phenomenon; it always has a history and it is linked to the whole character. Otherwise we may risk treating only the symptoms. Instead, we must always try to get a grip on the *whole* person. The task is to design an educational plan which will encompass the whole lifestyle of the juvenile.[60]

---

[58] Reining, 'Arbeitslosigkeit und Jugendkriminalität', 234.
[59] Jacoby, 'Kriminalität', 105.
[60] Walter Hoffmann, speech, in *Verhandlungen des 6. Deutschen Jugendgerichtstags in Heidelberg, 17–19 Sept. 1924* (Berlin, 1925), 46.

The following account of juvenile justice in practice attempts to assess the degree to which the juvenile justice system measured up to its stated aims. Developments in the Reich as a whole are outlined on the basis of published statistics and other material.[61] For Hamburg, published statistics are available for the years from 1926.[62] These statistics are supplemented by evidence from Hamburg juvenile court records for the period 1927–33.

Where appropriate, the young offender could be dealt with without the full apparatus of formal court proceedings. One of the aims of the reform of juvenile justice was to keep the courts clear of unnecessary cases. Several stages were involved in bringing a juvenile offender to court, and the reformed juvenile justice system enabled proceedings to be terminated at various points in this process. The first stage was the reporting to the state prosecuting authorities of an offence committed by a juvenile. The prosecuting authorities, who had the sole right to bring a prosecution (private prosecutions could not be brought against juveniles), then had to decide whether or not to prosecute. If there was judged to be insufficient public interest or justifiable private interest at stake, the prosecuting authorities could decide, generally in consultation with the juvenile court judge, not to bring charges. Proceedings could also be terminated at this stage if the young person was judged not to possess sufficient intellectual or moral maturity to be fully responsible for his or her actions (JGG, paragraph 3).

For the Reich as a whole, there are no official statistics on the number of juvenile offenders whose cases were dropped by the state prosecutor before charges were brought. The German Juvenile Courts Association estimated on the basis of figures for nine cities that in 1928 34 per cent of all cases were terminated before charges were brought.[63] Statistics for two Munich districts show comparable figures for the early 1930s: in one district, the prosecuting authorities decided not to bring charges in 30 per cent of cases of

---

[61] See Matthias, *Praxis*; in addition, the statistical reports published by the Deutsche Vereinigung für Jugendgerichte und Jugendgerichtshilfen examine the workings of the juvenile courts as well as trends in juvenile crime.

[62] *StJB Hamburg* (1926/7), 314–15; (1928/9), 319–20; (1929/30), 326–7; (1930/1), 310–11; (1931/2), 183–4; (1932/3), 176–7; (1933/4), 182–3. In the following, figures on the practice of the juvenile court are taken from these sources unless stated otherwise.

[63] Poelchau, 'Kriminalstatistik', 106–7.

reported juvenile offences, while in the other district charges were dropped in 44 per cent of cases.[64]

In Hamburg, a preliminary session with the juvenile court judge provided the basis on which the judge decided whether or not to continue to formal proceedings with the lay assessors (*Hauptverhandlung*).[65] In addition, even the formal court proceedings could be terminated before a verdict was reached. Statistics on the Hamburg juvenile courts for the period 1929–33 show that a rising proportion of cases was dropped before and during the formal proceedings. As we have already seen, the number of juveniles accused rose sharply from 625 in 1929 to 989 in 1932, a rise of 58 per cent, but the number of cases leading to a final verdict remained relatively stable. In 1928, the number of young persons whose cases reached a verdict was 409; in 1929, 394; in 1930, 445; in 1931, 423; in 1932, 424. The number of cases reaching a final verdict fell further between 1932 and 1933, but this was partly due to the amnesties declared on 20 December 1932 and 21 March 1933.[66] By reducing the number of cases brought to the juvenile courts, and by terminating some proceedings before a verdict was reached, the Hamburg judicial authorities could claim to have brought about within the new system of juvenile justice a substantial degree of rationalization.

Of the cases where formal court proceedings actually took place and ended with a verdict, acquittals were relatively infrequent. Acquittals occurred, firstly, where the accused juvenile denied the offence (these were a small minority of cases) and there was insufficient evidence to sustain a conviction. Secondly, acquittals could occur where the accused was deemed to lack an understanding of the criminal nature of his or her actions or the capacity to control his or her actions in accordance with this understanding (JGG, paragraph 3). Figures for the Reich as a whole show that in the years 1924–32 about 10 per cent of juveniles against whom charges were brought were acquitted, a proportion that fell to 7.5 per cent in 1933.[67] A verdict acquitting a juvenile did not mean,

---

[64] Matthias, *Praxis*, 13.
[65] Bruno Müller, 'Das Jugendgerichtsgesetz in der Praxis des Hamburger Jugendgerichts', MS (Hamburg, 1924), 7.
[66] Gesetz über Straffreiheit, 20 Dec. 1932, *RGBl* 1932, i. 559–60; Verordnung des Reichspräsidenten über die Gewährung von Straffreiheit, 21 Mar. 1933, *RGBl* 1933, i. 134–5.
[67] Matthias, *Praxis*, 20.

however, that the judge could not impose educational measures where they were considered necessary.

In the case of verdicts giving a conviction, the juvenile court judge could opt for one of several alternative courses of action. If the offence was a minor one classified as a misdemeanour (*Vergehen*) or minor infringement of the law (Übertretung), and the juvenile did not appear to be in need of educational measures, the judge could opt to order neither punishment nor educational measures (JGG, paragraph 9, section 4). If the crime was classified as a crime (*Verbrechen*), the judge could again opt not to impose a punishment. However, if he decided not to impose a punishment, he was obliged to order some form of educational measure instead (JGG, paragraph 6). Alternatively, he could—however trivial or severe the offence—impose punishment without educational measures, or punishment in combination with educational measures.

The decision on how to treat the convicted juvenile offender—whether or not to order punitive and/or educational measures, and if so of what kind—was taken by the juvenile judge in consultation with the lay assessors in the juvenile court. This decision was partly based on the outcome of the court proceedings and the impression made by the juvenile offender in court, but it was also based to a great extent on the recommendations in the report submitted by the Juvenile Court Assistance. In a smaller number of cases, the psychiatrist also played an important role: these were the cases where the judge required a psychiatrist to submit a report on whether the accused juveniles came under the category of paragraph 3, JGG: whether or not they were capable of understanding the criminal nature of their actions and of controlling their actions accordingly.

Under the National Youth Welfare Law of 1922, the task of Juvenile Court Assistance had been made the responsibility of local youth welfare departments. Youth welfare departments were entitled to delegate this task to voluntary youth welfare agencies, but in Hamburg the public youth welfare authorities chose to retain responsibility for and control of assistance to the courts. In Hamburg, an increasing proportion of the investigations undertaken for the courts were carried out by trained and salaried employees of the youth welfare department; however, since there were too many cases for them to handle alone, the services of unpaid volunteers continued to be called upon as well.

Juvenile Court Assistance reports followed a set pattern. The investigator was required to provide information on the occupation, past history, and present circumstances of the accused youngster's parents, on the conditions in the home, on the occupation and lifestyle of siblings, and finally on the accused: his or her health since birth, school record, work record, leisure activities, attitudes, and—particularly in the case of girls—sexual habits. This information was obtained from visits to the young person's home and conversations with the accused and with his or her family, with additional information supplied by teachers and by neighbours. The youngster's family was not always cooperative, particularly in cases where there had already been contact with the youth welfare authorities, for instance over taking children into care on grounds of alleged neglect. This was the case where Frau S. was concerned, the mother of a girl accused of performing an illegal abortion and tried in October 1932. Frau S. refused youth welfare officials access to her flat and was reported by the youth welfare department's psychiatrist to have said that she wished to have nothing to do with those 'pigs from the youth welfare'.[68]

Where family members were uncooperative or not to be found at home, the investigator was all the more dependent on information gleaned from neighbours. Some investigators faithfully recorded items of gossip: an investigator reporting in October 1927 on Erna W. (accused of theft) wrote that: 'People in the Fischerstraße think Erna is insolent and a liar. Erna has been seen a lot recently with gypsies. The neighbour who told me this added: "I'd like to know if Erna is teaching the gypsies her tricks or whether she can learn any new ones from them."'[69]

Investigators for the courts sometimes went into considerable detail in their efforts to build up a picture of the young person's personality, and the manner in which they selected and presented such details betrayed much about the categories in which they thought. Familiar clichés cropped up repeatedly. One key area for the investigator's attention was the accused juvenile's employment record. An irregular work record punctuated by spells of unemployment indicated to an investigator a state of latent, if not actual, delinquency. Even if the accused juvenile could not be shown to be work-shy, the unemployed were automatically designated as being 'at risk'. Where activities outside work were

[68] LGH A1879/1932.   [69] LGH A5799/1931.

concerned, investigators had fixed ideas regarding proper leisure pursuits for working-class youth. Membership of a sports club, or of a 'respectable' political organization such as the SPD youth organization, was acceptable; so was staying at home with suitable hobbies. 'Unhealthy' leisure activities, in the eyes of the investigators, included smoking and drinking, reading pulp literature, hanging around the streets or pubs, and getting involved with radical political organizations.

A few extracts from Juvenile Court Assistance reports may illustrate the workings of the investigators' minds. A report on Willi S. (born 1914), charged with theft, which was written for the court in June 1931 by a Lutheran church youth worker, described the boy in terms reminiscent of Clemens Schultz's classic description of the Hamburg *Halbstarker*:

> Willi S. has had no regular work since he left school apart from a few spells working on ships and a brief period of agricultural work. He lacks all real willpower and energy, in contrast to his brother Heinrich. . . . Heinrich, who is a competent and enthusiastic gymnast and is correspondingly disciplined, tries to influence Willi and has taken him along to youth and sports clubs. But Willi . . . has a total aversion to commitments and to discipline. What he likes best is standing with his hands in his pockets in the courtyard entrance.[70]

In the minds of youth welfare workers and investigators, the category of *Halbstarke* overlapped with the category of political radicals and rowdies. The report written in July 1930 on Hans L. (born 1914, charged with burglary) gives an example of this view and of the regard in which youth welfare officials held the SAJ (the Social Democratic youth organization) as opposed to Communist organizations:

> In order to find the boy some company in the evenings, his parents, with the best intentions, sent him to the SAJ. But he secretly transferred to the Communist youth and soon began mouthing propaganda for all sorts of causes about which he has no idea. Despite all his parents' requests, warnings and punishments, the boy has slithered gradually into radical political rowdyism. . . . He is an example of what one calls in Hamburg a 'proper hooligan' [*einen richtigen Briten*].[71]

Where girls were concerned, moral disapprobation was often focused on symptoms of 'delinquency' similar to those typical of

[70] LGH A2339/1933.   [71] LGH A149/1930.

the male *Halbstarker*: failing to work regularly, hanging round streets and pubs, and smoking. In addition, however, girls' appearance and sexual habits came in for particular comment. An appearance which did not conform to the norm could be singled out for comment, regardless of whether it was exaggeratedly 'feminine', indicating sexual precocity, abnormally 'masculine', or simply 'slovenly'. A social work report written in 1932 on Anna S. (born 1914) commented on her appearance as follows: 'The girl is strongly developed physically and gives the impression of being lethargic and ruled by her physical urges [*triebhaft*]. Despite the outward emphasis on a masculine style (man's haircut, dark glasses, man's shirt) her whole manner gives the effect of being strikingly careless and ill-bred.'[72] Juvenile Court Assistance reports sometimes revealed the clash between the moral norms of youth welfare workers and those of their clients. A report dated October 1928 on the 18-year-old Lissy J., accused of carrying out an illegal abortion, demonstrated this discrepancy in outlook. The social worker from the youth welfare department commented disapprovingly on the sleeping arrangements at Lissy J.'s home and on the girl's attitude: 'Lissy admits that she lives together with her fiancé as if they were married, but she finds nothing wrong with this: "But so many do it!" ' The social worker recommended that Lissy J. be forcibly separated from her fiancé and placed in correctional education; the court followed this recommendation.[73]

Where psychiatric reports on a juvenile were prepared for the juvenile court, these were undertaken on the basis of a physical and psychiatric examination of the accused juvenile and, often, an interview with his or her parents. From 1926 onwards most of the reports prepared for the Hamburg juvenile court were undertaken by Werner Villinger, who was appointed in that year as the youth welfare department's first full-time youth psychiatrist.[74] Villinger made hereditary factors a central focus in his assessment of criminal behaviour in juveniles. From information about a history of alcoholism, criminal activities, or insanity in the family, he would pronounce on the degree to which the accused juvenile could be regarded as 'hereditarily burdened' or degenerate. Gertrud S., for instance, according to Villinger came from a 'degenerative family':

[72] LGH A1412/1934.
[73] LGH A9142/1931.
[74] On Villinger, see Ch. 5, p. 175.

the evidence put forward for this was that most of her eight brothers and sisters had criminal records.[75]

The recommendations submitted to the juvenile court by the Juvenile Court Assistance carried considerable weight with the court. It was important for the juvenile court to cooperate with the youth welfare department, particularly where the ordering of educational measures was concerned, since the youth welfare department was responsible for implementing most of the educational measures which could be prescribed by the court.

Contemporary commentators on the development of juvenile justice under the new Juvenile Courts Law were interested in the extent to which juvenile courts throughout the Reich made use of their powers to refrain from punishment and order educational measures instead. In 1931, an official of the German Juvenile Courts Association commented that the trend since 1924 in the towns for which his organization collected statistics was clearly towards more educational measures and away from punishment.[76] However, striking regional variations existed: in cases of juveniles convicted for theft, juvenile courts in Bavaria refrained from punishment in 5.1 per cent of cases in 1926/7 and in 7.7 per cent of cases in 1931/2. The corresponding rates for the more 'progressive' Hanseatic towns of Bremen, Lübeck, and Hamburg, were 37.2 per cent in 1926/7 and 34.6 per cent in 1931/2.[77] A comparison of the figures for the Reich as a whole and for Hamburg shows that, taking convictions for all offences, the average rate in the Reich as a whole for refraining from punishment was 18 per cent of juveniles convicted in 1926, 20.7 per cent in 1931, and 18.2 per cent in 1932. The corresponding rate in Hamburg was 30.9 per cent in 1926, 43.6 per cent in 1931, and 35.9 per cent in 1932.[78]

There was thus a clear discrepancy between the rates for the Reich as a whole and those for Hamburg; however, a trend in 1931/2 in the Reich towards a more punitive approach towards convicted juvenile offenders was also reflected in Hamburg.[79] Statements made by the Hamburg juvenile court in its judgments in the period 1931–2 confirm the impression that the court was consciously tending towards a tougher approach to punishing convicted juveniles, particularly in cases of politically motivated offences

---

[75] LGH A4223/1930.
[76] Poelchau, 'Kriminalstatistik', 108–10.
[77] Matthias, *Praxis*, 46.
[78] See Table 8.
[79] Matthias, *Praxis*, 32.

involving violence. The following statement, taken from the appeal court's judgment on the case of Dora V., appealing unsuccessfully in December 1931 against her prison sentence of six weeks for insulting a policeman and resisting arrest, is typical: 'Above all at the present time, when politically motivated acts of violence are taking place on the streets, it appears absolutely vital to award severe penalties.'[80]

Punishments ordered by the juvenile court judge were of two kinds: fines and prison sentences. In the Reich as a whole, less than a third of all punishments imposed by the juvenile courts took the form of fines, and fines as a percentage of all punishments fell from their highest level of 32.1 per cent in 1928 to 24.3 per cent in 1932.[81] Prison sentences remained throughout this period, both in the Reich and in Hamburg, the prevalent form of punishment. Prison sentences varied considerably in their impact, not only because of their varying length but also due to the use of the juvenile court judge's power to grant suspension of sentences (*Strafaufschub* or *Strafaussetzung*). Suspended sentences were popular with the juvenile courts since they were thought to combine punishment with education: the threat of prison was used as a sanction to enforce good behaviour.[82] In the Reich as a whole between 1924 and 1933, roughly half of all juveniles convicted of offences were sentenced to prison. The percentage of convicted juveniles sentenced to prison fell from 56.8 per cent in 1925 to 48.6 per cent in 1929, rising thereafter to 57.4 per cent in 1932 and 62 per cent in 1933.[83] Over the same period in Hamburg, the proportion of convicted juveniles sentenced to prison was more variable, falling from 67.6 per cent in 1925 to 35.7 per cent in 1927 and rising again to around 50 per cent in 1928 to 1932. The increase in the proportion of convicted juveniles sentenced to prison in the years 1931/2 was a trend evident in Hamburg as well as in the Reich as a whole.

If juveniles were sent to prison, they were sent either to special youth prisons or to special sections of adult prisons: paragraphs 12 and 16 of the Juvenile Courts Law of 1923 laid down that juveniles had to be kept separate from adult prisoners and that prison should, without detracting from the seriousness of the juveniles' punishment, also promote their education. National guidelines issued by

[80] LGH A1769/1932. [81] Matthias, *Praxis*, 30.
[82] Ibid. 25. [83] Ibid. 29.

the government on prisons in 1923 also stipulated that 18–21-year-olds should be kept separate from adult prisoners; thus the special youth prisons and youth sections housed prisoners aged 14–21, while keeping the juveniles separate from the older age-group.[84] For young female offenders, there were no special institutions, since the numbers involved were so small; in Hamburg, female prisoners aged under 21 were kept in a special section of the Fühlsbüttel prison. For male juveniles aged 14–21, there were by the mid-1920s five special youth prisons in operation. The prison in Wittlich an der Mosel, founded in 1912, was the first juvenile prison to be set up in Germany. Two further youth prisons were located at Bruchsal in Baden and at Eisenach in Thuringia. The largest youth prison in Germany was at Wohlau in Silesia, with 550 places; the second largest, with 350 places, and one of the most famous, was Hahnöfersand, Hamburg's youth prison on an island in the Elbe.[85]

Hahnöfersand's fame derived largely from the publicity given to the educational experiment carried out there between November 1921 and July 1922 by Walter Herrmann and Curt Bondy. Their work with the juveniles in Hahnöfersand, inspired by Karl Wilker's work in the Berlin reformatory Lindenhof, sought to build up a more intensive pedagogical relationship between staff and inmates, to involve inmates actively in discussions and decisions concerning prison routine, and to create a progressive regime stressing incentives and rewards for good behaviour as well as punishments for misbehaviour.[86] The experiment ended after tensions between the reformers and the Hamburg prison administration grew to crisis point and Herrmann and Bondy resigned.[87] After their departure, the Hamburg prison administration continued, at least on paper, to uphold a policy in line with the spirit of the Juvenile Courts Law; its prison guidelines, like those of Saxony, remained more explicitly committed to the education of juvenile prisoners than those of some other *Länder*.[88] However, two years after the end of Herrmann

---

[84] Herbert Francke, 'Zum gegenwärtigen Stande des Jugendstrafvollzuges in Deutschland', *ZBl* 17 (1925/6), 166–9.
[85] Ibid. 167.
[86] Walter Herrmann, *Das Hamburgische Jugendgefängnis Hahnöfersand: Ein Bericht über Erziehungsarbeit im Strafvollzug* (Hamburg, 1923).
[87] Gustav Aschaffenburg, 'Hahnöfersand', *Monatsschrift für Kriminalpsychologie und Strafrechtsreform*, 15 (1924), 346–51, 347.
[88] Francke, 'Zum gegenwärtigen Stande des Jugendstrafvollzuges', 168.

and Bondy's experiment, critical observers found little to praise about Hahnöfersand.[89]

Prison sentences were rarely of more than three months' duration: in the Reich as a whole, about one-fifth of prison sentences imposed on juveniles were longer than three months.[90] In 1931/2, the proportion of sentences of three months and more rose both in the Reich and in Hamburg. Of probably greater significance than the length of sentence imposed was the frequency with which prison sentences imposed on juveniles were suspended. Figures for the Reich as a whole give the proportion of prison sentences which were suspended at the time of the verdict: these amounted to around three-quarters of all prison sentences in the years 1925–30, falling to 70 per cent in 1931 and 67 per cent in 1932.[91] In Hamburg, it was less common to declare a suspension of sentence immediately at the time of the verdict: less than a third of sentences were suspended in this way in the years 1925–33. Instead, the decision on whether a suspension should be granted was often deferred for several weeks or months with the aim of increasing the educational impact of the measure.[92] However, the deferred decision did usually result in the sentence being suspended. Nor were many suspensions of sentences revoked as a result of the juvenile reoffending: about three quarters of suspended sentences were ultimately cancelled (*Strafe erlassen*).[93] Some juveniles escaped being sent to prison because they were in correctional education—even though they might well have preferred the shorter prison sentence to the indefinite period in the reformatory.

Figures on the Hamburg prison population show that only a very few juveniles actually ended up in prison as the result of being sentenced in court. The majority of young people in custody were sent there after arrest pending their trial (*Untersuchungshaft*). In 1929, for instance, 184 juveniles were sent to prison in the course of the year, but 126 of these were on remand. Only fifty-eight juveniles (fifty-six boys and two girls) were sent to prison after being sentenced: this was compared to a total of 165 prison sentences imposed by the juvenile court during that year. However,

---

[89] Aschaffenburg, 'Hahnöfersand', 351.
[90] Matthias, *Praxis*, 29.
[91] Poelchau, 'Kriminalstatistik', 111; Matthias, *Praxis*, 26, 29.
[92] Kruse, 'Straffälligkeit', 513–14.   [93] Ibid. 514.

the subsequent years showed some increase in the number of juveniles sent to prison in Hamburg: in 1932, a total of 218 juveniles were sent to prison, 102 of which (ninety-seven boys, five girls) were sent after being sentenced by the courts.[94]

The factors which appear to have weighed most in cases where the juvenile court decided to send a juvenile to prison immediately were, firstly, the assessment of the youngster's milieu, and, secondly, his or her previous record. One youth was sent to Neumünster prison for six months in September 1932 for the theft of a bicycle, an offence for which many juveniles were merely warned and placed on probation. However, Felix W. had several previous convictions; he was described as having been brought up 'in darkest St Pauli', and he was unemployed. The juvenile court judgment made it clear that Felix W. was not considered a suitable case for 'educational' treatment:

It is clear, particularly in view of the previous convictions of the accused, and in view of other aspects of his record hitherto which have not been the subject of criminal prosecution, that the accused is thoroughly asocial and a certain candidate for future security detention [*Sicherungsverwahrung*]. Lighter punishments and educational measures appear to be a waste of time.[95]

Where the juvenile courts chose to order educational measures as well as or instead of punishment, they had a range of measures to choose from. These varied considerably in the frequency with which they were imposed and in the impact they had on a young person's life. One of the most commonly ordered educational measures was the caution (*Verwarnung*). The caution was often used in cases where no punishment was imposed: if an offence classified as a crime was involved, some educational measures had to be ordered if punishment was not, and the caution was used by juvenile court judges as a convenient and relatively harmless measure to order to comply with the law in such cases.[96] From 1926 onwards in Hamburg, the caution was the educational measure most frequently ordered by the juvenile court.[97]

---

[94] *StJB Hamburg* (1925), 312; (1926/7), 353; (1927/8), 370; (1928/9), 356: (1929/30), 366; (1932/3), 190–1.   [95] LGH A1394/1934.
[96] Bruno Müller, 'Die praktischen Aufgaben des Jugendrichters und der Jugendgerichtshilfe in der Gegenwart', in Max Grünhut und Bruno Müller, *Zwei Vorträge über Jugendgerichtsbarkeit*, (n.p., 1927), 35–53, 49.
[97] See Table 9.

Probation was another frequently ordered educational measure, ordered sometimes in conjunction with a caution but often in conjunction with a suspended prison sentence.[98] In Hamburg, the youth welfare authorities were heavily involved in administering probation. The youth welfare department had considerable influence over whether probation was ordered in the first place—since the Juvenile Court Assistance was responsible for advising the juvenile court on whether educational measures for juvenile offenders were necessary and likely to be effective.[99] In the light of his experience with probation, Hamburg's youth welfare director warned in 1931 against an over-estimation of its benefits:

> There has been a gradual shift away from the idea that probation is a panacea for all 'lighter' cases. Experience has shown—though unfortunately not all juvenile court judges have grasped this yet—that a family which has virtually broken down and which instinctively resists anything done by 'the authorities' is not a good basis for successful probation.[100]

One case where the social worker advised the court not to order probation on the grounds that it was bound to fail in such an allegedly immoral and criminal milieu was that of Paula N. (born 1909), who was charged with causing a disturbance, insulting and obstructing police while she was drunk. Reporting in April 1927, the social worker wrote that:

> Paula has been without work since December 1925. She is already heavily involved in the world of prostitution in the city centre. . . . The girl finds support from her circle of female friends for her thoughtless, work-shy way of life. . . . She encounters no countervailing influence from her family, which had broken down completely. . . . Influencing the girl through probation has so far proved useless; only a longer period of systematic education in a reformatory can make a respectable person out of this girl.

Paula N. was accordingly placed in correctional education.[101]

Probation was judged to be more likely to succeed in 'intact' families where the social worker was confident that the parents would back up the youth welfare authorities with regard to their wayward child. The conservative social values which informed such

---

[98] Ibid.
[99] On the implementation of probation orders, see Ch. 7.
[100] Wilhelm Hertz, 'Heraufsetzung der Strafmündigkeitsgrenze?', *ZGS* 51 (1931), 877–91, 884.   [101] LGH A6763/1931.

judgements are illustrated in a report on Meta A., who was convicted in December 1932 of theft from her employers:

> Herr A. was on active service for the duration of the war. . . . He takes the education of his children very seriously. . . . Frau A. is a very sensible, orderly woman. . . . The apartment consists of three rooms; it is kept in a state of exemplary cleanliness and is decorated and furnished in a pleasant, respectable style [nett-bürgerlich eingerichtet].[102]

On the basis of the social worker's recommendation, Meta A. was placed on probation.

Possibly due to the growing caution of the youth welfare authorities, the Hamburg juvenile court became more sparing in its use of probation in sentencing juvenile offenders in the years before 1933: probation orders comprised nearly half of the total number of educational measures ordered by the juvenile court in 1924–5, but only 21 per cent in 1931, and 13 per cent in 1932. In absolute terms, the number of juveniles for whom probation was ordered by the court fell from over 100 in 1924 to seventy-one in 1927, rising to ninety-three in 1931 and falling again to seventy in 1932 and sixty-three in 1933.[103] In the Reich as a whole, only a slight decline in the application of probation was evident over the same period: 12.2 per cent of all convicted juveniles were placed on probation in 1925, a proportion which fell to between 10 and 11 per cent in the years 1929–32.[104]

The decline in probation orders did not, however, lead to an increase in the number of cases where the more drastic measure of correctional education was imposed. This was true both in the Reich as a whole and in Hamburg. Only 4.7 per cent of convicted juveniles were placed in correctional education by the juvenile courts in 1925, and this proportion fell to 3.0 per cent in 1932.[105] In Hamburg, the proportion of convicted juveniles who were referred to correctional education by the juvenile court was higher than in the Reich as a whole, and rose—in contrast to the Reich as a whole—from 1926/7 levels to a maximum in 1930, when thirty-nine boys and nine girls were placed by the juvenile court in correctional education.[106] This represented 12 per cent of all convicted juveniles in that year. Thereafter, referrals fell; only thirty-three convicted

---

[102] LGH A115/1934.
[103] See Table 9.
[104] Matthias, *Praxis*, 23.
[105] Ibid. 24.
[106] See Table 9.

juveniles were placed by the court in correctional education in 1932, equivalent to 8.5 per cent of the total number of convicted juveniles. Nevertheless, referrals in Hamburg still represented a higher proportion of total convicted juveniles than in the Reich as a whole. This discrepancy can be explained in terms of the Hamburg juvenile court's overall inclination to opt for educational measures as opposed to punishments. It appears that in cases where other courts elsewhere in the Reich sent a youngster to prison, the 'progressive', educationally minded Hamburg juvenile judges placed him or her in correctional education.

The juvenile court usually justified the ordering of correctional education by referring to the lifestyle and previous record of the juvenile concerned. A standard formula used by the court was to refer to the need for 'strict and well-regulated education to guide the accused onto the right path'. Not surprisingly, cases where the juvenile court ordered correctional education—which entailed an indeterminate period of separation of youngsters from their families—could result in conflicts between the court and the juvenile's parents. According to a survey of juvenile courts throughout the Reich, correctional education was commonly perceived as an excessive 'punishment' for a slight offence. A juvenile court judge commented that

> it is true that the educational measure is not meant to 'compensate' for the offence: the offence is only the occasion for a referral to correctional education and it is never the only reason. The young people and their parents, however, do not appreciate this, all that they see is that 'just because of a little thing' correctional education has been ordered.[107]

Juveniles and their parents, in his view, had obviously not grasped that the purpose of the new juvenile justice system was to treat the offender, not to punish schematically according to the severity of the offence.

New Directions in Juvenile Justice? The Debate on Revisions to the Juvenile Courts Law

Contemporary opinion was divided over whether the juvenile court system as constituted in the Juvenile Courts Law of 1923 was

---

[107] Van Dühren, 'Die Erziehungsmaßregeln des Jugendgerichtsgesetzes', *ZBl* 17/4 (1925/6), 77–82, 81.

satisfactory. Moves to revise the law were concentrated on two issues, both of which proved to be highly controversial within the specialist circles of youth welfare and juvenile justice.

The first issue was whether or not juvenile courts were the most appropriate way of dealing with juvenile offenders aged 14 to 18. Even during the debates on the drafting of the Juvenile Courts Law, for instance at the Fifth Juvenile Courts Conference in 1920, there had been calls for setting the new age of criminal responsibility not at 14 but at 16 or even 18, leaving juvenile offenders below that age to be dealt with entirely by the educational measures administered by the youth welfare authorities. These calls did not cease with the introduction of the Juvenile Courts Law, and the controversy reached a climax in the years 1927–31.[108]

A particularly energetic opponent of the juvenile court for 14–18-year-olds was Heinrich Webler, a member of the Gilde Soziale Arbeit and an editor of the leading specialist youth welfare journal, the *Zentralblatt für Jugendrecht und Jugendwohlfahrt*. In 1929, he published his proposals for the abolition of the juvenile courts for the 14–18-year-old age-group altogether. He argued that punishments imposed by a criminal court could never be justified for juveniles under the age of 18, since in his opinion they lacked the necessary 'social maturity' that would make them fully responsible for their actions. The educational measures appropriate for this age-group which were currently ordered by the juvenile courts would, argued Webler, be better left to the guardianship courts.[109]

The reaction of many juvenile court judges to the proposals put forward by Webler and others to abolish the juvenile courts for the 14–18-year-old age-group was predictably negative. Those who defended the juvenile court system put forward a number of arguments. At one level, the different sides in the controversy reflected different views of the rights of the individual and the state. Some advocates of the juvenile justice system focused on the protection of a young person's legal rights and liberties, a concern which has been termed the 'constitutionalist' approach by Anthony

---

[108] C. Noppel and E. von Düring, 'Jugendzeit und Strafmündigkeit' pt. 1, *ZBl* 19/8 (1927/8), 203–7; Herbert Francke, 'Jugendzeit und Strafmündigkeit' pt. 3, *ZBl* 19/9 (1927/8), 227–9.

[109] Heinrich Webler, *Wider das Jugendgericht* (Berlin, 1929); id., 'Zur Problematik des Jugendgerichts', *ZBl* 22/1 (1930/1), 1–14.

Platt in his discussion of the American juvenile justice system.¹¹⁰ In the German context, the 'constitutionalists' argued that young people's rights were better protected in the existing juvenile court than they would be if the juvenile courts were abolished and juveniles were referred only to the guardianship court. Juvenile courts were preferable from this point of view, for instance with regard to appeals, or the possibility of having a defence lawyer.¹¹¹ To abolish the juvenile court would be to deny altogether the responsibility of juvenile offenders in this age-group for their actions and to stress only their need of education and 'treatment'. This was, some argued, to deprive them of their rightful autonomy. At a conference in 1929, Carl Mennicke, founder and director of the social work school at the Deutsche Hochschule für Politik and a prominent mentor of the Gilde Soziale Arbeit, warned of the dangers of an 'uncontrolled educational fanaticism' removing people's rights of self-determination, particularly the rights of young people. Mennicke proposed, given the economic independence of the great majority of the population upon leaving school, that their legal responsibility be likewise confirmed and the juvenile courts retained.¹¹²

A more practical consideration which was brought up in favour of the juvenile courts was the problem of the 'incorrigible' offenders under the age of 18—the small number of 'hard cases' for whom prison appeared to be the only answer. If prison sentences were abolished for the under-18s, this group of offenders would have to be placed in correctional education. A number of prominent members of the German Juvenile Courts Association declared their opposition to any 'deportation of inmates from the youth prisons into the secure wings of the reformatories'. Such a transfer of responsibility would create insoluble problems for the reformatories and endanger the liberalization of reformatory education.¹¹³

---

¹¹⁰ Anthony Platt, *The Child Savers: The Invention of Delinquency*, 2nd edn. (Chicago and London, 1977), 152.
¹¹¹ Walter Friedländer, 'Zur Problematik des Jugendgerichts', *AW* 5/11 (1930), 349.
¹¹² Mennicke's arguments quoted in Friedländer, 'Bericht über eine Sachverständigenkonferenz über Aufhebung der Jugendgerichte am 20. April 1929', *AW* 4/9 (1929), 273–5, 274.
¹¹³ Deutsche Vereinigung für Jugendgerichte und Jugendgerichtshilfen, Kurzbericht über die kleine Jugendgerichtskonferenz in Rolandseck, 19 Oct. 1929. StAH, JB I, 493b, vol. 2.

Those who, like Webler, advocated the total abolition of the juvenile courts for 14–18-year-old offenders were in a small minority in the specialist circles of youth welfare and juvenile justice, and the idea was never considered seriously by the Reich Ministry of Justice. However, a wide degree of consensus within specialist circles was reached by 1931 in favour of raising the minimum age of criminal responsibility to 16. A vote in favour of this reform was passed by the Criminal Law Committee of the Reichstag in January 1931; however, the Reichstag rejected the proposal.[114]

As far as older juvenile offenders were concerned, the consensus among youth welfare specialists was that juvenile courts should be retained as the most appropriate and effective method of dealing with the age-group 16–18. Punishments were considered to be an indispensable part of the range of measures at the disposal of the juvenile court to deal with the problem of juvenile crime. This attitude appears to have been a reflection of the times. The Depression with its rising juvenile criminality rate and the growing problem of offences involving political violence was not a favourable environment for proposing the abolition of punishments for juvenile offenders. As we have seen, there was a trend in the juvenile courts in the final years of the Weimar Republic emphasizing the punitive element in the treatment of young criminals. Although the juvenile justice system had been conceived as a means of promoting an educationally oriented treatment of juvenile offenders, it was flexible enough to accommodate a more punitive approach.

The second question which aroused controversy within specialist juvenile justice circles was not so much whether the juvenile courts were fulfilling their function as far as their existing target group of 14–18-year-olds was concerned, but whether the target age-group was the right one. At a special conference convened by the German Juvenile Courts Association in 1927, a number of juvenile court judges proposed having offenders in the 18–21 age-group included within the jurisdiction of the juvenile courts.[115] Institutional politics within the judicial system almost certainly played a role in this proposal. The inclusion of a large and important group of offenders

[114] Von Liszt, 'Kriminalität', 251.
[115] Deutsche Vereinigung für Jugendgerichte und Jugendgerichtshilfen, Bericht über eine Sachverständigenkonferenz in Potsdam am 30. April 1927 über die strafrechtliche Behandlung der über 18 Jahre alten Minderjährigen. ZStA Potsdam, 30.01, 5568.

within the sphere of responsibility of the juvenile courts would have expanded the influence of the juvenile sector and would be likely to strengthen the campaign to carry the principles applying in juvenile justice into the criminal justice system as a whole.

The lobby pressing for the inclusion of 18–21-year-olds in the sphere of juvenile justice also claimed that their proposals would have a number of practical benefits. One argument concerned the possibility of educating rather than punishing the young adult offender. If it was thought possible, for the purposes of correctional education, to educate young people up to the age of 21, then, it was argued, the courts should also have the option of prescribing educational measures for this age-group and refraining from punishment.[116] At the 1927 conference, Hamburg's youth welfare director argued that educational treatment of this kind would not represent a soft option, but individualized, flexible 'treatment' for young adult criminals: 'the proposals are not about a softer, but a fairer treatment of this age group'.[117] A prominent juvenile court judge added the point that as the 'juniors' in the adult courts rather than as the 'seniors' in the juvenile courts, offenders aged 18–21 were currently treated too leniently.[118]

The campaign to include the 18–21 age group in the jurisdiction of the juvenile courts had some success in practice. Like the introduction of the juvenile courts in the years before the Juvenile Courts Law, reforms took place at a local level on the initiative of the local judicial administration. From 1925 onwards, juvenile courts in a number of towns and cities in Prussia began to include 18–21-year-old offenders within their jurisdiction. (This meant offenders who were aged up to 20 years at the time of the offence and up to 21 at the time of the charge.) The first court where this was introduced was Berlin-Mitte, followed by Altona, Dortmund, and Flensburg. Their reforms were officially encouraged by the Prussian Ministry of Justice in a decree dated 20 January 1928.[119]

At Reich level, change appeared to be on the way when in 1930 the draft of an introductory law to the Criminal Code was

---

[116] Präses des Jugendamts Hamburg an die Senatskommission für die Justizverwaltung, 11 Nov. 1927. StAH, Justizverwaltung, I, D, d1, vol. 4.
[117] Wilhelm Hertz, at Sachverständigenkonferenz, 30 Apr. 1927.
[118] Paul Blumenthal, at Sachverständigenkonferenz, 30 Apr. 1927.
[119] Paul Blumenthal, 'Die strafrechtliche Behandlung der 18–21jährigen', *ZBl* 19/12 (1927/8), 321–2.

published which defined 18–21-year-olds as an intermediate group between juveniles and adults. Sentencing for this age-group was to be modified, and there was to be the option of ordering educational measures instead of punishment.[120] However, this draft legislation never became law. In the Depression, with rising public concern about juvenile crime and with growing calls from the Right for the tough treatment of young offenders, circumstances were not favourable for an expansion of juvenile justice as a special category within the judicial system.[121] Rather the reverse: the Papen government, seeking to cut public expenditure by rationalizing the administration of the juvenile courts, removed in the process one of the important features that distinguished juvenile courts from other courts. Under an emergency decree of 14 June 1932, lay assessors were to be dispensed with in juvenile courts for hearings in cases of certain categories of offences committed by juveniles—categories which made up the majority of juvenile court cases.[122] As a leading member of the German Juvenile Courts Association pointed out, this decree contravened the principle underlying the Juvenile Courts Law that the individual personality of the offender, not the offence, should determine a juvenile's treatment. Now, the severity of the offence alone determined the nature of the court which the juvenile was to face. This, she argued, was a sign that the Reich government was no longer in tune with the ethos of the juvenile justice movement. The juvenile court as it was originally conceived was under threat; it was time, she declared, for all supporters of youth welfare to rally to the defence of its special status and its educational idea.[123]

Assessing the Impact of Juvenile Justice

The impact of the juvenile justice system put in place and codified by the Juvenile Courts Law can be assessed both in terms of its

---

[120] Friedländer, 'Eine Novelle zum Jugendgerichtsgesetz', *AW* 5/23 (1930), 705–10.
[121] Matthias, *Praxis*, 32. See also Stachura, *Weimar Republic and the Younger Proletariat*, 152–3.
[122] Verordnung des Reichspräsidenten über Maßnahmen auf dem Gebiete der Rechtspflege und Verwaltung, 14 June 1932, *RGBl* 1932, i. 285; von Liszt, 'Das neue Jugendgericht', *Freie Wohlfahrtspflege* 7/5 (1932), 222–3.
[123] Von Liszt, 'Das neue Jugendgericht', 223.

expressed aims and in the wider context of the relationship between the state and the problem adolescent.

One of the aims which the juvenile justice movement set out to achieve was an overall reduction in juvenile crime through 'individual prevention'—educating offenders so that they did not reoffend. Assessing the degree to which this was achieved is difficult. As we have seen above, the proportion of convicted juveniles who had received punishments for previous convictions fell for some years after the Juvenile Courts Law was implemented, but then rose again. However, that rise is not easy to interpret: it could mean either a growth in the number of hardened young criminals, or an increased success in dealing with first-time offenders outside the courts. Similarly, it is hard to assess the impact of juvenile justice on overall juvenile crime. Reported juvenile crime was on the increase during the Depression. Both its volume and its nature were affected by mass unemployment and political tension, even though 14–18-year-olds were by no means the worst affected by unemployment or the most heavily involved in radical political activity. If a study of crime among the 18–25-year-olds were possible, the results would probably be considerably more dramatic. The rise in juvenile crime during the Depression was admittedly less than contemporaries expected. Whether this can be seen as an achievement of the juvenile justice system is harder to say, and even those most closely involved in implementing that system were notably cautious in making such claims.

Another, more modest aim of the Juvenile Courts Law was to unclog the courts and free them of trivial cases. This would appear to have been achieved: despite the rise in juvenile crime during the Depression, the juvenile courts were not flooded with cases as a result. Juvenile justice thus appeared to be achieving a hoped-for rationalization of the judicial system; however, this was not enough for the Papen government, which decided in 1932 that the need for further rationalization of the judicial system could be best met by cuts in the juvenile court system itself.

Juvenile courts could also be seen to be implementing their principle of looking at the criminal rather than at the crime as a guide to sentencing. The welfare bureaucracy of social workers and psychiatrists provided detailed reports scrutinizing the personality, medical history and domestic circumstances of individual offenders, and the courts in Hamburg tended to incorporate parts of such reports in their written verdicts. On the basis of these reports, flexible sentencing was practised, tailoring 'educational' and 'punitive' measures to the offender.

Acting in line with the precepts of the Juvenile Courts Law, juvenile court judges made extensive use of educational measures. After the implementation of the Juvenile Courts Law, the proportion of convicted youngsters sentenced to prison fell, a trend particularly marked in Hamburg; widespread use of the powers to suspend sentences meant that the majority of juveniles with prison sentences stayed out of prison; and probation established itself as a staple of the juvenile court. However, juvenile justice experts saw signs of a more punitive approach returning during the Depression. In the last 18 months of the Republic, juvenile courts ordered probation and correctional education less frequently. Instead, more prison sentences were imposed and more of them resulted in youngsters actually going to prison.

The impact of the juvenile justice system can also be seen in terms of an extension of the powers of the welfare bureaucracy. The implications of flexible sentencing for the juveniles concerned were considerable. First, the investigations by social workers and psychiatrists were significant invasions of privacy. Secondly, it was clear that more education instead of punishment did not necessarily represent a lesser degree of intervention. Some 'educational' measures prescribed by the courts did, it is true, represent a less heavy-handed method of dealing with an offender. A caution combined with probation meant that young people could stay with their families and in their jobs. Nor was probation combined with a suspended prison sentence, which in the end would often be cancelled, a radical intervention into a young person's life. However, this was precisely the drawback of probation and a reason for the doubts about its effectiveness which set in during the later years of the Republic. By contrast, if the educational measure ordered was correctional education, this represented a drastic intervention and one which had the disadvantage, compared with a prison sentence, that it could be of indefinite duration up to the age of majority. For all the efforts of educational reformers, correctional education retained its stigma and continued to be regarded by juveniles and their families as a punishment.

The situation of juvenile justice in the Depression was complex. On the one hand, juvenile court judges were responding to the

Juvenile Crime and Juvenile Justice 225

pressures upon them to take a more punitive line with young offenders, both to deter them as individuals and to set an example to others. At the same time, the juvenile justice lobby sought to resist these pressures. They condemned the erosion of the juvenile court apparatus, demanded that the priority of the educational idea be upheld, and even advocated the extension of educational measures, via an expanded juvenile court system, to offenders above the age of 18. However, such demands came precisely at a time when the youth welfare system, vital to the implementation of educational measures for young offenders, was reaching a crisis point. Under the pressure of increased social problems and reductions in public funding, probation work and correctional education were being cut back. As we shall see below, those already trying to use educational means to influence problem adolescents, particularly those in the older age-groups, were increasingly pessimistic about their success rates as the Depression deepened.

7

Reforming the Delinquent? Probation and Correctional Education

The Weimar governments' policies for resocializing delinquents depended on the provision of appropriate youth welfare measures. Probation (Schutzaufsicht) and correctional education (Fürsorgeerziehung or *FE*) were central to this provision, being the chief methods whereby young offenders and other adolescents considered delinquent or 'at risk' were placed under the supervision and control of the youth welfare authorities. Of these, correctional education was by far the most controversial, being throughout the Weimar period the subject of public debate and the focus of major scandals.

In the mid-1920s, a period of expanding welfare provision, educational reformers were still optimistic about the prospects of improving the standard of youth welfare personnel and facilities. In the Depression, however, youth welfare proved to be particularly vulnerable to cuts in public expenditure. Under the impact of right-wing attacks on the Weimar Republic's welfare system, the earlier discussions on methods of treating the problem adolescent widened into a debate on the function of youth welfare provision generally. Educationalists' debates regarding the usefulness of their efforts when directed at older, 'hardened' delinquents became overlaid by a more brutal discourse focused on racial hygiene and a selective approach to welfare.

Probation in Practice

Probation aimed to reform and educate difficult juveniles without

Part of this chapter has already appeared elsewhere in a different form: E. Harvey, 'Die Jugendfürsorge in der Endphase der Weimarer Republik: Das Beispiel der Fürsorgeerziehung', in Hans-Uwe Otto and Heinz Sünker (eds.), *Soziale Arbeit und Faschismus* (Frankfurt am Main, 1989), 198–227.

removing and isolating them from their environment.¹ It was believed to be particularly appropriate for older juveniles, firstly because this group was held to be the most difficult to educate in custodial institutions, and secondly because removing them from their environment would in many cases also remove them from their jobs. Although probation was thus a less drastic intervention in a young person's life than correctional education, it was nevertheless supposed to go beyond merely superficial checks on a youngster's activities.²

Several routes could lead a youngster to be placed on probation. The route via the juvenile court has been described in Chapter 6. In addition, the youth welfare authorities could intervene after being notified of children and adolescents thought to be at risk or delinquent. Alternatively, parents themselves might contact the youth welfare department in cases where their offspring appeared uncontrollable. Where parents consented, probation could be exercised by the youth welfare authorities without a court order; otherwise, it was backed up by an order from the guardianship court or the juvenile court.

In Hamburg, the majority of probation orders were undertaken with the parents' consent and without a court order.³ The total number on probation in Hamburg peaked in 1930 at 3,576, dropping to 3,194 in 1932.⁴ The youth welfare department reported in 1925 that one of the reasons for the decline in referral to correctional education was the substantial number of juveniles placed under probation instead.⁵

Where probation was embarked upon, the social workers and volunteer investigators were faced with the task of carrying out 'therapy' in accordance with the 'diagnosis' of behavioural difficulties and educational needs. One major task for the person supervising adolescents on probation was to ensure that they had jobs, and that the jobs were suitable. Youth welfare departments

---

¹ Willy Leisten, 'Die Schutzaufsicht in der Praxis', *ZBl* 24/10 (1932/3), 358–66.
² Amtsgerichtsrat van Dühren, 'Die Erziehungsmaßnahmen des JGG', *ZBl* 17/4 (1925/6), 77–82, 81.
³ Hertz, 'Zehn Jahre Hamburger Jugendamt 1923–1933', MS (Hamburg, 1934), 83–4.
⁴ *Statistisches Handbuch für den hamburgischen Staat* (1920), 375; *StJB Hamburg* (1925), 276; (1928/9), 307; (1931/2), 176; (1933/4), 175.
⁵ Landesjugendamt und Jugendamt Hamburg, *Jahresbericht 1925*, 8, 13. On the decline in FE referrals, see Table 10.

attempted to place young people in skilled apprenticeships and to keep them out of jobs like 'newspaper or ice-cream seller, cigarette boy, or pedlar'.[6] Particular efforts were made where girls were thought to be in morally dangerous jobs as 'artistes' and night-club dancers.[7]

An example from Hamburg records of such efforts was the case of Wilhelmine S. (born 1912), who was placed on probation by the guardianship court in November 1930. The volunteer supervising the girl wrote in November 1931 that Wilhelmine S. had, after being given a 'firm talking-to', taken a hairdressing job, but had lost it when the shop closed down; she had then taken a job as a dancer in the 'Alkazar' night-club. She was told to find a different job, but she 'declared that if she were forced to take another job she would still carry on at the Alkazar in the evenings'. The report concluded that the girl had a 'very sensual nature' and that probation in her case was a waste of time.[8]

A second area of attention for the social workers supervising adolescents on probation was that of leisure activities.[9] A Hamburg social worker supervising Bruno K., a 17-year-old unskilled factory worker earning 36 marks per week, reported that 'he is very addicted to pleasures and distractions. Visits to the cinema, dance-floors, and ballrooms are his passion. My efforts to change this have so far been in vain'.[10] In another case, that of Herbert K., the boy's father had called upon the youth welfare authorities for assistance after Herbert, aged 14, had given up his apprenticeship, joined an SA Sturmabteilung troop and left home for an SA barracks. The social worker succeeded in recovering Herbert K. from the SA barracks and finding him a new job, but 'all my efforts have so far failed to dissuade the youth from his political activity'.[11]

It was difficult to persuade youngsters simply to abandon their preferred activities. Social workers and youth experts, particularly those with a background in the youth movement, thought that the answer was to offer working-class youngsters something more

[6] Leisten, 'Die Schutzaufsicht in der Praxis', 361.
[7] Clara Thorbecke, 'Die Gefährdung jugendlicher Artistinnen und Tänzerinnen unter der Berücksichtigung der Fürsorgemöglichkeiten', *ZBl* 16/10 (1924/5), 234–7.
[8] LGH A953/1931.
[9] Walter Hoffmann, speech, *Verhandlungen des 6. Deutschen Jugendgerichtstags in Heidelberg, 17–19 Sept. 1924* (Berlin, 1925), 46.
[10] LGH A2327/1933.
[11] LGH A990/1932.

positive instead.[12] They sought to integrate youngsters 'at risk' into suitable youth groups and youth clubs, hoping that they would thereby come to absorb and adopt the values and ethos of the youth movement. In Hamburg, cooperation was sought by the public youth welfare department with youth movement groups generally, and one result of this cooperation was the setting up of the group of so-called 'young helpers' who volunteered to take on a number of youngsters on probation. After initial abortive attempts to allot young people on probation to volunteers on a one-to-one basis, a new strategy was adopted whereby volunteers ran group activities with children and youngsters 'at risk', offering hikes, sports, and indoor activities. By 1927 there were fifteen such groups, comprising about 350 children and young people.[13]

There were, nevertheless, major obstacles to contacts between 'organized' youth and the youngsters under the supervision of the youth welfare department. There was a great difference between the lifestyle of the young people on probation and that of the members of élitist and consciously self-disciplined youth organizations, with their puritan sexual morality and their rejection of alcohol, tobacco, commercial entertainments, and trash literature. This was not so much a class as a cultural divide: in terms of their lifestyle and ethos, working-class members of the SPD's youth organization, the SAJ, had, despite political differences, more in common with bourgeois youth organizations than with the boys and girls classified as 'at risk'. As a result, young people on probation did not necessarily want to have anything to do with youth clubs or youth groups prescribed for them, nor did most youth groups want unwilling members foisted upon them. The director of the Hamburg youth welfare department ignored this when he proposed in 1931 that juvenile courts should exert more pressure on young offenders on probation to join a youth group.[14]

Studies of probation for delinquent juveniles have argued that one of the main purposes of such non-custodial forms of supervision is

---

[12] August Oswalt, 'Die ehrenamtliche Mitarbeit der Jugendbewegung in der sozialen Arbeit', in *Bericht über die Schulungswoche der Gildenschaft 'Soziale Arbeit' vom 23.-29. Juni 1927 in Ludwigslust*, n.p., n.d., 20–32.

[13] Gertrud Embden, 'Die Schutzaufsicht in der Praxis', *JV* 2/3 (1926), 16; W. Hertz an den Senat, 16 Sept. 1926. StAH, JB I, 340; Herbert Bökel, 'Die Mitwirkung der Jugendbünde in der Jugendfürsorge', *JV* 3/1 (1927), 18–21.

[14] Hertz, 'Heraufsetzung der Strafmündigkeitsgrenze', *ZGS* 51 (1931), 877–91, 887.

to influence not just the juveniles themselves but also their milieu.[15] Although in the Weimar period the attention of social workers carrying out probation work was primarily focused on the juvenile, the 'family care' (*Familienfürsorge*) school of thought, which was increasingly fashionable in social work during this period, favoured an approach which 'treated' the family as well.[16] In Hamburg, social workers sometimes reported that they had admonished the juvenile's parents about their educational practices, or even about their housekeeping. One (male) social visitor noted that the mother of one of his juvenile clients 'has from time to time to be reminded firmly to take care of the apartment—admittedly a very poor one—and to keep the remains of its furnishings in proper order'.[17]

Probation represented an invasion by the public authorities of the domestic sphere. However, such visits might only take place twice a year, and for the juvenile the advantages of probation compared to custodial care were considerable. From the point of view of the state authorities, probation might not be a panacea, but it was cheaper than correctional education, and it accorded better with the spirit of the National Youth Welfare Law to educate individual juveniles in their normal environment than to remove them to a reformatory. However, the effectiveness of probation depended on the commitment and energy of social workers, and, as far as 'education for work' was concerned, on the state of the job market. Meanwhile, for the 'hard cases', custodial care in the reformatory continued.

Corrctional Education in the Post-War Period

Taking a juvenile into correctional education was the most drastic measure that the state youth welfare system could resort to.

[15] Jacques Donzelot, *The Policing of Families: Welfare versus the State* (London, 1980), 137.

[16] The *Familienfürsorge* approach to social work pioneered by Marie Baum had three dimensions: firstly as a 'philosophy' which put the family at the centre of social reform and social work efforts; secondly as a method of social casework which stressed dealing with a family as an entity; thirdly as an approach to organizing home visiting, based around generic social workers (*Familienfürsorgerinnen*) with responsibility for a particular district. See C. Sachße, *Mütterlichkeit als Beruf: Sozialarbeit, Sozialreform und Frauenbewegung 1871–1929* (Frankfurt am Main, 1986), 244; on the relationship between youth welfare and 'family care', see Hanna Hellinger, 'Grenzen der Familienfürsorge in der Erziehungsfürsorge', *ZBl* 17/9 (1925/6), 216–18.

[17] Heitmann, report on Hermann M., 16 Sept. 1927. LGH A1325/1933.

Juveniles under 20 years of age considered to be endangered by their social environment (RJWG paragraph 63, section 1.1) or already delinquent (paragraph 63, section 1.2) could, on the basis of a court order, be removed from their homes and placed either with a foster family or employer, or, as in nearly half of all cases, in a reformatory.

For a brief period during the revolution of 1918, it had seemed that the whole institution of correctional education was on the point of being swept away. The breakdown of state authority undermined discipline in the reformatories, and in a number of places Workers' and Soldiers' Councils ordered the release of inmates.[18] This development was only gradually brought under control with the suppression of the revolutionary movement. Nevertheless, to the dismay of conservatives, public confidence in correctional education had yet to be restored. 'The loud-mouthed *Halbstarker* has gained new power and influence in the workplace and on the street,' wrote one outraged judge in the spring of 1921. And yet, he complained, the courts were over-cautious in referring youngsters to correctional education: 'What is to become of today's youth, which lacks the stern hand of discipline and against whom no one dares to order the necessary measures of correctional education?'[19]

Meanwhile, left-wing and liberal critics of correctional education pointed out that it meant an effective deprivation of liberty, the duration of which was never determined in advance (in contrast to a prison sentence), and which often lasted for several years. They attacked its clumsy referral and review procedures and its discriminatory class character. Middle-class parents, it was alleged—not without reason—usually had the means to prevent their children being taken into public care.[20] The worst accusations concerned the reformatories, the majority of which were still run (with the aid of

---

[18] Preußisches Ministerium des Innern an den Regierungspräsidenten Arnsberg, 7 Aug. 1919. ZStA Merseburg, Rep. 191, 2296. See also Richard Bessel, 'State and Society in Germany in the Aftermath of the First World War', in W. R. Lee and E. Rosenhaft (eds.), *The State and Social Change in Germany 1880–1980* (Oxford, 1990), 200–1.

[19] Amtsgerichtsrat Schumacher, 'Die FE unter der Einwirkung der Revolution', *Deutsche Tageszeitung*, 31 Mar. 1921 (in ZStA Potsdam, 30.01, 1515).

[20] Dr Wagner-Roemnitz, 'Fürsorgeerziehung und Arbeiterschaft', *SP* 28/52 (1918/19), cols. 953–5; Ernst Schellenberg, 'FE und Proletariat', *Proletarische Sozialpolitik* 4/1 (1931), 21–3. On the social background of those referred to correctional education, see D. Peukert, *Grenzen der Sozialdisziplinierung: Aufstieg und Krise der deutschen Jugendfürsorge 1878–1932* (Cologne, 1986), 338–9, 355.

state subsidies) by the confessional welfare agencies. Liberal critics attacked the rigidity of institutions whose traditional goal was to save souls and turn out God-fearing subjects who knew their place in life and respected the existing order of society.

Liberal demands for reform concentrated initially on reformatory conditions. A symbol of the spirit of reform and renewal in reformatory education was the work of Karl Wilker at the Lindenhof in Berlin in the years 1917–20. Wilker took his inspiration from his experiences in the youth movement. As director of the Lindenhof, Wilker abolished the system of punishments which had prevailed under the previous regime, introduced elements of self-administration by the inmates and, together with his colleagues, endeavoured to create a 'pedagogical relationship' (*pädagogischen Bezug*) between staff and inmates which would be characterized by trust rather than fear.[21]

In Hamburg too, Wilker and the Lindenhof were a rallying cry for critics of conditions in the local reformatories. Under Direktor Schallehn and Oberin Rothe, the old regime in the city's two reformatories for older juveniles had survived the revolutionary upheavals of 1918/19. Inmates were subjected to a strict routine: in Schallehn's words, 'the cure for the inmates is strictly regulated work'.[22] For the boys, work entailed cultivating the land belonging to the reformatory; for the girls, it consisted of domestic tasks in the institution, including washing and mending the laundry for other Hamburg residential institutions. Punishments for insubordination or refusal to work ranged from solitary confinement to corporal punishment. Escapees brought back to the reformatory after being caught on the run were commonly greeted by a beating or being locked up in isolation. Both Schallehn and Rothe defended corporal punishment as an indispensable means of educating the inmates and deterring them from escaping.[23]

The critics of reformatory education in Hamburg were closely identified with the political Left. Towards the end of 1919, the

---

[21] Karl Wilker, 'Erziehungsheim Lindenhof: Ein Stück Tat gewordene Jugendbewegung', *Internationale Erziehungs-Rundschau*, 11 (Nov. 1920), 91–104; id., *Fürsorgeerziehung als Lebensschulung: Ein Aufruf zur Tat* (Berlin, 1921). On the ideas of the educational reformers, see Peukert, *Sozialdisziplinierung*, 199–206.

[22] Niederschrift über die 3. Sitzung der Kommission zur Beratung der Strafordnungen in den Erziehungsanstalten für Mädchen und für Knaben, 29 Nov. 1922. StAH, JB I, 479.

[23] Ibid.

organ of the Hamburg KPD, the *Hamburger Volkszeitung*, began publishing articles denouncing the physical conditions and educational methods in Hamburg's reformatories and in the orphanage.[24] In October 1920, a group of Hamburg ex-inmates set up their own organization, the Union of Ex-Reformatory Inmates (Verein ehemaliger Fürsorgezöglinge).[25] The organization was backed by Communist delegates in the Hamburg city assembly. In the spring of 1921, the organization began producing its own newspaper, *Die Stimme* ('The Voice'), which carried articles on Wilker and his work in the Lindenhof as well as exposing scandals in local reformatories. *Die Stimme* soon acquired notoriety in conservative youth welfare circles and was denounced by the chairman of the Conference on Correctional Education as part of a nationwide movement to undermine FE.[26]

The editor of *Die Stimme* was prosecuted in 1921 by the Hamburg youth welfare authorities for offences against Hamburg's press laws.[27] By May 1922, the paper had stopped appearing, and the organization faded away after 1923. Though the organization was short-lived, it succeeded in exposing the youth welfare authorities to unwelcome publicity, and from 1919 onwards representatives of the SPD and USPD in the newly-constituted youth welfare board used cases cited by the Verein as ammunition in their campaign for the liberalization of educational methods in the reformatories.[28] However, it was not until a new director and deputy director took over the youth welfare department in 1923 (Wilhelm Hertz and August Hellmann) that the advocates of liberalization begin to find support from the city authorities.[29] In

[24] 'Aus dem Waisenhaus entflohen', *Hamburger Volkszeitung*, 20 Dec. 1919.
[25] 'Verein ehemaliger Fürsorgezöglinge', *Der Pranger*, 22 (1920), 'Weiße Sklaven', *Der Verfemte: Kampfschrift der Deklassierten*, 4 (1920).
[26] Pastor Backhausen, 'Die neueste Entwicklung der FE in Deutschland', *ZBl* 13/11–12 (1921/2), 114–18, 116.
[27] Amtsgericht Hamburg, Urteil in der Strafsache gegen Karl Dopf, 23 May 1921. StAH, JB I, 8, vol. 4.
[28] Niederschrift über die außerordentliche Sitzung der Behörde für öffentliche Jugendfürsorge, 17 Mar. 1921. StAH, JB I, 420; 1. Sitzung der Kommission zur Abfassung einer Strafordnung der Erziehungsanstalt für Mädchen, 6 Dec. 1921; 2. Sitzung der Kommission zur Beratung der Strafordnung für die Erziehungsanstalt für Mädchen, 1 Nov. 1922; 3. Sitzung der Kommission zur Beratung der Strafordnungen in den Erziehungsanstalten, 29 Nov. 1922. StAH, JB I, 479.
[29] Niederschrift über die 4. Sitzung der Kommission zur Beratung der Strafordnung für die Erziehungsanstalten, 21 Mar. 1923. StAH, JB I, 479.

1923, under the 'new regime', corporal punishment was formally banned in both reformatories, and Hertz and Hellmann announced plans to bring about a complete transformation of the institutions.[30]

Not all referrals to correctional education meant referral to a reformatory; a proportion of juveniles referred were boarded out with foster families. In the Reich as a whole between 1927 and 1933, the number of juveniles in reformatories as a proportion of all juveniles in correctional education fluctuated between 41 and 48 per cent.[31] In Hamburg at the end of 1919, only 32.7 per cent of the juveniles in correctional education were in reformatories, though this proportion rose to 38.7 per cent in 1922, to 40.3 per cent in 1925, and reached a peak of 44.2 per cent in 1929.[32] This trend towards custodial care in Hamburg reflected the fact that a rising proportion of juveniles referred to correctional education in the course of the 1920s were aged 14 and over. The older age groups were more difficult to place in foster families than the under-14s, and were thus more likely to end up in a residential institution. Of the inmates of the state-run reformatories in Hamburg, 28.5 per cent were 14 and over in 1919: this proportion rose to 31.7 per cent in 1924, 45.1 per cent in 1926, and reached a maximum level of 49.3 per cent in 1928.[33] In the years 1927–33 (statistics being unavailable for the years up to 1925), more than 50 per cent of reformatory inmates over 14 in Hamburg were girls.[34]

The Hamburg innovation of 'voluntary correctional education', introduced in 1910, was retained in Hamburg's law to implement the National Youth Welfare Law of 1922/24.[35] From the point of

[30] Auszug aus dem Protokoll der Behörde für öffentliche Jugendfürsorge, 13 Dec. 1923. StAH, JB I, 465 vol. 2.
[31] These statistics and those referred to in the following are based, firstly, on those collected by the Allgemeiner Fürsorgeerziehungstag, since official statistics for the Reich as a whole on correctional education were only introduced in 1935: A. Ohland, 'Statistik über die FE in Deutschland', *ZBl* 23/8 (1931/2), 272–9; 24/6–7 (1932/3), 248–53; 25/12 (1933/4), 354–65; 26/10–11 (1934/5), 304–17. Secondly, they are based on the official statistics on FE in Prussia: 'Statistik über die FE in Preußen für das Rechnungsjahr 1929', *Volkswohlfahrt*, Beilage zu Jg. 13 (1932), 162–86; 'Statistik über die FE in Preußen 1930', ibid. 694–723; 'Statistik . . . 1932', *Zeitschrift des Preußischen Statistischen Landesamtes* 72 (1934), 413–30; 'Statistik . . . 1933', *Vierteljahreshefte für preußische Statistik* 1 (1935), 182–201. References in the following to FE statistics are, if not otherwise specified, from these sources.
[32] See Table 10.   [33] Ibid.   [34] Ibid.
[35] Gesetz zur Ausführung des RJWG vom 2. Januar 1924, in *Hamburgisches Gesetz- und Verordnungsblatt*, 3, (6. Jan 1924), 6. On voluntary correctional education before 1914, see Ch. 2.

the youth welfare authorities voluntary referral was a convenient device to reduce administration and—so it was thought—lessen popular hostility to the institution of correctional education. By the mid-1920s, around three-quarters of new referrals were on this 'voluntary' basis, and around half the juveniles entering institutional care in any one year were placed there by their parents under voluntary arrangements.[36] However, it was easier to put one's troublesome children into public care than to get them out again: if parents tried to remove their offspring from correctional education 'too soon', the authorities usually ensured that the guardianship court passed a court order placing the child in 'normal' correctional education and depriving the parents of their authority over the child.[37] Hamburg was seen by other youth welfare authorities as a pioneer in its use of voluntary correctional education, and the model was copied in other *Länder*, including Saxony, Bremen, and Lübeck, during the course of the 1920s.

Reformatory Scandals and Reform Efforts

Opportunities for reform opened up to some extent with the increase in public welfare spending in the second half of the 1920s. Youth welfare authorities committed to reform, such as the SPD-controlled Landesjugendamt in Berlin, set up new public reformatories which endeavoured to apply the new educational principles.[38] The Hamburg youth welfare department attempted a similar strategy, opening two new reformatories for older boys in 1925 and 1926. These two institutions were smaller and more modern in design, contrasting with the prison-like premises of Ohlsdorf. 'Lighter' cases tended to be transferred to the new institutions, while Ohlsdorf became increasingly a dumping ground for boys considered particularly intractable.

However, the real pressure for changes in reformatory conditions in the Reich as a whole came from a series of reformatory scandals in the late 1920s. Peter Martin Lampel's play about a riot in a reformatory, based on his reportage *Jungen in Not*, caused a

---

[36] Hertz, 'Zehn Jahre Hamburger Jugendamt', 94.
[37] Hertz, 'Die Entwicklung der FE in Deutschland und ihre Auswirkungen auf Hamburg', *JV* 6/6–7 (1930), 108–13.
[38] *Fünf Jahre Landesjugendamt* Berlin 1925–1930 (Berlin, 1931), 26–9.

sensation in the winter of 1928–9 in Berlin and sparked off public meetings on the issue.[39] In August 1929 the authorities, attempting vainly to damp down the furore surrounding Lampel's work, banned the film version of the play.[40] Other writers, journalists, and film-makers also turned their hand to the subject,[41] to the extent that a leading Catholic exponent of reformatory education complained of a coordinated 'frontal attack' on correctional education by the media.[42]

With the public thus highly sensitized to the issue, it was inevitable that two major scandals which broke around this time attracted all the more public attention. These occurred in a reformatory run by the Innere Mission in Rickling, where inmates were maltreated in the secure wing of the reformatory,[43] and in one run by the Berlin public youth welfare authorities, Scheuen, where a number of inmates were exposed, with the knowledge of the director, to what amounted to lynch justice by other inmates. As a result, one of the inmates had died of his injuries.[44] The incidents in Rickling and Scheuen led to widely-publicized court cases. One youth welfare administrator commented in 1932 that 'it is beyond doubt that the general mistrust of correctional education has grown and that the so-called reformatory scandals... have undermined the trust in correctional education even amongst otherwise sensible people'.[45]

The climate of opinion in the late 1920s encouraged liberal and left-wing educational reformers to step up their reform campaigns.

[39] On Lampel's work and its public impact, see Peukert, *Sozialdisziplinierung*, 240–5; on the Berlin public meeting, see Max Fürst, *Talisman Scheherezade* (Frankfurt am Main, 1976), 180–90.

[40] Peter Martin Lampel, *Jungen in Not. Berichte von Fürsorgezöglingen* (Berlin, 1929); id., *Revolte im Erziehungshaus; Schauspiel der Gegenwart in 3 Akten* (Berlin, 1929); 'Verbot des Films "Revolte im Erziehungshaus" ', *Evangelische Jugendhilfe* 5/11 (1929), 349–55.

[41] By 1930, apart from Lampel's works, two films had been made dealing with reformatory education ('Das gottlose Mädchen' and 'Tagebuch einer Verlorenen') and a novel, *Die in ihre Hände fallen* (H. Richter).

[42] Gustav von Mann, 'Um die Zukunft unserer Anstalten', *Jugendwohl* 19 (1930), 2–4.

[43] W. Ehlers, 'Ist das christliche Erziehung?', *Schleswig-Holsteinische Volkszeitung*, 23 June 1928. On Rickling, see Peukert, *Sozialdisziplinierung*, 244.

[44] B. Frei, G. Löwenthal, and A. Brandt, *Scheuen: Gericht über die Schuldigen* (Berlin, 1931); Curt Bondy, *Scheuen* (Berlin, 1931); Peukert, *Sozialdisziplinierung*, 243–4; C. Kuhlmann, *Erbkrank oder erziehbar?* (Weinheim, 1989), 32–3.

[45] I. Fischer, 'Zur heutigen Lage in der Jugendfürsorge', *ZBl* 24/3 (1932/3), 81–6, 83.

The Gilde Soziale Arbeit set up a working party to press for the reform of correctional education in 1927.[46] The youth welfare committee of the Arbeiterwohlfahrt published guidelines for the reform of FE in 1929.[47] These groups' proposals summarized and reiterated many demands already voiced in the course of the 1920s regarding reformatory conditions. These entailed in the first place the basic reforms propagated by Karl Wilker (for instance greater self-government for inmates, skilled vocational training, and a ban on corporal punishment). The Gilde stressed furthermore the need to create a sophisticated and differentiated system of education tailored scientifically to the needs of different types of children; reformatories should be staffed by personnel adequately trained in educational psychology and run in accordance with the insights of psychiatry and psychotherapy.[48] In addition, Social Democrats emphasized the importance of combating the tendency of reformatory education to 'keep children in cloister-like isolation from the outside world, to alienate them from their social class, to educate them according to outdated authoritarian principles, and inculcate in them petty bourgeois values'.[49]

The reforms called for by the Arbeiterwohlfahrt extended to administrative and legal aspects of correctional education as well as reformatory conditions. These included the expansion of state as opposed to private reformatory provision, the imposition of a tighter system of inspection on privately-run reformatories, and the strengthening of the legal rights of juveniles in correctional education. In addition, Social Democrats proposed the transfer of the administration of correctional education in Prussia from regional control (Provinzialausschüsse) to local control. The costs of correctional education in Prussia were borne by the regional welfare associations (Provinzialverbände), which could claim back two-thirds of the cost of correctional education from the Prussian state. The larger municipal youth welfare departments in Prussia were keen to take on these extra responsibilities as long as financial

[46] Justus Ehrhardt, 'Die Gilde "Soziale Arbeit" und der AFET', *Der Zwiespruch* 12/44 (1930), 523.
[47] 'Richtlinien des Hauptausschusses für Arbeiterwohlfahrt zur Umgestaltung der FE mit Erläuterungen', *AW* 4/10 (1929), 289–320.
[48] Justus Ehrhardt, 'Die Krise der Anstaltserziehung', *Der Zwiespruch* 12/15 (1930), 169–70.
[49] 'Richtlinien des Hauptausschusses für Arbeiterwohlfahrt zur Umgestaltung der FE', 298.

arrangements were made to compensate them for the extra costs involved. The Prussian regional authorities and the Prussian welfare ministry (which was controlled by the Centre Party) opposed such a change, alleging that it was an attack on private welfare agencies and confessional education.[50] This dispute was a specifically Prussian problem and the Arbeiterwohlfahrt proposals did not apply to, for instance, Saxony and Hessen, where the local authorities were responsible for the administration and costs of correctional education, or to Oldenburg, or city-states like Bremen and Hamburg, where the *Land* authorities were responsible for running correctional education.[51]

By the end of the 1920s, the reform lobby was beginning to elicit a positive response from the state authorities. In 1929, the Prussian welfare ministry issued a circular banning corporal punishment in reformatories, and new guidelines on reformatory administration and inspection were issued in June 1931.[52] The correctional education establishment, in which the confessional welfare agencies played a key role, also began to make concessions. The leading Catholic journal for reformatory education published in 1930 a measured response to the left-wing critics.[53] Meanwhile, the Conference on Correctional Education (Allgemeiner Fürsorgeerziehungstag or AFET) was being pushed in the direction of reform by left-wingers within its ranks. Two leading members of the Gilde Soziale Arbeit were elected on to its executive at the AFET conference in 1930.[54] In 1931, the AFET executive issued a statement expressing a measure of self-criticism on behalf of reformatory administrators and staff.[55]

While liberal educational principles were becoming increasingly

[50] Landeshauptmann der Provinz Sachsen an den Verband preußischer Provinzen, 28 Aug. 1928; Auszug aus der Niederschrift über die Konferenz der FE-Dezernenten der preußischen Provinzen, 2 Sept. 1928. BA Koblenz, R36, 1997; Karl Vossen, 'Verschiebung der Trägerschaft in der FE', *Jugendwohl* 18/3 (1929), 89–98.

[51] C. Hasenclever, *Jugendhilfe und Jugendgesetzgebung seit 1900* (Göttingen, 1978), 112.

[52] Preußisches Ministerium für Volkswohlfahrt an alle Oberpräsidenten, 12 July 1929. StAH, JB I, 493; 'Runderlaß des Preußischen Ministeriums für Volkswohlfahrt vom 20.6.1931 betr. Fürsorgeerziehung', *Volkswohlfahrt* 12 (1931), col. 620.

[53] P. Petto, 'Aktuelle Fragen der Heimerziehung', *Blätter für Anstaltspädagogik: Zeitschrift für Pflege der katholischen Anstaltserziehung* 20/2 (1930), 33–47.

[54] Hertz, Kurzer Aktenbericht über die Tagung des Hauptausschusses des AFET am 21. und 22.10.1930 in Weimar. StAH, JB I, 444; Justus Ehrhardt, 'Die Gilde "Soziale Arbeit" und der AFET', *Der Zwiespruch* 12/44 (1930), 523.

[55] 'Erklärung des Allgemeinen Fürsorgeerziehungstags', *ZBl* 23/6 (1931/2), 193.

accepted in theory by reformatory directors and youth welfare administrators, much still remained to be done to put them into practice.[56] However, there were some generally-acclaimed examples of the new social education methods in practice which were seen as reform models. Pioneering reformatories of the Weimar period included Bräunsdorf, Heiligenstedten, Selent, Lindenhof (Berlin), and the Westendheim (Frankfurt). The latter was notable for its 'half-open' principle: the inmates lived in the reformatory but had normal jobs outside the institution.[57]

Unique among the experiments in correctional education of the 1920s in being an institution for girls, the Immenhof, founded by the Arbeiterwohlfahrt in 1927, was a consciously 'socialist' reformatory, set up to demonstrate that Social Democratic reform demands could be realized in practice.[58] Under the Immenhof's director from 1928 to 1931, Hanna Eisfelder, rules and sanctions were kept to a minimum: the girls could dress as they liked and organize their dormitories as they pleased.[59] The only punishment was to be sent away from the Immenhof to another reformatory. The socialist youth movement provided a basis for contacts between the reformatory and the outside world: pupils set up their own SAJ group and in 1930 half the pupils were reported to belong to it.[60] The Immenhof's unorthodox educational approach did not find the wholehearted backing of the more conventionally minded on the Arbeiterwohlfahrt executive,[61] and tensions mounted which underlay Hanna Eisfelder's resignation from the Immenhof in the summer of 1931 on grounds of ill-health. Nevertheless, under her direction the Immenhof provided a striking contrast to those regimented institutions dedicated above all to inculcating chastity, penitence, and humility into 'fallen girls'.

[56] Walter Herrmann, 'Ist Methodenwechsel in der FE nötig?', *Erziehung* 7/7 (1931/32), 412–18.
[57] On the Westendheim, see P. Dudek, *Leitbild: Kamerad und Helfer* (Frankfurt am Main, 1988), 167–75.
[58] E. Kirschmann-Röhl, in *Jahrbuch der Arbeiterwohlfahrt 1930* (Berlin, 1931), 16.
[59] Hilde Köster-Richter, letter of 18 Mar. 1985; interview with Lotte Lemke, 28 July 1984.
[60] 'Verfassungstag im Immenhof', *AW* 4/17 (1929), 536–7; 'Revolutionsfeier im Immenhof', *AW* 5/1 (1930); Hanna Eisfelder, 'Erziehungsfragen auf dem Immenhof', *Jahrbuch der Arbeiterwohlfahrt 1930* (Berlin, 1931), 31–44; Hilde Köster-Richter, letter to the author, 18 Mar. 1985.
[61] Information from Lotte Lemke, interview 28 July 1984.

Successful reform experiments were few in number and often short-lived. In some places, reforms were never attempted; in others, haphazard attempts to liberalize had ended in disaster. While Rickling was a reformatory where authoritarian methods had never been abandoned, Scheuen was an example of an ill-conceived and poorly executed 'liberal' experiment which had ended in violent anarchy, with 'self-government' degenerating into a situation where a group of privileged inmates victimized the rest.[62]

While the public controversies created pressure for reform in the longer term, they tended in the short term to exacerbate the problems inside the reformatories. The growing public mistrust of correctional education increased the reluctance on the part of the courts to refer any but the most intractable juveniles; these tended to be the older age-groups. The number of children under 14 years who were referred as a percentage of total referrals in Prussia came to 43.5 per cent in 1926/7 and fell to 22.8 per cent in 1931/2. Meanwhile, there were growing disciplinary problems in the reformatories as inmates became increasingly aware of their rights, or rather their lack of them. Opposition to the reformatory regime was sometimes encouraged and assisted by the Communists' campaign against correctional education, which intensified towards the end of the 1920s.[63]

In Hamburg, after 1923, reform efforts under the new leadership of the youth welfare department produced some changes in the girls' reformatory. Oberin Rothe was persuaded to resign, and Bertha Paulssen, from her position as *Regierungsrätin* in the department, instituted a number of changes. The new director of the girls' reformatory, Margarete Cornils, was more sympathetic to reforming ideas than her predecessor, and a systematic attempt was made to 'individualize' and to differentiate between the needs of the new referrals.[64]

Changes proved more difficult to implement in the boys' reformatory in Ohlsdorf, where Schallehn retained his post as

---

[62] Peukert, *Sozialdisziplinierung*, 243. Carola Kuhlmann plays down this dimension of the background to the Scheuen debacle: see *Erbkrank oder erziehbar*, 37.

[63] August Brandt, 'Zwischenbilanz der Fürsorgeerziehungskampagne der IAH', *Proletarische Sozialpolitik* 2/6 (1929), 179–83; Ernst Schellenberg, 'FE und Proletariat', *Proletarische Sozialpolitik* 4/1 (1931), 21–3; 4/2, 57–60; Georg Glaser, *Geheimnis und Gewalt* (Reinbek, 1983), 41.

[64] Interview with Alice Borchert, 29 Feb. 1984.

Probation and Correctional Education 241

director. Embarrassingly for the youth welfare department, Ohlsdorf scandals continued to be reported in the local Communist press.[65] Escapes from Ohlsdorf continued to be a major problem, and a subculture of absconded reformatory inmates developed in certain quarters of Hamburg. Two absconders, Friedrich S. and Otto S., were tried for robbery and assault in 1929. It emerged that on his day out from the Ohlsdorf reformatory, Otto S. went to the Speisehaus Neuenberg in St Pauli, where he met Friedrich S.: he 'knew that you can always find boys from Ohlsdorf and that it's easy to sell reformatory uniforms there.' It was the man who supplied them with different clothing who ended up as the victim of their assault.[66]

Despite the pledge by the new directors of the Hamburg youth welfare authorities to transform the reformatories in line with the new liberal educational principles, it seems that their efforts brought limited success. In 1928, Wilhelm Hertz had to admit that the principles he advocated were not fully realized in practice in the public reformatories run by his own department in Hamburg.[67] Even if Hamburg managed to avoid any major revolts or scandals in its institutions, developments in the Hamburg reformatories did not enhance the image of the Hamburg youth welfare department, which liked to present itself as a model for the rest of the Reich.

Public Youth Welfare on the Defensive, 1929–1932

The system of public youth welfare was hardly consolidated when it was confronted with the problems created by the economic crisis from 1929 onwards. Adolescents 'at risk', whose numbers escalated as a result of unemployment and poverty, became a mass phenomenon. Assistance to unemployed youth was not expressly designated as a task for public youth welfare by the National Youth

---

[65] 'Das Lehrlingsheim Ohlsdorf', *Hamburger Volkszeitung*, 11 Aug. 1927; 'Skandalöse Zustände im Arbeiterheim Ohlsdorf', ibid. 18 Aug. 1927; Schallehn an das Jugendamt Hamburg, 20 Aug. 1927; A. Hellmann, Vermerk 22 Aug. 1927; H. Eisenbarth (Präses der Jugendbehörde) an Schallehn, 26 Aug. 1927. StAH, JB I, 465 vol. 2. 'Revolte gegen das Zwangserziehungssystem', *Hamburger Volkszeitung*, 13 Apr. 1929; 'Kommißmethoden vernichten das Leben der Proletarierjugend', ibid. 15 Aug. 1930; 'Der jugendliche Selbstmörder', ibid. 26 Aug. 1930.
[66] LGH 1196/1928.
[67] Hertz an Schwering, Jugendamt Köln, 24 July 1928. StAH, JB I, 465, vol. 2.

Welfare Law, which had been passed at a time of low youth unemployment. Nevertheless, as outlined in Chapter 4, youth welfare departments in large cities tried to improvise measures to organize and supervise unemployed youth.

While the tasks confronting public youth welfare multiplied in scale and complexity, its resources were vanishing. As we have seen in Chapter 4, the dismantling of unemployment insurance at national level led to a large part of the costs for supporting the unemployed being transferred to the welfare budgets of the municipalities.[68] Municipal expenditure on other areas of welfare, including youth welfare, was reduced correspondingly.

The impact of the cuts in Hamburg is illustrated by figures on youth welfare expenditure between 1924 and 1933. The total expenditure on public youth welfare in the city of Hamburg rose steadily from 4.8m. RM in the financial year 1924 to 8m. RM in 1927, reaching a maximum level of 9.7m. RM in 1929. Thereafter expenditure fell to 7.5m. RM in 1932 and 6.1m. RM in 1932.[69] In 1931, the director of the youth welfare department declared that the whole range of tasks undertaken by his department was being placed in jeopardy by the cuts.[70]

At the same time as cuts in youth welfare were taking effect throughout the Reich, public welfare became the target for bitter ideological attacks from the Right. Right-wing publicists declared that state expenditure on welfare benefits and facilities benefited primarily the eugenically inferior section of the population and hence functioned in a counter-selective manner. Particularly in the economic crisis, they argued, where those not supported by state welfare were living on the poverty line themselves, the state had to cut its expenditure on the weak and 'unfit' to 'realistic' levels; the public authorities should only undertake the education of deprived and delinquent juveniles insofar as the costs involved did not exceed the use of such measures for the 'national whole'. These Social Darwinist arguments were not new, but they were expressed more openly and frequently in the period of economic crisis than before.[71] Moreover, they were gaining greater respectability, both

---

[68] See Ch. 4, pp. 117–19.
[69] *StJB Hamburg* (1930/1), 298; (1933/4), 175.
[70] Hertz, 'Die gegenwärtige Lage der Jugendwohlfahrt', memo, 26 Nov. 1931. BA Koblenz, R36, 1460.
[71] Helene Wessel, *Lebenshaltung aus Fürsorge und aus Erwerbstätigkeit* (Berlin, 1931), 73–81, 192; Gudula Kall, 'Der Kampf um die Aufrechterhaltung der

within welfare and educational circles and in government. In a ministerial discussion in 1932, a civil servant in the Prussian welfare ministry argued that the resources available for youth welfare should be concentrated on the 'healthy' rather than being wasted on less 'valuable' youngsters:

> In the field of youth welfare the key principle must be that the bulk of resources be channelled into preserving the physical and mental fitness of that portion of the youthful population which is still healthy, but which is due to the crisis exposed to all sorts of dangers to a greater extent than previously. Sick and delinquent juveniles should not exactly be abandoned to their fate, but should be cared for only to an extent which is in reasonable proportion to the resources used for preventive youth work [*Jugendpflege*] and which is also in proportion to the milieu from which these juveniles come and to their usefulness as future citizens. One does not need to labour the point that in this respect mistakes have not infrequently been made. Resources have been used on ineducable or otherwise inferior juveniles which would have sufficed to support entire working-class families with several children.[72]

A resolution adopted by the Prussian State Council in January 1932 reflected the same trend, calling on the public authorities at all levels in Prussia to 'reduce the costs of the care and education of the mentally and physically inferior to a level which can be borne by a nation which has been completely impoverished and sucked dry'.[73] In Hamburg, these views were echoed in the complaints of officials in the general welfare department that enormous sums were being wasted on the 'asocial elements which because of psychological defects have been kept in institutions for years'.[74]

A successful resistance to cuts in youth welfare was hampered by the fact that youth welfare circles were not united among themselves. Some representatives of the voluntary sector welcomed cuts in the state youth welfare bureaucracy. They thought that their chance had come to revise the hard-fought compromise of the

---

Aufrechterhaltung der Wohlfahrtspflege', *ZBl* 23/10–11 (1931), 341–6. On the links between the Depression and the changing climate of eugenic thought, see P. Weindling, *Health, Race and German Politics* (Cambridge, 1989), esp. pp. 442–6.

[72] Kurt Richter, in Bericht über eine Sitzung im Volkswohlfahrtsministerium betr. Jugendpflege, 22 Jan. 1932. ZStA Merseburg, Rep. 191, 924, 1, vol. 3.

[73] *Drucksache des Preußischen Staatsrates*, 222 (1931), (Gayl, Steiniger und Genossen). ZStA Merseburg, Rep. 2.1.7, 168.

[74] Niederschrift über die Leitersitzung der Wohlfahrtsbehörde Hamburg, 7 Oct. 1931. StAH, SB I, VG 24.31.

National Youth Welfare Law between the state and the voluntary sector and to restore the primacy of the voluntary agencies. In the course of the 1920s, private welfare agencies had found themselves increasingly excluded from youth welfare work as a consequence of the expansion of public youth welfare.[75] Now things looked about to change: 'Private welfare is now coming back into its own, after having been pronounced dead ten years ago and despite efforts by the public authorities in some places to kill it off', proclaimed a representative of the German Red Cross at a congress in September 1930.[76] Admittedly, this was not an attitude adopted by the entire private welfare sector, some of whose spokesmen were ready to admit that the private agencies were dependent on a flourishing public welfare sector for much of their funding.[77]

Meanwhile, divisions were emerging within the ranks of those seeking to maintain and expand the state youth welfare system. Radical left-wing views were growing among the rank and file of social workers as a response to the political threat from the Right, a mood that became clear at a series of meetings among social workers in Berlin in the winter of 1931/2.[78] Prominent liberal and Social Democratic reformers noted this development with alarm.[79] They themselves remained on the defensive, confronted constantly with the problem of how far to resist and how far to compromise with the cuts and with right-wing plans for education and youth welfare.[80]

---

[75] Pastor Ruhnke, 'Die private Jugendhilfe in ihrem Verhältnis zur öffentlichen Jugendhilfe', *Evangelische Jugendhilfe* 5/3 (1929), 65–79.

[76] Dr Kessler, 'Wirtschaftskrise und Wohlfahrtsarbeit', *Bl. DRK* 9 (1930), 576–82, 576.

[77] Hasenclever, *Jugendhilfe*, 125; Grüneisen, 'Wie geht es weiter?', *Bl. DRK* 4 (1932), 210–22; Johannes Sunder, 'Gegenwartslage und -leistungen der freien Wohlfahrtspflege', *SP* 41/42 (1932), cols. 1343–9, col. 1344.

[78] 'Gilde und Politik', *Rundbrief der Gilde*, 21 (Nov. 1931); 'Hat soziale Arbeit heute noch einen Sinn?', *Der Zwiespruch*, 14/10 (1932), 116–17; 'Bericht über die zweite Internationale Konferenz für soziale Arbeit', *Proletarische Sozialpolitik*, 5/8 (1932), 248–51; Henry Jacoby, *Von des Kaisers Schule zu Hitlers Zuchthaus* (Frankfurt am Main, 1980), 155.

[79] Hedwig Wachenheim, 'Fürsorger und Fürsorgerinnen! Wo steht ihr im politischen Kampf?', *AW* 6/23 (1931), 727–30; Hans Muthesius, 'Fürsorge und fürsorgerische Haltung', in Deutscher Verband der Sozialbeamtinnen (ed.), *Fürsorgerinnen-Not, Fürsorgerinnen-Wille* (Berlin, 1932), 5–9.

[80] Gertrud Bäumer, 'Die Jugendnot—ein unpolitischer Appell', *Soziale Arbeit*, 10/12 (1933), 69–70.

The Impact of the Depression on Reformatory Education

A crisis already existed in correctional education before the economic crisis made itself felt, but the existing problems were exacerbated by the effects of the Depression. At a meeting of one of the AFET's subcommittees on 9 December 1932, the mood of the inmates and staff in the reformatories was characterized as one of deep gloom. Rudolf Schlosser, the director of the reformatory in Bräunsdorf, reported that 'the vitality of our work and our morale are suffering greatly, not just through the unemployment outside but because of the shockingly pessimistic attitude of the pupils themselves'.[81]

Some inmates may have been grateful for the food and shelter which the reformatory provided.[82] In 1930, it was reported that some reformatory inmates deliberately spent the winters 'inside' and escaped regularly for the duration of the summer.[83] However, it is likely that for most inmates their view of correctional education as a dead end was reinforced by the almost certain prospect of unemployment upon release.[84] For the administrators of correctional education, the social reintegration of juveniles in correctional education through work became an increasingly elusive goal. Domestic service or agricultural labour was the most that could be hoped for in the way of work and even this was becoming difficult to obtain.[85] For the more conservative reformatories, this merely confirmed their view that old ways were the best ways. For the reformers who had campaigned for facilities to train inmates—including girls—for skilled trades, it was a dilemma. Some called for a revision of reform objectives: Hans Achinger, for example, speaking at a meeting of the Gilde Soziale Arbeit in July 1932,

---

[81] Bericht über die Sitzung des Fachausschusses 1 des AFET, 9/10 Dec. 1932. StAH, JB I, 232, vol. 1.

[82] Immanuel Fischer, 'Zur heutigen Lage in der Jugendfürsorge', *ZBl* 24/3 (1932), 81–6, 84.

[83] Otto Voss and Herbert Schön, 'Die Cliquen jugendlicher Verwahrloster als sozialpädagogisches Problem', in Carl Mennicke (ed.), *Erfahrungen der Jungen* (Potsdam, 1930), 69–89, 75.

[84] Hertz, Kurzer Aktenbericht über die Tagung des Hauptausschusses des AFET am 21. und 22.10.1930 in Weimar. StAH, JB I, 444.

[85] 'Auszug aus dem Jahresbericht über die FE Minderjähriger in der Provinz Hannover für die Zeit April 1931 bis März 1932', *Volkswohlfahrt*, 13/21 (1932), cols. 941–5, col. 943.

pleaded for an abandonment of 'unrealistic' demands. Sophisticated vocational training facilities for the juveniles in correctional education were, he argued, a waste of resources at a time 'when thousands of normal youngsters are glad to escape from perpetual unemployment into the most primitive work on the land'.[86]

That young people in reformatories had it too good in comparison with adolescents outside was a constant accusation thrown at correctional education by those who advocated drastic cuts in welfare spending, particularly on such 'undeserving' juveniles as reformatory inmates. However, signs of luxury in reformatories would have been hard to find in these years. The cuts forced the correctional education administrations to reduce their costs, particularly the most expensive item on their budget, reformatory costs. Under the slogan of rationalization, reformatories were merged or closed down: an estimated 10–15 per cent of all the confessionally run reformatories in the Reich were closed during the years 1928–32.[87] The Prussian welfare ministry instructed that the cuts should be used as an opportunity to close down substandard institutions.[88] Hamburg put this principle into practice when it shut down the boys' reformatory in Ohlsdorf in 1932; but it is impossible to judge the extent to which the institutions shut down elsewhere in the Reich were selected according to educational criteria.

Reducing the costs of running the reformatories took the form of cuts in the menu, in clothing allowances, in leisure activities, in staffing levels, and vocational training. In February 1931, the Prussian welfare ministry instructed the Prussian correctional education authorities to cut costs by ensuring that the standard of living in the institutions was appropriate for the austere times.[89] Another strategy pursued by the reformatories was to exploit the

---

[86] Hans Achinger, 'Fürsorge und Wirtschaftskrise', *Rundbrief der Gilde*, 23 (July, 1932), 8–10, 9–10.

[87] Estimate by Rudolf Schlosser, in Bericht über die Sitzung des Fachausschusses 1 des AFET, 9/10 Dec. 1932. StAH, JB I, 232, vol. 1. According to another estimate, 20% of Protestant reformatories shut down during the Depression: 'Zur Lage der evangelischen Jugendfürsorge und Erziehungsheime', *Evangelische Jugendhilfe*, 9/1 (1933), 5–9.

[88] 'Runderlaß des Preußischen Ministeriums für Volkswohlfahrt vom 20.6.1931 betr. Fürsorgeerziehung', *Volkswohlfahrt*, 12 (1931), cols. 620–4, col. 622.

[89] Preußisches Ministerium für Volkswohlfahrt an die Oberpräsidenten, betr. Fürsorgeerziehungskosten, 26 Feb. 1931. BA Koblenz, R36, 1976.

labour of their inmates more effectively. In Hamburg, in September 1931, the youth welfare department noted that ten female staff in the residential homes had been replaced by older reformatory pupils.[90]

Reductions in reformatory standards were a blow to the correctional education reform movement, whose slogan had been 'better no reformatories than bad reformatories'.[91] The reformatory director Rudolf Schlosser warned against allowing the standard of living in the reformatories to sink to that of impoverished working-class families. Living standards in the reformatory should, according to Schlosser, encourage rather than dampen the inmates' aspirations for a decent and civilized existence.[92] However, the reaction of liberal and left-wing educational reformers to such cuts was not unanimous. Some, like Hans Achinger, considered a certain lowering of the standards of reformatory facilities necessary and justified.[93]

The declining standards in the reformatories exacerbated the existing educational difficulties brought on by the fall in referrals of the younger and more tractable 'material' and the discontent of the adolescent inmates.[94] Revolts, escapes and violent reactions by staff against inmates continued.[95] The unrest fuelled a call for tougher discipline: hardly had the liberal reformers got their ideas across to the establishment than a right-wing backlash against liberalization began.[96] One reformatory director gave vent to his feelings in an article in the Catholic reformatory journal attacking soft-hearted liberals for ignoring the problem of violent and disruptive inmates in reformatories. He complained that correctional education was being jeopardized by the actions of such 'scum' and that a 'tyranny of the inferior' (*Herrschaft der Minderwertigen*) now prevailed in

---

[90] Niederschrift über die Vollversammlung des LJA und JA Hamburg, 29 Sept. 1931. StAH, JB I, 3, vol. 1.
[91] Curt Bondy, 'Kritisches zur FE', *ZBl* 22/5 (1930/1), 145–9, 148.
[92] Rudolf Schlosser, in Bericht über die Sitzung des Fachausschusses 1 des AFET, 9/10 Dec. 1932. StAH, JB I, 232, vol. 1.
[93] Hans Achinger, 'Fürsorge und Wirtschaftskrise', *Rundbrief der Gilde*, 23 (July, 1932), 8–10.
[94] Landesrat Hecker, 'Neue Wege in der FE', *WRP* 8/8 (1932), 123–4; Bondy, *Scheuen*, 32.
[95] Herbert Francke, 'Von Scheuen bis Strausberg', *SP* 41/10 (1932), cols. 296–301.
[96] 'Erklärung des Landesdirektors der Provinz Brandenburg zu den Vorgängen in der Provinzialanstalt Strausberg am 16./17. Februar 1932', quoted in Webler, 'Neue Anstaltsprozesse', *ZBl* 24/2 (1932/3), 58–9, 59.

the reformatories.[97] In line with this new, tougher mood, the correctional education authorities in the Prussian provinces of the Rhineland and in Westphalia issued instructions in 1930 and 1931 to the reformatories in their region allowing the punishment of solitary confinement to be made more severe. They argued that this step was necessary in view of growing difficulties in maintaining discipline, which they ascribed to the abolition of corporal punishment.[98]

In the autumn of 1932, some educational reformers appeared ready to compromise on this issue. The liberal reformers had previously responded unanimously to calls for 'back to the birch' with the argument that revolts in reformatories were not so much the consequence of the new liberal educational methods as of their false application.[99] Now, however, prominent voices from the liberal reform lobby could be heard questioning the wisdom of excessively liberal disciplinary methods and complaining that the pendulum had swung too far in the liberal direction. Justus Ehrhardt, a senior social worker in the Berlin youth welfare office, wrote in October 1932 that 'there will have to be an end to the overemphasis on banning punishments. This has now reached a stage where on account of someone's ear being boxed whole commissions are set in motion, questions are asked in parliament, [and] thick files are accumulated'.[100] On 26 October 1932, Curt Bondy, professor of educational science in Göttingen and director of the Eisenach youth prison, spoke at a public meeting called by education and welfare organizations 'against the reaction in education'. Bondy rejected the right-wing calls for a simple return to authoritarian methods. He emphasized, however, the necessity for discipline and obedience to the demands of the social group as key principles of modern social education. He warned against the degeneration of an educational style which was too heavily oriented to the 'sentimentality' and individualism of the youth movement and which in his view no longer corresponded to the needs of the times. These remarks were interpreted by left-wing critics in the audience as a tactical

---

[97] Direktor Moll, 'Zucht oder Auflösung in der FE', *Blätter für Anstaltspädagogik* 22/4 (1932), 101–8.
[98] Landeshauptmann der Provinz Westfalen, Anweisung betr. Verschärfung der Strafmaßnahmen in der FE in besonderen Fällen, 17 Mar. 1931. BA Koblenz, R36, 1982.   [99] Bondy, *Scheuen*, 19.
[100] Justus Ehrhardt, 'Gefahren in der Jugendfürsorge', *ZBl* 24/7 (1932/3), 225–32, 229.

withdrawal from previous liberal positions in an attempt to present the line of least resistance to the growing forces of the Right. These critics—among them the former director of the Immenhof, Hanna Eisfelder—declared that the adoption of Bondy's position would bring the educational reform movement itself into the reactionary camp.[101]

The Problem of the 'Ineducables' and the Reorientation of Correctional Education, 1931/2

The strength of the 'reaction in education' became evident as the debate on reformatories shifted from discussing educational methods towards the more fundamental issue of defining the tasks and target group of correctional education. This debate reflected the search for a new policy which would both reduce costs and solve the educational problems in the reformatories.

The increasing financial pressure on correctional education produced, in 1931/2, a growing lobby of administrators and reformatories who sought to cope with spending cuts by altering the categories of juveniles for whom correctional education could be ordered. There were two driving forces within this predominantly Prussian lobby. One was the organization of Prussian regional authorities (Verband der Preußischen Provinzen); the other was a group of reformatory directors and correctional education administrators who comprised the still dominant conservative wing of the AFET. This lobby, which may be characterized as the conservative correctional education establishment in Prussia, sought to cut costs while improving the 'success rates' of correctional education,[102] maintaining the viability of existing public and private reformatories, upholding the principle of confessional education, and preserving the regionally-based structure of correctional education administration.

In the summer of 1931, the head of the regional authority in the Rhineland presented to the Prussian state government a plan for

---

[101] 'Gegen die pädagogische Reaktion', *ZBl* 24/9 (1932/3), 343–4; 'Pädagogische Bewegung oder pädagogische Reaktion', *Rundbrief der Gilde*, 1 Jan. and 1 Feb. 1933; Jacoby, *Kaisers Schule zu Hitlers Zuchthaus*, 169–70.

[102] For some examples of the somewhat dubious 'success statistics' produced by the Prussian confessional education authorities, see Peukert, *Sozialdisziplinierung*, 346, 358.

legislative changes.[103] The general aim of this plan was to concentrate the resources of correctional education on younger children and adolescents 'at risk' instead of on those who were actually delinquent. Its advocates argued that catching and 'treating' potentially asocial juveniles at an early stage would prove in the long run to be an economy measure. The crisis in correctional education, in their eyes, was not so much due to the institutions but to the unsuitable and defective 'material' with which the system was called upon to deal.

Such a reorientation of correctional education required, firstly, an increase in the number of younger and 'lighter' cases referred. As we have seen above, the National Youth Welfare Law of 1922 contained a clause (paragraph 63, section 1) which was generally read as giving priority to fostering or other care at local authority expense over 'preventive' referrals to correctional education.[104] This interpretation of the law was confirmed by a decision by the Reichsgericht in April 1929. The Reichsgericht decision displeased those with a vested interest in confessional reformatory education: whereas the principle of placing a child according to its confession was laid down for correctional education (RJWG, paragraph 69), it was not prescribed for fostering at local authority expense under paragraph 63, section 1.[105] The new plans for correctional education drawn up in 1931/2 were based on the regulations enabling 'preventive referrals' which had applied in Prussia under the ruling of 1915 but had been superseded by the National Youth Welfare Law.[106] The advocates of 'preventive' referrals sought to restore the 1915 regulations in Prussia and extend them to the rest of the Reich.

The controversy over a change of referral practice was fiercest in Prussia, where rivalries between local authority youth welfare departments and regional correctional education authorities were most intense.[107] Liberal and Social Democratic reformers and administrators had welcomed and encouraged the decline in referrals of younger children to correctional education as long as the local youth welfare departments had been in a position to provide

---

[103] 'Abbruch der vorbeugenden Erziehungsfürsorge?', *WRP* 7/15 (1931), 239–40.
[104] See Ch. 5, p. 170. Dr Memelsdorff, Denkschrift über die Abgrenzung zwischen Fürsorgepflicht und Fürsorgeerziehung, 8 May 1928. BA Koblenz, R36, 1997.
[105] G. von Mann, 'Um die Zukunft unserer Anstalten', *Jugendwohl*, 19 (1930), 2–4. [106] See Ch. 2, p. 52.
[107] Landeshauptmann der Provinz Sachsen an den deutschen Städtetag, 18 May 1931. BA Koblenz, R36, 1996.

alternative methods of care on the local level. They condemned the right-wingers' demands for amendments to the law to enable earlier referral as a ploy on the part of the confessional organizations and the regional correctional education authorities to consolidate their power at the expense of the local youth welfare authorities.[108] However, local youth welfare authorities were not in a strong position to challenge the correctional education lobby: under the impact of Brüning's financial cuts, the local youth welfare services could not in practice provide the care they advocated as an alternative to correctional education.[109]

Despite the reluctance of the Prussian state government to support the change,[110] the advocates of 'preventive referral' got their way: the Reich Ministry of the Interior inserted clauses designed to enable 'preventive referral' into the first draft of an emergency decree on correctional education in November 1931.[111]

The other aspect of the Prussian correctional education lobby's plans to change its target group was to exclude and debar from it the more troublesome categories of juveniles: the older age groups and the 'ineducables' (*Unerziehbare*). This entailed, firstly, the reduction of the average age of juveniles in correctional education. This was to be achieved through lowering the upper age limit for referral (hitherto 18 years, but up to 20 years where the prospects of educational success were deemed to be good) and for release (hitherto 21 years). Secondly, 'ineducables' were to be excluded from correctional education. This would entail both the release of such juveniles who were already in correctional education and a stricter selection at the referral stage according to the likelihood of educational success. The definition of what constituted 'ineducability' was deliberately left vague: 'ineducables' included not only those characterized as having 'hereditary mental or emotional abnormalities', but also those juveniles who were simply rebellious.

---

[108] Herbert Francke an Paul Blumenthal, 5 Nov. 1931; Wilhelm Hertz, 'Vorbericht für die Sitzung des Wohlfahrtsausschusses des Deutschen Städtetags', 13 Nov. 1931. StAH, JB I, 232, vol. 1.

[109] Walter Friedländer, 'Abbau der FE durch Notverordnung?' *AW* 6/21 (1931), 641–6.

[110] Preußisches Ministerium für Volkswohlfahrt an den RMdI, 23 Aug. 1931. ZStA Merseburg, Rep. 120, BB XV 61; Preußisches Min. für Volkswohlfahrt an den RMdI, Feb. 1932. BA Koblenz, R36, 2005.

[111] Entwurf des RMdI einer Notverordnung zur Fürsorgeerziehung, Nov. 1931. StAH, JB I, 232, vol. 1.

The exclusion of the ineducables would end a 'misuse' and an 'inflation' of correctional education; it would restore order to reformatory life and improve the reformatories' public image. In addition, according to this view, it would save valuable resources squandered at a time of national economic crisis on juveniles unresponsive to and undeserving of such care and attention.[112]

Unlike the demand for an increase in 'preventive referral', the issue of the older and more 'difficult' juveniles in correctional education was not a specifically Prussian concern. Nor was it a new one: throughout the Weimar period, youth welfare experts had been discussing whether there were 'limits of educability' and, if so, how they could be defined. As Detlev Peukert has argued, it was a question made more complicated in the Depression by the intertwining of two basically distinct approaches to the problem of educational difficulty.[113]

On the one hand, an essentially pedagogical debate on the limits of education was in progress. This was partly a product of the far-reaching ambitions and ideals of the educational reformers: education, in their view, should not merely drill the youngster into outer conformity, but bring about profound and inward change in the young person's attitudes and behaviour. This was to be achieved in a pedagogical atmosphere of freedom and comradeship between educator and educated. If a young person's development was irreversible, if the influences of their milieu had already shaped them so far as to make them resistant to all educational efforts, went the argument, then education had found its limits. It was in the context of this debate that Bertha Paulssen, senior administrator in the Hamburg youth welfare department and prominent representative of the campaign to modernize and liberalize reformatory education for girls, wrote, in November 1931, that youth welfare institutions should cut their losses where certain categories of adolescents were concerned. Despite its racist overtones, her argument stressed above all the cultural and environmental limits of educability:

I am thinking here particularly of artistes, dancers, girls from gypsy families, girls of mixed race, and others. These girls are generally very experienced. Their development is complete; respectable middle-class life

---

[112] 'Abbruch der vorbeugenden Erziehungsfürsorge?', *WRP* 7/15 (1931), 239–40.
[113] Peukert, *Sozialdisziplinierung*, 248–50.

with its rules is something quite alien to them, and they have no possibility of integrating themselves into an existence based on such precepts.[114]

It was regrettable, she concluded, that existing laws did not allow for the release of such persons from correctional education.

Not all representatives of liberal reforming opinion shared Bertha Paulssen's views. Some educational reformers agreed with her that limiting the numbers of juveniles in correctional education was preferable to cutting standards for all, and that it would be sensible to limit numbers where educational success appeared least likely. Others rejected the idea of excluding the allegedly 'tough cases'; they pointed out that labelling adolescents as 'ineducable' would prove a temptation for reformatories to shirk their responsibilities.

The dangers of educationalists deciding—on whatever grounds—that certain youngsters would prove perpetually resistant to educational efforts were all the greater in the Depression given the growing prevalence of a more sinister discourse about 'ineducability' based on biologistic premisses. The rise of the 'science of delinquency'[115] and the development by the experts of increasingly sophisticated categories of delinquency had brought with it attempts to diagnose and treat more successfully those juveniles seen as hard or impossible to educate. The racial hygienists' contribution was to focus on the degree to which juveniles' educability was affected by their genetic makeup. A prominent exponent of this approach was Werner Villinger, a colleague of Bertha Paulssen in the Hamburg youth welfare office. In his reports for the juvenile court, he consistently sought to highlight the hereditary dimension to the psychological defects and intellectual inadequacies he diagnosed. In 1931, he declared that correctional education in Hamburg was 'most severely burdened by constitutionally abnormal children and juveniles, most of whom display intellectual weakness and psychopathic tendencies, often in combination'.[116] Villinger, it was true, emphasized that 'abnormal' children were not *necessarily* ineducable; he, after all, was interested in promoting psychiatric expertise as the key to treating even unpromising cases.[117] However, such subtleties could easily get lost

---

[114] Bertha Paulssen (Landesjugendamt Hamburg) to Gertrud Bäumer (RMdI), 11 Nov. 1931. StAH, JB I, 232, vol. 1.
[115] The term is used by Peukert, *Sozialdisziplinierung*, 151.
[116] Dienstbesprechung des Jugendamtes, 17 Dec. 1931. StAH, JB I, 3, vol. 1.
[117] Ibid.

when a biologistic approach was taken up by others more interested in ridding the Weimar welfare state of its 'burdens'. A particularly forthright position was formulated by Helmuth Schreiner in 1931 in the journal of the Innere Mission, the Protestant welfare organization: it was hubris, he argued, to assume that everyone was educable. Limits were set by nature; no educational efforts could redeem anything from 'ruined hereditary material' (*einer zerstörten Erbmasse*). Any solution to the current problems of correctional education, he argued, had to be based on an awareness of the biological limits of educability.[118]

Notions of biological inferiority and of genetically determined conditions of being 'difficult to educate' or 'ineducable' fitted well into the climate in the Depression of targeting education and welfare resources more effectively on the 'valuable'. Meanwhile, with proposals for legislative change still under discussion, the exclusion of the older age groups and of allegedly 'ineducable' juveniles from correctional education was already beginning in practice. In Hamburg, there was a clear decline in the number of older juveniles referred to correctional education from 1930 onwards. In 1930, 254 boys and 184 girls over 14 were taken into correctional education in Hamburg for the first time: in 1931, only 168 boys and 144 girls over 14 were referred.[119] A social worker admitted in a published article that this decline in referrals was not due to any reduction in delinquency or deprivation but to the youth welfare department deliberately holding back.[120]

At the same time, the more recalcitrant inmates of Hamburg's reformatories were being released. Some were released permanently, on the grounds that the aim of correctional education had been fulfilled; others were released temporarily, 'on parole', to look for work. In addition, there were many released more informally: the authorities simply stopped making any effort to fetch back determined escapees.[121] It soon became known in the reformatories

---

[118] Helmuth Schreiner, 'Der Kampf um die Fürsorgeerziehung', *Innere Mission im evangelischen Deutschland*, 26 (1931), 194–9, 198, cited by Peukert, *Sozialdisziplinierung*, 250.
[119] Bericht der Verwaltungsreformkommission 1932. StAH, JB I, 119.
[120] A. Borchert-Gölling, 'Statistik über die durch die Aufnahmeabteilung laufenden schulentlassenen Mädchen beim Jugendamt Hamburg', *JV* 8/3 (1932), 91–4, 93.
[121] Wilhelm Hertz an die Finanzdeputation Hamburg, 13 Jan 1932. StAH, JB I, 232, vol. 1.

that one way to get released was to create as much trouble as possible. This emerged in the court case against Friedrich B., a former reformatory inmate who in January 1932 after half a dozen escapes from the reformatory was released from correctional education:

In answer to the question why he had absconded so often he said: 'There's too little freedom and you only get 75 pfennigs a week'. Also, he said, he knew that the more often you ran away and the worse you behaved the sooner you got released. That was how it had been with lots of people and that's what he had done too. And it had worked.[122]

Still more controversial than the proposal to remove the more difficult categories of juvenile from correctional education was the issue of what should be done with such youngsters if they were released. A number of suggestions were made regarding what should be done with the 'ineducables' who were expelled or debarred from correctional education. Only a minority of youth welfare experts regarded with equanimity the prospect of simply releasing the 'ineducables' back into society. Many supported proposals for alternative forms of detention which were intended to be cheaper and tougher than correctional education.

One proposed alternative to the reformatory for the 'ineducables' was the workhouse (*Arbeitshaus*). This was suggested by the organization of Prussian regional authorities to the Reich Ministry of the Interior in November 1931. The Prussian regional authorities argued that it was necessary to stop 'ineducables' deliberately misbehaving to effect their release and that a 'greater evil' should threaten those expelled from correctional education on grounds of ineducability.[123] In November 1931, drawing up the first draft of the emergency decree on correctional education, the Reich Ministry of the Interior proposed that paragraph 73 of the National Youth Welfare Law be amended to allow juveniles aged between 18 and 21 who had 'demonstrated an obstinate resistance, not attributable to a pathological constitution, to the educational measures of correctional education' to be referred to the workhouse.[124]

An outcry from educational reformers greeted this plan. The

[122] Fachärztliches Gutachten über Friedrich B., 22 June 1932. LGH A11017/1932.
[123] Verband der preußischen Provinzen an den RMdI, 23 Nov. 1931. BA Koblenz, R36, 1983.
[124] Entwurf des RMdI einer Notverordnung zur Fürsorgeerziehung, Nov. 1931. StAH, JB I, 232, vol. 1.

workhouse was an institution which in the Weimar period hitherto had been reserved for the detention of adult 'asocials' who were referred there by the police after convictions for vagrancy, pimping, drunkenness, prostitution, etc. The proposal to send juveniles there was denounced as a return to an educational Dark Age.[125]

In December 1931 the liberal reformers succeeded in getting the clause on the workhouse removed from the government draft, and the Ministry of the Interior omitted any mention of special provision for released 'ineducables' from the second draft of the emergency decree, dated January 1932. In response, the right-wing correctional education lobby threw itself into a campaign for the introduction of the long-debated 'protective detention' (Bewahrung), specifically to cope with juveniles excluded from correctional education who would 'put themselves and society at risk' if they were left to their own devices.

Protective detention appeared to be a simple way for the welfare services to deal with a number of 'problem' categories of people. In theory, it was to protect those regarded as weak-willed and eugenically unfit 'from themselves' as well as protecting society from their anti-social behaviour.[126] The demand for a law on protective detention was not simply a product of a right-wing backlash in the final years of the Republic. On the contrary, it had been discussed since the beginning of the Weimar Republic by welfare specialists ranging in political affiliation from the Right to the Social Democratic Left, and had been proposed in Reichstag resolutions backed by the Social Democrats between 1925 and 1927. In 1927, the Reich Ministry of the Interior drafted a law which envisaged protective detention for persons over 18 years who were, or were in danger of becoming, *verwahrlost*, and who had either been placed under public care and authority (*entmündigt*) on the grounds of 'mental weakness', or who were alcoholic, or who had been convicted for begging, vagrancy, or prostitution.[127] The decisive obstacle to the realization of these plans had been the problem of financing them. Now, with the economy and public

---

[125] Hedwig Wachenheim, 'Arbeitshaus! die letzte Weisheit der Bürokratie', *Vorwärts*, 5 Dec. 1931.
[126] On protective detention, see Peukert, *Sozialdisziplinierung*, 263–301.
[127] Niederschrift über die Verhandlungen der Kommission zur Beratung eines Entwurfs zu einem Bewahrungsgesetz, 13 Jan. 1927. ZStA Potsdam, 15.01, 1373; RMdI an die Landesregierungen betr. Bewahrungsgesetz, 26 Jan. 1928. StAH, Medizinalkollegium, II U 3.

finances in crisis, undeterred by the fate of all previous attempts to introduce protective detention, the correctional education lobby tried once more. In January 1932, the AFET demanded the immediate introduction of a law on protective detention, in order to close the loophole opening up as a result of the cuts in correctional education.[128]

With regard to alternative and stricter forms of detention for youngsters released from correctional education, practice again anticipated legislative change. Legal forms presented few obstacles to enterprising administrators in the Prussian province of the Rhineland, where the regional youth welfare authority introduced such detention for older girls in the summer of 1932.[129]

Meanwhile, the efforts of the Prussian FE establishment to obtain the legal changes they sought were bearing little fruit. After consultations with the governments of the *Länder* in the spring of 1932, the Brüning government made no further moves to issue the planned emergency decree. In the summer of 1932, however, Papen's Minister of the Interior, Freiherr von Gayl, took up the plans once more.[130] A long silence on the part of the ministry ensued; then, on 4 November 1932, the Papen government suddenly issued an emergency decree revising the regulations regarding correctional education, taking specialist youth welfare circles by surprise.[131]

The details of the emergency decree fulfilled the wishes of the conservative correctional education establishment with regard to the exclusion of 'difficult' juveniles. While the upper age-limit for referral in normal cases continued, as in the RJWG, to be the juvenile's 18th birthday, the upper age-limit for referral in exceptional cases was reduced from the 20th birthday to the 19th birthday. In the law of 1922, the upper age-limit for release had been the young person's 21st birthday: now, the upper age-limit for release in all but exceptional cases was to be the 19th birthday. In special cases, the authorities could apply for an extension of correctional education up till the young person's 21st birthday. The release of 'ineducables' was legalized and the referral to correctional

---

[128] AFET, Rundschreiben, 25 Jan. 1932. StAH, JB I, 232, vol. 1.
[129] Agnes Neuhaus, 'FE und Bewahrung', *WRP* 8/12 (1932), 188–190, 190.
[130] RMdI an den Staatssekretär in der Reichskanzlei, 29 July 1932. ZStA Potsdam, 30.01, 1518.
[131] Verordnung des Reichspräsidenten über Jugendwohlfahrt, 4 Nov. 1932, *RGBl* 1932, i. 522.

education was made conditional in every case on the prospect of educational success.

In one important respect, however, the decree did not satisfy the Prussian correctional education lobby. No provisions were made for alternative forms of detention for the older and/or 'ineducable' juveniles who would be released from correctional education as a result of the decree. The paradox that at the height of the political and social crisis the state was voluntarily relinquishing an important means of control over a group of particularly troublesome adolescents was not lost on critics. The youth welfare director in Lübeck had already pointed out the possible consequences for law and order of a restriction of correctional education: 'with public order in its present state, and the so-called *Halbstarken* playing such a prominent role, a retreat by the state in its function as educator will seem like the bankruptcy of state authority'.[132]

In so far as the decree of 4 November 1932 restricted the categories of juveniles eligible for referral to correctional education, it could be seen as a measure which, while being designed to fulfil a number of goals, was largely motivated by financial considerations. However, financial factors played a minor role with regard to other provisions of the decree. These provisions extended the powers and responsibilities of the correctional authorities at the expense of the local youth welfare departments, in order to bring about an increase of 'preventive' referrals to correctional education of younger juveniles 'at risk'.[133] This was clearly not an economy measure; indeed, it seemed that the resulting costs of extra referrals might well outweigh the savings made by excluding the older adolescents.

The effects of the emergency decree were less dramatic in practice than widely predicted or feared; in particular, the chaos expected to result from releasing the older inmates of the reformatories did not ensue. This was for two reasons. First, not all the 19- and 20-year-olds in correctional education were released immediately: a supplementary decree issued on 28 November 1932 in response to reformatory directors' protests enabled FE authorities to postpone the release of these age-groups until March 1933. About a fifth of 19- and 20-year-olds in correctional education had their release

---

[132] Behörde für Arbeit und Wohlfahrt Lübeck an den Lübecker Senat, 29 Sept. 1931. StAH, JB I, 232, vol. 1.
[133] Verordnung des Reichspräsidenten über Jugendwohlfahrt, 4 Nov. 1932, *RGBl* 1932, i. 522: deletion of paragraph 55, amendment of paragraph 63 of RJWG.

postponed in this way.[134] Secondly, a large number of those who were released from correctional education as a result of the decree turned out not to have been in reformatories anyway. They were either living with their employers or foster families, were on parole at home or had escaped and were untraceable. In the course of the financial year 1932/3 the number of juveniles in reformatories fell by 20.7 per cent, while the number of juveniles in foster families and with employers fell by 37 per cent. For the latter group of juveniles, the release from correctional education was more or less a formality. In such cases, the efforts to rid correctional education of its older cases were more a matter of rationalization than of setting a new course for youth welfare policy.

What actually happened to the 19- and 20-year-olds who were in fact released from reformatories must remain a matter for speculation. Their numbers were estimated to be 7,000 in Prussia, 250 in Württemberg, only twenty-five in Hamburg.[135] A Prussian report mentioned that 'the voluntary labour service and the nationalist organizations have given some of them a temporary home'.[136]

Though so much had been talked about the problem of the 'ineducables' before the emergency decree was issued, the number of youngsters actually released from correctional education on the grounds of 'ineducability' rather than age was very small: one estimate put it between 6 per cent and 7 per cent of those released.[137] It was pointed out that many 'ineducables' were released on grounds of age anyway. On the other hand, the lack of alternative detention facilities may have inhibited large-scale expulsions. By the end of the financial year 1932/3, 218 juveniles in the Reich, of whom 192 were from Prussia, had been released on the grounds of 'significant mental or emotional abnormality' and sixty-seven on the grounds of 'character'. Of those released, it was

[134] RMdI an den Staatssekretär in der Reichskanzlei, 22 Nov. 1932. BA Koblenz, R43II, 785; VO des Reichspräsidenten über Fürsorgeerziehung, 28 Nov. 1932, *RGBl* 1932, i. 531; Loebich, 'Neuerungen in der Fürsorgeerziehung', *BWW* 86/1 (1933) 5–8.

[135] Estimates for Prussia: Konferenz der Landesvertreter im RMdI, 15 Nov. 1932. StAH, JB I, 232, vol. 1; for Württemberg: Loebich, 'Neuerungen in der FE'; for Hamburg: Hertz, 'Die Notverordnung des Reichspräsidenten über Jugendwohlfahrt', *JV* 8/4 (1932).

[136] Franz Zengerling, 'Die Fürsorgeerziehung in Preußen nach dem neuen Recht', *ZBl* 25/4 (1933/4), 125–30, 127.

[137] Ina Hundinger, 'Zur Auswirkung der Notverordnung', *Evangelische Jugendhilfe*, 9 (1933), 130–5, 133.

reported that the majority had already been in mental hospitals and asylums. Here again, the ending of correctional education was of more significance for the correctional education authorities than for the juveniles concerned, who simply remained where they were with merely the legal basis having changed.[138]

Regarding the pattern of new referrals, within the first few months the decree had the expected effect of increasing the proportion of referrals of younger children on the grounds of 'prevention'. Between April and the end of November 1932, 203 juveniles were referred to correctional education in Prussia on the grounds of 'risk' and 2,866 on the grounds of delinquency. Between 1 December 1932 and 31 March 1933, 207 were referred on the grounds of 'risk', 1,313 on the grounds of delinquency. Referrals of older juveniles to correctional education fell: however, here the decree merely confirmed a trend already evident in 1931/2 both in Hamburg and in the Reich as a whole.

The 'Dictatorship of Poverty' and New Trends in Youth Welfare Policy at the End of the Weimar Republic

The correctional education system released a few thousand adolescents at the end of 1932 on to the streets and left the municipal welfare services to deal with them. This merely added to the dilemma of the local authority youth welfare facilities which were already unable to cope with the tens of thousands out of work and 'at risk'. In one sense, what a later critic called the 'declaration of bankruptcy'[139] by the reformatories with regard to their more recalcitrant inmates was of limited significance compared with the scale of the overall problem of adolescent destitution and delinquency. Justus Ehrhardt pointed out in a pessimistic article of October 1932 that correctional education had become an increasingly arbitrary measure anyway, 'a sort of lottery, where you don't know whether you will lose or win, get referred or not'.[140]

The problems confronting youth welfare workers in the Depres-

---

[138] Zengerling, 'Fürsorgeerziehung in Preußen', 126.

[139] Ernst Braunschweig, 'Die Situation von Fürsorgeerziehung und Jugendstrafvollzug vor und nach 1933', pt. 2, *Die deutsche Sonderschule*, 6/4 (1939), 281–9, 285.

[140] Justus Ehrhardt, 'Gefahren in der Jugendfürsorge', *ZBl* 24/7 (1932/3), 225–32, 228.

sion who tried to educate and influence young people 'at risk' by means of probation were spelled out by a leading Social Democratic spokesman on youth welfare issues in January 1932.[141] He pointed out that unemployment not only made it impossible to find a job for a youngster on probation, it also created tensions in families which placed a young person in a situation of additional risk. Nor were youth organizations able to fill the gap.[142] Other commentators pointed out the impact of staffing cuts: many probation cases which were still officially on the books were in practice simply abandoned.[143]

Justus Ehrhardt summed up the sense of powerlessness felt by social workers dealing with unemployed youngsters 'at risk': 'When a youngster proves to the social worker down to the last penny that he cannot survive on his benefit and that he has to get the rest of what he needs from begging, stealing, or prostituting himself, even the most positive attitude on the part of the social worker is useless.'[144] Not only with regard to probation work, but in relation to youth welfare work generally, social workers were reported to be suffering from 'a fatal feeling of resignation' in face of the tasks confronting them and the inadequacy of the means available to enable them to intervene.[145] At a meeting of the Gilde Soziale Arbeit in October 1932, the Berlin juvenile court judge Herbert Francke was reported as having given an accurate summary of the situation: 'he demonstrated how dependent we are today on the state of the economy and spoke of the dictatorship of poverty, which finds in youth welfare the point of least resistance'.[146]

The morale of the left-wing and liberal reformers was further undermined in the last weeks before the National Socialist take-over by the erosion of their institutional base in youth welfare and education. The pioneering reformatory in Frankfurt am Main, the Westendheim, was closed at the end of December 1932 because of the sharp decline in the number of inmates. Herbert Francke was

---

[141] Walter Friedländer, in Niederschrift über die Besprechung eines Notprogramms für Kinder- und Jugendfürsorge im Preußischen Ministerium für Volkswohlfahrt, 29 Jan. 1932. BA Koblenz R36, 1460.   [142] Ibid.
[143] August Oswalt, 'Die Lage der Sozialarbeit', *Rundbrief der Gilde*, 23 (July, 1932), 5–8, 6.
[144] Ehrhardt, 'Gefahren in der Jugendfürsorge', 226.   [145] Ibid.
[146] Egon Behnke, reporting on Gilde meeting of 27 Oct. 1932, *Rundbrief der Gilde*, 25 (1 Dec. 1932).

transferred away from the juvenile courts in November 1932; Curt Bondy was dismissed from his post as director of the youth prison in Eisenach in December 1932. These were presentiments of the more comprehensive purge that was to come.[147]

Correctional Education and Probation in the Weimar Period: An Assessment

By the end of the 1920s, the overhaul of correctional education had taken place only on a limited scale. Many reformatories continued to operate much as they had before 1918, and new 'model' reformatories were still the exception. Nevertheless, in this period the reform lobby did gain institutional footholds in youth welfare departments and in reformatories, and at the end of the 1920s there were signs that correctional education administrators generally were moving in the direction desired by the liberal reformers. Meanwhile, the expansion of public youth welfare provision following the implementation of the National Youth Welfare Law encouraged the development of probation as an alternative form of supervision for 'problem' adolescents.

These developments were overtaken by the effects of the Depression. Social Democrats and liberals in local government found the ground cut from beneath them by the economic and financial crisis. Social workers were increasingly deployed on tasks other than youth welfare, and those who did undertake probation work had little in the way of advice or assistance to offer unemployed youngsters 'at risk'. At the same time, reformatory education was cut back under the impact of the fiscal crisis, and conditions deteriorated for the inmates who remained.

The efforts of the reform lobby were also undermined by the swing to the Right in Reich politics. Divisions widened within the youth welfare camp; youth welfare became the subject of intense debate as conservative opponents of public welfare and of liberal experiments in education sensed a shift in central government circles in their favour. They called not only for more discipline in the reformatories, but also for a fundamental redefinition of the target

---

[147] 'Versetzung von Landgerichtsdirektor Francke', *Rundbrief der Gilde* (Nov. 1932); 'Curt Bondy gekündigt: Ein Erfolg der Reaktion', *Rundbrief der Gilde* (Dec. 1932); Jacoby, *Von Kaisers Schule zu Hitlers Zuchthaus*, 169–70.

group for educational efforts. A tougher attitude towards rebellious and 'pathological' behaviour was to open the way to discussions of more far-reaching solutions to the problem of the 'ineducables'.

A few representatives of the liberal reform lobby proved to be susceptible to some of the new currents of thinking evident in central government circles. This could be interpreted as being in part a reaction against the optimism prevailing in the early Weimar years regarding the possibility of educating all 'problem' adolescents using non-authoritarian methods. This seemed to be the case, for instance, when some prominent educationalists in the final phase of the Weimar Republic called for a return to a tougher style of education for delinquents. But it was also a question of resources: it had been easier to cope with the problem of the 'hard cases' during a period of expanding provision than it was in the crisis, when the allocation of resources became an acute and daily-recurring dilemma. While many educational reformers resisted calls for the exclusion of the 'ineducables' from correctional education, others were inclined to accept the idea.

For the young people concerned, being excluded from an institution commonly regarded more as a punishment than as a form of welfare may not have been experienced as much of a deprivation. Nevertheless, the reform of correctional education in November 1932 represented a major break with the principle of the 'child's right to education', and it was to be of considerable significance for the subsequent direction of youth welfare. Rather than emphasizing general social rights to welfare, such as the child's right to education laid down in the National Youth Welfare Law, the new current in youth welfare policy stressed the tasks of selection and exclusion: selecting those deemed worthy of welfare and likely to respond to education, and excluding the 'undeserving', the 'unfit' and the 'ineducable'.

8
From Republic to Third Reich

The Crisis of Weimar Welfare

On taking over in June 1932 at the head of an openly reactionary government in the Reich, von Papen declared an offensive on the policies of the parliamentary governments which had allegedly turned the state into a 'welfare institution'.[1] However, by this time the actual institutions of the Weimar welfare state were already being transformed into an instrument to protect employers' interests and to police the unemployed. Already under Brüning the system of unemployment insurance was being dismantled, and the employment administration was put on to the task of running voluntary labour schemes; local welfare offices were in practice increasingly engaged on controlling the poor rather than combating poverty. Papen's take-over brought further turns of the screw. Whereas Brüning had stopped short of attacking the framework of collective agreements, one of the foundation stones of the Republic's social compromise between capital and labour, the Papen government had no such inhibitions.[2] A bastion of the Republic's welfare policies also fell victim to the recasting of political priorities: one of the acts of the new government in Prussia, after its forcible installation in July 1932, was to abolish the Prussian welfare ministry.[3]

By this stage, the reformist Left, as the traditional advocate of state social policy, was in disarray. Though protesting against the erosion of social rights, the labour movement could not agree on plans for tackling mass unemployment. The 'cuts consensus' which

---

[1] H. Winkler, *Der Weg in die Katastrophe* (Berlin and Bonn, 1987), 615.
[2] Ibid. 709.
[3] Ibid. 763; P. Weindling, *Health, Race and German Politics between National Unification and Nazism 1870–1945* (Cambridge, 1989), 443.

united much of the political spectrum in the Depression, extended well into the ranks of the SPD.[4] While, by 1932, the free trade unions were becoming bolder in demanding job creation on a large scale, the SPD remained stuck in its rejection of any measures which might be inflationary.[5]

With no prospect of a solution to the economic crisis in sight, the employees in public sector welfare institutions faced the dilemma of being part of a shrinking system with which many could no longer identify. Mass poverty made a farce of a welfare system geared to the individual scrutiny of cases which linked assistance to personal guidance and 'therapy'. The practice of 'individualized' welfare was now increasingly a channel for the application of negative eugenics, sorting those 'worthy of support' from the 'asocial' and 'inferior'. Social workers and welfare administrators lamented the way welfare departments had been reduced to bureaucratic skeletons, machines for selecting and rejecting applicants for inadequate welfare assistance.[6] But divisions opened up in the Depression between those who pleaded for a political response to the crisis and those who insisted, on the grounds of their obligations as professionals, on a stance of political neutrality.[7] Neither faction, however, was able to halt the process of dismantling which made a mockery of Weimar's social welfare pledges.

In the sphere of youth work and welfare, cuts in staff and pressure to allocate priorities for resources meant that it was impossible to intervene in all cases of educational need. Meanwhile, the basis of the Weimar welfare state's approach to preventing and curing delinquency was undermined. Integrating the adolescent into the world of work would, it had been hoped, reduce the occurrence of deviant behaviour. Welfare and educational measures aimed at reforming 'delinquent' adolescents depended not least on the provision of material security and employment opportunities for them. As the crisis worsened, it seemed to youth welfare experts that a whole generation of children and young people was being driven into delinquency, and—in the context of the politically

---

[4] Winkler, *Weg in die Katastrophe*, 176.   [5] Ibid. 637.
[6] 'Hat soziale Arbeit heute noch einen Sinn?', *Der Zwiespruch*, 14/10 (1932), 116–17.
[7] Clara Israel, 'Und dennoch—wir halten durch', in Deutscher Verband der Sozialbeamtinnen (ed.), *Fürsorgerinnen-Not, Fürsorgerinnen-Wille* (Berlin, 1932), 23–4.

charged atmosphere of the final years of the Weimar Republic—
increasingly into political disaffection as well.[8]

Mobilizing Youth for the State?

Growing concern on the part of the right-wing Reich governments after 1930 with the problem of the political radicalization of youth produced a new departure in state youth policy. The policies towards young people pursued hitherto by state and local authorities in the Weimar period had not attempted to mobilize young people directly in line with national goals; the efforts in that direction which had been made during the pre-war years and in wartime had been abandoned with the founding of the Republic. After 1930, however, there were moves in central government circles towards implementing a more ambitious 'youth policy' targeted not at specific categories of young workers, the young unemployed, and problem working-class adolescents, as had been the case with Weimar social and welfare policies towards youth hitherto, but at the 'young generation' as a whole—or, more precisely, the young *male* generation—with the aim of 'integrating youth into the state'.

The justification for such a policy was provided by evidence of growing political disaffection and radicalism among youth. Although Weimar electoral statistics gave no detailed breakdown according to the age of voters, political analysts writing at the end of the Weimar Republic used evidence of an increased turn-out among first-time voters to conclude that the successes of the anti-Republican parties of both Left and Right in the polls from 1930 onwards were partly due to their mobilization of young voters.[9] Some analyses stressed the specific attraction of National Socialism for young voters.[10]

[8] Immanuel Fischer, 'Zur heutigen Lage der Jugendfürsorge', *ZBl* 24/2 (1932–3); Paul Honigsheim, 'Jugend, Familie, Gegenwartskrise', *ZBl* 24/4 (1932/3).
[9] Arthur Dix, 'Die deutsche Reichstagswahl von 1930 und die Wandlungen in der Volksgliederung', in Otto Büsch (ed.), *Wählerbewegungen in der deutschen Geschichte: Analyse und Bericht zu den Reichstagswahlen 1871–1933* (Berlin, 1978), 225–35, 227; Bruno Gleitze, 'Die politischen Wahlen im Zeichen des Wirtschaftsniederganges', *Die Arbeit*, 9/5 (1932), 304–10.
[10] Carlo Mierendorff, 'Gesicht und Charakter der nationalsozialistischen Bewegung', *Die Gesellschaft*, 1 (1930), 489–504. See also the survey of the literature in Jürgen Falter, 'The National Socialist Mobilization of New Voters: 1928–1933', in Thomas Childers (ed.), *The Formation of the Nazi Constituency 1919–1933* (London, 1986), 202–31. Falter's recent investigation on a region-by-region basis of

Contemporary observers saw the political crisis and levels of day-to-day political conflict activating groups of young people who had hitherto been relatively indifferent to politics, such as unskilled and 'unorganized' working-class youngsters.[11] A clear sign of the increase in activism was the growing involvement of young men in paramilitary organizations, particularly those of the radical anti-Republican organizations such as the KPD's banned Roter Frontkämpferbund and other Communist self-defence organizations,[12] and the SA.[13] Political mobilization was taking place among young people still in work, as shown by evidence on, for instance, the Nazi factory cell organization.[14] However, links clearly existed between the growth of paramilitary anti-Republican organizations in the final years of the Republic and the rise of mass unemployment among young people.[15] For young unemployed men, paramilitary organizations provided a type of alternative welfare provision in the form of soup kitchens, clothing, and shelter; moreover, an organization such as the right-wing Stahlhelm had good contacts to

the impact on the vote for the NSDAP of changes in turn-out and the percentage of young voters has confirmed a positive correlation for 1930 onwards between the proportion of 20–30-year-olds in the population and an increase in the NSDAP vote. However, the data do not enable an analysis of the 'youth factor' in voting behaviour which would also take account of gender and social class.

[11] Gertrud Staewen-Ordemann, *Menschen der Unordnung* (Berlin, 1933), 161; Mierendorff, 'Gesicht und Charakter der nationalsozialistischen Bewegung', 497.

[12] On the banned RFB and other Communist self-defence organizations, see E. Rosenhaft, *Beating the Fascists?* (Cambridge, 1983), 88–110.

[13] On the debate over the class composition of the SA and on the extent of the National Socialists' success in recruiting, organizing, and mobilizing working-class members, see Dick Geary, 'Jugend, Arbeitslosigkeit und politischer Radikalismus am Ende der Weimarer Republik', *Gewerkschaftliche Monatshefte*, 5 (1983), 304–9; Richard Bessel, *Political Violence and the Rise of Nazism: The Storm Troopers in Eastern Germany 1925–1934* (New Haven and London, 1984), 44–53; Mathilde Jamin, *Zwischen den Klassen: Zur Sozialstruktur der SA-Führerschaft* (Wuppertal, 1984), 77–89; Conan Fischer, *Stormtroopers: A Social, Economic and Ideological Analysis, 1929–1935* (London, 1983), 25–45; id., 'Class Enemies or Class Brothers? Communist–Nazi Relations in Germany 1929–1933', *European History Quarterly* 15 (1985), 259–79; Dick Geary, 'Nazis and Workers: A Response to Conan Fischer's "Class Enemies or Class Brothers" ', ibid. 453–64.

[14] Volker Kratzenberg, *Arbeiter auf dem Weg zu Hitler? Die Nationalsozialistische Betriebszellen-Organisation, ihre Entstehung, ihre Programmatik, ihr Scheitern 1927–1934* (Frankfurt am Main, 1987), 236; C. Fischer, *The German Communists and the Rise of Nazism* (London, 1991), 175–6.

[15] On the age composition of the SA, see Fischer, *Stormtroopers*, 48–50. Fischer estimates unemployment levels in the SA at around 70%: ibid. 46. In Rosenhaft's sample of communist streetfighters, 84% were under 30, over a third were under 21, and 57% were unemployed. Rosenhaft, *Beating the Fascists?*, 194.

employers and could act as an unofficial employment referral agency.[16] There were other, less tangible attractions as well, such as the way the organizations offered a structure for action and excitement to relieve the tedium of unemployment—as well as a way of escaping from the tensions in the family into a peer-group environment.[17] However, membership of radical political organizations in the crisis was characterized by high fluctuation—which has been seen as a sign that the unemployed passed through radical political organizations quickly, unable to keep up payments of dues or possessing only a tenuous commitment to the cause they had joined.[18]

Girls and young women were absent from most contemporary discussions of the political radicalization of the young and of the young unemployed. Here it seems that traditions of political activity continued to shape politics in the Depression. Girls were generally less highly 'organized' than boys; young women were in a minority in all political youth groups, and were in a particularly small minority in the radical anti-Republican groups and organizations.[19] One bourgeois feminist commentator speculated that the experience of unemployment, together with the growing domination of political life on the street and in the neighbourhood by the 'streetfighters', was marginalizing girls from political life and public affairs to an even greater extent than was the case already, in spite of the Republic having granted full citizenship rights to women for the first time. Writing in October 1932 on the impact of unemployment on young women, she observed that only the 'more robust' of the unemployed were becoming the followers of radical political movements, and only the 'wildest and most uncontrollable' were landing up on the street. The rest ran the danger of being absorbed into a petty bourgeois world of domesticity and becoming cut off from the world outside and from public affairs altogether.[20]

---

[16] C. Fischer, 'Turning the Tide? The KPD and Right Radicalism in German Industrial Relations, 1925–1928', *Journal of Contemporary History*, 24 (1989), 575–97, 580.

[17] Detlev Peukert, 'The Lost Generation', in R. J. Evans and D. Geary (eds.), *The German Unemployed* (London, 1987), 188–9.

[18] C. Fischer, *German Communists and the Rise of Nazism*, 132, 135.

[19] Josepha Fischer, *Die Mädchen in den deutschen Jugendverbänden: Stand, Ziele und Aufgaben* (Leipzig, 1933), 12–14.

[20] Hilde Lion, 'Die Aufgabe der Frau im freiwilligen Arbeitsdienst', *Frankfurter Zeitung*, 23 Oct. 1932.

The response of the Papen government to the evidence of the political radicalization of youth was partly defensive. The evidence about the impact of the 'youth factor' on the dramatic electoral realignments of the final Weimar elections was more impressionistic than conclusive. However, the calls from bourgeois and conservative political circles for the voting age to be raised became louder, and Papen and his Interior Minister von Gayl took them up in the electoral reform plans which they saw as fundamental to the realization of the government's blueprint for an authoritarian 'New State'. When, in October 1932, von Gayl made public the government's electoral reform proposals, he announced that the voting age would be raised from 20 to 25 years. These proposals, however, were abandoned when Papen resigned and was succeeded by Schleicher.[21]

Meanwhile, the Papen government was implementing a more offensive strategy on youth policy in response to the growing political mobilization of young men, especially the young unemployed. Unemployment, according to the Reich government's view, sapped young men's physical fitness, destroyed their 'self-discipline', and produced mass disaffection against the state authorities. The new youth policy accordingly stressed political aims in its measures targeted at the young unemployed and launched other measures targeted at young men in general. Conceived and promoted by Wilhelm Groener and Kurt von Schleicher, the aim was to 'toughen' male youth, improve young men's military fitness, subject the young unemployed to a programme of discipline and hard work, and subordinate the younger generation as a whole to the authority of the state.[22]

Groener's campaign for such measures had begun during his period in office as Brüning's Defence Minister and, subsequently, Interior Minister: his idea was to channel resources currently granted to private sports organizations and courses for the unemployed into a vast state-organized paramilitary sports programme which would instil discipline into the ranks of the young through tough physical training. Such a scheme, he argued, would

---

[21] On the electoral reform efforts of the Papen government, see Eberhard Schanbacher, *Parlamentarische Wahlen und Wahlsysteme in der Weimarer Republik* (Düsseldorf, 1982), 119, 147–8.

[22] Reichswehrminster Schleicher an den Reichskanzler, 17 Oct. 1932. BA Koblenz, R43 II, 519.

not only serve the interests of the state in preventing the young unemployed drifting into delinquency, but also promote the fitness of young men generally with an eye to their military potential.[23] It was this scheme which Groener floated, in the spring of 1932, as part of his response to the escalating problem of political violence. Banning the most troublesome organizations could not, in his view, be the final answer; instead, the paramilitary organizations could be brought under state control and harnessed to the task of paramilitary sports training, as a transitional phase towards forming a national militia.[24] In a statement to the Press on 16 April 1932, Groener declared that he aimed to 'organize the whole of German youth regardless of party in sports organizations, in order to toughen young people physically and mentally, and to instil in them the notion of the state and the will to serve it'.[25]

Groener failed to realize any of his plans during his term of office, but similar ideas were taken up by Kurt von Schleicher, who pursued them initially whilst defence minister under Papen and then in the weeks when he himself was chancellor. Schleicher's main initiative on youth policy, launched in September 1932, was the so-called National Committee for Youth Fitness (Reichskuratorium für Jugendertüchtigung), a state-funded body under the responsibility of the Interior Ministry. In the decree setting up the National Committee on 13 September 1932, the government declared that 'making youngsters physically tougher, and instilling in them a sense of discipline, order, comradeship, and readiness to sacrifice themselves for the public good are tasks which the state has a duty to perform'.[26] The National Committee, headed by General Edwin von Stülpnagel, was in the longer term supposed to lay the basis for a future militia;[27] in the short term, it was to coordinate and promote the activities of existing clubs and organizations undertaking paramilitary sports (*Wehrsport, Geländesport*) by organizing

[23] Vermerk der Reichskanzlei 21.1.1931 betr. Wehrhaftigkeit der Jugend; Groener, Notizen für eine Kabinettsdiskussion, Mar. 1931. BA Koblenz, R43 II, 519.
[24] Protokoll der Ministerbesprechung, 5 Apr. 1932; Groener to Brüning, 10 Apr. 1932. ZStA Potsdam, 15.01, 25871.
[25] Groener an die Presse, 16 Apr. 1932. ZStA Potsdam, 15.01, 25871; on Groener's initiative, see also Winkler, *Weg in die Katastrophe*, 535.
[26] 'Körperliche Ausbildung der Jugend', *Kölnische Zeitung*, 15 Sept. 1932. On the Reichskuratorium, see also Winkler, *Weg in die Katastrophe*, 736–77, 753, 787, 821; P. Dudek, *Erziehung durch Arbeit* (Opladen, 1988), 185–6.
[27] Schleicher an den Reichskanzler, 17 Oct. 1932. BA Koblenz, R43 II, 519.

three-week courses in seventeen paramilitary sports schools for young trainee instructors, beginning in November 1932.[28] The programme was targeted at young men aged 16–26 who were members of youth and sports organizations; it provided free accommodation and tuition and subsidized travelling costs. Apart from the daytime tuition in paramilitary sports, other sports and small-bore shooting, participants were expected to attend lectures on topics such as 'Poison Gases', 'Germany's Borders', and 'Wartime Experiences'.[29]

Apart from its military aims, the National Committee had social and political goals. The publicly declared aim of the programme defined its purpose with reference to the social and economic context: to 'restore morale and fitness to young men whose courage and hope for the future have been undermined by the economic crisis'.[30] While it did not specifically target the young unemployed, one participant reported that the paramilitary organizations sending their members on the course had made a point of sending their unemployed members, who had the time to spare and for whom three weeks' free board and lodging held particular appeal.[31]

The Committee was conceived as an instrument of the broad political front which Schleicher was trying to construct, extending from the Free Trade Unions and the Reichsbanner to the SA; its courses would be a means of integrating and disciplining political elements hostile to the state, including elements within National Socialism. In practice, the SA and HJ proved eager to participate, and these two organizations together agreed to provide a third of the 2,150 participants in the first courses held in November 1932.[32] Recruiting from the trade unions and the Reichsbanner was more problematic, given the SPD's hostility to the National Committee and to cooperation with Schleicher generally;[33] nevertheless, Schleicher did find some encouragement for his broad-front concept initially from the Reichsbanner, who planned to send

[28] Reichszentrale für Heimatdienst, Richtlinie 233, Feb. 1933: 'Das Hilfswerk für die deutsche Jugend', 11.
[29] Erich Korsukewirtz, 'Aus der Praxis des Reichskuratoriums', *Jungnationale Stimmen*, 8/3–4 (1933), 5–6, 5.
[30] Reichszentrale für Heimatdienst, 'Das Hilfswerk für die deutsche Jugend', 2.
[31] Korsukewirtz, 'Aus der Praxis des Reichskuratoriums', 5.
[32] Präsident des Reichskuratoriums für Jugendertüchtigung an das RMdI, 7 Nov. 1932. ZStA Potsdam, 15.01, 25674.
[33] On the conflict between SPD and Reichsbanner over the question of the *Reichskuratorium*, see Winkler, *Weg in die Katastrophe*, 753, 787, 821.

twenty-five members to courses in November 1932,[34] and from the Free Trade Unions, who sent a representative to talks in the Interior Ministry in January 1933 to discuss the National Committee's programme.[35]

Apart from the National Committee initiative, Schleicher sought to coordinate and give a new profile to existing government policies towards young people under the slogans of 'fitness' and 'integration into the state'.[36] Under the Papen government, the voluntary labour service was expanded and increasingly oriented towards the political disciplining of its volunteers in the interests of the state; Schleicher declared in October 1932 that the voluntary labour service was proving itself to be a vital source of new 'community spirit'.[37] Links between the FAD and the paramilitary sports training run by the National Committee were encouraged—labour service leaders were to introduce paramilitary sports activities into camp life, while sports instructors were encouraged to volunteer for the labour service.[38] Together with plans for other measures such as Emergency Aid for German Youth (*Notwerk der deutschen Jugend*), a compulsory labour service scheme for university candidates (*Akademisches Werkjahr*) and miscellaneous measures for sending youngsters from cities to work on the land, the voluntary labour service, and the National Committee for Youth Fitness were presented by Schleicher to the public in the autumn of 1932 as a comprehensive package to tackle political disaffection among the young as well as the material needs of the young unemployed. Acutely aware of the political importance of these problems, Schleicher argued in October 1932 that

the effects of the various measures to integrate youth into the state will depend not least on the extent to which their significance is grasped by national public opinion. It is therefore vital that all available means of *propaganda* are continually employed to put across what the state is doing

[34] Präsident des Reichskuratoriums für Jugendertüchtigung an das RMdI, 7 Nov. 1932, ZStA Potsdam, 15.01, 25674.
[35] Vermerk über Besprechung im RMdI über das Kuratorium für Jugendertüchtigung, 24 Jan. 1933. ZStA Potsdam, 15.01, 25674.
[36] Schleicher an den Reichskanzler, 17 Oct. 1932. BA Koblenz, R43 II, 519.
[37] Schleicher an den Reichskanzler, 17 Oct. 1932; on the reorientation of the voluntary labour service in 1932, see Ch. 4, pp. 139–41.
[38] 'Das Reichskuratorium für Jugendertüchtigung', *Das junge Volk. Nachrichtenblatt der bündischen Jugend Deutschlands*, 13/3 (1932), repr. in Werner Kindt (ed.), *Dokumentation der Jugendbewegung*, iii. *Die bündische Zeit* (Düsseldorf and Cologne, 1974), 1621.

to promote the fitness of youth. Of primary importance in this context is the radio, which—perhaps under the overall title 'Youth's Way to the State'—would broadcast reports about the labour service, paramilitary sports, farm work, and the Emergency Aid for German Youth scheme.[39]

How much, if any, propaganda success was derived from Schleicher's youth policy initiatives is hard to say; however, those initiatives have a certain significance as a model of youth policy. Schleicher stopped short of using compulsion, and his measures merely entailed distributing resources in such a way as to channel activities in the direction determined by the central government. He thus refrained from directly attacking the autonomy of youth and sports organizations. In this respect his National Socialist successors had fewer qualms. However, in contrast to previous Weimar policies, which had not directly sought to influence and mobilize young people for national ends, Schleicher's approach represented a precedent for a highly centralized, state-oriented, and regimented approach to organizing and educating youth in the mass.

Beyond 1933: Policies Towards Adolescents after the Nazi Take-over

With the installation of the National Socialist regime, a movement had come to power which had always sought to project its 'youthful' dynamism and which portrayed its take-over as the 'revolution of youth'. Youth, proclaimed the National Socialists, would enjoy a special place in the Third Reich.[40] Beneath the rhetoric lay the conviction that mobilizing the young for National Socialist goals was a key to ensuring the future of the regime: in its drive to mould society in line with National Socialist objectives, the Nazi 'educator state' (*Erziehungsstaat*) had youth as one of its primary objects.[41] Social and welfare policies towards young people

[39] Schleicher an den Reichskanzler, 17 Oct. 1932. BA Koblenz, R43 II, 519 (emphasis in original).

[40] Adelheid Gräfin zu Castell Rüdenhausen and Jürgen Reulecke, 'Aspekte der nationalsozialistischen Gesellschaftspolitik am Beispiel der Jugend- und Rassenpolitik', in Kurt Düwell and Wolfgang Köllmann (eds.), *Rheinland-Westfalen im Industriezeitalter*, iii. *Vom Ende der Weimarer Republik bis zum Land Nordrhein-Westfalen* (Wuppertal, 1984), 161.

[41] Arno Klönne, *Jugend im Dritten Reich: Die Hitler-Jugend und ihre Gegner* (Köln, 1984), 7; Jürgen Reulecke, ' ". . . und sie werden nicht mehr frei ihr ganzes Leben!" Der Weg in die "Staatsjugend" von der Weimarer Republik zur NS-Zeit', in

became a vital part of the regime's 'dual strategy' to mobilize support and enforce conformity. On the one hand, young people who were, according to political and 'racial' criteria, judged to be potentially valuable and useful members of the community were to receive improved and upgraded vocational training, leisure facilities, and welfare provision. This 'positive' strand of National Socialist policy was at the same time indissolubly linked with its negative counterpart. The welding together of the new *Volksgemeinschaft* entailed not only incentives for political conformity, but also terror against 'alien elements', resulting in a ruthless persecution of the 'undeserving', the 'asocial', and the 'unfit'.[42] Accordingly, young people who refused to conform politically, who transgressed Nazi codes of conduct, or who were defined as biologically or racially 'inferior', soon ran up against the coercive power of the Nazi state.

A detailed analysis of National Socialist policies towards young workers, and towards youth more generally, lies outside the scope of this study. The growing interest in these issues is reflected in the growing literature on the Hitler Youth and the Bund Deutscher Mädel,[43] together with a number of studies of young people's resistance and opposition to the Nazi regime.[44] The focus of the

Ulrich Herrmann and Jürgen Oelkers (eds.), *Pädagogik und Nationalsozialismus* (Weinheim and Basle, 1988), 244. The term *Erziehungsstaat* was already in use in 1933: for instance, see D. Stahl, 'Jugendwohlfahrtspflege im alten und neuen Staat', *Die Wohlfahrtspflege in der Rheinprovinz* (1933), 175.

[42] Detlev Peukert, *Volksgenossen und Gemeinschaftsfremde: Anpassung, Ausmerze und Aufbegehren unter dem Nationalsozialismus* (Cologne, 1982), 89, 214.

[43] For a general account of the Hitler Youth, see Klönne, *Jugend im Dritten Reich*; on the BDM, see Martin Klaus, *Mädchenerziehung zur Zeit der faschistischen Herrschaft in Deutschland: Der Bund Deutscher Mädel*, 2 vols. (Frankfurt am Main, 1983); and Dagmar Reese, 'Straff aber nicht stramm—herb aber nicht derb': Zur Vergesellschaftung von Mädchen durch den Bund Deutscher Mädel im sozial-kulturellen Vergleich zweier Milieus (Weinheim, 1989). See also Gerhard Rempel, *Hitler's Children: The Hitler Youth and the SS* (Chapel Hill, NC, and London, 1989).

[44] On forms of youth protest and youth opposition to National Socialism, see Klönne, 'Jugendwiderstand und Jugendopposition: Von der HJ-Erziehung zum Cliquenwesen der Kriegszeit', in Martin Broszat, Elke Fröhlich, and Anton Grossmann (eds.), *Bayern in der NS-Zeit IV: Herrschaft und Gesellschaft im Konflikt*, pt. C (Munich, 1981), 527–62; Detlev Peukert, *Die Edelweißpiraten: Protestbewegungen jugendlicher Arbeiter im Dritten Reich* (Cologne, 1980); Heinrich Muth, 'Jugendopposition im Dritten Reich', *VjZG* 30 (1982), 369–417; on the mentality and experience of young miners in the Third Reich, see Michael Zimmermann, 'Ausbruchshoffnungen: Junge Bergleute in den dreißiger Jahren', in Lutz Niethammer (ed.), *'Die Jahre weiß man nicht, wo man die heute hinsetzen soll': Faschismus-Erfahrungen im Ruhrgebiet* (Berlin and Bonn, 1983).

following survey of developments in social and welfare policies towards young people after 1933 is the question of continuities and discontinuities between the policies of the Weimar Republic and those of the Third Reich. Within that context, however, issues are raised which are of relevance for a social history of young workers in the Third Reich.

Some discontinuities between the Weimar years and the onset of the Third Reich are obvious. In terms of institutions, for instance, the policy-making structures of the Weimar period were in 1933 quickly Nazified and purged of politically suspect personnel. With the removal of Jews, socialists, and other known political opponents of the Nazi regime from central and local government and from all organs of public administration, together with the suppression of the labour movement and its welfare organizations, what remained of the liberal and left-wing social reforming lobby of the Weimar years was destroyed.[45] A new constellation in the field of social and welfare policies emerged in which the National Socialist People's Welfare (NSV) and the Labour Front (DAF) vied for influence with the public authorities, with the Hitler Youth, and with each other.

The transformation of the Hitler Youth from the youth wing of the NSDAP into an all-encompassing state youth organization was in itself a further obvious sign of a break between the Weimar era and the Third Reich. In the final months of the Weimar Republic, Papen and Schleicher had toyed with the idea of a state youth organization, but they had conceived it in the limited terms of a quasi-militia for young men; the Nazis put the idea into practice in far more comprehensive fashion. The twofold 'total claim' of the Hitler Youth was made clear from the outset: the state youth organization aimed to encompass the whole of German youth of both sexes and penetrate all aspects of young people's lives.[46] Accordingly, the Hitler Youth quickly moved to establish its

[45] For an analysis of this process in relation to the medical profession and the health insurance funds, see Stephan Leibfried and Florian Tennstedt, *Berufsverbote und Sozialpolitik 1933: Die Auswirkungen der nationalsozialistischen Machtergreifung auf die Krankenkassenverwaltung und die Kassenärzte* (Bremen, 1981); on the Nazi take-over and its impact on the welfare services in a district of Berlin, see Elizabeth Harvey, *Youth Welfare and Social Democracy in Weimar Germany: The Work of Walter Friedländer* (New Alyth, 1987), 76–80.

[46] Klönne, *Jugend im Dritten Reich*, 19. On the concept of the 'total claim' made by the Nazi dictatorship upon its subjects generally, see Ian Kershaw, *The Nazi Dictatorship: Problems and Perspectives of Interpretation*, 2nd edn. (London, 1989), 40.

monopoly as the sole organization of German youth[47] and to assert its influence over its members at the expense of that of the family, school, or church. Using a combination of propaganda, incentives, and informal coercion (which became formal from March 1939), the Hitler Youth expanded the membership of its various branches[48] with the result that by the outbreak of war, according to official statistics, practically all young people aged between 10 and 18 were members; girls, by this stage, were as comprehensively 'organized' as boys.[49] The Hitler Youth's ambitions to exert authority in all matters concerning young people meant that it soon sought to intervene in areas of policy ranging from vocational training to juvenile justice and the control and suppression of dissent and opposition.[50]

There are thus important discontinuities which cannot be overlooked. However, a number of questions concerning possible continuities also arise. Some involve continuities between policies pursued by the Weimar governments in the period of post-war expansion and developments after 1933, since the National Socialists did not simply dismantle the instruments developed during the Weimar period to intervene in and organize the labour market, nor the welfare services developed to investigate and monitor adolescents at risk, nor the juvenile courts. Here, questions arise about the use to which these institutions and policies of the Weimar welfare state were put under the Nazi regime, the ease with which they were adapted to National Socialist purposes and the extent to which the Nazi regime developed them further. A second set of questions arises concerning the Depression years, when the political basis of the post-war expansion of welfare was crumbling: here, what is at issue is the extent of direct continuity between certain right-wing trends in the ideology and practice of welfare at the end of the Weimar Republic and the policies of the Third Reich. The following survey of developments in youth policy after 1933 looks at both sets

---

[47] Matthias von Hellfeld, *Bündische Jugend und Hitlerjugend: Zur Geschichte von Anpassung und Widerstand 1930–1939* (Cologne, 1987), 75–9.

[48] The Deutsches Jungvolk for boys aged 10–14, the Hitler-Jugend for boys aged 14–18, the Jungmädel-Bund for girls aged 10–14, the Bund Deutscher Mädel for girls aged 14–18 (from 1939, 17–21-year-old girls were organized in the BDM-Werk Glauben und Schönheit). Klönne, *Jugend im Dritten Reich*, 42–3; Klaus, *Mädchenerziehung*, i. 189.   [49] *Jugend im Dritten Reich*, 34.

[50] Ibid. 93; Jörg Wolff, 'Hitlerjugend und Jugendgerichtsbarkeit 1933–1945', *VjZG* 33 (1985), 640–67; Rempel, *Hitler's Children*, 47–63.

of questions, firstly in relation to policies towards young workers and the young unemployed, and secondly in relation to youth welfare policies and juvenile justice.

POLICIES TOWARDS YOUNG WORKERS AND UNEMPLOYED YOUTH AFTER 1933

National Socialist policies towards young workers in the early years of the regime were focused on measures which would reduce or disguise youth unemployment and combat its alleged effects—such efforts being combined with an attempt to relieve the labour shortage in agriculture and domestic service. After the mid-1930s, the primary task of policy was to mobilize youthful labour to solve the problem of labour shortages, not only in agriculture but also in specific sectors of industry. In this phase, increasing attention was given to planning and promoting vocational training, while attempts were made to channel young workers into particular sectors of the economy to assist the regime's economic preparations for war. Throughout, the regime used every opportunity to thrust the Nazi message upon the young worker, whether this took the form of indoctrination sessions in labour service camps or through propaganda efforts by party organizations at the workplace.

In the measures adopted by the state authorities towards the young unemployed in the early phase of the National Socialist regime, there were clear continuities with the policies of the late Weimar years. One dimension of continuity lay in the fact that the Nazi regime had no coherent strategy towards youth unemployment. This partly reflected the regime's priorities: although unemployed youth had to be supervised and provided with some form of occupation, it was older male workers with families who were to have priority in access to 'real' jobs. This priority was clearly expressed in a decree of August 1934 instructing employers to replace unmarried workers under the age of 25 by unemployed fathers of families.[51] Meanwhile, the hotchpotch of uncoordinated measures targeted at the young unemployed in the initial phase of

---

[51] Rüdiger Hachtmann, 'Arbeitsmarkt und Arbeitszeit in der deutschen Industrie 1929–1939', *AfS* 27 (1987), 177–227, 182–3; Fritz Petrick, *Zur sozialen Lage der Arbeiterjugend in Deutschland 1933–1939* (Berlin, 1974), 12–14; Timothy W. Mason, *Sozialpolitik im Dritten Reich: Arbeiterklasse und Volksgemeinschaft*, 2nd edn. (Opladen, 1978), 133–4.

the regime were, like the policies of the late Weimar Republic, largely aimed at removing youngsters for a time from the labour market, getting them off the streets, and toughening their moral fibre.

One such initiative was the 'Farm Aid' scheme (*Landhilfe*). During the periods of labour market crisis during the Weimar Republic, attempts had been made, with limited success, to induce the young unemployed from urban areas to take jobs on the land. This policy was taken up in the 'Farm Aid' programme launched by the national employment administration in March 1933. The scheme subsidized farmers to take on up to two 'farm helpers' (*Landhelfer*) from the ranks of the young unemployed, who were to receive board and lodging and a nominal wage.[52] The scheme expanded quickly: by July 1933, there were approximately 145,000 'farm helpers', of whom 33,000 were women.[53] Theoretically, candidates were to volunteer for the scheme; however, in August 1933 local welfare offices were encouraged to lean on recipients of welfare benefit to volunteer.[54] The function of the programme in bringing about a reduction in the unemployment figures was clear: from August 1933 onwards, 'farm helpers' were no longer counted as unemployed.[55]

A further initiative to cut youth unemployment by sending urban youngsters to work on the land was the 'Farm Year' (*Landjahr*), set up in Prussia in March 1934 and imitated in a number of other states subsequently.[56] This scheme took up the idea much canvassed during the Weimar Republic of raising the school-leaving age, and like that proposal was presented as combining economic and pedagogical goals. However, instead of the final compulsory year being spent in the schoolroom, the 'Farm Year' entailed 14-year-olds being sent to educational camps in the countryside, where

---

[52] Präsident der RAVAV an die LAÄ und AÄ betr. Landhilfe, 3 Mar. 1933. BA Koblenz, R36, 1520. The monthly remuneration for farm helpers was initially set at a maximum of 25 M for men and 20 M for women (later reduced). On the *Landhilfe*, see Petrick, *Arbeiterjugend*, 8.

[53] Präsident der RAVAV an die LAÄ, 3 Aug 1933. BA Koblenz, R36, 1520.

[54] Ibid.

[55] Hachtmann, 'Arbeitsmarkt', 186; Petrick, *Arbeiterjugend*, 8; B. Wulff, *Arbeitslosigkeit und Arbeitsbeschaffungsmaßnahmen in Hamburg 1933–1939* (Frankfurt am Main, 1987), 147.

[56] Theo Wolsing, *Untersuchungen zur Berufsausbildung im Dritten Reich* (Düsseldorf, 1977), 134.

pupils worked on farms for a number of hours per day. The remaining hours were taken up with physical training and instruction in subjects such as history, geography and 'race lore' (*Rassenkunde*).[57] The goal of the scheme was to relieve pressure on the urban labour market—this was a matter of urgency, given that the number of 14-year-old school-leavers in 1934 was double that of 1933[58]—while (in line with ruralist ideology) encouraging life on the land. The 'Farm Year' was never implemented as a compulsory measure for all school-leavers. After the mid-1930s, as unemployment among male youth declined, its purpose as a labour market measure shifted to channelling girls into work on the land.[59]

Inducing girls to take up occupations which would fit them physically and mentally for their future tasks as mothers to the nation was a fundamental goal of Nazi girls' education.[60] At the same time, the labour of young women was to be harnessed for reproductive work in households and for productive work in horticulture and agriculture. In some ways this represented little of a departure from the proposals and practices of the Weimar years. During the Weimar period, labour exchanges had pressed young women to take jobs in domestic service and on the land; domestic science had been a central part of the curriculum of the vocational school for unskilled girls; and preparation for the tasks of housewife and mother together with training in gardening and agricultural tasks had been built into the guidelines for girls' labour service schemes. Where the National Socialists were different was in their greater readiness to use coercive means. Similar in conception to the 'Farm Aid' scheme, but targeted specifically at female school-leavers, was the 'Domestic Service Year' (*Hauswirtschaftliches Jahr*), introduced in May 1934. Households were subsidized to employ girls as domestic servants; the state authorities attempted to put pressure on girls to volunteer for the scheme by instructing craft employers to give preference to applicants for apprenticeships who had done a year's domestic service.[61] While the Domestic Service

---

[57] 'Einführung des Landjahrs in Preußen', *Nachrichtendienst*, 15/2–3 (1934), 61. On the *Landjahr*, see Petrick, *Arbeiterjugend*, 10–11.
[58] 'Das Gesetz über das Landjahr', *Nachrichtendienst*, 15/5 (1934), 130.
[59] Wolsing, *Untersuchungen zur Berufsausbildung*, 138–9.
[60] J. Stephenson, *Women in Nazi Society* (London, 1975), 85–6, 116–23; Klaus, *Mädchenerziehung*, i. 136–7; L. Willmot, 'National Socialist Youth Organisations for Girls', D. Phil. (Oxford, 1980), 49.
[61] Wolsing, *Untersuchungen zur Berufsausbildung*, 130.

Year had originally been targeted at unemployed girls, it was soon used as a means to influence girls' vocational choice in favour of domestic service and agriculture.

A major role in absorbing the young unemployed in the early years of the Nazi regime was played by the voluntary labour service, which after January 1933 was taken over, purged of non-National Socialist influence and expanded, its growing apparatus headed from May 1933 by Konstantin Hierl.[62] Like participants in the *Landhilfe* scheme, labour service 'volunteers' from mid-1933 were no longer counted in the statistics as unemployed.[63] While Henning Köhler has stressed the contrast between the 'self-help ethos' of the Weimar voluntary labour service and the authoritarianism of the labour service of the National Socialists,[64] the elements of formal continuity are striking, particularly in the phase lasting until the introduction of compulsion in 1935. Hierl, whose grandiose visions of the labour service as not only the 'school of the nation' but also as the instrument for re-agrarianizing Germany were not entirely shared by Hitler,[65] tried in 1933 to force the immediate introduction of compulsion. He was unsuccessful, and until 1935 the labour service continued to be based on the decree of July 1932: the main organizational changes in this phase, carried through in the summer of 1933, being the banning of non-Nazi organizations from running labour service schemes and the extension (from six months to one year) of the period for which volunteers could be financed.[66]

The voluntary labour service for young women before 1933 had never taken off on the scale of the men's FAD. While it was expanded following the Nazi take-over, it continued to be considered a matter of relatively low priority. After a number of organizational vicissitudes, the women's labour service was administratively reunited with the men's labour service under Hierl's command in 1936.[67] A clear definition of its purpose proved elusive: there were

---

[62] On development of the labour service under National Socialism see Köhler, *Arbeitsdienst*, 245 ff.   [63] Hachtmann, 'Arbeitsmarkt', 186.

[64] Köhler, *Arbeitsdienst*, 266–7. Köhler also stresses, less convincingly, the contrast between the 'guaranteed principle of voluntary participation' before 1933 and the growing extent of compulsion after the Nazi take-over (p. 266).

[65] Ibid. 256–7.

[66] Verordnung zur Änderung der Ausführungsvorschriften zur VO über den FAD, 29 Aug. 1933, *RGBl* 1933, i. 621.

[67] Stephenson, 'Women's Labor Service in Nazi Germany', *Central European History*, 15 (1982), 241–65, 246–51.

unresolved tensions between its ideological goals of instilling Nazi values into young women and preparing them for their role in the *Volksgemeinschaft*, and its economic function of absorbing young unemployed women from the labour market and utilizing their labour for agricultural work and resettlement projects.[68]

Between 1933 and 1935, the labour service for both sexes remained formally on a voluntary basis; however, this status was highly problematic. The public welfare authorities, a number of which had, before 1933, already been putting pressure on young people to 'volunteer', saw the 'national revolution' as a signal to apply coercion openly. Local welfare offices now felt free to deny welfare benefits to 'work-shy' youngsters who refused to go into the labour service; at the same time, correctional education authorities increasingly sought to use the labour service as a place to send ex-reformatory inmates.[69] Such practices contradicted Hierl's vision of the labour service as the vanguard of the *Volksgemeinschaft*, and sharp exchanges ensued between Hierl and representatives of local authorities over the issue of whether particular youngsters who were considered 'work-shy' or 'at risk' should be singled out and compelled to volunteer.[70]

In 1935, the law on compulsory labour service for men was introduced: it was to apply to men aged 18–25 and was to be of six months' duration.[71] What the final Weimar regimes had not been able to carry through for financial reasons and due to their inability to enforce such a measure was now, belatedly, reality. However, with the introduction of conscription the potential role of the

---

[68] Ibid. 242–6; Gisela Miller, 'Erziehung durch den Reichsarbeitsdienst für die weibliche Jugend: Ein Beitrag zur Aufklärung nationalsozialistischer Erziehungsideologie', in Manfred Heinemann (ed.), *Erziehung und Schulung im Dritten Reich* (Stuttgart, 1980), i. 177.

[69] Ausschnitt aus der Niederschrift über die Verhandlungen der Arbeitsgemeinschaft der preußischen FE-Dezernenten am 28.7.1934 in Berlin. BA Koblenz, R36, 1939.

[70] Reichsleitung des Arbeitsdienstes an die Innenministerien der Länder, 23 Oct. 1933. StAH, SB I, AW 49.10, vol. 5; Oberbürgermeister der Stadt Berlin an die Reichsleitung des Arbeitsdienstes, 10 Feb. 1934; Deutscher Gemeindetag an die Reichsleitung des Arbeitsdienstes, 2 Mar. 34; Reichsleitung des Arbeitsdienstes an den Dt. Gemeindetag, 9 Mar. 1934. BA Koblenz, R36, 1939.

[71] Reichsarbeitsdienstgesetz, 26 June 1935, *RGBl* (1935), i. 769; 'Das Reichsarbeitsdienstgesetz', *Nachrichtendienst*, 16 (1935), 214–15. An element of formal compulsion for particular categories of people had already been in place before 1935: for instance, a decree of Feb. 1934 had made a 6-month period of labour service a condition of obtaining a place at university. Köhler, *Arbeitsdienst*, 260.

labour service as a quasi-military 'school of the nation' became largely irrelevant.[72] While the women's labour service continued on a voluntary basis after the 1935 law, preparations were under way to make it compulsory as well,[73] and a decree to that effect was issued immediately after the outbreak of war. While the labour service leadership continued to stress the political and 'educational' dimensions of the women's labour service, wartime pressures increasingly pushed into the foreground the goal of mobilizing female labour, particularly for agriculture.[74]

In the first three years of Nazi rule, a marked fall in youth unemployment figures was recorded: while in June 1933 1.7 million 14–25-year-olds were officially counted as being out of work, this figure fell to 500,000 in June 1934 and 420,000 in October 1935.[75] The expansion of employment for young people produced by economic recovery was unmistakeable. At the same time, the removal of young workers from the labour market through the various schemes outlined above also played a role: in October 1935 there were an estimated 350,000 young people under 25 years who were not included in the unemployment figures, but who were not in normal paid employment, being engaged instead on a variety of schemes ranging from 'Farm Aid' to the labour service.[76] After 1935, compulsory labour service and military conscription removed further cohorts of young men from the labour market, reducing unemployment still further—to the extent that a growing shortage of youthful labour began to make itself felt.

Hamburg's economy recovered from the Depression less quickly than that of most other areas of the Reich. This was largely due to Hamburg's dependence on foreign trade, which suffered from the regime's efforts to promote autarky. The city continued to be designated an 'emergency relief area' until 1939, and signs that the economic situation was adversely affecting the morale of the city's population were a matter of concern to the regime.[77] However, the arms boom did in due course bring an economic upswing: while the

[72] Köhler, *Arbeitsdienst*, 267.
[73] 'Der Frauenarbeitsdienst', *Nachrichtendienst*, 17/1 (1936), 74–6.
[74] Stephenson, 'Women's Labor Service', 256–63.
[75] Figures for 1934 and 1935 cited in Petrick, *Arbeiterjugend*, 22.
[76] Ibid.
[77] Birgit Wulff, 'The Third Reich and the Unemployed: National Socialist Work-Creation Schemes in Hamburg 1933–1934', in Evans and Geary (eds.), *The German Unemployed*, 292.

city's commercial sector continued to stagnate, naval contracts to the shipyards helped pull Hamburg's economy as a whole out of recession.[78]

Unemployment in Hamburg started to fall in 1933, though it fell more slowly there than in other parts of the Reich.[79] In so far as unemployment did fall, this was due more to general economic recovery than to specific measures targeted at the unemployed. The work creation schemes financed by the Reich government in the initial phase of the regime did little to give work to Hamburg's jobless; the regulations governing the allocation of funding benefited other parts of the Reich more.[80] Other labour market measures did not create work at all, but merely redistributed the work available. In line with national policy, Hamburg firms used financial inducements to persuade women employees to give up their jobs,[81] and in 1934 local employers' organizations called for member firms to replace young workers under 25 with older male workers.[82]

A major factor in keeping Hamburg's unemployment statistics down was the crackdown on suspected 'scroungers'. After 1933, the local labour administration and welfare authorities zealously 'combed out' the ranks of unemployed claimants in order to remove the allegedly work-shy from the lists of jobless. This was nothing new: before 1933 the Hamburg welfare department, under its director Oskar Martini and senior official Kurt Struve, had already been employing coercive means to discipline the unemployed. Both men remained in their posts after 1933. Martini now spelled out in tough terms as official policy the approach which he had already sought to apply in the welfare department before 1933: while the deserving would be assisted, he declared, 'anti-social elements' (*Gemeinschaftswidrige*) would be pursued and dealt with by 'firm, even severe means'.[83]

Much of the Hamburg welfare authorities' coercive efforts were directed at the young unemployed of both sexes. Though they were implemented on a larger scale, the policies pursued after 1933 were basically similar to those adopted in the Depression. Between 1934

[78] Ibid. 298.   [79] Wulff, *Arbeitsbeschaffungsmaßnahmen*, 145.
[80] Ibid. 133–4; id., 'The Third Reich and the Unemployed', 291.
[81] Wulff, *Arbeitsbeschaffungsmaßnahmen*, 149.
[82] Ibid.
[83] Oskar Martini, 'Aus 150 Jahren sozialer Arbeit in Hamburg', in Hauptverwaltung Hamburg (ed.), *Die Sozialverwaltung* [= *Hamburg im Dritten Reich*, 10] (Hamburg, 1939), 25.

and 1935, over 2,000 unemployed female claimants of welfare benefit under the age of 25 were summoned before the welfare authorities and given the option of taking part in a six-month residential re-training course for domestic service or, in the absence of acceptable reasons for refusing to participate, of losing their benefit. The course set out not only to accustom the participants, among whom were former clerks and factory workers, to the lack of freedom which they were to expect in domestic service, but also to subject them to a programme to enforce personal hygiene, physical fitness, and political conformity.[84] Three-quarters of those summoned refused to go on the course, of whom most were deprived of their benefits.[85] This measure replicated on a much larger scale the compulsory labour scheme for young women started up by the Hamburg welfare department in Fleestedt in 1932 (which also continued its re-training of young women for agricultural work after 1933). However, new dimensions of physical control were now added to what had been before 1933 primarily a measure to impose work discipline upon young working-class women. This was reflected in the fact that those who went on the re-training course were given medical examinations, which in a number of cases led to the young women concerned being referred for sterilization.[86]

Where unemployed young men were concerned, a number were required to work, in return for their benefit, on residential 'compulsory labour' (*Pflichtarbeit*) schemes outside Hamburg.[87] However, the welfare department's main answer to the problem of young male unemployed claimants was to dispatch them on to the newly-introduced 'Farm Aid' programme[88] or to the labour service. It was with satisfaction that the welfare department reported that between August 1933 and spring 1935 over 11,000 young men from

---

[84] Hamburger Staatsamt (ed.), *Hamburgs Fürsorgewesen im Kampf gegen die Arbeitslosigkeit*, [= *Hamburg im Dritten Reich*, 6] (Hamburg, 1935), 34–5.

[85] Kurt Struve, 'Bericht über die ersten Erfahrungen in der Umschulung junger Mädchen in den Staatskrankenanstalten und in den Staatlichen Wohlfahrtsanstalten', 12 June 1934. StAH, SB I, AW 92.10, vol. 2; *Hamburgs Fürsorgewesen im Kampf gegen die Arbeitslosigkeit*, 32–7.

[86] Kurt Struve an die Direktion der Staatlichen Wohlfahrtsanstalten Hamburg, 27 June 1934. StAH, SB I, AW 92.10, vol. 2.

[87] *Hamburgs Fürsorgewesen im Kampf gegen die Arbeitslosigkeit*, 27.

[88] Präsident des LAA Nordmark an Bürgermeister Krogmann, 24 April 1933. StAH, Staatsamt 90, vol. 1. Girls were sent on the 'Farm Aid' programme as well.

Hamburg had been 'persuaded' to go to labour service camps, many of them being sent as far away as East Prussia and Silesia.[89]

In the late 1930s, the focus of National Socialist policies towards young workers shifted away from the 'battle against unemployment' towards the problem of relieving labour shortages both in agriculture and in industry. Labour supply considerations had already played a role in the measures of the earlier years, steering school-leavers into agricultural and domestic work, and a concern with supplying agriculture in particular with youthful labour continued to dictate efforts to mobilize young women's labour in the late 1930s. In February 1938, Goering announced the conversion of the hitherto voluntary 'Domestic Service Year' into a compulsory year (*Pflichtjahr*).[90] Initially, the decree was to apply to all young women seeking employment in specific consumer goods industries and as clerical workers in any branch of the economy; its application was later widened. There was some economic rationale in measures to steer young women into agriculture, where there was an acute labour shortage. Significantly, however, the conscription of female labour was not employed to tackle the urgent problem of the labour shortage in industries vital to the regime's preparations for war.[91]

The regime's response to the shortage of skilled male labour for the booming arms-related industries, a shortfall partly due to the decline in training during the Depression, was to intensify vocational training efforts targeted at male school-leavers.[92] With a determination to intervene in the economy which went far beyond that of Weimar governments, the state authorities drew up national goals for vocational training and imposed controls over the labour market in order to match the supply of youthful labour to the needs of the arms economy. Industrial employers were prevailed upon to take on an increased share of apprentice training, rather than relying upon a supply of skilled workers trained in craft workshops. The

---

[89] *Hamburgs Fürsorgewesen im Kampf gegen die Arbeitslosigkeit*, 38–9.
[90] Stephenson, *Women in Nazi Society*, 103–4; Wolsing, *Untersuchungen zur Berufsausbildung*, 199–206.
[91] Mason, *Sozialpolitik im Dritten Reich*, 275–6.
[92] Wolsing, 'Die Berufsausbildung im Dritten Reich im Spannungsfeld der Beziehungen von Industrie und Handwerk zu Partei und Staat', in Manfred Heinemann (ed.), *Erziehung und Schulung im Dritten Reich*, i. *Kindergarten, Schule, Jugend, Berufserziehung* (Stuttgart, 1980), 301.

employers' response, as the dimension of the problem became clear, led to an increasing proportion of apprentices training in industrial firms.[93] In 1938, the state authorities went a stage further in their interventionist strategy, introducing a system whereby apprentices were allocated to firms by the labour market administration according to the regime's training priorities.[94]

Meanwhile, state institutions and party organizations undertook the ideological mobilization of young workers for the national effort. Vocational schools placed increasing emphasis after 1933 on 'national-political instruction', while various forms of collaboration developed between the vocational school authorities on the one hand and the Labour Front and the Hitler Youth on the other. In Hamburg, for instance, vocational school teachers were involved in preparing participants for the National Vocational Competitions (*Reichsberufswettkämpfe*) organized by the Hitler Youth and the DAF.[95] These aimed to 'mobilize German youth for their vocation', the aim being to boost the image of skilled training and provide incentives to apprentices to improve their performance—while improving the profile of the party youth organization among young workers.[96]

Although the political and economic context of policy-making on vocational training was transformed after 1933, some of the concerns of social reformers in the Weimar period were clearly echoed in National Socialist deliberations on the subject. There was, firstly, the desire to reduce, for socio-political as well as economic reasons, the number of male school-leavers from the *Volksschule* going into unskilled work. The Hitler Youth, for instance, together with the Labour Front, called for a comprehensive law on vocational training to cover the unskilled as well as the skilled, with the aims of 'gradually eradicating the type of the rootless, unskilled

[93] Wolsing, *Untersuchungen zur Berufsausbildung*, 160–70; Petrick, *Arbeiterjugend*, 61.

[94] From Mar. 1938, every school-leaver was obliged to register with the labour office, which was to be notified of every apprenticeship place, and no firm was to take on a person under 25 without the labour office's permission: Erwin Runge, 'Industrielle Lehrlingsausbildung und Leistungssteigerung mit besonderer Würdigung Hamburger Verhältnisse', Diss. phil. (Hamburg, 1941), 23; Wolsing, *Untersuchungen zur Berufsausbildung*, 172; Petrick, *Arbeiterjugend*, 64; John Gillingham, 'The "Deproletarianization" of German Society: Vocational Training in the Third Reich', *Journal of Social History*, 19/3 (1986), 423–32, 426–7.

[95] Hamburger Staatsamt (ed.), *Die Neugestaltung der Schule*, 95–106.

[96] Petrick, *Arbeiterjugend*, 30–1.

worker'.[97] However, for all the regime's initiatives and growing intervention in the field of vocational training, the plans of the Economics Ministry to introduce a law on vocational training were not realized[98]—just as the drafts of the vocational training law prepared during the Weimar Republic had come to nothing. Although the number of school-leavers forced into unskilled work for lack of training opportunities declined as the demand for apprentices grew, the 'eradication of the unskilled worker' never happened.

One reform envisaged during the Weimar period which was belatedly achieved, at least on paper, by the National Socialists, was the law on compulsory schooling of July 1938: this introduced, for the first time nationwide, three years of compulsory vocational schooling to follow the *Volksschule* (except for youngsters in agricultural jobs, who were required to attend for only two years).[99] This law did not affect places like Hamburg, where three years of vocational schooling following the *Volksschule* had already been the rule in the Weimar period. Nationwide, however, the new law's implementation ran into difficulties when the outbreak of war led to cuts in vocational schooling provision.[100]

Some historians have seen the material benefits gained by young workers under the Third Reich as a key aspect of the regime's appeal to the young. It has been claimed that 'National Socialist vocational education policies must be classed as a popular feature of the Third Reich',[101] and that 'in contrast to the Weimar Republic, which had done virtually nothing for youth, the years 1933 to 1939 brought undoubted benefits for young people—above all for young workers'.[102] A study of young miners in the Ruhr has suggested that National Socialist policies towards young workers contained a potential appeal which went beyond the obvious benefit of

---

[97] Wolfgang Siebert, 'Jugendarbeitsrecht', *Deutsches Recht: Zentralorgan des Bundes Nationalsozialistischer Deutscher Juristen*, 6/3–4 (1936), 63. See also Martin Kipp, ' "Überwindung der Ungelernten"? Vorstudien zur Jungarbeiterschulung im Dritten Reich', in H. Biermann, W. Greinert, and R. Janisch (eds.), *Berufsbildungsreform als politische und pädagogische Verpflichtung* (Velbert, 1981).

[98] Petrick, *Arbeiterjugend*, 104–5.

[99] Klaus Kümmel, 'Zur schulischen Berufserziehung im Nationalsozialismus: Gesetze und Erlasse', in Heinemann (ed.), *Erziehung und Schulung im Dritten Reich*, 278–9.

[100] Ibid. 279.

[101] J. Campbell, *Joy in Work, German Work: The National Debate 1800–1945* (Princeton, NJ, 1989), 365.

[102] Giesecke, *Vom Wandervogel bis zur Hitlerjugend*, 195 (my translation).

increasing job opportunities.[103] Further exploration of these issues would entail, for instance, looking at how the growing demand for youthful labour increased the leverage of the Hitler Youth, which took up and pursued energetically some of the social policy demands formulated during the Weimar period by the Youth Organizations Council. The granting in 1938 of increased holidays to young workers in the context of new protective legislation for juvenile labour was apparently the fruit of such efforts.[104] One could explore, too, the role of the *Reichsberufswettkämpfe* in feeding young people's individual vocational aspirations and in particular the enthusiasm of boys for modern technology.[105] However, any such benefits and any potential appeal arising from Nazi policies have to be seen in a context in which the youthful workforce was increasingly regimented and manipulated, in which the interests of individuals were subordinated to the requirements of an economy being geared to war, and in which, during wartime, a strategy of positive incentives gave way to draconian penalties to enforce work discipline.[106]

YOUTH WELFARE AND JUVENILE JUSTICE UNDER NATIONAL SOCIALISM

Under the National Socialist regime, the system of public youth welfare departments and juvenile courts established before 1933 was preserved and adapted to National Socialist ends. Despite the expectations expressed by those in the youth welfare establishment who had welcomed the new regime in 1933 in the hope that the National Socialist state would bring about a fundamental revision of youth welfare legislation,[107] no fundamental reform of the National Youth Welfare Law took place. Such demands for revision stemmed from a range of criticisms of the Weimar Republic's youth welfare legislation. A reformed youth welfare system, it was argued, should emphasize more strongly the work with 'healthy' youth and define

---

[103] Zimmermann, 'Ausbruchshoffnungen', 100–5.
[104] Hasenclever, *Jugendhilfe*, 139–40.
[105] Zimmermann, 'Ausbruchshoffnungen', 101–3.
[106] Stephen Salter, 'Structures of Consent and Coercion: Workers' Morale and the Maintenance of Work Discipline, 1939–1945', in David Welch (ed.), *Nazi Propaganda: The Power and the Limitations* (London, 1983), 106–7.
[107] Gottlieb Storck, 'Jugendwohlfahrt im neuen Staat', *ZBl* 25/1 (1933/4), 1–7; 'Reform des RJWG', *Wohlfahrtswoche*, 8/49 (1933), 401–2.

more clearly the place of youth welfare in relation to other aspects of youth and education policy;[108] it should stress more strongly the role of private welfare alongside public welfare provision;[109] and it should define the goals of youth welfare in terms of the interests of the community, state, and nation rather than in the 'individualistic' terms of the rights of the child.[110] In the event, the National Youth Welfare Law remained in force, the only changes being to abolish the local youth welfare boards.[111]

In the field of juvenile justice, too, the Nazi take-over prompted in some quarters a reaction against aspects of the 'Weimar system' of juvenile courts, which was accused of having blurred the distinction between education and punishment and having thereby watered down the idea of punishment. One radical solution proposed was to reserve the juvenile court for the most serious offences and for 'hopelessly criminal' offenders, leaving other cases to be dealt with only through educational measures, to be ordered by the guardianship court.[112] However, the juvenile court establishment represented in the German Juvenile Courts Association argued strongly against such reforms on the grounds that the juvenile courts were flexible enough to deal with all young offenders in line with Nazi educational goals.[113] In the end, no fundamental reform of the juvenile courts system took place; however, a clear shift towards stressing the punitive dimension of juvenile justice was evident in the practice of the courts from 1933 onwards[114] and in formal terms in the new National Juvenile Courts Law of 1943, which codified a

[108] 'Reform des RJWG', 401–2; Christian Klumker, 'Die Zukunft des Jugendamtes' pt. 3, *SP* 42/21 (1933), 633–7.
[109] Ina Hundinger, 'Umgestaltung des RJWG', *Evangelische Jugendhilfe*, 7 (1933), 289–93, 293.
[110] 'Reform des RJWG', 401–2; Hundinger, 'Umgestaltung des RJWG', 291.
[111] The RJWG had laid down in paragraph 9 that private welfare organizations and representatives of youth organizations should be represented on local youth welfare boards; these boards were now replaced by advisory committees including representatives of the NSV, the Hitler Youth, and the Bund Deutscher Mädel. Gesetz zur Änderung des RJWG, 1 Feb. 1939, cited in C. Kuhlmann, *Erbkrank oder erziehbar?* (Weinheim, 1989), 159–61; see also Hasenclever, *Jugendhilfe*, 130.
[112] Friedrich Schaffstein, 'Strafe und Erziehung im künftigen Jugendstrafrecht', *Deutsches Recht: Zentralorgan des Bundes Nationalsozialistischer Deutscher Juristen*, 6/3–4 (1936), 64–8.
[113] Kohlrausch u.a. an das Reichsjustizministerium (Denkschrift zur Reform des JGG), 18 Oct. 1936. StAH, JB I, 493b, vol. 2; Eduard Kohlrausch, 'Für das Jugendgericht', *ZGS* 56 (1937), 460–8.
[114] H. Matthias, *Die Praxis der Jugendgerichte 1924–1933 an Hand der Reichskriminalstatistik*, Diss. jur. (Cologne, 1937), 32–3.

number of changes in juvenile justice since 1939,[115] introduced the death penalty for juveniles, and lowered the age limit of criminal responsibility from 14 to 12. At the same time, however, the idea underlying the 1923 law of applying educational measures where appropriate was preserved and extended, with additional educational measures such as 'youth arrest'[116] being added to the range available to be ordered by the juvenile court judge.[117] Meanwhile, the ambitions of the Hitler Youth to be involved in all aspects of youth and educational policy in the Third Reich were reflected in a clause specifying the role of the Hitler Youth alongside the Juvenile Court Assistance in advising and assisting court proceedings.[118]

One of the tasks of youth welfare and juvenile justice after 1933 was to enforce political conformity. At the same time, the youth welfare authorities and the juvenile courts were agencies of Nazi racial policies, applying racial hygiene measures against 'inferior' members of the population and discriminatory measures directed against 'non-Aryans'. In the interests of the politically and racially defined *Volksgemeinschaft*, youth welfare departments and the juvenile courts were to apply a rigorous policy of selection to the children and young people coming under their jurisdiction, classifying youngsters according to their potential value, defining them as 'educable' or 'ineducable', 'hereditarily sound' or 'hereditarily burdened', and treating them accordingly.[119] This selectivity had antecedents in the 'scientific' practices prevalent in psychiatry and social work during the Weimar years. Nevertheless, it is necessary to stress within this broad continuity of technocratic welfare practice the specific trend towards the exclusion of the 'ineducable' from the welfare system and towards the punitive treatment of the 'asocial' which was fostered under the particular political and economic conditions of the Depression years.[120] This punitive variant of the welfare utopia of universal health and social harmony is a striking illustration of the direct and immediate

[115] Hasenclever, *Jugendhilfe*, 151.
[116] 'Jugendarrest' was introduced by a decree of 1940; it was a 'short sharp shock' of up to 3 months' solitary confinement, often served in prison, which was, however, classified as an 'educational measure' and did not count as a full-blown prison sentence on a young person's record.
[117] *Zum neuen Jugendstrafrecht. Vorträge* [= *Deutsches Jugendrecht*, 4] (Berlin, 1944). On juvenile justice under National Socialism, see Hasenclever, *Jugendhilfe*, 151. [118] Wolff, 'Hitlerjugend und Jugendgerichtsbarkeit', 666–7.
[119] Kuhlmann, *Erbkrank oder erziehbar*, 128.
[120] Peukert, *Volksgenossen*, 51.

continuities between Weimar welfare and the racial policies of the Third Reich.

In 1933, the confessional correctional education establishment had high hopes of the new regime.[121] There was optimism among reformatory administrators that the position of confessional reformatories would be consolidated;[122] that in the absence of 'Communist agitation' and through a tougher, simpler form of education in line with Nazi principles, order and discipline would be restored in the reformatories;[123] and that the introduction of legislation on protective detention (Bewahrung) would prevent reformatories having to cope with the various types of 'ineducables'— ranging from the 'psychopaths' to the 'feeble-minded'—who had allegedly burdened correctional education before 1933.[124]

Some of these expectations were borne out. At any rate, a tougher disciplinary regime, including corporal punishment, was implemented in the reformatories, along with a programme of political indoctrination for inmates.[125] Reformatories for boys were instructed to put greater emphasis on paramilitary sports;[126] girls were to be oriented strictly towards the ideal of true German womanhood based on service and self-sacrifice.[127] No legislation on protective detention was passed, but protective detention became increasingly common in practice within the institution of correctional education.[128]

However, any hopes that correctional education could be freed of its stigma among the public at large were wiped out by the sterilization law, which loomed over the reformatories from July 1933 onwards.[129] Both Protestant and Catholic reformatory staff

[121] Kuhlmann, *Erbkrank oder erziehbar*, 58–71.
[122] 'Der AFET zur Gestaltung der FE', *Nachrichtendienst*, 14/8 (1933), 183–4.
[123] Moll, 'Rückblicke und Ausblicke in der FE', *Blätter für Anstaltspädagogik*, 23/5 (1933), 132–42, 136.
[124] 'Der AFET zur Gestaltung der FE', 183–4; Ina Hundinger, 'Arbeitsbericht des Evangelischen Reichs-Erziehungs-Verbandes e.V. für die Zeit vom 1.4.1932 bis 31.1.1933', *Evangelische Jugendhilfe*, 9/5 (1933), 102–24, 104.
[125] Kuhlmann, *Erbkrank oder erziehbar*, 112–14.
[126] 'Nationale Erziehung der FZ und ihre Zugehörigkeit zu nationalen Verbänden', *Nachrichtendienst*, 14/6 (1933), 115–16.
[127] Kuhlmann, *Erbkrank oder erziehbar*, 100.   [128] Ibid. 143–8.
[129] Adalbert Gregor, 'Über die Sterilisierung minderwertiger Fürsorgezöglinge', in Ernst Rüdin (ed.), *Erblehre und Rassenhygiene im völkischen Staat* (Munich, 1934); Kuhlmann, *Erbkrank oder erziehbar*, 132–43; Peukert, *Sozialdisziplinierung*, 276–9; A. Ebbinghaus et al. (eds.), *Heilen und Vernichten im Mustergau Hamburg* (Hamburg, 1984), 26–40, 136–61.

were painfully aware of the impact of sterilization on morale among reformatory pupils, and of the dilemma posed particularly for the education of girls. If the goal of girls' education in the Nazi state was preparation for motherhood, for what did one educate a girl destined to be sterilized?[130] The growing mistrust of parents who feared that a child taken into correctional education would be sterilized led to the (probably futile) recommendation that such suspicions could be allayed if the application for sterilization were made by a doctor unconnected with the reformatory, and if the operation were delayed until after the sterilization 'candidate' was released from the institution.[131]

The way in which the doubts and qualms concerning sterilization policy expressed by Protestant and Catholic welfare organizations[132] were ignored by the Nazi state authorities underlined the fact that the position of the Christian confessional organizations was anything but consolidated under the new regime. This was also evident in the way that confessional correctional education soon found itself on the defensive in face of the NSV's efforts to assume responsibility for children and young people with mild educational difficulties who were to be regarded as 'hereditarily fit'. The NSV aimed to have the privately-run confessional reformatories turned into the dumping ground for the rest—the 'hard cases' and those classified as 'hereditarily inferior'.[133] With their inmates branded as eugenically inferior and designated as prime candidates for sterilization, the confessional reformatories had an uphill struggle to portray their inmates as potentially valuable members of the national community and their educational work as being a vital part of National Socialist education policy.[134] Meanwhile, the NSV, in cooperation with the Hitler Youth, began setting up homes for the 'light cases' on 'modern' lines. These homes (known as *NSV-Jugendheimstätten* or *Kameradschaftsheime*) consciously applied some of the ideas of educational reformers in the Weimar period,

---

[130] 'Betr. Sterilisation', *Jugendwohl*, 23/4 (1934), 73; 'Über die Besonderheit der Sterilisierung Jugendlicher', *Nachrichtendienst*, 14/12 (1934), 365–7; Gertrud Wüstenhagen, 'Seelsorge an Sterilisierten', *Evangelische Jugendhilfe*, 14/4 (1938), 70–80.

[131] 'Der AFET zu grundsätzlichen Fragen der FE', *Nachrichtendienst*, 15/8 (1934), 229–31.

[132] Kuhlmann, *Erbkrank oder erziehbar*, 138.   [133] Ibid. 172.

[134] 'Ist Fürsorgeerziehung gleichbedeutend mit einer Fürsorge für Minderwertige?', *Nachrichtendienst*, 14/11–12 (1933), 296–7.

for instance the principle of 'half-open' residential homes where youngsters would live while continuing to work in their jobs outside.[135]

The 'modern' Hitler Youth reform homes represented an aspect of National Socialist policies towards delinquents where some continuity with the reforming principles of liberal educationalists in the Weimar period was evident. However, in so far as less authoritarian educational methods were actually introduced in reform homes reserved for an 'élite' among children and young people with educational problems, these showcases were unthinkable without the rigorous selection which separated out 'hard cases' and punished them ruthlessly. Under cover of the wartime 'emergency' in which a crackdown on domestic opposition could be carried through all the more easily, the police and SS empire became increasingly involved in 'educating' young people defined by the regime as deviant, delinquent, or politically suspect. Following an order by Himmler in December 1939, the SS, from the summer of 1940 onwards, began operating concentration camps (*Jugendschutzlager*) for 'asocial' juveniles over the age of 16.[136] These institutions, to which not only the police but also the youth welfare authorities referred cases, provided an ultimate sanction against juvenile criminals, delinquents, and youthful opponents of the regime.[137] Wartime also saw the exclusion of Jewish and gypsy children from youth welfare institutions; for some, this was the first stage on their journey to death camps.[138]

Hamburg, it has been argued, emerged as a model Nazi 'Gau' in terms of the enthusiasm with which its welfare authorities took up National Socialist policies and the efficiency with which they

[135] Hans Schwinn, 'Die Aufgabe des "Kameradschaftsheimes" der Hitler-Jugend', *Das junge Deutschland*, 30/4 (1936), 32–5; 'Neue Formen der Heimerziehung', *Nachrichtendienst*, 18/9 (1937), 268–9. On the NSV-Jugendheimstätten, see Kuhlmann, *Erbkrank oder erziehbar*, 183–6, 220.
[136] Peukert, *Sozialdisziplinierung*, 287–91.
[137] Martin Guse and Andreas Kohrs, 'Zur Entpädagogisierung der Jugendfürsorge in den Jahren 1922–1945', in Hans-Uwe Otto and Heinz Sünker (eds.), *Soziale Arbeit und Faschismus* (Frankfurt am Main, 1989), 234–49; Michael Hepp, 'Vorhof zur Hölle: Mädchen im "Jugendschutzlager" Uckermark', in Ebbinghaus (ed.), *Opfer und Täterinnen: Frauenbiographien im Nationalsozialismus* (Nördlingen, 1987); Kuhlmann, *Erbkrank oder erziehbar*, 202–7.
[138] In contrast to the official exclusion of Jewish children, the exclusion of gypsy children from correctional education took place unofficially: it never reached the stage of becoming official policy. Kuhlmann, *Erbkrank oder erziehbar*, 225–37.

implemented them.[139] This hypothesis, which argues that Hamburg's above-average readiness and capacity to implement Nazi goals is linked to its welfare authorities' systematic drive against the 'asocial' before 1933, has been convincingly argued with regard to the key area of sterilization.[140] However, with detailed research into youth welfare at national and regional level in the Third Reich having only recently got under way, this hypothesis is hard to substantiate for the area of youth welfare and juvenile justice: the basis for comparing Hamburg's youth welfare practices with those in the rest of the Reich is lacking. All that can be attempted here is to point out how the trends in youth welfare outlined above can be traced in Hamburg after 1933 and to what extent continuities with pre-1933 trends are evident.

The Nazi take-over brought a number of institutional changes to Hamburg youth welfare. 'Politically unreliable' and 'non-Aryan' personnel, including Wilhelm Hertz, August Hellmann, and Bertha Paulssen, were sacked.[141] In May 1933 the director of the general welfare department, Oskar Martini, launched a sharp attack on the youth welfare department and its work since 1918. In its efforts to provide a comprehensive educational service for young people generally, argued Martini, the youth welfare department had overextended its field of activity, while the level of care it had lavished on delinquents had been extravagant.[142] On Martini's initiative, the youth welfare department was dismantled at the end of May 1933—against the protests of its new Nazi director Radusch—and its tasks were taken over by the general welfare department.[143] This did not, however, end the disputes over who was responsible for the provision of youth welfare. The historically strong position of

[139] Karl Heinz Roth, 'Ein Mustergau gegen die Armen, Leistungsschwachen und "Gemeinschaftsunfähigen" ', in Ebbinghaus et al. (eds.) *Heilen und Vernichten*, 7–8.

[140] Friedemann Pfäfflin, 'Zwangssterilisation: Ein Überblick', and Andrea Brücks and Christiane Rothmaler, ' "In dubio pro Volksgemeinschaft": Das "Gesetz zur Verhütung erbkranken Nachwuchses" in Hamburg', in Ebbinghaus et al. (eds.), *Heilen und Vernichten*, 26–30, 30–6.

[141] Hertz was sent on leave in Apr. 1933, then retired in Aug. 1933; Bertha Paulssen went into exile in 1935.

[142] O. Martini, Grundsätzliches zur Aufhebung der Jugendbehörde und Übertragung ihrer Aufgaben auf andere Behörden, 25 May 1933. StAH, Senatskanzlei, Präsidialabteilung A 54.

[143] Radusch to Kurt Struve, 24 May 1933. StAH, Senatskanzlei, Präsidialabteilung A 54; Martini, Grundsätzliches; Gesetz, betreffend Aufhebung der Jugendbehörde, 31 May 1933, in *Hamburgisches Gesetz- und Verordnungsblatt*, 50 (1933), 186–7.

public youth welfare in Hamburg meant, at least initially, that the public welfare authorities were able to fend off the NSV's attempts to take over responsibility for measures aimed at 'healthy' children and young people, such as kindergartens. However, towards the end of the 1930s the NSV was able to gain control of a growing slice of youth welfare provision.[144]

The take-over of youth welfare by the general welfare department facilitated the smooth integration of youth welfare into the general welfare department's drive to cut expenditure and discipline the asocial. Where the leading figures of Hamburg's youth welfare before 1933 had stressed the principle of the 'child's right to education', the spokesmen of the new regime stressed the 'good of the community'.[145]

The year 1933 thus did bring an explicit shift of priorities for youth welfare in Hamburg. Nevertheless, policy statements must not be allowed to mask certain lines of continuity. The principles of racial hygiene, for instance, did not have to be imported after 1933 as an entirely alien concept into Hamburg's youth welfare administration. Villinger, the youth welfare department's chief psychiatrist, had before 1933 declared his conviction that, heredity being one among several factors determining behaviour, 'preventive eugenic measures' were a vital part of a strategy to combat delinquency.[146] Villinger remained in the public youth welfare administration after the Nazi take-over, leaving in 1934 to take up a post as chief psychiatrist at the mental asylum at Bethel.[147] While the principles of negative eugenics had been under discussion in Hamburg's youth welfare department before 1933, the systematic application of racial hygiene and anti-Semitic policies after 1933 marked a clear break. The implementation of the sterilization law of July 1933 became a major task of youth welfare work: children and young people in correctional education were high on the list of

---

[144] Peter Zolling, *Zwischen Integration und Segregation: Sozialpolitik im Dritten Reich am Beispiel der Nationalsozialistischen Volkswohlfahrt in Hamburg* (Frankfurt am Main, 1986), 108–12, 242–62.

[145] Paul Prellwitz, 'Öffentliche Jugendhilfe in Hamburg', in Hauptverwaltungsamt Hamburg (ed.), *Die Sozialverwaltung* [= *Hamburg im Dritten Reich*, 10] (Hamburg, 1939), 114.

[146] Villinger, in Protokoll über die Dienstbesprechung des Jugendamts, 17 Dec. 1931. StAH, JB I, 3, vol. 1.

[147] In 1939 he became professor for neurology and psychiatry at the University of Breslau. Kuhlmann, *Erbkrank oder erziehbar*, 136.

potential candidates for sterilization.[148] Anti-Semitic policies led to the exclusion of Jewish children from access to public youth welfare services, while Jewish parents were deprived of their rights as parents and as guardians.[149]

A further shift in youth welfare practice in Hamburg after 1933 was the increased emphasis on the punitive treatment of 'antisocial elements', the rejection of 'liberal' tendencies in youth welfare, and, in wartime, the increasing cooperation with the police/SS apparatus. Corporal punishment was officially reintroduced into Hamburg reformatories in April 1934.[150] During wartime, the setting up by the SS of concentration camps for young people was greeted with mixed reactions in the Hamburg welfare department;[151] nevertheless, a number of boys and girls were referred to Moringen and to Uckermarck respectively.[152] Prominent among the young people in Hamburg singled out for the concentration camps were those identified as adherents of the 'swing youth'—a phenomenon, particularly associated with Hamburg, of middle-class youth whose opposition to the Nazi regime was expressed outwardly through subcultural forms such as jazz music and clothing styles and who in Nazi eyes were decadent, sexually promiscuous, work-shy, and un-German: the antithesis of the Nazi youth ideal.[153]

Assessment: Policies towards Youth from Weimar and the Third Reich: Continuity or Break?

The drive by the Nazi regime to mobilize young people for state ends through the Hitler Youth and to enforce social and political

---

[148] 'Dokumentation: Fürsorgerinnen in Hamburg 1933–1939', in Ebbinghaus (ed.), *Opfer und Täterinnen*, 132–43. The exact number of sterilizations carried out on young people in correctional education in Hamburg is not known.

[149] Victor Huvalé, 'Der 9. November und das Jugendamt', *ZBl* 65/10 (1978), 413–15.

[150] Radusch, Vermerk betr. Anwendung körperliche Züchtigung, 3 Apr. 1934. StAH, JB I, 493.

[151] Hepp, 'Vorhof zur Hölle', in Ebbinghaus (ed.), *Opfer und Täterinnen*, 196.

[152] Oliver Hermann, 'Jugendhilfe im Dritten Reich, aufgezeigt am Beispiel der Fürsorgeerziehung im Stadtstaat Hamburg', Diplomarbeit für Sozialpädagogik (Hochschule Lüneburg, 1988), 78; Hepp, 'Vorhof zur Hölle', in Ebbinghaus (ed.), *Opfer und Täterinnen*, 201.

[153] Peukert, *Volksgenossen*, 198–200; Thorsten Müller, 'Furcht vor der SS im Alsterpavillon', in Deutscher Werkbund (ed.), *Schock und Schöpfung* (Darmstadt and Neuwied, 1986), 324–5.

conformity upon youth in the mass stood in clear contrast to the more indirect and partial efforts of the Weimar public authorities to promote the social, political, and economic integration of young workers into the existing order. The Weimar state authorities, subject to the conflicting pressures of the reformist Left, bourgeois conservative forces, and the churches, while concurring on what youth should *not* be and *not* do, had never proclaimed clear educational goals beyond that of promoting young people's physical, emotional, and social 'fitness', nor a unitary image to which young people were to conform. The Nazi state, by contrast, laid down explicitly the roles into which youth was to be moulded: the German soldier and the German mother.

The methods used by the National Socialists to implement their policies, positive incentives combined with an uninhibited application of force, also contrasted with the more limited means at the disposal of the Weimar state authorities. With the installation of the Nazi regime, measures to organize the labour market, put the young unemployed to work, and discipline the work-shy were quickly made more comprehensive and more coercive. As the power of the SS grew, the ultimate sanctions used against youngsters defying the Nazi order grew more draconian. For the 'ineducables' in Weimar, there was nothing beyond the reformatory and the prison; after 1940, there was the concentration camp.

However, patterns of continuity between Weimar and the Third Reich can also be identified. Many of the concerns of the state authorities with respect to the problems posed by the young worker, the young unemployed, and the delinquent adolescent remained fundamentally unchanged from the Weimar Republic to the Third Reich. The negative images observable in Weimar discussions of youth policy of shiftless, unskilled boy labourers and sexualized girls, feeding into a class of socially and politically dangerous 'asocial' adults, continued to shape policies towards adolescents after 1933. Moreover, for all the institutional shake-ups in and after 1933 and the purge of politically 'unreliable' personnel, the mechanisms developed by the state authorities in the Weimar period for reaching, investigating, monitoring, categorizing, and controlling young people, particularly groups of working-class adolescents defined as 'at risk', were found by the National Socialists to be adaptable to Nazi purposes.

These broad lines of continuity have to be distinguished from the more immediate continuities involved where the dismantling and reorientation of welfare and social policies as a consequence of the Depression and the right-wing shift in politics in the final years of the Weimar Republic produced trends in policies towards young people which directly paved the way for Nazi policies. Such trends signified a turn away from the liberal and reformist left-wing panaceas of welfare and education as the answer to social problems and social conflict. Instead, a model emerged which envisaged the renewal of German society through positive measures to integrate the deserving and healthy into the *Volksgemeinschaft*, and negative measures to exclude, punish, and ultimately eliminate the 'alien'.

APPENDIX: TABLES

TABLE 1. *Occupational structure of the youthful labour force compared to the total workforce in the Reich, 1925 and 1933*

	1925: *Erwerbspersonen* aged 14–20 years					
	Male	%	Female	%	Total	%
Agriculture	902,811	27.0	966,094	37.0	1,868,905	30.5
Industry and crafts	1,986,926	59.5	771,635	29.5	2,758,561	42.9
Transport and commerce	356,374	10.7	329,799	12.6	686,173	13.9
Admin., services	89,632	2.7	77,264	3.0	166,896	4.8
Domestic service	3,629	0.1	466,533	17.9	470,162	7.9
TOTAL all sectors	3,339,372	100.0	2,611,325	100.0	5,950,697	100.0

	1925: Total *Erwerbspersonen* (all ages)					
	Male	%	Female	%	Total	%
Agriculture	4,793,147	23.3	4,969,279	43.3	9,762,426	30.5
Industry and crafts	10,497,387	51.1	2,988,875	26.1	13,486,262	42.1
Transport and commerce	3,684,506	18.0	1,550,864	13.5	5,235,370	16.4
Admin., services	1,519,356	7.4	611,900	5.3	2,131,256	6.7
Domestic service	36,892	0.2	1,357,094	11.8	1,393,986	4.3
TOTAL all sectors	20,531,288	100.0	11,478,012	100.0	32,009,300	100.0

TABLE 1. (continued):

1933: *Erwerbspersonen* aged 14–20 years

	Male	%	Female	%	Total	%
Agriculture	597,034	28.3	567,922	33.3	1,164,956	31.4
Industry and crafts	1,177,370	55.8	461,270	27.0	1,638,640	46.4
Transport and commerce	230,613	10.9	301,516	17.7	532,129	11.5
Admin., services	104,959	5.0	77,881	4.5	182,840	2.8
Domestic service	1,445	0.0	298,565	17.5	300,010	7.9
TOTAL all sectors	2,111,421	100.0	1,707,154	100.0	3,818,575	100.0

1933: Total *Erwerbspersonen* (all ages)

	Male	%	Female	%	Total	%
Agriculture	4,694,003	22.5	4,648,782	40.5	9,342,785	28.9
Industry and crafts	10,294,180	49.5	2,758,802	24.0	13,052,982	40.4
Transport and commerce	4,011,311	19.3	1,920,758	16.7	5,932,069	18.4
Admin., services	1,797,593	8.6	901,063	7.9	2,698,656	8.4
Domestic service	19,946	0.1	1,249,636	10.9	1,269,582	3.9
TOTAL all sectors	20,817,033	100.0	11,479,041	100.0	32,296,074	100.0

Notes:
1. *Erwerbspersonen* includes *Erwerbstätige* and *Erwerbslose*.
2. 'Agriculture' includes forestry and fisheries; 'Transport and commerce' includes retail trade, commerce, transport, hotels, and catering; 'Administration and services' includes armed forces, churches, hospitals, education, private services such as hairdressing.

Source: H. Siemering, *Deutschlands Jugend in Bevölkerung und Wirtschaft* (Berlin, 1937), 132, 139, 141.

TABLE 2. *Occupational structure of the youthful labour force compared to the total workforce in the city of Hamburg, 1933*

	Erwerbspersonen aged 14–20 years					
	Male	%	Female	%	Total	%
Agriculture	482	1.9	86	0.4	568	1.2
Industry and crafts	13,454	52.3	6,147	27.8	19,601	40.9
Transport and commerce	10,769	41.8	9,348	42.2	20,117	42.0
Admin., services	996	3.9	1,476	6.6	2,472	5.2
Domestic service	24	0.1	5,091	23.0	5,115	10.7
TOTAL all sectors	25,725	100.0	22,148	100.0	47,873	100.0
	Total *Erwerbspersonen* (all ages)					
	Male	%	Female	%	Total	%
Agriculture	4,504	1.2	422	0.2	4,926	0.9
Industry and crafts	145,619	37.4	43,949	25.6	189,568	33.8
Transport and commerce	194,619	50.0	70,557	41.1	265,176	47.3
Admin., services	43,939	11.3	26,970	15.7	70,909	12.6
Domestic service	394	0.1	29,901	17.4	30,295	5.4
TOTAL all sectors	389,075	100.0	171,799	100.0	560,874	100.0

Note: Erwerbspersonen includes *Erwerbstätige* and *Erwerbslose*.
Source: StJB Hamburg, Nachtrag zum Jahrgang 1933/4, p. 30.

TABLE 3. *Economic participation rates of the youthful population in the Reich, 1925 and 1933*

	Economically active young people as % of resident population in age-group					
	1925			1933		
	Male	Female	Overall	Male	Female	Overall
14–16 years	72.4	52.0		62.8	46.3	
16–18 years	88.9	72.1		84.6	70.8	
18–20 years	93.6	77.4		92.4	78.6	
TOTAL 14–20 years	85.0	67.0	76.0	82.6	68.3	75.5

Sources: Siemering, *Deutschlands Jugend*, 122–3; Johanna Ernst, 'Die wirtschaftliche und berufliche Lage der weiblichen Jugend im Winter 1931/2', *Arbeit und Beruf*, 7/8 (1932), 93.

TABLE 4. *Apprentices and unskilled young workers in Hamburg: survey of vocational school pupils, Dec. 1926*

	Male	As % of total male pupils	Female	As % of total female pupils	Overall	As % of total pupils
Craft apprentices	14,185	58.6	2,639	14.1	16,824	39.2
Commercial trainees	6,514	26.9	4,421	23.7	10,935	25.5
Unskilled workers, domestic servants	3,045	12.6	5,005	26.8	8,050	18.8
'Without occupation' e.g. *Haustöchter*	—	—	5,864	31.4	5,864	13.7
Unemployed	450	1.9	735	4.0	1,203	2.8
TOTAL	24,194	100	18,682	100	42,876	100

Source: 'Berufsgliederung der Jugend in Hamburg. Stand Dezember 1926', in *Jahresbericht des Ortsausschusses Groß-Hamburg des ADGB*, 30. Geschäftsjahr (1926), 98–101.

TABLE 5. *The unemployed as a proportion of the economically active population in different age-groups in the city of Hamburg and in the Reich in June 1933*

	City of Hamburg 16 June 1933		Reich 16 June 1933	
	No. of unemployed	As % of EAP in age-group	No. of unemployed	As % of EAP in age-group
14–18 yrs				
M	1,215	11.0	90,624	8.9
F	1,549	18.6	57,462	7.3
TOTAL	2,764	14.3	148,086	8.2
18–20 yrs				
M	5,234	35.6	265,526	24.4
F	3,452	25.0	107,618	11.7
TOTAL	8,686	30.5	373,144	18.6
20–25 yrs				
M	20,758	47.2	900,752	30.8
F	10,168	26.7	293,222	13.6
TOTAL	30,926	37.7	1,193,974	23.5
Total 14–25 yrs				
M	27,207	39.0	1,256,902	25.0
F	15,169	25.2	458,302	11.9
TOTAL	42,376	32.6	1,715,204	19.3
Total all ages				
M	127,373	32.7	4,712,432	22.6
F	41,053	23.9	1,142,586	9.9
TOTAL	168,426	30.0	5,855,018	18.1

Source: For Hamburg: *Aus Hamburgs Verwaltung und Wirtschaft*, 12/9 (1935) 171–5, 174; for Reich: Siemering, *Deutschlands Jugend*, 139,

TABLE 6. *Youth unemployment compared to total unemployment in Hamburg and in the Reich in July 1932*

	City of Hamburg 31 July 1932		Reich 31 July 1932	
	No. of unemployed	As % of total male, female and overall unemployed	No. of unemployed	As % of total male, female and overall unemployed
14–18 yrs				
M	1,629	1.6	79,323	1.8
F	1,918	5.6	70,751	6.5
TOTAL	3,547	2.6	150,074	2.8
18–25 yrs				
M	19,975	19.5	957,373	22.3
F	10,552	31.1	349,407	32.0
TOTAL	30,527	22.4	1,306,780	24.2
14–25 yrs				
M	21,604	21.1	1,036,696	24.1
F	12,470	36.7	420,158	38.7
TOTAL	34,074	25.0	1,456,854	27.0
Total all ages				
M	102,142		4,299,294	
F	33,970		1,092,954	
TOTAL	136,112		5,392,248	

Sources: For Hamburg: Sondererhebung über die Zahl der jugendlichen Arbeitslosen im Arbeitsamtsbezirk Hamburg, 31 July 1932, StAH, Arbeitsbehörde I, 16; for Reich: Sondererhebung über die Zahl der jugendlichen Arbeitslosen, 31 July 1932, ZStA Merseburg, Rep. 120, BB VII, 1, 181.

TABLE 7. *Youth unemployment rates in different sectors of the economy*

	14–25-year-olds				
	Male	As %	Female	As %	Total
Agriculture					
Unemployed	68,574	5.5	14,995	3.3	83,56
Economically active	1,303,997	25.9	1,159,862	30.1	2,465,85
Unemployed as % of econ. active		5.2		1.3	
Industry and crafts					
Unemployed	993,348	79.0	210,938	46.0	1,204,28
Economically active	2,769,929	55.0	1,076,652	27.9	3,846,58
Unemployed as % of econ. active		35.9		19.6	
Transport and commerce					
Unemployed	155,255	12.3	112,275	24.5	267,53
Economically active	654,176	13.0	690,225	17.9	1,344,40
Unemployed as % of econ. active		23.7		16.3	
Admin., services					
Unemployed	38,515	3.1	30,176	6.6	68,6
Economically active	302,337	6.0	229,539	6.0	531,8
Unemployed as % of econ. active		12.7		13.1	
Domestic service					
Unemployed	1,210	0.1	89,918	19.6	91,1
Economically active	4,674	0.1	698,425	18.1	703,0
Unemployed as % of econ. active		25.9		12.9	
TOTAL all sectors					
Unemployed	1,256,902	100.0	458,302	100.0	1,715,2
Economically active	5,035,113	100.0	3,854,703	100.0	8,889,8
Unemployed as % of econ. active		25.0		11.9	
Unemployed as % of resident population		22.2		8.2	

Source: Siemering, *Deutschlands Jugend*, 132, 139, 253, 262, 266–7.

Appendix: Tables

...mpared with total unemployment in the Reich, 16 June 1933

	Total population					
As %	Male	As %	Female	As %	Total	As %
4.9	262,822	5.6	46,329	4.0	309,151	5.3
27.7	4,694,003	22.5	4,648,782	40.5	9,342,785	28.9
3.4		5.6		0.9		3.3
70.2	3,607,062	76.5	589,834	51.6	4,196,896	71,7
43.3	10,294,180	49.5	2,758,802	24.0	13,052,982	40.4
31.3		35.0		21.4		32.1
15.6	677,202	14.4	245,143	21.4	922,345	15.7
15.1	4,011,311	19.3	1,920,758	16.7	5,932,069	18.4
19.9		16.9		12.8		15.5
4.0	160,431	3.4	83,357	7.3	243,788	4.2
6.0	1,797,593	8.6	901,063	7.9	2,698,656	8.4
2.9		8.9		9.2		9.0
5.3	4,915	0.1	177,923	15.6	182,838	3.1
7.9	19,946	0.1	1,249,636	10.9	1,269,582	3.9
3.0		24.6		14.2		14.4
0.0	4,712,432	100.0	1,142,586	100.0	5,855,018	100.0
0.0	20,817,033	100.0	11,479,041	100.0	32,296,074	100.0
9.3		22.6		9.9		18.1
5.3		1 14.8		3.4		9.0

TABLE 8. *Education and punishment in the practice of the juvenile courts in the Reich and in Hamburg, 1924–1933*

	Reich			
	Total juveniles convicted (*verurteilt*)	Cases where no punishment imposed as % of *Verurteilte*	Cases where punishment imposed as % of *Verurteilte*	Juveniles with previous convictions as % of *Verurteilte*
1924	41,196	14.5	85.5	16.7
1925	22,578	16.8	83.2	13.0
1926	21,623	18.0	82.0	10.6
1927	21,219	20.0	80.0	9.7
1928	23,050	18.6	81.4	10.8
1929	22,509	19.7	80.2	11.6
1930	23,410	20.4	79.5	11.9
1931	20,245	20.7	79.8	12.1
1932	18,852	18.2	81.7	14.1
1933	14,269	16.5	83.4	13.4

Hamburg

	Total juveniles convicted (verurteilt)	Cases where no punishment imposed as % of Verurteilte	Cases where punishment imposed as % of Verurteilte	Juveniles with previous convictions as % of Verurteilte	Juveniles with previous convictions as % of accused (Beschuldigte)
1924	708	21.4	78.5	43.7	38.9
1925	461	19.1	80.9	29.0	26.3
1926	494	30.9	69.1	18.2	18.3
1927	514	34.4	65.6	—	—
1928	344	38.3	61.6	17.7	13.6
1929	344	43.6	56.3	18.0	9.9
1930	400	41.5	58.5	24.7	13.9
1931	380	43.6	56.3	14.2	7.3
1932	384	35.9	64.1	15.9	6.2
1933	290	38.9	61.0	13.8	6.1

Source: Hubert Matthias, *Die Praxis der Jugendgerichte 1924–1933 an Hand der Reichskriminalstatistik* (Cologne, 1937), 52–3; *StJB Hamburg* (1926/7), 314–15; (1928/9), 175–6; (1933/4), 181–2.

TABLE 9. *Educational measures ordered by the Hamburg juvenile courts, 1924–1933*

	Total no. of juveniles accused (*Beschuldigte*)	Total no. of juveniles convicted (*Verurteilte*)*	No. of juveniles sentenced to punishments	No. of juveniles for whom educational measures ordered		
				With punishment	Without punishment	Total
1924	796	708	556	—	—	—
1925	510	461	373	—	—	—
1926	—	494	341	—	—	—
1927	544	514	337	—	—	—
1928	449	344	212	90	150	240
1929	625	344	194	56	211	267
1930	711	400	234	104	278	382
1931	732	380	214	70	365	435
1932	989	384	246	60	429	489
1933	658	290	177	57	351	408

Appendix: Tables

	Made up of				
	Total no. of educational measures ordered	Caution (*Verwarnung*)	Probation (*Schutzaufsicht*)	Public care (*Fürsorgeerziehung*)	Other
1924	232	29	109	—	94
1925	196	24	93	—	79
1926	218	93	72	27	26
1927	243	132	71	24	16
1928	261	105	72	38	46
1929	309	174	84	26	25
1930	382	206	96	48	32
1931	435	273	93	43	26
1932	536	408	70	33	25
1933	405	287	63	27	28

Note: Number of juveniles for whom educational measures ordered includes juveniles against whom proceedings dropped before court verdict reached.

* i.e. the number on whom judgment was passed (*Abgeurteilte*) less those acquitted (*Freigesprochene*).

Source: StJB Hamburg (1926/7), 314–15; (1928/9), 318–19; (1929/30), 325–6; (1930/1), 309–10; (1931/2), 182–3; (1932/3), 175–6; (1933/4), 181–2.

TABLE 10. *Correctional education in Hamburg, 1919–1934*

| | Juveniles in public care (*Fürsorgezöglinge*, or *FZ*) in public reformatories run by Landesjugendamt ||||||||
| | Total all ages ||| Over-14s ||| |
	Male	Female	Total	Male	Female	Total	As % of public reformatory inmates
1919	—	—	2,161	—	—	617	28.5
1920	—	—	2,460	—	—	664	27.0
1921	—	—	2,547	—	—	683	26.8
1922	—	—	2,897	—	—	781	26.9
1923	—	—	3,160	—	—	972	30.7
1924	—	—	2,732	—	—	866	31.7
1925	—	—	2,573	—	—	892	34.6
1926	1,323	1,065	2,388	542	536	1,078	45.1
1927	1,279	1,122	2,401	529	595	1,124	46.8
1928	1,085	1,045	2,130	464	586	1,050	49.3
1929	1,142	947	2,089	477	499	976	46.7
1930	1,125	958	2,083	455	480	935	44.9
1931	957	892	1,849	358	450	808	43.7
1932	865	834	1,699	332	451	783	46.1
1933	799	639	1,438	217	297	514	35.7
1934	636	623	1,259	258	281	539	42.8

	FZ in other reformatories and institutions (incl. private)	Total FZ in all institutions	Total FZ in institutions/ foster care	FZ in institutions as % of total FZ
1919	135	2,296	7,008	32.8
1920	124	2,584	7,399	34.9
1921	116	2,663	7,552	35.3
1922	135	3,032	7,827	38.7
1923	172	3,332	7,821	42.6
1924	171	2,903	6,942	41.8
1925	210	2,783	6,896	40.3
1926	257	2,645	6,563	40.3
1927	403	2,804	6,636	42.2
1928	515	2,645	6,486	40.8
1929	622	2,711	6,128	44.2
1930	440	2,523	5,821	43.3
1931	303	2,152	4,995	43.1
1932	268	1,967	4,586	42.9
1933	203	1,641	3,954	41.5
1934	180	1,439	3,753	38.3

Source: StJB Hamburg (1925), 277; (1930/1), 298; (1933/4), 176.

BIBLIOGRAPHY

I. UNPUBLISHED SOURCES

Note: The following list gives the *Bestände* used in each archive: individual files used within each *Bestand* are not listed separately.

Staatsarchiv, Hamburg
Jugendbehörde I.
Arbeitsbehörde I.
Sozialbehörde I.
Justizverwaltung.
Medizinal-Kollegium.
Berufsschulbehörde I and II.
Oberschulbehörde V.
Staatliche Pressestelle I–IV.

Archiv der Handelskammer, Hamburg
Arbeitsrecht, Arbeitsschutz (Abt. 25).
Wohlfahrtspflege, Fürsorgewesen (Abt. 31).
Gesundheitswesen (Abt. 32).
Sozialversicherung (Abt. 34).
Arbeitsvermittlung, Arbeitslosenversicherung (Abt. 66).
Lehrlingswesen, Berufsausbildung (Abt. 67).

Kirchenarchiv, Hamburg
Kirchliches Jugendamt.
Kirchenrat.
Mitternachtsmission und Volkswachtbund.

Landgericht, Hamburg
Juvenile court records (uncatalogued).

Bundesarchiv, Koblenz
Reichskanzlei (R43).
Reichsfinanzministerium (R2).
Reichsjustizministerium (R22).
Reichsgesundheitsamt (R86).

Deutscher Gemeindetag (R36).
Reichsarbeitsministerium (R41).

Zentrales Staatsarchiv, Potsdam
Reichsministerium des Innern (15.01).
Reichsjustizministerium (30.01).
Reichsarbeitsministerium (39.01).
Reichsministerium für Wissenschaft, Erziehung und Volksbildung (49.01).
Reichstag (0.1).
Vorläufiger Reichswirtschaftsrat (04.01).
Präsidialkanzlei (06.01).
Reichslandbund Pressearchiv (61 Re 1).
Reichsanstalt für Arbeitsvermittlung und Arbeitslosenversicherung (39.03).
Reichskommissar für Arbeitsbeschaffung (39.05).

Zentrales Staatsarchiv, Merseburg
Preußisches Ministerium für Volkswohlfahrt (Rep. 191).
Preußisches Ministerium für Handel und Gewerbe (Rep. 120).
Preußisches Finanzministerium (Rep. 151).
Preußisches Innenministerium (Rep. 77).
Preußischer Staatsrat (Rep. 2.1.7).
Preußisches Ministerium für Wissenschaft, Kunst, und Volksbildung (Rep. 76).
Preußischer Landtag (Rep. 169).

II. CONTEMPORARY PRINTED SOURCES

1. Periodicals

Note: Articles from contemporary periodicals are not listed individually.

a. Periodical Volumes: Series

Die Arbeit. Zeitschrift für Gewerkschaftspolitik und Wirtschaftskunde, 1 (1924) to 9 (1932).

Arbeit und Beruf. Monatsschrift für Fragen der Berufsberatung und verwandter Gebiete im Deutschen Reich und in Österreich, 1 (1926) to 8 (1933).

Arbeit und Wohlfahrt. Hamburger Blätter für Arbeitswesen, Wohlfahrtspflege und Jugendfürsorge, 1 (1922) to 2 (1923) (from 1923, see *Jugend- und Volkswohl*).

Der Arbeitgeber. Zeitschrift der Vereinigung der Deutschen Arbeitgeber-Verbände, 1918–33.

Arbeiterwohlfahrt. Herausgegeben vom Hauptausschuß der Arbeiterwohlfahrt, 1 (1926) to 8 (1933).
Berliner Wohlfahrtsblatt. Herausgegeben von der Zentralarbeitsgemeinschaft der öffentlichen und freien Wohlfahrtspflege in Berlin, 1 (1925) to 9 (1933).
Blätter des Deutschen Roten Kreuzes, 8 (1929) to 12 (1933).
Blätter für die Hamburgische Waisenpflege und Jugendfürsorge. Amtliches Organ des Waisenhauskollegiums, 1 (1902) to 9 (1910) (from 1910 see *Blätter für die Hamburgische öffentliche Jugendfürsorge*).
Blätter für die Hamburgische öffentliche Jugendfürsorge. Amtliches Organ der Behörde für öffentliche Jugendfürsorge, 9 (1910) to 21 (1922).
Blätter für die Wohlfahrtspflege (Sachsen). Herausgegeben vom Sächsischen Landesamt für Wohlfahrtspflege, 1 (1921) to 5 (1925).
Blätter der Zentralleitung für Wohltätigkeit in Württemberg (Neue Folge), 71 (1918) to 86 (1933).
Correspondenzblatt der Generalkommission der Gewerkschaften Deutschlands, 27 (1917) to 33 (1932) (from 1924 see *Gewerkschafts-Zeitung*).
Deutsche Arbeitgeber-Zeitung. Zentralblatt deutscher Arbeitgeberverbände), 16 (1917) to 23 (1924).
Erziehung. Monatsschrift für den Zusammenhang von Kultur und Erziehung in Wissenschaft und Leben, 1 (1925/6) to 8 (1932/3).
Die Frau, 38 (1930/1) to 40 (1932/3).
Die Gemeinde. Halbmonatsschrift für sozialistische Arbeit in Stadt und Land, 1 (1924) to 7 (1930).
Gewerkschafts-Zeitung, 34 (1924) to 44 (1933).
Jugend- und Volkswohl. Hamburgische Blätter für Wohlfahrtspflege und Jugendhilfe, 1 (1925) to 8 (1932).
Jugendwohl. Katholische Zeitschrift für Kinder- und Jugendfürsorge, 20 (1930) to 22 (1933).
Das Junge Deutschland. Überbündische Zeitschrift, 13 (1919) to 26 (1932).
Jungvolk. Mitteilungsblatt des Arbeiterjugendbundes Groß-Hamburg, 1 (1919) to 4 (1922).
Kommunale Praxis. Wochenschrift für Kommunalpolitik und Gemeindesozialismus, 1 (1914) to 5 (1918).
Nachrichten des Hamburger Landesverbandes für Jugendpflege, 1 (1915) to 6 (1920).
Nachrichtendienst des Deutschen Vereins für öffentliche und private Fürsorge, 7 (1926) to 14 (1933).
Der Pranger. Organ der Hamburg-Altonaer Kontrollmädchen, 1 to 29 (1920–1).
Proletarische Sozialpolitik. Organ der Arbeitsgemeinschaft sozialpolitischer Organisationen, 1 (1928) to 6 (1933).
Rundbrief der Gilde Soziale Arbeit, 1926–32.
Soziale Praxis und Archiv für Volkswohlfahrt, 28 (1918/19) to 42 (1933).

Die Stimme. Blätter für Kinderschutz und Kinderfürsorge, 1 (1921) to 2 (1922).
Volkswohlfahrt. Amtsblatt des Preußischen Ministeriums für Volkswohlfahrt, 1 (1920) to 13 (1932).
Die Wohlfahrtspflege in der Rheinprovinz, 1 (1925) to 9 (1933).
Zeitschrift für die gesamte Strafrechtswissenschaft, 35 (1914) to 52 (1932).
Zentralblatt für Jugendrecht und Jugendwohlfahrt, 16 (1924/5) to 27 (1935).
Zentralblatt für Vormundschaftswesen, Jugendgerichte und Fürsorgeerziehung. Organ des Archivs Deutscher Berufsvormünder, des Allgemeinen Fürsorgeerziehungstages und des Deutschen Kinderschutzverbandes, 10 (1918/19) to 15 (1923/4) (from 1924 see *Zentralblatt für Jugendrecht und Jugendwohlfahrt*).

b. *Periodicals: Single Volumes or Parts of Volumes*

Deutsche Richterzeitung, 24 (1932).
Freie Wohlfahrtspflege, 7 (1932).
Kölner Vierteljahreshefte für Sozialwissenschaften. Zeitschrift des Forschungsinstituts für Sozialwissenschaften in Köln, 6 (1926).
Mitteilungen der Kriminalbiologischen Gesellschaft, 4 (1933).
Monatsschrift für Kriminalbiologie und Strafrechtsreform, 28 (1937).
Schmollers Jahrbuch, 39 (1915).
Der Verfemte. Kampfschrift der Deklassierten, 1 (1920).

2. Official Reports and Gazettes

Bericht über den dritten Kongreß für Psychopathenfürsorge (Heidelberg, 1924).
Bericht über die Sitzung des Gesamtausschusses und des Rechtsausschusses des AFET am 27. Mai 1920 im Ständehaus Hannover (Hanover, 1920).
Bericht über die Verhandlungen des 7. Deutschen Jugendgerichtstags: Die Durchführung des Jugendgerichtsgesetzes als Personenfrage (Berlin, 1928).
Bericht über die Verhandlungen der Tagung des AFET in Heidelberg am 15. und 16. September 1924 (Hanover, 1924).
Bericht über die Verhandlungen der Tagung des AFET in Dresden am 12. und 13. Oktober 1925 (Hanover, 1925).
Bericht über die Verhandlungen des Hauptausschusses des AFET in Würzburg am 19./20.10.1928 (Hanover, 1929).
Bericht über die Sitzung des Bildungsausschusses des Deutschen Industrie- und Handelstages, 9.12.1926 (1926).
Bericht über die Schulungswoche der Gildenschaft 'Soziale Arbeit' vom 23.–29. Juni 1927 in Ludwigslust (n.p., n.d.).
Deutscher Verein für öffentliche und private Fürsorge (ed.), *Jugendämter*

als Träger der öffentlichen Jugendfürsorge im Reich: Bericht über die Verhandlungen des Deutschen Jugendfürsorgetags am 20. und 21. September 1918 in Berlin (Berlin, 1919).
Deutscher Verein für öffentliche und private Fürsorge (ed.), *Die Verwertung der Arbeitskraft als Problem der Fürsorge: Vorbericht für den 40. Deutschen Fürsorgetag des Deutschen Vereins, Hamburg 1927* (Karlsruhe, 1927).
Deutsche Vereinigung für Jugendgerichte und Jugendgerichtshilfen (ed.), *Bericht über die Sachverständigenkonferenz über das Thema: 'Die Bedeutung des Anlagefaktors beim Verbrechen' am 11. März 1929* (Berlin, 1928).
Gesetzsammlung der Freien und Hansestadt Hamburg, 23 (1887) to 57 (1920).
Hamburgisches Gesetz- und Verordnungsblatt, 1921–33.
Hauptausschuß für Arbeiterwohlfahrt (ed.), *Jahrbuch der Arbeiterwohlfahrt 1930* (Berlin, 1931).
Hauptausschuß für Arbeiterwohlfahrt (ed.), *Jahrbuch der Arbeiterwohlfahrt 1931* (Berlin, 1932).
Jahrbuch des Bundes Deutscher Frauenvereine 1927 (1921–7) (Mannheim, 1927).
Jahresberichte des Ortsausschusses Groß-Hamburg des Allgemeinen Deutschen Gewerkschaftsbundes, 26. Geschäftsjahr (1922) to 35. Geschäftsjahr (1931).
Jahresberichte des Hamburgischen Gewerbeaufsichtamtes, 1922–30.
Jahresberichte der Berufsschulbehörde 1915–1924 (Hamburg, n.d.).
Landesjugendamt und Jugendamt Hamburg, *Jahresbericht 1925* (Hamburg, 1926).
Protokoll über die Verhandlungen des Parteitags der SPD in Kassel vom 10. bis 16. Oktober 1920 (Berlin, 1920).
Reichs-Arbeitsblatt. Amtsblatt des Reichsarbeitsministeriums und des Reichsamts für Arbeitsvermittlung, New Series (1921–33) (I = official section, II = unofficial section).
Reichsgesetzblatt, 1918–33.
Verhandlungen des Ersten Deutschen Jugendgerichtstages in Charlottenburg am 15.–17. März 1909 (Berlin, 1909).
Verhandlungen der 5. Generalversammlung der Gesellschaft für Soziale Reform am 12. und 13. Mai 1911 in Berlin [= Gesellschaft für Soziale Reform (ed.), *Die jugendlichen Arbeiter in Deutschland*, 5/6] (Jena, 1911).
Verhandlungen des Reichstags. Stenographische Berichte und Anlagen 1. Wahlperiode 1920–4 (Berlin, 1924); 2. Wahlperiode 1924 (Berlin, 1924); 3. Wahlperiode 1924–8 (Berlin, 1929); 4. Wahlperiode 1928–30 (Berlin, 1932); 5. Wahlperiode 1930–2 (Berlin, 1932); 6. Wahlperiode 1932 (Berlin, 1932).

Verhandlungen der Verfassunggebenden Deutschen Nationalversammlung 1919–1920. Stenographische Berichte und Anlagen (Berlin, 1920).
Verwaltungsbericht der Stadt Berlin für die Zeit 1924–1928 (Berlin, 1930).

3. Statistics

Aus Hamburgs Verwaltung und Wirtschaft, 4 (1927) to 15 (1938).
Hamburger Statistische Monatsberichte, 1 (1924) to 3 (1926) (from 1927, see *Aus Hamburgs Verwaltung und Wirtschaft*).
Statistik des Hamburgischen Staates, 27 (1918) to 34 (1928).
Statistisches Handbuch für den Hamburgischen Staat, 1920 (for later years, see *Statistisches Jahrbuch für die freie und Hansestadt Hamburg*).
Statistisches Jahrbuch für die freie und Hansestadt Hamburg, 1925, 1926/7, 1927/8, 1928/9, 1929/30, 1930/1, 1931/2, 1932/3, 1933/4, 1934/5 (with supplement, 1935).

4. Other Pre-1945 Material

Note: Individual periodical articles are not listed separately. Where only one essay from a volume of essays has been cited, that essay is listed separately below; where more than one essay from a collection has been cited, only the collection is included below.

BAERNREITER, J. M., *Jugendfürsorge und Strafrecht in den Vereinigten Staaten von Amerika* (Leipzig, 1905).
BARSCHAK, ERNA, *Die Schülerin der Berufsschule und ihre Umwelt* (Berlin, 1926).
BARTH, A., BODE G., and ERBEN, H. (eds.), *Die Beschulung der Ungelernten* (Wittenberg, 1928).
BAUM, MARIE, *Familienfürsorge* (Karlsruhe, 1927).
BERUFSSCHULBEHÖRDE DER FREIEN UND HANSESTADT HAMBURG (ed.), *Das Berufsschulwesen im Groß-Hamburgischen Städtegebiet* (Hamburg, 1925).
BINDER, GOTTLOB, *Die Arbeiterwohlfahrtspflege—ihre Entwicklung, Motive und Ziele* (Münster, 1926).
BLAUM, C., RIEBESELL, P., and STORCK, C. (eds.), *Reichsjugendwohlfahrtsgesetz* (Mannheim, 1923).
BÖHM, C. M., 'Berufsumschichtung und Berufsumstellung in der Nachkriegszeit mit besonderer Berücksichtigung hamburgischer Verhältnisse', Diss. phil. (Hamburg, 1932).
BÖHME, HILDEGARD, 'Die Entwicklung des gewerblichen Lehrlingswesens in Preußen während und nach dem Krieg', Diss. jur. (Hamburg, 1923).
BOHM-SCHUCH, CLARA, *Willst Du mich hören? Weckruf an unsere Mädel* (Berlin, 1922).
BONDY, CURT, *Scheuen* (Berlin, 1931).

BUES, HERMANN, *Die Stellung der Jugendlichen zum Beruf und zur Arbeit* (Bernau, 1926).
BUNDESVORSTAND DES ALLGEMEINEN DEUTSCHEN GEWERKSCHAFTSBUNDES (ed.), *Hilfe für die erwerbslose Jugend: Die Stellung der Gewerkschaften zum Freiwilligen Arbeitsdienst* (Berlin, 1932).
CLOSTERMANN, LUDWIG, HELLER, THEODOR, and STEPHANI, P. (eds.), *Enzyklopädisches Handbuch des Kinderschutzes und der Jugendfürsorge*, 2nd edn. (Leipzig, 1930).
DANZIGER, G., and KAWERAU, S. (eds.), *Jugendnot* (Dresden, 1923).
DEHEN, PETER, *Die deutschen Industriewerkschulen in wohlfahrts-, wirtschafts- und bildungsgeschichtlicher Beleuchtung* (Munich, 1928).
DEHN, GÜNTHER, *Proletarische Jugend: Lebensgestaltung und Gedankenwelt der großstädtischen Proletarierjugend* (Berlin, 1929).
DEUTSCHE ZENTRALE FÜR JUGENDFÜRSORGE (ed.), *Der Kampf der Parteien um die Jugend* (Berlin, 1912).
DEUTSCHER VERBAND DER SOZIALBEAMTINNEN (ed.), *Fürsorgerinnen-Not, Fürsorgerinnen-Wille* (Berlin, 1932).
DEUTSCHER VEREIN FÜR ÖFFENTLICHE UND PRIVATE FÜRSORGE (ed.), *Jugendämter als Träger der öffentlichen Jugendfürsorge im Reich: Bericht über die Verhandlungen des Deutschen Jugendfürsorgetages am 20. und 21. September 1918 in Berlin* (Berlin, 1919).
DEUTSCHES ARCHIV FÜR JUGENDWOHLFAHRT (ed.), *Fürsorge für erwerbslose Jugendliche: Ergebnisse einer Umfrage des Deutschen Archivs für Jugendwohlfahrt über jugendpflegerische Maßnahmen bei jugendlichen Erwerbslosen* (Berlin, 1924).
—— (ed.), *Aus der Praxis der Erwerbslosenhilfe an Jugendlichen* (Eberswalde and Berlin, 1931).
ELSTER, LUDWIG, WEBER, ADOLF, and WIESER, FRIEDRICH, *Handwörterbuch der Staatswissenschaften*, 4th edn. (Jena, 1927).
ERICH, G., 'Die Kriminalität der 12–14jährigen im Deutschen Reiche', *ZGS* 35/21 (1914), 21–5.
ERICHSON, KURT, *Die Fürsorge in Hamburg. Ein Überblick über ihre Entwicklung, Stand, Grundlagen* (Hamburg, 1930).
FELISCH, PAUL, *Ein deutsches Jugendgesetz* (Berlin, 1917).
FINCK, BERTHA (ed.), *Was können wir für unsere arbeitslose Jugend tun? Bilder aus der Arbeit der evangelischen Liebestätigkeit* (Berlin, 1931).
FISCHER, JOSEPHA, *Die Mädchen in den deutschen Jugendverbänden: Stand, Ziele, und Aufgaben* (Leipzig, 1933).
FRANCKE, HERBERT, *Jugendverwahrlosung und ihre Bekämpfung* (Berlin, 1926).
FRANZEN-HELLERSBERG, LISBETH, *Die jugendliche Arbeiterin: Ihre Arbeitsweise und Lebensform* (Tübingen, 1932).
FREI, BRUNO, LÖWENTHAL, G., and BRANDT, A. *Scheuen: Gericht über die Schuldigen* (Berlin, 1931).

FRIEDLÄNDER, WALTER, and MYERS, EARL, *Child Welfare before and after Nazism* (Chicago, 1940).
Fünf Jahre Landesjugendamt Berlin 1925–1930 (Berlin, 1930).
FÜRTH, HENRIETTE, *Zur Sozialisierung der öffentlichen Wohlfahrtspflege* (Berlin, 1928).
GAEBEL, KÄTHE, *Die deutsche Wirtschaft und das Berufsschicksal der Frau* (Berlin, 1932).
GLEITZE, BRUNO, *Die Konjunkturkriminalität: Eine statistische Untersuchung über die konjunkturellen und demographischen Einflüsse auf die Kriminalitätsentwicklung* (Stuttgart and Berlin, 1941).
GREGOR, ADALBERT, *Rassehygiene und Jugendfürsorge* (Berlin, 1919).
—— 'Über die Sterilisierung minderwertiger Fürsorgezöglinge', in Ernst Rüdin (ed.), *Erblehre und Rassenhygiene im völkischen Staat* (Munich, 1934).
GRÜNHUT, MAX, and MÜLLER, BRUNO, *Zwei Vorträge über Jugendgerichtsbarkeit* (n.p. 1927).
Gutachten zur Arbeitslosenfrage, erstattet von der Gutachterkommission zur Arbeitslosenfrage (Brauns-Kommission) (Berlin, 1931).
HALL, W. CLARKE, *Children's Courts* (London, 1926).
HAMBURGER STAATSAMT (ed.), *Hamburg im Dritten Reich: Arbeiten der hamburgischen Verwaltung in Einzeldarstellungen*, i. *Die Neugestaltung der Schule*; vi. *Hamburgs Fürsorgewesen im Kampf gegen die Arbeitslosigkeit* (Hamburg, 1935); x. *Die Sozialverwaltung* (Hamburg, 1939).
HEIMANN, HILDEGARD VON, *Studien zur Erziehungsarbeit an verwahrlosten Mädchen* (Hamburg, 1923).
HERRMANN, WALTER, *Das hamburgische Jugendgefängnis Hahnöfersand: Ein Bericht über Erziehungsarbeit im Strafvollzug* (Hamburg, 1923).
HERRNSTADT, ERNST, *Die Lage der arbeitslosen Jugend in Deutschland* (Berlin, 1927).
HERTZ, WILHELM, 'Zehn Jahre Hamburger Jugendamt 1923–1933', MS (Hamburg, 1934).
HINRICHS, MARIA, *Handbuch für den Hamburger Wohlfahrtspfleger* (Hamburg, 1922).
JACOBY, HEINZ, 'Verwahrlosung und Verbrechen als sozialpathologische Erscheinungen', MS (Staatsexamensarbeit) (Berlin, 1930).
KASTEN, A., u.a., *Die kommende Angestelltengeneration: Eine sozialstatistische Untersuchung des Gewerkschaftsbundes der Angestellten über Herkunft, Arbeitsverhältnisse und Berufsausbildung der Lehrlinge in Angestelltenberufen* (Berlin, 1933).
KELCHNER, MATHILDE, *Kummer und Trost jugendlicher Arbeiterinnen* (Berlin, 1929).
KIESSLING, WILHELM, and ENDER, EMMA, *Hamburgische Jugendpflege in und nach dem Krieg* (Hamburg, 1919).

KITZINGER, FRIEDRICH, *Die Internationale Kriminalistische Vereinigung: Betrachtungen über ihr Wesen und ihre bisherige Wirksamkeit* (Munich, 1905).
KLOPFER, BRUNO, *Jugendpflege an erwerbslosen Jugendlichen: Erfahrungen und Vorschläge* (Berlin, 1926).
KÖHNE, PAUL, *Kriminalität und sittliches Verhalten der Jugendlichen* [= Gesellschaft für Soziale Reform (ed.), *Die jugendlichen Arbeiter in Deutschland*, 2] (Jena, 1910).
KÜHNE, A. (ed.), *Handbuch für das Berufs- und Fachschulwesen* (Leipzig, 1929).
LAHANN, SIGURD, 'Die Kriminalität Hamburgs 1926–1933', Diss. jur. (Hamburg, 1937).
LAMM, ALBERT, *Betrogene Jugend: Aus einem Erwerbslosenheim* (Berlin, 1932).
LAMPEL, PETER MARTIN, *Jungen in Not. Berichte von Fürsorgezöglingen* (Berlin, 1929).
—— *Revolte im Erziehungshaus: Schauspiel der Gegenwart in 3 Akten* (Berlin, 1929).
LEHRKÖRPER DER ALLGEMEINEN BERUFSSCHULEN FÜR DIE WEIBLICHE JUGEND (ed.), *Von dem Leben und der Arbeit unserer allgemeinbildenden Mädchenberufsschulen in Hamburg* (Hamburg, 1927).
—— et al. (eds.), *Frauenarbeit und öffentliche Berufserziehung in Hamburg* (Hamburg, 1929).
LEMKE, H., *Öffentliche Jugendhilfe in Hamburg* (Hamburg, 1925).
LUSCH, MARIA, *Fürsorge an Mädchenberufsschulen und Wege zu ihrer Durchführung* (Cologne, 1930).
MAGNUS, ERNA, *Werkheime für erwerbslose Jugendliche* (Berlin, 1927).
MATTHIAS, HUBERT, *Die Praxis der Jugendgerichte 1924–1933 an Hand der Reichskriminalstatistik*, Diss. Jur. (Cologne, 1937).
MENNICKE, CARL (ed.), *Erfahrungen der Jungen* (Potsdam, 1930).
MEWES, BERNHARD, *Die erwerbstätige Jugend: Eine statistische Untersuchung* (Berlin and Leipzig, 1929).
MISCHKE, HILDEGARD, 'Bedeutung von Anlage und Milieu bei weiblichen Fürsorgezöglingen Mecklenburgs', Diss. phil. (Rostock, 1932).
MUCHOW, MARTHA, and MUCHOW, H. H., *Der Lebensraum des Großstadtkindes* (Hamburg, 1935).
MÜLLER, BRUNO, 'Das Jugendgerichtsgesetz in der Praxis des Hamburger Jugendgerichts', MS (Hamburg, 1924).
MUSER, HANS, *Homosexualität und Jugendfürsorge: Eine soziologische und fürsorgerische Untersuchung* (Paderborn, 1933).
NAILIS, ANNA, *Zur Geschichte und Theorie der Verwahrlosung* (Düsseldorf, 1933).
NIFFKA, ERWIN, 'Die berufliche Lage der Jugend in der Gegenwart unter besonderer Berücksichtigung der männlichen Jugendlichen im Alter von

14–21 Jahren', in *Handbuch der Jugendpflege*, 1/2 (Eberswalde and Berlin, 1932).
NOACK, VICTOR, *Das soziale Sexualverbrechen: Wohnungsnot und Geschlechtsnot: Ein Kampfwort auch für die Jugend* (Stuttgart, 1932).
OBERDÖRFFER, PAULA, *Von der Wertwelt der Gefährdeten auf Grund psychologischer Untersuchungen in rheinischen Erziehungsheimen für schulentlassene Mädchen* (Paderborn, 1928).
PETERSEN, JOHANNES, *Die hamburgische öffentliche Jugendfürsorge* (Hamburg, 1911).
POLLIGKEIT, WILHELM (ed.), *Familie und Fürsorge* (Langensalza, 1927).
REICHSARBEITSVERWALTUNG (ed.), *Berufsberatung, Berufsauslese, Berufsausbildung: Beiträge zur Förderung des gewerblichen Nachwuchses* (Berlin, 1925).
—— (ed.), *Entwurf eines Berufsausbildungsgesetzes nebst amtlicher Begründung* (*Reichsarbeitsblatt*, Sonderheft 39) (Berlin, 1927).
REICHSMINISTERIUM DES INNERN (ed.), *Notprogramme für die Jugendwohlfahrt* (Berlin, 1932).
RICHTER, KURT, 'Maßnahmen zur Betreuung der erwerbslosen Jugend', in *Handbuch der Jugendpflege*, 14 (Eberswalde and Berlin, 1933).
RUNGE, ERWIN, 'Industrielle Lehrlingsausbildung und Leistungssteigerung mit besonderer Würdigung Hamburger Verhältnisse', Diss. phil. (Hamburg, 1941).
RUSCHEWEYH, HERBERT, *Die Entwicklung des deutschen Jugendgerichts* (Weimar, 1918).
SAARBOURG, 'Maßnahmen zur Betreuung der unorganisierten Jugend', in *Handbuch der Jugendpflege*, 14 (Eberswalde and Berlin, 1933).
SAVE THE CHILDREN INTERNATIONAL UNION (ed.), *Children, Young People and Unemployment: A Series of Enquiries into the Effects of Unemployment on Children and Young People* (Geneva, 1933).
SCHELLENBERG, ERNST, *Der Freiwillige Arbeitsdienst auf Grund der bisherigen Erfahrungen* (Berlin, 1932).
SCHOLZ, OTTO, 'Ursachen der Verwahrlosung und Kriminalität der Jugendlichen untersucht an Zöglingen der Fürsorgeerziehungsanstalt Ohlsdorf', Diss. Jur. (Hamburg, 1935).
SCHULTZ, CLEMENS, *Die Halbstarken* (Leipzig, 1912).
SIEMERING, HERTHA, *Deutschlands Jugend in Bevölkerung und Wirtschaft* (Berlin, 1937).
—— and SPRANGER, EDMUND (ed.), *Weibliche Jugend in unserer Zeit: Beobachtungen und Erfahrungen von Jugendführerinnen* (Leipzig, 1932).
SIMON, HELENE, *Aufgaben und Ziele der neuzeitlichen Wohlfahrtspflege* (Stuttgart and Berlin, 1922).
STAEWEN-ORDEMANN, GERTRUD, *Menschen der Unordnung: Die proletarische Wirklichkeit im Arbeitsschicksal der ungelernten Großstadtjugend* (Berlin, 1933).

STEIGERTHAL, GEORG, *Zwangsfürsorgerische Maßnahmen gegenüber erwachsenen Personen: Ein Beitrag zur Geschichte des Arbeitshauswesens und zum Problem der Bewahrung* (Berlin, 1932).
STELZNER, HELENE FRIEDERIKE, *Weibliche Fürsorgezöglinge* (Berlin, 1929).
STERN, JACQUES, *Der Weg zum deutschen Jugendgesetz* (Berlin, 1918).
STUHLMANN, ADOLF, *Das staatliche Gewerbeschulwesen zu Hamburg bis zum Jahre 1902: Ein Rückblick* (n.p., n.d.).
TAYLOR, JOHN W., *Youth Welfare in Germany: A Study of Governmental Action Relative to the Care of the Normal German Youth* (Nashville, 1936).
THURNWALD, RICHARD (ed.), *Die neue Jugend* (Leipzig, 1927).
WEBLER, HEINRICH, *Wider das Jugendgericht* (Berlin, 1929).
WEICKER, HANS, *Bildung und Erziehung außerhalb der Schule (Jugendpflege)* [= Gesellschaft für Soziale Reform (ed.), *Die jugendlichen Arbeiter in Deutschland*, 4] (Jena, 1911).
WESSEL, HELENE, *Lebenshaltung aus Fürsorge und aus Erwerbstätigkeit* (Berlin, 1931).
WILKER, KARL, *Fürsorgeerziehung als Lebensschulung: Ein Aufruf zur Tat* (Berlin, 1921).

III. POST-1945 MONOGRAPHS, DISSERTATIONS, ESSAYS, AND ARTICLES

ABELSHAUSER, WERNER (ed.), *Die Weimarer Republik als Wohlfahrtsstaat: Zum Verhältnis von Wirtschafts- und Sozialpolitik in der Industriegesellschaft* (Stuttgart, 1987).
ABRAHAM, DAVID, *The Collapse of the Weimar Republic: Political Economy and Crisis*, 2nd edn. (New York, 1986).
ABRAMS, LYNN, 'Prostitutes in Imperial Germany, 1870–1918: Working Girls or Social Outcasts?', in Richard J. Evans (ed.), *The German Underworld: Deviants and Outcasts in German History* (London, 1988).
ARNDT, HELMUT, 'Zu einigen Aspekten sozialdemokratischer Kommunalpolitik in der Weimarer Republik', *Jahrbuch für Regionalgeschichte*, 9 (1982).
AUTORENKOLLEKTIV, *Gefesselte Jugend: Fürsorgeerziehung im Kapitalismus* (Frankfurt am Main, 1971).
BAJOHR, STEFAN, *Die Hälfte der Fabrik. Geschichte der Frauenarbeit in Deutschland 1914–1945* (Marburg, 1979).
BARON, RÜDEGER, ' "Ballastexistenzen"—Sparmaßnahmen in der Krise: Fürsorgeerziehung im Übergang zum Dritten Reich', in Georg Vobruba (ed.), *'Wir sitzen alle in einem Boot': Gemeinschaftsrhetorik in der Krise* (Frankfurt am Main and New York, 1983).

BARON, RÜDEGER and LANDWEHR, ROLF, 'Von der Berufung zum Beruf: Zur Entwicklung der Ausbildung für die soziale Arbeit', in R. Baron (ed.), *Sozialarbeit und Soziale Reform: Zur Geschichte eines Berufs zwischen Frauenbewegung und öffentlicher Verwaltung* (Weinheim and Basle, 1983).

BARTZ, JOACHIM, and MOR, DAGMAR, 'Der Weg in die Jugendzwangsarbeit: Maßnahmen gegen Jugendarbeitslosigkeit zwischen 1925 und 1935', in Gero Lenhardt (ed.), *Der hilflose Sozialstaat: Jugendarbeitslosigkeit und Politik* (Frankfurt am Main, 1979).

BESSEL, RICHARD, *Political Violence and the Rise of Nazism: The Storm Troopers in Eastern Germany 1925–1934* (New Haven, Conn., and London, 1984).

—— and FEUCHTWANGER, E. J. (eds.), *Social Change and Political Development in Weimar Germany* (London, 1981).

BLACKBOURN, DAVID, 'Between Resignation and Volatility: The German Petite Bourgeoisie in the 19th Century', in Geoffrey Crossick and Hans-Georg Haupt (eds.), *Shopkeepers and Master Artisans in Nineteenth-Century Europe* (London, 1984).

BORCHARDT, KNUT, 'Zwangslagen und Handlungsspielräume in der großen Wirtschaftskrise der frühen dreißiger Jahre', in Michael Stürmer (ed.), *Die Weimarer Republik: Belagerte Civitas* (Königstein/Ts., 1980).

—— *Perspectives on Modern German Economic History and Policy* (Cambridge, 1991).

BRIDENTHAL, RENATE, 'Class Struggle Around the Hearth: Women and Domestic Service in the Weimar Republic', in M. Dobkowski and I. Wallimann (eds.), *Towards the Holocaust: The Social and Economic Collapse of the Weimar Republic* (Westport, Conn., 1983).

—— GROSSMANN, ATINA, and KAPLAN, MARION (eds.), *When Biology Became Destiny: Women in Weimar and Nazi Germany* (New York, 1984).

BRIGHT, CHARLES, and HARDING, SUSAN (eds.), *Statemaking and Social Movements: Essays in History and Theory* (Ann Arbor, Mich., 1984).

BRUCH, RÜDIGER VOM (ed.), *Weder Kommunismus noch Kapitalismus: Bürgerliche Sozialreform in Deutschland vom Vormärz bis zur Ära Adenauer* (Munich, 1985).

BÜHLER, KARL, 'Die pädagogische Problematik des Freiwilligen Arbeitsdienstes', Diss. phil. (Aachen, 1978).

BÜSCH, OTTO (ed.), *Wählerbewegungen in der deutschen Geschichte: Analyse und Bericht zu den Reichstagswahlen 1871–1933* (Berlin, 1978).

BÜTTNER, URSULA, *Hamburg in der Staats- und Wirtschaftskrise 1928–1931* (Hamburg, 1982).

CAIN, MAUREEN (ed.), *Growing Up Good: Policing the Behaviour of Girls in Europe* (London, 1989).

CAMPBELL, JOAN, *Joy in Work, German Work: The National Debate, 1800–1945* (Princeton, 1989).
CASBURN, MAGGIE, *Girls Will Be Girls* (London, 1979).
CASTELL RÜDENHAUSEN, ADELHEID GRÄFIN ZU, 'Die Überwindung der Armenschule: Schülerhygiene an den Hamburger öffentlichen Volksschulen im Zweiten Kaiserreich', *AfS* 22 (1982), 201–77.
—— and REULECKE, JÜRGEN, 'Aspekte der nationalsozialistischen Gesellschaftspolitik am Beispiel der Jugend- und Rassenpolitik', in Kurt Düwell and Wolfgang Köllmann (eds.), *Rheinland-Westfalen im Industriezeitalter*, iii: *Vom Ende der Weimarer Republik bis zum Land Nordrhein-Westfalen* (Wuppertal, 1984).
CHILDERS, THOMAS (ed.), *The Formation of the Nazi Constituency 1919– 1933* (London, 1986).
COHEN, STANLEY, *Folk Devils and Moral Panics: The Creation of the Mods and Rockers*, 2nd edn. (Oxford, 1980).
COMFORT, RICHARD, *Revolutionary Hamburg: Labour Politics in the Early Weimar Republic* (Stanford, 1966).
CREW, DAVID, 'German Socialism, the State and Family Policy 1918–1933', *Continuity and Change*, 1/2 (1986), 256–63.
CROON, HELLMUTH, 'Jugendbewegung und Arbeitdienst', *Jahrbuch des Archivs der deutschen Jugendbewegung*, 5 (1973), 66–84.
DANIEL, UTE, 'Funktionalisierung von Frauen und Familien in der Kriegswirtschaft 1914–1918: Tendenzen und Gegentendenzen', in *Historikerinnentreffen März 1983: Dokumentation* (Berlin, 1983).
DEUTSCHER WERKBUND E.V and WÜRTTEMBERGISCHER KUNSTVEREIN STUTTGART (eds.), *Schock und Schöpfung: Jugendästhetik im 20. Jahrhundert* (Darmstadt and Neuwied, 1986).
DITTMER, PETER, 'Zur Geschichte der Zwangs- und Fürsorgeerziehung', Diss. jur. (Hamburg, 1960).
DOMANSKY, ELISABETH, and HEINEMANN, ULRICH, 'Jugend als Generationserfahrung: Das Beispiel der Weimarer Republik', *SOWI* 13/1 (1984), 14–21.
DONZELOT, JACQUES, *The Policing of Families: Welfare versus the State* (London, 1980).
DOWE, DIETER (ed.), *Jugendprotest und Generationenkonflikt in Europa im 20. Jahrhundert: Deutschland, England, Frankreich und Italien im Vergleich* (Bonn, 1986).
DRECHSEL, WILTRUD ULRIKE, 'Ausbildung für zwei Berufe: Zur Geschichte der hauswirtschaftlichen Pflichtfortbildungsschule für Mädchen in Bremen 1920–1933', in Jutta Dalhoff, Uschi Frey, and Ingrid Schöll (eds.), *Frauenmacht in der Geschichte: Beiträge des Historikerinnentreffens 1985 zur Frauengeschichtsforschung* (Düsseldorf, 1986).
Dreihundertfünfzig Jahre Jugendwohlfahrt in Hamburg: Vom Waisenhauskollegium zur Jugendbehörde (Hamburg, 1955).

DUDEK, PETER, *Erziehung durch Arbeit: Arbeitslagerbewegung und Freiwilliger Arbeitsdienst 1920–1935* (Opladen, 1988).
—— *Leitbild: Kamerad und Helfer: Sozialpädagogische Bewegung in der Weimarer Republik am Beispiel der 'Gilde Soziale Arbeit'* (Frankfurt am Main, 1988).
EBBINGHAUS, ANGELIKA (ed.), *Opfer und Täterinnen: Frauenbiographien im Nationalsozialismus* (Nördlingen, 1987).
—— KAUPEN-HAAS, HEIDRUN and ROTH, KARL HEINZ (eds.), *Heilen und Vernichten im Mustergau Hamburg: Bevölkerungs- und Gesundheitspolitik im Dritten Reich* (Hamburg, 1984).
EBERTS, ERICH, *Arbeiterjugend 1904–1945: Sozialistische Erziehungsgemeinschaft—Politische Organisation* (Frankfurt am Main, 1979).
EHNI, HANS-PETER, *Bollwerk Preußen? Preußen-Regierung, Reich-Länder-Problem und Sozialdemokratie 1928–1932* (Bonn–Bad Godesberg, 1975).
EMIG, BRIGITTE, *Die Veredelung des Arbeiters: Sozialdemokratie als Kulturbewegung* (Frankfurt am Main, 1980).
EPPE, HEINRICH, *Selbsthilfe und Interessenvertretung: Die sozial- und jugendpolitischen Bestrebungen der sozialdemokratischen Arbeiterjugendorganisation 1904–1933* (Bonn, 1983).
EVANS, RICHARD J., *Sozialdemokratie und Frauenemanzipation im deutschen Kaiserreich* (Berlin and Bonn, 1979).
—— ' "Red Wednesday" in Hamburg: Social Democrats, Police and Lumpenproletariat in the Suffrage Disturbances of 17 January 1906', *Social History*, 4 (1979), 1–31, repr. in id. *Rethinking German History* (London, 1987).
—— (ed.), *The German Working Class 1888–1933: The Politics of Everyday Life* (London, 1982).
—— *Death in Hamburg: Society and Politics in the Cholera Years 1830–1910* (Oxford, 1987).
—— and DICK GEARY (eds.), *The German Unemployed: Experiences and Consequences of Mass Unemployment from the Weimar Republic to the Third Reich* (London, 1987).
FALTER, JÜRGEN, LINDENBERGER, THOMAS, and SCHUMANN, SIEGFRIED, *Wahlen und Abstimmungen in der Weimarer Republik* (Munich, 1986).
FELDMAN, GERALD, *Army, Industry and Labor in Germany 1914–1918* (Princeton, 1966).
FIEDLER, GUDRUN, *Jugend im Krieg; Bürgerliche Jugendbewegung, Erster Weltkrieg und sozialer Wandel 1914–1923* (Cologne, 1989).
FISCHER, CONAN, *Stormtroopers: A Social, Economic and Ideological Analysis 1929–1935* (London, 1983).
—— *The German Communists and the Rise of Nazism* (London, 1991).

FRAUENGRUPPE FASCHISMUSFORSCHUNG (ed.), *Mutterkreuz und Arbeitsbuch: Zur Geschichte der Frauen in der Weimarer Republik und im Nationalsozialismus* (Berlin, 1981).

FREVERT, UTE, 'Vom Klavier zur Schreibmaschine: Weiblicher Arbeitsmarkt am Beispiel der weiblichen Angestellten in der Weimarer Republik', in Annette Kuhn and Gerhard Schneider (eds.), *Frauen in der Geschichte* (Düsseldorf, 1979).

—— 'Traditionale Weiblichkeit und moderne Interessenorganisation: Frauen im Angestelltenberuf 1918–1933', *GG* 7 (1981), 507–53.

—— 'The Civilizing Tendency of Hygiene: Working-Class Women under Medical Control in Imperial Germany', in John C. Fout (ed.), *German Women in the Nineteenth Century: A Social History* (New York and London, 1984).

—— *Women in German History: From Bourgeois Emancipation to Sexual Liberation* (Oxford, 1989).

FRIEDLÄNDER, WALTER, *Helene Simon: Ein Leben für soziale Gerechtigkeit* (Bonn, 1962).

FÜHRER, KARL CHRISTIAN, *Arbeitslosigkeit und die Entstehung der Arbeitslosenversicherung in Deutschland 1902–1927* (Berlin, 1990).

Fünfzig Jahre Gilde Soziale Arbeit 1925–1975 (n.p., 1975).

FÜRST, MAX, *Talisman Scheherezade: Die schwierigen zwanziger Jahre* (Frankfurt am Main, 1976).

GEARY, DICK, 'Jugend, Arbeitslosigkeit und politischer Radikalismus am Ende der Weimarer Republik', *Gewerkschaftliche Monatshefte*, 5 (1983), 304–9.

—— 'The Industrial Élite and the Nazis', in Peter D. Stachura (ed.), *The Nazi Machtergreifung* (London, 1983).

GIESECKE, HERMANN, *Vom Wandervogel bis zur Hitlerjugend: Jugendarbeit zwischen Politik und Pädagogik* (Munich, 1981).

GILLINGHAM, JOHN, 'Vocational Training in the Third Reich', *Journal of Social History*, 19/3 (1986), 423–32.

GILLIS, JOHN R., *Youth and History: Tradition and Change in European Age Relations, 1770–Present*, 2nd edn. (London, 1981).

GLASER, GEORG, *Geheimnis und Gewalt* (Reinbek, 1983).

GÖTZ VON OLENHUSEN, IRMTRAUD, *Jugendreich, Gottesreich, Deutsches Reich: Junge Generation, Religion und Politik 1928–1933* (Cologne, 1987).

GREINERT, WOLF-DIETRICH, *Schule als Instrument sozialer Kontrolle und Objekt privater Interessen: Der Beitrag der Berufsschule zur politischen Erziehung der Unterschichten* (Hanover, 1975).

GROSSMANN, ATINA, 'The "New Woman", the New Family and the Rationalization of Sexuality', Ph.D. (Rutgers University, 1983).

GRÜTTNER, MICHAEL, *Arbeitswelt an der Wasserkante: Sozialgeschichte der Hamburger Hafenarbeiter 1886–1914* (Göttingen, 1984).

HACHTMANN, RÜDIGER, 'Arbeitsmarkt und Arbeitszeit in der Industrie 1929–1939', *AfS* 27 (1987), 177–227.

HAGEMANN, KAREN, *Frauenalltag und Männerpolitik: Alltagsleben und gesellschaftliches Handeln von Arbeiterfrauen in der Weimarer Republik* (Bonn, 1990).

HALL, STUART, and JEFFERSON, TONY (eds.), *Resistance through Rituals: Youth Subcultures in Post-war Britain* (London, 1976).

HAMMER, FRANZ, *Traum und Wirklichkeit: Die Geschichte einer Jugend* (E. Berlin, 1982).

HANSEN, ECKHARD, HEISIG, MICHAEL, LEIBFRIED, STEPHAN, and TENNSTEDT, FLORIAN, *Seit über einem Jahrhundert . . .: Verschüttete Alternativen in der Sozialpolitik: Sozialer Fortschritt, organisierte Dienstleistermacht und nationalsozialistische Machtergreifung: Der Fall der Ambulatorien in den Unterweserstädten und Berlin* (Cologne, 1981).

HANSMEYER, KARL-HEINRICH (ed.), *Kommunale Finanzpolitik in der Weimarer Republik* (Stuttgart, 1973).

HARNEY, KLAUS, *Die preußische Fortbildungsschule: Eine Studie zum Problem der Hierarchisierung beruflicher Schultypen im 19. Jahrhundert* (Berlin, 1980).

HARVEY, ELIZABETH, 'Sozialdemokratische Jugendhilfereform in der Praxis: Walter Friedländer und das Bezirksjugendamt Prenzlauer Berg in der Weimarer Republik', *Theorie und Praxis der sozialen Arbeit*, 36/6 (1985), 218–29.

—— *Youth Welfare and Social Democracy in Weimar Germany: The Work of Walter Friedländer* (New Alyth, 1987).

HASENCLEVER, CHRISTA, *Jugendhilfe und Jugendgesetzgebung seit 1900* (Göttingen, 1978).

HAUSEN, KARIN, 'Mütter, Söhne und der Markt von Symbolen und Waren: Der deutsche Muttertag 1923–1933', in Hans Medick und David Sabean (eds.), *Emotionen und materielle Interessen: Sozialanthropologische und historische Beiträge zur Familienforschung* (Göttingen, 1984).

HEINEMANN, MANFRED (ed.), *Sozialisation und Bildungswesen in der Weimarer Republik* (Stuttgart, 1976).

—— *Erziehung und Schulung im Dritten Reich*, i: *Schule, Jugend, Berufserziehung* (Stuttgart, 1980).

HELLFELD, MATTHIAS VON, *Bündische Jugend und Hitlerjugend: Zur Geschichte von Anpassung und Widerstand 1930–1939* (Cologne, 1987).

HEMPEL-KÜTER, CHRISTA, ' "Gestempelt wurde jeden Tag": Zur Situation der Arbeitslosen in Altona in den ersten Jahren der Weimarer Republik, November 1918–Ende 1923', in Arnold Sywottek (ed.), *Das andere Altona: Beiträge zur Alltagsgeschichte* (Hamburg, 1984).

HENTSCHEL, VOLKER, *Geschichte der deutschen Sozialpolitik 1880–1980* (Frankfurt am Main, 1983).

HERMANN, OLIVER, 'Jugendhilfe im Dritten Reich aufgezeigt am Beispiel der FE im Stadtstaat Hamburg', Diplomarbeit (Lüneburg, 1988).

HERMANNS, MANFRED, *Jugendarbeitslosigkeit 1926–1988: Ein sozialgeschichtlicher und zeitgeschichtlicher Vergleich* (Opladen, 1988).

HERRMANN, GERTRUD, *Die sozialpädagogische Bewegung der zwanziger Jahre* (Weinheim and Berlin, 1956).

HERRMANN, ULRICH (ed.), *'Neue Erziehung', 'neue Menschen': Ansätze zur Erziehungs- und Bildungsreform in Deutschland zwischen Kaiserreich und Diktatur* (Weinheim, 1987).

—— (ed.), *'Die Formung des Volksgenossen': Der 'Erziehungsstaat' des Dritten Reichs'* (Weinheim, 1985).

HERZIG, ARNO, LANGEWIESCHE, DIETER, and SYWOTTEK, ARNOLD, (eds.), *Arbeiter in Hamburg: Unterschichten, Arbeiter und Arbeiterbewegung seit dem ausgehenden 18. Jahrhundert* (Hamburg, 1983).

HOLTFRERICH, CARL-LUDWIG, *Die deutsche Inflation 1914–1923: Ursachen und Folgen in internationaler Perspektive* (Berlin and New York, 1980).

HONG, YOUNG SUN, 'Femininity as a Vocation: Gender and Class Conflict in the Professionalization of German Social Work', in Konrad Jarausch and Geoffrey Cocks (eds.), *German Professions 1800–1950* (Oxford, 1990).

HORNUNG, KLAUS, *Der Jungdeutsche Orden* (Düsseldorf, 1958).

HUMPHRIES, STEPHEN, *Hooligans or Rebels? An Oral History of Working-class Childhood and Youth 1889–1939* (Oxford, 1981).

JACOBY, HENRY (= Heinz), *Von des Kaisers Schule zu Hitlers Zuchthaus* (Frankfurt am Main, 1980).

JAHNKE, KARL-HEINZ, et al., *Geschichte der Arbeiterjugendbewegung 1904–1945* (Berlin, 1973).

JAMES, HAROLD, *The German Slump: Politics and Economics 1924–1936* (Oxford, 1986).

JAMIN, MATHILDE, *Zwischen den Klassen: Zur Sozialstruktur der SA-Führerschaft* (Wuppertal, 1984).

JASPER, GOTTHARD, *Die gescheiterte Zähmung: Wege zur Machtergreifung Hitlers 1930–1934* (Frankfurt am Main, 1985).

JONES, LARRY EUGENE, 'German Liberalism and the Alienation of the Younger Generation in the Weimar Republic', in Konrad M. Jarausch and Larry Eugene Jones (eds.), *In Search of a Liberal Germany: Studies in the History of German Liberalism from 1789 to the Present* (Oxford, 1990).

JORDAN, ERWIN, and MÜNDER, JOHANNES (eds.), *65 Jahre Reichsjugendwohlfahrtsgesetz—ein Gesetz auf dem Weg in den Ruhestand?* (Münster, 1987).

JOST, WOLFDIETRICH, *Gewerbliche Schulen und politische Macht: Zur*

Entwicklung des gewerblichen Schulwesens in Preußen in der Zeit von 1850–1880 (Weinheim and Basle, 1982).

KATER, MICHAEL, 'Generationskonflikt als Entwicklungsfaktor in der NS-Bewegung vor 1933', *GG* 11 (1985), 217–43.

KERSHAW, IAN, *The Nazi Dictatorship: Problems and Perspectives of Interpretation* (London, 1985).

—— (ed.), *Weimar: Why Did German Democracy Fail?* (London, 1990).

KINDT, WERNER (ed.), *Grundschriften der deutschen Jugendbewegung* (Düsseldorf and Cologne, 1963).

—— (ed.), *Dokumentation der Jugendbewegung*, iii: *Die bündische Zeit* (Düsseldorf and Cologne, 1974).

KIPP, MARTIN, ' "Überwindung der Ungelernten"? Vorstudien zur Jungarbeiterschulung im Dritten Reich', in H. Biermann, W. Greinert, and R. Janisch (eds.), *Berufsbildungsreform als politische und pädagogische Verpflichtung* (Velbert, 1982).

KLAUS, MARTIN, *Mädchenerziehung zur Zeit der faschistischen Herrschaft in Deutschland: Der Bund Deutscher Mädel*, 2 vols. (Frankfurt am Main, 1983).

KLÖNNE, ARNO, 'Jugendwiderstand und Jugendopposition: Von der HJ-Erziehung zum Cliquenwesen der Kriegszeit', in Martin Broszat, Elke Fröhlich, and Anton Grossmann (eds.), *Bayern in der NS-Zeit IV: Herrschaft und Gesellschaft im Konflikt*, pt. C (Munich, 1981).

—— *Jugend im Dritten Reich: Die Hitler-Jugend und ihre Gegner* (Cologne, 1984).

KOCKA, JÜRGEN, *Facing Total War: German Society 1914–1918* (Leamington Spa, 1984).

KOEBNER, THOMAS, JANZ, ROLF-PETER, and TROMMLER, FRANK (eds.), *'Mit uns zieht die neue Zeit': Der Mythos Jugend* (Frankfurt am Main, 1985).

KÖHLER, HENNING, *Arbeitsdienst in Deutschland: Pläne und Verwirklichungsformen bis zur Einführung der Arbeitsdienstpflicht im Jahre 1935* (Berlin, 1967).

KRABBE, WOLFGANG R., *Kommunalpolitik und Industrialisierung: Die Entfaltung der städtischen Leistungsverwaltung im 19. und im frühen 20. Jahrhundert: Fallstudien zu Dortmund und Münster* (Stuttgart, 1985).

KRAFELD, FRANZ JOSEF, *Geschichte der Jugendarbeit: Von den Anfängen bis zur Gegenwart* (Weinheim and Basle, 1984).

KRAMER, HELGARD, 'Veränderungen der Frauenrolle in der Weimarer Republik', *Beiträge zur feministischen Theorie und Praxis*, 5 (1981), 17–25.

KRATZENBERG, V., *Arbeiter auf dem Weg zu Hitler? Die nationalsozialistische Betriebszellen-Organisation, ihre Entstehung, ihre Programmatik, ihr Scheitern 1927–1934* (Frankfurt am Main, 1987).

KRUEDENER, JÜRGEN VON, 'Die Überforderung der Weimarer Republik als Sozialstaat', *GG* 11 (1985), 358–76.
—— (ed.), *Economic Crisis and Political Collapse: The Weimar Republic 1924–1933* (New York, Oxford, and Hamburg, 1990).
KUHLMANN, CAROLA, *Erbkrank oder erziehbar? Jugendhilfe als Vorsorge und Aussonderung in der Fürsorgeerziehung in Westfalen von 1933–1945* (Weinheim and Munich, 1989).
LANDWEHR, ROLF, and BARON, RÜDEGER (eds.), *Geschichte der Sozialarbeit: Hauptlinien ihrer Entwicklung im 19. und 20. Jahrhundert* (Weinheim and Basle, 1983).
LAQUEUR, WALTER, *Young Germany: A History of the German Youth Movement* (London, 1962).
LEE, W. R. and ROSENHAFT, EVE (eds.), *The State and Social Change in Germany 1880–1980* (New York, Oxford, and Munich, 1990).
LEIBFRIED, STEPHAN, and TENNSTEDT, FLORIAN, *Berufsverbote und Sozialpolitik 1933: Die Auswirkungen der nationalsozialistischen Machtergreifung auf die Krankenkassenverwaltung und die Kassenärzte* (Bremen, 1981).
—— and TENNSTEDT, FLORIAN, *Politik der Armut und die Spaltung des Sozialstaats* (Frankfurt am Main, 1985).
—— HANSEN, ECKARD, and HEISIG, MICHAEL, 'Politik mit der Armut: Notizen zu Weimarer Perspektiven anläßlich bundesrepublikanischer Wirklichkeiten', *Prokla*, 56 (1984), 105–26.
LENNHOFF, FRIEDRICH GEORG, *Die Zugscharen: Eine Jugendhilfe-Organisation* (Munich, 1983).
LINTON, DEREK S., 'Between School and Marriage, Workshop and Household: Young Working Women as a Social Problem in Late Imperial Germany', *European History Quarterly*, 18 (1988), 387–408.
—— *'Who Has the Youth, Has the Future': The Campaign to Save Young Workers in Imperial Germany* (Cambridge, 1991).
LOEWENBERG, PETER, 'The Psychohistorical Origins of the Nazi Youth Cohort', *AHR* 76 (1971), 1457–502.
LORENT, HANS-PETER DE, and ULLRICH VOLKER (eds.), *Der Traum von der freien Schule: Schule und Schulpolitik in Hamburg während der Weimarer Republik* (Hamburg, 1988).
LUNDGREEN, PETER, *Sozialgeschichte der deutschen Schule im Überblick*, ii: *1918–1980* (Göttingen, 1981).
McROBBIE, ANGELA, and NAVA, MICA (eds.), *Gender and Generation* (London, 1984).
MARCON, HELMUT, *Arbeitsbeschaffungspolitik der Regierungen Papen und Schleicher* (Frankfurt am Main, 1974).
MASON, TIMOTHY W., *Sozialpolitik im Dritten Reich: Arbeiterklasse und Volksgemeinschaft* (Opladen, 1978).

MIEHE, OLAF, and SCHAFFSTEIN, FRIEDRICH (eds.), *Weg und Aufgabe des Jugendstrafrechts* (Darmstadt, 1968).
MOMMSEN, HANS, PETZINA, DIETMAR, and WEISBROD, BERND (eds.) *Industrielles System und Politische Entwicklung in der Weimarer Republik* (Düsseldorf, 1977).
MOMMSEN, WOLFGANG J. and MOCK, WOLFGANG (eds.), *The Emergence of the Welfare State in Britain and Germany 1850–1950* (London, 1981).
MONAT, ANNELIESE, *Sozialdemokratie und Wohlfahrtspflege: Ein Beitrag zur Entstehungsgeschichte der Arbeiterwohlfahrt* (Stuttgart, 1961).
MORGAN, DAGMAR, *Weiblicher Arbeitsdienst in Deutschland* (Darmstadt, 1978).
MÜLLER, C. WOLFGANG, *Wie Helfen zum Beruf wurde: Eine Methodengeschichte der Sozialarbeit* (Weinheim and Basle, 1982).
MUTH, HEINRICH, 'Jugendopposition im Dritten Reich', *VjZG* 30 (1982), 369–417.
MUTH, WOLFGANG, *Berufsausbildung in der Weimarer Republik* (Stuttgart, 1985).
NASSMACHER, KARL-HEINZ (ed.), *Kommunalpolitik und Sozialdemokratie: Der Beitrag des demokratischen Sozialismus zur kommunalen Selbstverwaltung* (Bonn, 1977).
NAUJOKS, MARTINA, *Mädchen in der Arbeiterjugendbewegung in der Weimarer Republik* (Hamburg, 1984).
NEULOH, O., and SYRUP, F., *Hundert Jahre Staatliche Sozialpolitik* (Stuttgart, 1957).
NIETHAMMER, LUTZ, 'Some Elements of the Housing Reform Debate in Nineteenth-Century Europe, or, On the Making of a New Paradigm of Social Control', in Bruce M. Stave (ed.), *Modern Industrial Cities: History, Policy, and Survival* (Beverly Hills and London, 1981).
NOAKES, JEREMY, 'Nazism and Eugenics: the Background to the Nazi Sterilisation Law of 14 July 1933', in R. J. Bullen *et al.* (eds.), *Ideas into Politics: Aspects of European History 1880–1950* (London, 1984).
NOLAN, MARY, ' "Housework Made Easy": the Taylorized Housewife in Weimar Germany's Rationalized Economy', *Feminist Studies*, 16/3 (1990), 549–77.
NYE, ROBERT, A., *Crime, Madness and Politics in Modern France: The Medical Concept of National Decline* (Princeton, 1984).
OTTO, HANS-UWE, and SÜNKER, HEINZ (eds.), *Soziale Arbeit und Faschismus* (Frankfurt am Main, 1989).
PÄTZOLD, GÜNTER (ed.), *Quellen und Dokumente zur betrieblichen Berufsbildung 1918–1945* (Cologne, 1980).
—— (ed.), *Quellen und Dokumente zur Geschichte des Berufsbildungsgesetzes 1875–1981* (Cologne, 1982).
PETRICK, FRITZ, *Zur sozialen Lage der Arbeiterjugend in Deutschland 1933–1939* (Berlin, 1974).

PEUKERT, DETLEV J. K., *Die Edelweißpiraten: Protestbewegungen jugendlicher Arbeiter im Dritten Reich* (Cologne, 1980).
—— 'Arbeitslager und Jugend-KZ: Die Behandlung "Gemeinschaftsfremder" im Dritten Reich', in D. Peukert and J. Reulecke (eds.), *Die Reihen fast geschlossen: Alltag im Nationalsozialismus* (Wuppertal, 1981).
—— *Volksgenossen und Gemeinschaftsfremde: Anpassung, Ausmerze und Aufbegehren unter dem Nationalsozialismus* (Cologne, 1982).
—— *Grenzen der Sozialdisziplinierung: Aufstieg und Krise der deutschen Jugendfürsorge 1878–1932* (Cologne, 1986).
—— *Jugend zwischen Krieg und Krise: Lebenswelten von Arbeiterjungen in der Weimarer Republik* (Cologne, 1987).
—— *Die Weimarer Republik 1918–1933: Krisenjahre der klassischen Moderne* (Frankfurt am Main, 1987).
PIETSCHMANN, HORST, 'Probleme der Massenarbeit des KJVD: Zur Einführung der "neuen Arbeitsmethoden" 1926–1928', *Wissenschaftliche Zeitschrift der Wilhelm-Pieck-Universität Rostock*, 31 (1982), Gesellschaftswiss. Reihe, 1/2, 19–25.
PLATT, ANTHONY, *The Child Savers: The Invention of Delinquency*, 2nd edn. (Chicago and London, 1977).
PRELLER, LUDWIG, *Sozialpolitik in der Weimarer Republik* (Düsseldorf, 1978).
PRINZ, DETLEF, and REXIN, MANFRED, *Gewerkschaftsjugend im Weimarer Staat* (Cologne, 1983).
PROJEKT ARBEITERKULTUR (ed.), *Vorwärts und nicht vergessen: Arbeiterkultur in Hamburg um 1930* (Berlin, 1982).
PROJEKTGRUPPE FÜR DIE VERGESSENEN OPFER DES NS-REGIMES (ed.), *'Verachtet, verfolgt, vernichtet'* (Hamburg, 1986).
PROKOP, DIETER (ed.), *Massenkommunikationsforschung* iii. *Produktanalysen* (Frankfurt am Main, 1977).
RAMCKE, WILHELM, 'Die Jugendstrafgerichtsbarkeit in Hamburg während der Zeit 1909–1923', Diss. jur. (Hamburg, 1959).
RAS, MARION E. P. DE, *Körper, Eros und weibliche Kultur: Mädchen im Wandervogel und in der bündischen Jugend 1900–1933* (Pfaffenweiler, 1988).
RASCHE, EDITH, 'Die Entwicklung des Freiwilligen Arbeitsdienstes in den Jahren der Weltwirtschaftskrise und der Kampf des KJVD gegen den FAD 1930–1933', Diss. phil. (Dresden, 1967).
REESE, DAGMAR, *'Straff aber nicht stramm—herb aber nicht derb': Zur Vergesellschaftung von Mädchen durch den Bund Deutscher Mädel im sozial-kulturellen Vergleich zweier Milieus* (Weinheim, 1989).
REMPEL, GERHARD, *Hitler's Children: The Hitler Youth and the SS* (Chapel Hill and London, 1989).

REULECKE, JÜRGEN, 'Bürgerliche Sozialreformer und Arbeiterjugend im Kaiserreich', *AfS* 22 (1982), 299–329.

—— ' "... und sie werden nicht mehr frei ihr ganzes Leben!": Der Weg in die "Staatsjugend" von der Weimarer Republik zur NS-Zeit', in Ulrich Herrmann and Jürgen Oelkers (eds.), *Pädagogik und Nationalsozialismus* (Weinheim and Basel, 1988).

—— and CASTELL RÜD–HAUSEN, ADELHEID GRÄFIN ZU, (eds.) *Stadt und Gesundheit: Zum Wandel von 'Volksgesundheit' und kommunaler Gesundheitspolitik im 19. und frühen 20. Jahrhundert* (Stuttgart, 1991).

RIMLINGER, GASTON V., 'Welfare Policy and Economic Development: a Comparative Historical Perspective', *JEH* 26 (1966), 556–71.

—— *Welfare Policy and Industrialization in Europe, America and Russia* (New York and London, 1971).

RITTER, GERHARD A., *Sozialversicherung in Deutschland und England: Entstehung und Grundzüge im Vergleich* (Munich, 1983).

—— 'Entstehung und Entwicklung des Sozialstaates in vergleichender Perspektive', *HZ* 243 (1986), 1–90.

—— *Der Sozialstaat: Entstehung und Entwicklung im internationalen Vergleich* (Munich, 1989).

RÖHL, FRITZMICHAEL, *Marie Juchacz und die Arbeiterwohlfahrt* (Hanover, 1961).

ROSENHAFT, EVE, 'Organising the "Lumpenproletariat": Cliques and Communists in Berlin during the Weimar Republic', in Richard J. Evans (ed.), *The German Working Class 1888–1933: The Politics of Everyday Life* (London, 1982).

—— *Beating the Fascists? The German Communists and Political Violence 1929–1933* (Cambridge, 1983).

ROTH, KARL HEINZ, 'Schein-Alternativen im Gesundheitswesen: Alfred Grotjahn—Integrationsfigur etablierter Sozialmedizin und nationalsozialistischer "Rassenhygiene" ', in Karl Heinz Roth (ed.), *Erfassung zur Vernichtung: Von der Sozialhygiene zum 'Gesetz über Sterbehilfe'* (Berlin, 1984).

ROTHMALER, CHRISTIANE, and GLENSK, EVELYN (eds.), Kehrseiten der Wohlfahrt: Die Hamburger Fürsorge auf ihrem Weg von der Weimarer Republik in den Nationalsozialismus (Hamburg, 1992).

ROUETTE, SUSANNE, 'Zur Geschichte von Sozialpolitik und Sozialstaat in Deutschland: Einige neuere Veröffentlichungen', *SOWI* 18/1 (1989), 3–11.

RYERSON, ELLEN, *The Best-Laid Plans: America's Juvenile Court Experiment* (New York, 1978).

SACHßE, CHRISTOPH, *Mütterlichkeit als Beruf: Sozialarbeit, Sozialreform und Frauenbewegung 1871–1929* (Frankfurt am Main, 1986).

—— and TENNSTEDT, FLORIAN, *Geschichte der Armenfürsorge in*

Deutschland, i: *Vom Spätmittelalter bis zum Ersten Weltkrieg* (Stuttgart, 1980), ii. *Fürsorge und Wohlfahrtspflege 1871–1929* (Stuttgart, 1988).

——— *Soziale Sicherheit und soziale Disziplinierung: Beiträge zu einer historischen Theorie der Sozialpolitik* (Frankfurt am Main, 1986).

SALDERN, ADELHEID VON (ed.), *Stadt und Moderne: Hannover in der Weimarer Republik* (Hamburg, 1989).

SALTER, STEPHEN, 'Structures of Consent and Coercion: Workers' Morale and the Maintenance of Work Discipline, 1939–1945', in David Welch (ed.), *Nazi Propaganda: The Power and the Limitations* (London, 1983).

SAUL, KLAUS, 'Der Kampf um die Jugend zwischen Volksschule und Kaserne: Ein Beitrag zur "Jugendpflege" im Wilhelminischen Reich', *MM* 9/1 (1971), 98–144.

SCHANBACHER, EBERHARD, *Parlamentarische Wahlen und Wahlsysteme in der Weimarer Republik* (Düsseldorf, 1982).

SCHERPNER, HANS, *Geschichte der Jugendfürsorge* (Göttingen, 1966).

SCHILDT, AXEL, 'Hanseatische Vernunft kontra Extremismus? Zum antifaschistischen Kampf der Hamburger Sozialdemokratie 1929–1933', in Jörg Berlin (ed.), *Das andere Hamburg* (Cologne, 1981).

SCHLEY, CORNELIUS, 'Die jugendpolitischen Vorstellungen und Aktivitäten des "Reichsausschusses der deutschen Jugendverbände" in den letzten Jahren der Weimarer Republik', Diplomarbeit (Göttingen, 1980).

SCHLICKER, WOLFGANG, 'Arbeitsdienstbestrebungen des deutschen Monopolkapitalismus in der Weimarer Republik', *Jahrbuch für Wirtschaftsgeschichte* (1971), pt. 3, 95–122.

SCHLÜTER, ANNE, *Neue Hüte—alte Hüte? Gewerbliche Berufsbildung für Mädchen zu Beginn des 20. Jahrhunderts: Zur Geschichte ihrer Institutionalisierung* (Düsseldorf, 1987).

——— (ed.), *Quellen und Dokumente zur Geschichte der gewerblichen Berufsbildung von Mädchen* (Cologne and Vienna, 1987).

SCHRÖDER, HEINZ, 'Die Geschichte der hamburgischen öffentlichen Jugendfürsorge 1863–1924', Diss. jur. (Hamburg, 1966).

SCHULZ, ELLEN, *Die Mädchenbildung in den Schulen für die berufstätige Jugend: Ihre geschichtliche Entwicklung und ihre gegenwärtige Problematik* (Hamburg, 1963).

SEUBERT, ROLF, *Berufserziehung und Nationalsozialismus: Das berufspädagogische Erbe und seine Betreuer* (Weinheim, 1977).

SILVERMAN, DAN P., 'A Pledge Unredeemed: The Housing Crisis in Weimar Germany', *Central European History*, 3/1–2 (1970), 112–39.

SIMONSOHN, BERTHOLD, *Jugendkriminalität, Strafjustiz und Sozialpädagogik* (Frankfurt am Main, 1969).

SPREE, REINHARD, *Soziale Ungleichkeit vor Krankheit und Tod: Zur Sozialgeschichte des Gesundheitsbereichs im Deutschen Kaiserreich* (Göttingen, 1981).

STACHURA, PETER D. (ed.), *Unemployment and the Great Depression in Weimar Germany* (London, 1986).
—— *The Weimar Republic and the Younger Proletariat: An Economic and Social Analysis* (London, 1989).
STEPHENSON, JILL, *Women in Nazi Society* (London, 1975).
—— 'Women's Labor Service in Nazi Germany', *Central European History*, 15 (1982), 241–65.
STIEG, MARGARET F., 'The 1926 German Law to Protect Youth against Trash and Dirt: Moral Protectionism in a Democracy', *Central European History*, 23/1 (1990), 22–56.
TENFELDE, KLAUS, 'Großstadtjugend in Deutschland vor 1914: Eine historisch-demographische Annäherung', *VSWG*, 69/2 (1982), 182–218.
TENNSTEDT, FLORIAN, *Sozialgeschichte der Sozialpolitik in Deutschland vom 18. Jahrhundert bis zum Ersten Weltkrieg* (Göttingen, 1981).
TILSNER-GROLL, ROTRAUD, *Die Jugendbildungsarbeit in den freien Gewerkschaften 1919–1933* (Frankfurt am Main, 1982).
TOLLMIEN, CORDULA, *Die Geschichte der Arbeiterwohlfahrt in Hann. Münden* (Hann. Münden, 1983).
TORNIEPORTH, GERDA, *Studien zur Frauenbildung: Ein Beitrag zur historischen Analyse lebensweltorientierter Bildungskonzeptionen* (Weinheim and Basle, 1977).
ULLRICH, VOLKER, *Kriegsalltag: Hamburg im ersten Weltkrieg* (Cologne, 1982).
VIERHAUS, RUDOLF, 'Auswirkungen der Krise um 1930 in Deutschland: Beiträge zu einer historisch-psychologischen Analyse', in Werner Conze and Hans Raupach (eds.), *Die Staats- und Wirtschaftskrise des Deutschen Reichs 1929–1933* (Stuttgart, 1967).
VOLKOV, SHULAMIT, *The Rise of Popular Antimodernism in Germany* (Princeton, 1978).
WALSER, KARIN, 'Prostitutionsverdacht und Geschlechterforschung: Das Beispiel der Dienstmädchen um 1900', *GG* 11 (1985), 99–111.
WEBER, HARALD, *Die geschichtliche Entwicklung des Waisenhauses und der Jugendhilfe in Hamburg* (Hamburg, 1978).
WEBER, HERIBERT, 'Ratlosigkeit und Rebellion: Jugend und politische Erziehung in der zweiten Hälfte der Weimarer Republik', Diss. Phil. (Tübingen, 1972).
WEHLER, HANS-ULRICH, *Das deutsche Kaiserreich 1871–1918* (Göttingen, 1973).
WEINDLING, PAUL, 'Die Preußische Medizinalverwaltung und die "Rassenhygiene" 1905–1933', in A. Thom and H. Spaar (eds.), *Medizin im Faschismus* (Berlin, 1983).
—— 'Eugenik und medizinische Praxis: der Fall Alfred Grotjahn', *Das Argument*, 119 (1984), 6–24.
—— 'The Medical Profession, Social Hygiene and the Birth Rate in

Germany, 1914–1918', in Richard Wall and Jay Winter (eds.), *The Upheaval of War: Family, Work and Welfare in Europe, 1914–1918* (Cambridge, 1988).

—— *Health, Race and German Politics between National Unification and Nazism 1870–1945* (Cambridge, 1989).

WEISBROD, BERND, *Schwerindustrie in der Weimarer Republik: Interessenpolitik zwischen Stabilisierung und Krise* (Wuppertal, 1978).

—— 'Die Befreiung von den "Tariffesseln": Deflationspolitik als Krisenstrategie der Unternehmer in der Ära Brüning', *GG* 11 (1985), 295–325.

WELLNER, GABRIELE, 'Industriearbeiterinnen in der Weimarer Republik: Arbeitsmarkt, Arbeit und Privatleben 1919–1933', *GG* 7 (1981), 534–54.

WILLMOT, LOUISE, 'National Socialist Youth Organisations for Girls: A Contribution to the Social and Political History of the Third Reich', D. Phil. (Oxford, 1980).

WINKLER, HEINRICH A., *Mittelstand, Demokratie und Nationalsozialismus: Die politische Entwicklung von Handwerk und Kleinhandel in der Weimarer Republik* (Cologne, 1972).

—— *Von der Revolution zur Stabilisierung: Arbeiter und Arbeiterbewegung in der Weimarer Republik 1918–1924* (Berlin and Bonn, 1984).

—— *Der Weg in die Katastrophe: Arbeiter und Arbeiterbewegung in der Weimarer Republik 1930–1933* (Berlin and Bonn, 1987).

—— *Der Schein der Normalität: Arbeiter und Arbeiterbewegung in der Weimarer Republik 1924–1930* (Berlin and Bonn, 1988).

WINTER, JAY, and WALL, RICHARD (eds.), *The Upheaval of War: Family, Work and Welfare in Europe 1914–1918* (Cambridge, 1989).

WITT, FRIEDRICH WILHELM, *Die Hamburger Sozialdemokratie in der Republik, unter besonderer Berücksichtigung der Jahre 1929/30–1933* (Hanover, 1971).

WITT, PETER-CHRISTIAN, 'Finanzpolitik als Verfassungs- und Gesellschaftspolitik', *GG* 8 (1982), 386–414.

WOLFF, JÖRG, 'Hitlerjugend und Jugendgerichtsbarkeit 1933–1945', *VjZG* 33 (1985), 640–67.

WOLSING, THEO, *Untersuchungen zur Berufsausbildung im Dritten Reich* (Düsseldorf, 1977).

WULFF, BIRGIT, *Arbeitslosigkeit und Arbeitsbeschaffungsmaßnahmen in Hamburg 1933–1939: Eine Untersuchung zur nationalsozialistischen Wirtschafts- und Sozialpolitik* (Frankfurt am Main, 1987).

ZELLER, SUSANNE, *Volksmütter: Frauen im Wohlfahrtswesen der zwanziger Jahre* (Düsseldorf, 1987).

ZIMMERMANN, MICHAEL, 'Ausbruchshoffnungen: Junge Bergleute in den dreißiger Jahren', in Lutz Niethammer (ed.), *'Die Jahre weiß man nicht, wo man die heute hinsetzen soll': Faschismus-Erfahrungen im Ruhrgebiet* (Berlin and Bonn, 1983).

ZOLLING, PETER, *Zwischen Integration und Segregation: Sozialpolitik im*

Dritten Reich am Beispiel der NSV in Hamburg (Frankfurt am Main, 1986).

ZÖLLNER, DETLEV, 'Germany', in Peter Köhler, F. Zacher, and Martin Partington (eds.), *The Evolution of Social Insurance 1881–1981* (London, 1982).

ZWERSCHKE, MANFRED, *Jugendverbände und Sozialpolitik: Zur Geschichte der deutschen Jugendverbände* (Munich, 1963).

INDEX

abortion, prosecutions for 207, 209
Achinger, Hans 245–6, 247
agriculture 93
  exempted from vocational training legislation 98
  impact of Depression on 109–10
  as outlet for surplus young unemployed 115, 125, 278, 285
  proportion of young workers in 110
  shortage of labour in 125, 285
Allgemeiner Deutscher Gewerkschaftsbund (ADGB), see Free Trade Unions
Adler, Alfred 161, 162
adolescence:
  academic study of 64
  concept of 28–9
  'discovery of' 28–30
  as norm for working-class youth 30, 35
Allgemeine Armenanstalt (Hamburg) 22
Allgemeiner Deutscher Lehrerinnenverband 142
Allgemeiner Fürsorgeerziehungstag (AFET) (Conference on Correctional Education) 44, 154, 233, 238, 245, 249, 257
Altona:
  'bomb trials' in 193
  FAD schemes in 143, 147
  juvenile courts in 221
apprentices:
  and collective agreements 68, 94–5, 99
  contracts of 40, 67
  in craft trades 38–40, 67–8, 97
  dismissal of after training 110–11, 112
  and employers 38–40, 68, 76–7, 95
  entitlement to unemployment benefits 116–17
  exploitation of 67
  and Free Trade Unions 66–8, 101
  in industry 39, 68–70, 285–6
  as proportion of juvenile offenders 200

  as proportion of young workers 72–3, 74–5
  vocational schooling of 39–40, 79–80, 83, 87–8
  wages of 68, 86, 95–6, 99
Arbeiterwohlfahrt:
  co-operation with Hamburg youth welfare department 174
  founding of 157
  and reform of FE 237–8, 239
  and social work training 182
  as source of social work volunteers 158, 184
  working party on youth welfare 157
  and young unemployed 127
Archiv deutscher Berufsvormünder (German Professional Guardians' Association) 44, 154, 167
army 31
AVAVG, see Law on Labour Exchanges and Unemployment Insurance

Bavaria 210
Bavarian People's Party (Bayerische Volkspartei, BVP) 168
Bauer, Jeanne 162 n.
Baum, Marie 180
Berlin:
  day centres for unemployed in 128, 129, 130
  juvenile courts in 221
  public youth welfare in 176, 235, 236
  social workers in 244
  vocational schools in 92
  young unemployed in 119
Bernfeld, Siegfried 161
Berufsausbildungsgesetz (BAG), see vocational training, draft legislation on
Bewahrung, see protective detention
Bismarck, Otto von 36, 37
Blohm und Voß 73–4, 87
Blumenthal, Paul 221 n.
Bondy, Curt 155, 160, 212, 248–9, 262
boys' clubs, see Jugendpflege
Brauns, Heinrich 5, 100

Bräunsdorf (reformatory) 239, 245
Bremen 82, 210, 235, 238
Brüning, Heinrich 107, 118, 131, 137, 140, 191, 257, 264, 269
Bund Deutscher Mädel 274, 276 n.
Bund Deutscher Frauenvereine (League of German Women's Associations) 142
Bünde (lit. 'leagues'), *see* youth movement
bündische Jugend, *see* youth movement
Bürgerschaft (Hamburg) 22

Caritas 37
  see also private welfare organizations
Catholics:
  involvement in reformatory education of 236, 238
  and social welfare 162, 166
  see also Caritas; Centre Party; Churches; private welfare organizations
Centre Party 4, 5, 158, 166–7, 168, 176, 238
child health, *see* health
child labour, protection of 38, 156
child's right to education 16, 37, 45, 47, 165, 168, 263, 295
cholera epidemic of 1892 (Hamburg) 22, 47
Churches 42, 43, 60, 129, 139, 144–5, 154
cinema 33, 228
Civil Code of 1900 (*Bürgerliches Gesetzbuch*, BGB) 52–3, 170–1
Classen, Walter 42
Cliquen, *see* gangs, juvenile
commerce:
  training in 67, 69, 73, 75, 98–9
  and vocational schooling 80, 86
  youthful workforce in 31
Communist Youth (Kommunistischer Jugendverband Deutschlands, KJVD):
  campaign against FAD 146–7
  campaign in vocational schools 91–2
  members prosecuted in juvenile courts 194
Communist Party of Germany (Kommunistische Partei Deutschlands, KPD) 134, 233, 267
compulsory labour schemes (*Pflichtarbeit*) 115, 132–6

  hardship of participants in 201–2
  under National Socialism 284
compulsory savings schemes (*Lohnsparzwang*) 59
concentration camps for juveniles (*Jugendschutzlager*) 293, 296
Conference on Correctional Education, *see* Allgemeiner Fürsorgeerziehungstag
continuation schools, *see* vocational schools
Cornils, Margarete 240
correctional education (Zwangserziehung, Fürsorgeerziehung) 50–3, 170–1, 230–60
  Communist attacks on 233
  impact of 1918 revolution on 152, 231
  of juvenile offenders 216–17
  under National Socialism 291–3
  as placement in foster families 170, 231, 234
  reform of (1932) 249–60
  see also reformatories
Council of People's Delegates (*Rat der Volksbeauftragten*) 93, 94
craft trades:
  apprenticeship in 38–9, 66–8, 72–3, 75, 76, 77, 92, 94–6, 97
  as source of skilled labour for industry 285
  and vocational schooling 39–40, 80
crime:
  explanations of 48–9
  prevention of 54–5
  see also juvenile crime
crime rates 188–9, 197
  during 1923 189, 202
  impact of Depression on 189–90, 197–8, 202–3
  see also juvenile crime
Criminal Code 50–1, 54, 177

dance-halls 33, 127, 163, 228
degeneration, fears of 7, 18, 32, 45
delinquency:
  definitions of 159, 163–5, 208–9
  environmental versus hereditary explanations of 48–9, 160–2, 209, 254–5
  gender and perceptions of 20, 163–4, 209
  medical models of 159, 253–4

Index

demobilization:
 and expansion of vocational schooling 78–9
 unemployment as result of 104, 105
Depression (1929–33) 23–5
 and correctional education 245–9
 and labour market 76–8, 92, 107–12, 121–6
 and local welfare provision 116, 118–19, 260–1, 265
 and political radicalization of youth 91–2, 137–8, 191–5, 266–70
 and public spending cuts 90–1, 117, 242–4, 264–5
 and unemployment insurance 117–19
Deutsche Zentrale für Jugendfürsorge (German Central Association for Youth Welfare) 44, 61 n., 154, 167
Deutscher Städtetag 90, 150, 171–2
Deutscher Verein für Armenpflege und Wohltätigkeit (German Association for Poor Relief and Welfare), see Deutscher Verein für öffentliche und private Fürsorge
Deutscher Verein für öffentliche und private Fürsorge (German Association for Public and Private Welfare) 45, 60 n., 154, 167, 172
Deutsche Vereinigung für Jugendgerichte und Jugendgerichtshilfen, see German Juvenile Courts Association
Deutscher Ausschuß für technisches Schulwesen (DATSCH) 68–9
Deutschnationaler Handlungsgehilfen-Verband (DHV) 144, 148
DINTA (Deutsches Institut für technische Arbeitsschulung) 69, 80, 137
docks, Hamburg 22, 34, 35
domestic science, see home economics
domestic servants 33
 offences committed by 196
 unemployment of 76, 124
 vocational schooling of 86, 90
domestic service 33, 69, 70, 75, 93, 245, 277
 young women pressed to enter 115, 135–6, 279–80, 283–4, 285
 young women's attitudes towards 74, 76, 284
Domestic Service Year (Hauswirtschaftliches Jahr) 279–80
 converted to Pflichtjahr 285

educational reform movement 18, 154–5, 159
Ehrhardt, Justus 248, 260, 261
eight-hour day 4, 68, 85, 92–3, 94
Eiserne Front 194
Eisfelder, Hanna 239, 249
Elberfeld system 46
Emergency Aid for German Youth (Notwerk der deutschen Jugend) 25, 147–50, 151, 272–3
employers 6, 62, 66–8, 75–6, 77, 277, 285–6
 and apprentices' contracts 40, 68, 94–5
 and draft law on vocational training 98–100
 and eight-hour day 92–3
 offences committed against 196, 198
 and vocational schools 39–40, 80, 85–8, 90
Erzberger tax reform 21, 171
eugenics:
 and attacks on welfare state in Depression 242–3
 positive and negative 9, 162
 and youth welfare 162
 see also racial hygiene
Evangelisch-Sozialer Kongreß 37

factory legislation, see protective legislation
family:
 perceived crisis of 32, 33, 60, 152–3
 position of young unemployed in 119–20, 130, 145–6, 261, 268
 state powers of intervention in 2, 50–4, 165, 169–71
 surveillance of by social workers 230
Farm Aid (Landhilfe) 278, 280, 284
Farm Year (Landjahr) 278–9
Felisch, Paul 60 n., 157
female youth 10–11, 18–20
 and correctional education 232, 234, 239, 252
 and crime 193–4, 195–6, 197, 198–9
 and definitions of delinquency 20, 163–4, 207, 209
 and leisure 130
 preparation for motherhood of 33, 82, 142, 279, 292
 and youth organizations 130, 145
 see also young female workers; young unemployed, female

feminists:
and girls' vocational schools 80, 82
and girls' vocational training 64, 70
and girls' voluntary labour service 142
and social work training 182
fostering:
ordered by public authorities 50, 51, 170, 231, 234, 250, 259
state supervision of 44, 47, 169
Foucault, Michel 7
Francke, Herbert 179, 261–2
Frankfurt am Main 56, 261
Free Trade Unions 4, 129
and economic policy in Depression 265
and Emergency Aid for German Youth 148
and National Committee for Youth Fitness 271–2
and protective legislation for young workers 93–5
and vocational training 66–8, 70, 80, 98–100
Freiwilliger Arbeitsdienst (FAD), see voluntary labour service
Freud, Sigmund 161, 162
Friedländer, Walter 157 n., 261 n.
Fürsorgeerziehung (FE), see correctional education

gangs, juvenile 10, 128, 195, 196–7
Gängeviertel (Hamburg) 23, 34 n., 89
Gayl, Wilhelm Freiherr von 257, 269
Geary, Dick 26
generational conflict 2–3, 9, 11, 26–7
German Association for the Care of Juvenile Psychopaths (Deutscher Verein zur Fürsorge jugendlicher Psychopathen) 160
German Democratic Party (Deutsche Demokratische Partei, DDP) 4
German Juvenile Courts Association (Deutsche Vereinigung für Jugendgerichte und Jugendgerichtshilfen) 44, 187, 200, 201, 204, 210, 219, 220, 222, 289
German National People's Party (Deutschnationale Volkspartei, DNVP) 158
German People's Party (Deutsche Volkspartei, DVP) 22, 117, 128, 132
German Red Cross 244

Gesellschaft für soziale Reform (Society for Social Reform) 37
Gesetz über Arbeitsvermittlung und Arbeitslosenversicherung (AVAVG), see Law on Labour Exchanges and Unemployment Insurance
Gewerbeordnung, see Industrial Code
Gilde Soziale Arbeit 155, 164, 183, 218, 219, 237, 238, 245–6, 261
girls, see female youth; young female workers; young unemployed, female
Goering, Hermann 285
Grand Coalition government (1928–30) 100, 117
Groener, Wilhelm 269–70
guardianship courts (Vormundschaftsgerichte) 56, 218–19, 227
guilds 39, 68, 95
gypsies:
excluded from youth welfare provision 293
as target of gossip 207

Hahnöfersand (prison) 212–13
Halbstarke 34–5, 208, 209, 231, 258
Hamburg 21–3, 33–5, 283
correctional education in 232–5, 240–1, 246, 247, 252, 254–5, 259, 295–6
juvenile court in 56, 59, 124, 205, 210–11, 213, 214, 216–17
juvenile crime in 188–203
Social Democracy in 21, 22–3, 35, 59, 79, 86, 144, 174, 175, 233
vocational guidance in 74–5, 77, 78
vocational schools in 39–40, 79, 81, 83–5, 86–91
welfare department in 118–19, 128, 132–6, 143, 283–5
workforce in 33–4, 73–5, 111
young unemployed in 58, 105, 111–12, 119–20, 128–31, 132–6, 143–7, 149–50, 283–5
youth welfare department in 47–8, 53–4, 128–30, 163, 173–6, 183–4, 209–10, 227, 233–5, 240, 241, 242, 253, 294–6
health:
concepts of 163–4, 290–1
of infants and children 38, 44–8, 57–8, 63

Index

of young workers 33, 34–5, 121
health policies:
  towards infants and children 37, 44–8, 58, 166–9
  under National Socialism 290–2, 295–6
  towards working-class youth 64, 81–2, 97, 169
Heiligenstedten (reformatory) 239
Hellmann, August 174, 233, 234, 294
Herrmann, Walter 155, 212
Hertz, Wilhelm 56, 173, 174, 175, 183, 221, 233, 234, 241, 294
Hessen 238
Hierl, Konstantin 280, 281
Himmler, Heinrich 293
Hitler, Adolf 280
Hitler Youth 271, 274–6, 286, 288, 290, 292–3, 296
  see also Bund Deutscher Mädel
Hoffmann, Walter 203
holidays:
  for children 46, 156
  young workers', statutory 93–4, 288
home economics 82, 84–5, 279
homosexuality, prosecutions for 195
housewives' organizations 70, 82, 86
housework:
  education for 18, 82, 84–5, 279
  rationalization of 85
  unemployed girls and 119–20, 130, 135

illegitimate children 44–5, 47, 169, 175
Immenhof (reformatory) 239, 249
Independent Social Democratic Party of Germany (Unabhängige Sozialdemokratische Partei Deutschlands, USPD) 233
Industrial Code (*Gewerbeordnung*) 39, 67, 93, 95
industry:
  training in 39, 58–9, 63, 68–9, 73–4, 75, 80, 97, 285–6
  unemployment rates in 109–11
  workforce in 30–1
'ineducables' 23, 24, 251–60, 291
infant welfare 46, 166, 169
inflation:
  and crime 189, 202
  and unemployment 105–6
Innere Mission 37, 135, 254

Jacoby, Heinz (= Henry) 203
Jews:
  dismissal of 275, 294
  excluded from youth welfare provision 293, 296
Juchacz, Marie 157
Jugendämter, *see* youth welfare departments
Jugendpflege (recreational provision for youth) 14–15, 41–3, 243
  as basis for work with young unemployed 123, 127–31
Jungdeutscher Orden (Young German Order) 137
Jungdeutschlandbund (Young Germany League) 43
Juvenile Court Assistance (Jugendgerichtshilfe) 169, 181, 183, 206–9, 210, 215, 216, 223–4, 290
juvenile court judges 55–6, 179–80, 203, 210–11
juvenile courts:
  co-operation with youth welfare authorities 56, 181, 206, 215
  criticisms of 218–22
  emergency decree on (1932) 222
  in England 55
  lay assessors in 179, 222
  origins of 54–6
  rationalizing impact of 204–5, 223
  regional differences in practice of 210
  regulated by Juvenile Courts Law 179
  sentencing practices of 206, 210–17
  in USA 55
Juvenile Courts Association (Deutsche Vereinigung für Jugendgerichte und Jugendgerichtshilfen), *see* German Juvenile Courts Association
Juvenile Courts Law:
  introduction of 176–80
  origins of 56
  reform of (1943) 289–90
juvenile crime:
  as crimes against the person 192–3
  explanations of 48–9, 209–10
  fear of 31–2, 64, 103, 120
  gender differences in patterns of 163–4, 196, 198–9
  as political crime 190–5, 211
  as property crime 195–8
  rates of 32, 48, 59, 188–90, 197–8
  see also delinquency

juvenile offenders:
    females as minority of 198–9
    occupational background of 198–200
    policies in Kaiserreich towards 50–6
    re-offending rates among 199–200
    social background of 198, 200
    and unemployment 200–3

Kaiser, *see* Wilhelm II, Emperor of Germany
Kay, Ella 162 n.
Koch, Erich 78
Köhler, Henning 280
Kommunistischer Jugendverband Deutschlands (KJVD), *see* Communist Youth
Kommunistische Partei Deutschlands (KPD), *see* Communist Party

labour exchanges 71–2, 116
Labour Front (Deutsche Arbeitsfront, DAF) 275, 286
Lampel, Peter Martin 235–6
Law on Associations (1908) 41
Law on Labour Exchanges and Unemployment Insurance (Gesetz über Arbeitsvermittlung und Arbeitslosenversicherung, AVAVG) 71–2, 99, 113, 115–18
leisure activities 32–3, 41–3, 60, 127–31, 156, 163, 207–9, 228, 229
Lindenhof (reformatory) 212, 232, 239
Linton, Derek 13–14
Liszt, Elsa von 222 n.
Liszt, Franz von 55
local government 20–3, 153, 171–2
    in Depression 90, 118, 143, 149, 242, 264–5
    and welfare provision 44–8, 52
Lombroso, Cesare 49
Lübeck 210, 235, 258

male youth:
    and Schleicher's youth policy 266–8, 269–73
    as target of public policies in Kaiserreich 32–3, 34–5, 40–3
    and voluntary labour service 137–8
Martini, Oskar 132, 133, 283, 294
motherhood, education for 82, 279
Mennicke, Carl 219
Müller, Hermann 117, 118
Munich 56, 204
municipal welfare, *see* local government

National Committee for Youth Fitness (Reichskuratorium für Jugendertüchtigung) 270–3
National Liberals 36
National Socialist German Workers' Party (Nationalsozialistische Deutsche Arbeiterpartei, NSDAP) 137, 266
Nationalsozialistische Volkswohlfahrt (NSV) 275, 292, 295
National Socialist factory cell organization (Nationalsozialistische Betriebszellen-Organisation, NSBO) 267
National Socialist Vocational and Works School League 92
National Youth Welfare Law of 1922 (Reichsjugendwohlfahrtsgesetz, RJWG) 18, 153, 154, 165–73, 206, 230, 241–2, 244, 250
    amended (1932) 257
    amended under National Socialism 288–9
Nohl, Herman 160
Notwerk der deutschen Jugend, *see* Emergency Aid for German Youth
November revolution of 1918 1, 4, 60, 67, 152–3, 161, 231–2

Oestreich, Gerhard 7
Ohlsdorf (reformatory) 53, 232, 235, 240–1, 246
Oldenburg 238
orphans 5, 43, 44, 47, 166, 169, 175

Papen, Franz von 25, 90, 118, 139, 140, 141, 191, 194, 222, 223, 257, 264, 269, 270, 272
paramilitary organizations 11, 140, 267–8, 270–1
paramilitary training:
    in First World War 59
    in Jungdeutschlandbund 43
    and paramilitary sports (Wehrsport) 269–72, 291
Paulssen, Bertha 163–4, 174, 240, 252–3, 294
Petersen, Johannes 47
Peukert, Detlev 10, 12–13, 23, 252
Pflichtarbeit, *see* compulsory labour schemes
physical education 43, 79, 81–2, 86, 90, 269–72
Platt, Anthony 218–19

Index

police 88–9, 191–2, 193, 293
political education, *see* vocational schools
Polligkeit, Wilhelm 45
population 30
  policy 32, 37, 45–6, 57–8, 63
poor relief 44, 45, 46–7, 57
prisons, juvenile 211–14
private welfare organizations:
  confessional 37, 127, 176, 291–2
  and correctional education 238
  position of in RJWG 167–8, 169, 172, 181, 206, 243–4
probation (Schutzaufsicht) 226–30, 261
  before 1914 53–4
  involvement of youth organizations in 229
  ordered by juvenile courts 215–16
  regulated in RJWG 169–70
prostitution 20, 33, 114, 256
  male 195, 261
protective detention (Bewahrung) 256–7, 291
protective legislation 37, 64, 93–4, 156, 288
Protestant Church 144–5
  see also Churches; Innere Mission; private welfare organizations
Prussia 194
  correctional education in 51–2, 237–8, 240, 249–52, 259
  Jugendpflege in 42–3
  juvenile courts in 221
  ninth school year in 126
  vocational schools in 40, 90–1
Prussian Ministry of Justice 221
Prussian Ministry of Welfare 152, 238, 243, 246, 264
Prussian State Council 243
psychopaths 152, 159–61
psychiatry:
  involvement in juvenile justice of 206, 209–10
  as source of theories of delinquency 159–61
  and youth welfare in Hamburg 175–6, 253, 295
psychotechnical testing 75–6

racial hygiene 226, 253–4, 290–1, 295–6
  see also eugenics
rationalization:
  of housework 85
  in industry 62–3, 105–6

Rauhes Haus (reformatory) 53
reformatories:
  before 1914 51
  Communist campaigns against 240
  cuts in during Depression 246–7
  escapes from 241, 247, 255
  liberalized regimes in 239, 240
  under National Socialism 291–3
  proposed reforms of 237
  punishments in 232, 234, 238, 239, 248, 291
  revolts in 240, 247
  scandals concerning 235–6, 240
  vocational training in 245–6
Reich Ministry of Economics 95, 96, 98, 100, 287
Reich Ministry of Finance 167, 172
Reich Ministry of the Interior 78–9, 167, 251, 255, 256, 269, 270, 272
Reich Ministry of Justice 176, 220
Reich Ministry of Labour 5, 81, 93, 94–5, 96, 100, 101, 121–6, 148
Reichsausschuß der deutschen Jugendverbände (RddJ), *see* Youth Organizations Council
Reichsbanner:
  and FAD 140, 141, 144
  and National Committee for Youth Fitness 271, 272
Reichsberufswettkämpfe (National Vocational Competitions) 286, 288
Reichsjugendwohlfahrtsgesetz (RJWG), *see* National Youth Welfare Law
Reichskuratorium für Jugendertüchtigung, *see* National Committee for Youth Fitness
Reichsanstalt für Arbeitsvermittlung und Arbeitslosenversicherung (RAVAV):
  creation of 116
  and Emergency Aid for German Youth 149
  and FAD 140, 146
  financial difficulties of 117–18
  labour market strategy during Depression of 121–7
  and vocational guidance 77–8
revolution of 1918, *see* November revolution
Rhineland 176, 248, 249, 257
Rickling (reformatory) 236, 240
Riebesell, Paul 179
Rosenhaft, Eve 10

Roter Frontkämpferbund (RFB) 267
Rothe, Oberin 232, 240

SA (*Sturmabteilung*) see stormtroopers
St Pauli (Hamburg) 34, 134, 214, 241
Sassenbach, Johannes 67
Saxony:
　correctional education in 235, 238
　implementation of RJWG in 172–3
　juvenile prisons in 212
Schallehn, Direktor 232, 240–1
Scheuen (reformatory) 236, 240
Schiffer, Eugen 176
Schleicher, Kurt von 25, 147, 269, 270, 271–3
Schlosser, Rudolf 245, 247
Schreiner, Helmuth 254
schools, elementary, see *Volksschule*
Schultz, Clemens 34, 42, 208
Schulz, Heinrich 79, 157
Selent (reformatory) 239
Senat (Hamburg) 22
sexual behaviour, norms of 20, 33, 163–4, 207, 209, 228
shipbuilding 73, 111, 283
Simon, Helene 60 n., 157, 166, 177
smoking 60, 129, 130, 156, 208, 229
Social Darwinism 48, 242
Social Democratic Party of Germany (Sozialdemokratische Partei Deutschlands, SPD):
　and economic policy in Depression 117, 264–5
　and FAD 140–1
　and Hamburg youth welfare 174, 175–6, 233
　and municipal welfare 5, 21
　and protective detention 256
　and RWJG 166, 168
　as target of antisocialist measures in Kaiserreich 36, 40, 41–3
　and views on delinquency 161–2
　and vocational schooling 79, 86, 100
　women in 64, 156
　and working class 8
　and youth welfare reform 153, 156–8
　see also Arbeiterwohlfahrt; Social Democratic Youth
Social Democratic Youth (Sozialistische Arbeiterjugend, SAJ) 10
　attitude of social workers towards 208
　before 1914 41, 43, 67
　conflicts with Nazi youth 194

　cultural norms of 229
　during First World War 59
　girls in 41
　in Immenhof reformatory 239
social hygiene 45–6, 49, 57–8, 80, 162
social insurance 3, 6, 7, 36, 37
social work 164, 180–5
social workers 127, 158, 161–2, 180–4
　as investigators for juvenile courts 209, 215, 223–4
　and probation work 228–30
　reactions to cuts in Depression 265
socialist youth, see Social Democratic Youth; see also Communist Youth
sports 11, 42, 79, 82, 129, 229
　clubs 144
　and paramilitary training 269–72
　see also physical education
SS (*Schutzstaffel*) 293, 296, 297
Stachura, Peter 13–14, 23
Stahlhelm 77, 137, 143, 144, 267
Stegerwald, Adam 140
sterilization, compulsory 284, 291–2, 294, 295–6
stormtroopers (SA) 149, 228, 267, 271
strikes:
　on compulsory labour schemes 134–5
　during First World War 59
　of Hamburg dock workers (1896) 22, 35
　by vocational school pupils 87
　on voluntary labour service schemes 147
Struve, Kurt 283
Stülpnagel, Edwin von 270
subsidiarity principle (in RJWG) 168, 169, 172
'swing youth' 296
Syrup, Friedrich 71, 140, 142, 146

teachers 120
　in vocational schools 89, 286
trade unions, see Free Trade Unions
'trash' literature (*Schundliteratur*) 129, 163, 208, 229
Treviranus, Gottfried 140

unemployment 58, 76–8, 104–12, 264–8, 277–8, 282–3
　see also young unemployed; youth unemployment
unemployment benefits 113–18, 122–4, 127, 131–2, 133–4, 140, 144–5, 201–2, 284

unemployment insurance, *see* Law on Labour Exchanges and Unemployment Insurance; unemployment benefits
unskilled young workers, *see* young workers

vagrants 7, 256
Verein für Sozialpolitik (Association for Social Policy) 37
Verwahrlosung (delinquency/state of educational neglect), *see* delinquency
Villinger, Werner 175, 209–10, 253, 295
violence, political 191–5, 210–11, 270
vocational guidance 66, 70–8
vocational schools:
  for apprentices 39–40, 80, 83
  in Depression 90–2
  enforcement of attendance at 85, 86–90
  National Socialist legislation on 287
  political agitation in 91–2
  political education in 83, 286
  private provision of 39, 80, 87
  quest for national legislation on 78–9
  social function of 81–3
  for unskilled female workers 40, 80–3, 84–5, 86
  for unskilled male workers 40, 80–2, 83–4, 87–8
vocational training:
  draft legislation on 96–100
  policies in Kaiserreich 38–40, 58
  policies under National Socialism 285–88
  see also apprentices; commerce, training in; craft trades, apprenticeship in; industry, training in
Volkskörper (lit. 'body of the people') 8
Volksschule (elementary school) 31, 66, 73–4, 77, 78, 79, 125–6, 278
voluntary labour service (Freiwilliger Arbeitsdienst, FAD):
  campaign against 146–7
  for female unemployed 142, 144–6, 280–2
  for male unemployed 137–8
  under National Socialism 280–2, 285
  purpose of 136–9, 272–3
  regulations on 137
  recruitment to 143–5

and youth movement 138
voting patterns, age factors in 266, 269
voting rights:
  of women 10, 83
  of young people 269

wages 32, 59, 68, 69, 86, 88, 95–6
Wandervogel, *see* youth movement
welfare departments, local authority 118–19, 132–6, 143, 264–5, 283–5
Webler, Heinrich 218, 220
Weimar Constitution 4, 78, 83, 113, 165
welfare state:
  concept of 1
  evolution of 3
  in Depression 8–9, 117–18, 241–4, 264–6
  and National Socialism 276, 296–8
  and Weimar economy 5–6, 8–9
Westendheim (reformatory) 239, 261
Westphalia 248
Wichern, Johannes Heinrich 53
Wilhelm II, Emperor of Germany 43, 57
wilde Cliquen, *see* gangs, juvenile
Wilker, Karl 155, 212, 232, 233
Wissell, Rudolf 93, 100, 157
workers, *see* young workers
Workers' and Soldiers' Councils 231
workforce:
  age structure of 30–1, 65–6
  gender composition of 31
  size of 30–1, 65–6, 106
workhouse 255–6
working hours, *see* eight-hour day
works schools 73, 76, 80, 87
women:
  employment patterns of 109–11
  Reichstag members and RJWG 167
  Social Democratic 64, 156
  as social workers 158, 181–2
  voting rights of 10, 83
Württemberg 71, 259

young women, *see* female youth; young female workers; young unemployed, female
young female workers 10, 11, 19–20, 64, 101
  apprenticeship training of 72–3, 75
  commercial training of 73, 75
  in domestic service 33, 74, 75, 76, 93, 115
  in factories 33

young female workers (*cont.*):
  participation rates of 65–6
  as social problem 33
  vocational guidance for 73, 74
  vocational schooling of 19, 82–3, 84–5
  unskilled 69–70, 72
  in white-collar occupations 31, 33, 73, 75
  see also apprentices; vocational guidance; vocational schools; young unemployed; young workers; youth unemployment
young male workers 10, 19
  participation rates of 65
  as political threat 31, 41, 59, 60
  as social problem 31–2
  unskilled 31, 34, 72, 74
  vocational guidance for 73, 74
  see also apprentices; vocational guidance; vocational schools; young unemployed; young workers; youth unemployment
young workers:
  protective legislation for 93–4
  protests against First World War by 59
  as social problem 38, 64
  unskilled 13, 17–18, 31–2, 69–70, 72, 89–91, 95–6, 97–9, 112, 163, 200, 286–7
  wages of 32, 59, 68, 69, 86, 88, 95–6, 99
  working conditions of 92–5, 97–9
  working hours of 85–7, 93–4
  see also apprentices; vocational guidance; vocational schools; young female workers; young male workers; young unemployed; youth unemployment
youth clubs, *see Jugendpflege*
youth gangs, *see* gangs, juvenile
youth movement 3, 9
  cultural norms of 156, 163
  and development of *bündische Jugend* 9
  Schlesische Jungmannschaft 138
  and voluntary labour service 138
  Wandervogel tradition of 9, 29
  and youth welfare 9, 64, 154–6, 228–9, 248
youth organizations 127, 139–40, 145, 148–9, 155–6
  see also youth movement

Youth Organizations Council (Reichsausschuß der deutschen Jugendverbände), 64 n., 94, 155–6, 288
young unemployed:
  and crime 200–3
  day centres for 128–31
  during demobilization period 104
  during Depression 76–8, 107–112, 118–21
  and Emergency Aid for German Youth 148–50
  entitlement to unemployment benefits 113–21, 122–4, 127, 131–2, 133–4, 140, 144–5, 201–2, 284
  female 108–10, 119, 129–30, 135–6, 145–6, 268
  during First World War 58
  male 108–10, 129, 267–8
  under National Socialism 277–85
  perceptions of 103, 120–1, 127, 207
  and politics 26–7, 137–9, 266–8
  and position within family 119–20, 130, 145–6, 261, 268
  retraining of 121–6
  on work schemes 115, 131–47
youth unemployment:
  distribution of 107–12
  as labour market problem 121–6
  under National Socialism 277–85
  rates of 104–12
  as social and political problem 127–51
youth welfare departments (Jugendämter):
  before 1918 45, 47–8, 60–1
  cuts during Depression in expenditure of 242, 243–4, 265
  employment of trained social workers by 181, 182–5
  and juvenile justice system 56, 181, 206, 215
  and private welfare organizations 168, 169, 172, 176, 181
  tasks under RJWG of 166, 169–70, 172–3, 173–6
  and young unemployed 126–31, 242
youth welfare movement
  in Kaiserreich 37, 43–56, 60–1
  in Weimar Republic 152–65

Zentralarbeitsgemeinschaft (ZAG) 98
Zirker, Otto 155
Zwangserziehung, *see* correctional education